CW00945918

LOCAL PRESS
LIMITED

Local Press Limited prides itself on the quality of its publications.

As the owners of titles in Belfast, Londonderry and Donegal – including the News Letter, the oldest English language daily newspaper in the world – it has earned a high reputation for serving the community.

The Irish on the Somme is the second book published by Local Press Limited this year, following on the heels of the highly-successful *Last Days of the RUC – First Days of the PSNI* by Bobbie Hanvey.

Our aim is to publish books which, like our newspapers, go to the very heart of the community and feel confident that *The Irish on the Somme* will contribute to a better understanding of the First World War.

The Irish on the Somme

A BATTLEFIELD GUIDE TO THE IRISH REGIMENTS IN THE GREAT WAR AND THE MONUMENTS TO THEIR MEMORY

Steven Moore

Best wishes

Steven Moore

LOCAL PRESS LIMITED

Published by
LOCAL PRESS LTD.,
Boucher Crescent, Belfast, BT12 6QY
email: sales@local-press.net

© Steven Moore, 2005

ISBN 0-954 9715-1-5

A catalogue record for this title is available from the British Library
All rights reserved. No part of this publication may be reproduced, stored in or introduced into a retrieval system, or transmitted, in any form or by any means (electronic, mechanical, photocopying, recording or otherwise), without the prior written permission of both the copyright owner and publisher of this book

Printed in Northern Ireland by University Press Ltd

Cover Designed by: Tim Bell, Local Press Ltd

CONTENTS

This book is dedicated to two men with a shared name,

John Reid Moore;

one was a great uncle who died on July 1, 1916,
the opening day of the Battle of the Somme;

the other is my father,
a man of honour and integrity

NOT MUCH OF A PICNIC

There is no word of us going back to the trenches again and as far as I can hear we won't be back again until after Christmas and I don't care as it is not much of a picnic

Sergeant John Reid Moore, 14th (YCV) Royal Irish Rifles
(Letter home dated November, 1915)

Ireland's contribution to the First World War was significant, with perhaps close to a quarter of a million men and women from the island serving between 1914 and 1918. It was an Irishman, Private Ernest Thomas, of the Royal Irish Dragoons, who fired the first shot in anger in August, 1914, just 18 days after the declaration of war; another, Private George Edwin Ellison, of the Royal Irish Lancers, was possibly the last to die, shot dead by a German sniper almost at the eleventh hour of the eleventh day of the eleventh month of 1918; Lieutenant Maurice James Dease, from County Westmeath, was the first Victoria Cross winner of the war, dying in his heroic action of August 23, 1914, as he covered the British retreat at Mons; Captain Arthur Edward Bruce O'Neill, of Shane's Castle, Antrim, was the first Member of Parliament to be killed; and Louis James Lipsett, from Donegal, was the final British general to lose his life and the last senior officer to have commanded a Canadian division in the field. In the four years and three months of fighting, at least 35,000 Irishmen, most in the prime of life, died on battlefields across the world. In addition to the regular battalions already serving with the British Army at the outbreak of hostilities, three divisions were formed – the 10th (Irish) which took part in the ill-fated Gallipoli campaign; the 16th (Irish), largely made up of nationalists asserting their right to Home Rule for Ireland; and the 36th (Ulster), which contained the Ulster Volunteer Force, pledged to resist the severing of Ireland from the Crown. Despite the political make-up of

For John Moore, like so many others, going off to war was an adventure and patriotic duty

the units, the traditional differences of religion and creed were largely set aside for the duration of the war.

The sacrifices of the 1914-18 war and particularly those on the Somme have never been forgotten in Northern Ireland, where July 1 is marked each year with a series of parades and wreath-laying ceremonies. In more recent years, due to the efforts of the County Down-based Somme Association, an organisation which grew out of a cross-community initiative in west Belfast to make young people aware of the part played by Irishmen of all creeds in the First World War, a service has been held at the Ulster Tower at Thiepval, France, on the same date.

In the Republic of Ireland, following the upheaval of its creation as a separate state, the part played by fellow countrymen during the war was largely ignored. Seen as having fought for the British Crown, veterans found themselves isolated in a country which was struggling with the domestic and political difficulties which come with independence. In the past decade or more, however, there has been a reawakening to this aspect of Irish history and these men are, long after their deaths, receiving some of the recognition they deserve. That the Catholics and Protestants of the 16th and 36th divisions respectively served shoulder-to-shoulder

William Moore was a natural leader who took to soldiering better than his brother

at Messines in June, 1917, after the slaughter endured by both at the Battle of the Somme a year earlier, has been used as a tool to encourage closer community relations.

The authorities in France have also shown a renewed interest in the war sites in recent years, having now realised the tourist potential of making what remains of the battlefields more accessible to the public. Several museums dedicated to the First World War have been opened, most notably at Peronne, and a Circuit of Remembrance takes the visitor on a trek which includes many sites of Irish interest.

This book attempts to help the Irish reader find their way around the Somme battlefields, and to appreciate the scale of sacrifice made by their fellow countrymen. The 36th (Ulster) Division and 16th (Irish) Division entered the 1916 battle six weeks apart but their sacrifices were on a similar scale. All other Irish battalions took their turn on this front at some stage, as did the men of the Tyneside Irish, London Irish and Liverpool Irish. There were significant numbers of Irish volunteers – and they were all volunteers for there was no conscription in Ireland – who served elsewhere in the armed services, not least in the Royal Navy and the fledging Royal Flying Corps, both of which are largely outside the scope of this book. Many newly-commissioned Irish-born officers were posted to English, Scottish or Welsh regiments, while family connections often meant even rank-and-file soldiers opted for non-Irish regiments. The Black Watch, for example, actively recruited in the north of Ireland and boasted a sizeable Ulster contingent. Likewise, in a generation of mass emigration, the armies of Australia, Canada and South Africa were liberally dotted with the youth of Ireland.

My interest in the First World War began as a teenager when an old aunt passed on to me a Royal Irish Rifles badge which had belonged to my great uncle, Sergeant John Reid Moore, quoted at the start of this chapter. He, I learned, had died on July 1, 1916, on the first day of the Battle of the Somme. His death, at the age of just 22, had been devastating for the family and even then, some 60 years on, his loss was still keenly felt. It had been my great grandfather's wish to visit the grave of his son, a dream neither he, nor any other family member, achieved until my first trip there in the 1980s. I have been back to France many times since, on each occasion spending time at John's grave in Connaught Cemetery, close to the Ulster Tower. His older brother William, who had taken to soldiering better than John, was a Company Quartermaster Sergeant in 1916. He served with the 36th (Ulster) Division throughout the conflict, was wounded several times, was granted a commission in 1917 and won the Military Cross for an action in which he was wounded as he gave a wire cutting party covering fire. He survived the war and enjoyed a long life. Both men were members of the Orange Order and had belonged to the Young Citizen Volunteers, an anti-Home Rule paramilitary body which ran parallel to the Ulster Volunteer Force before merging into it, and later became the nucleus for the 14th (Y.C.V.) battalion of the Royal Irish Rifles. They considered themselves to be both Irishmen and British. They would, I believe, have felt a kinship despite their political differences with their fellow Irishmen seeking to

The brothers served together in No.1 Platoon of the 14th Royal Irish Rifles. While John took part in the Battle of the Somme on July 1, 1916, William was held back as part of the cadre kept in reserve

break the British link. I have, therefore, used the terms "Irish" and "Irishmen" liberally throughout this book without weighing them down with the political baggage which so often accompanies such labels today yet without ignoring the differences which drove men of such diverse political beliefs to unite in a common cause. Likewise, I have used "British" in the same context as it was applied in 1914-18, as a catch-all description of the forces which fought on the British-held sectors of the Western Front. It consequently includes not just the English, Scottish, Welsh and Irish soldiers but the contingents sent from the likes of Australia, New Zealand, Canada, and South Africa.

Finally, in preparing this guide I am acutely aware there are others who are vastly more knowledgeable of Ireland's part in the 1914-18 war than I am. My hope and intention has been to make it easier, and more beneficial, for others to visit the war sites and I beg indulgence for the subjective, simplified and hopefully reader-friendly form in which the information which follows is presented.

The family requested of the Imperial War Graves Commission photographs of John's grave. The first showed the rough wooded cross which marked the spot, while a subsequent image recorded its replacement with a standard headstone. Note the absence of a religious cross, which could only be omitted on the specific instructions of the next-of-kin

Many Irishmen, having moved 'Down Under' in pursuit of a better life, joined the Australian Expeditionary Force at the outbreak of war. This photograph, although the names inscribed on the back are hard to decipher, clearly states that all three are 'Belfast Boys'

Courtesy of the Somme Heritage Centre

IN THIS GRAVE HOUR

His Majesty's Government recognise with deep gratitude the loyal help which Ireland has offered in this grave hour. They hope to announce as soon as possible the arrangements by which this offer can be made use of to the fullest extent

From Prime Minister Herbert Asquith to the Lord Lieutenant in Dublin, August 1914

Just how many Irishmen served during the First World War is still a matter of some conjecturer and debate. Estimates have varied from close to half-a-million to just 100,000. As early as 1919, a publication prepared by Belfast City Council was estimating the number to have joined the army in Ireland at 145,000, of which 50,000 enlisted in the first six months alone. Investigations in recent years by eminent historians have in essence confirmed that original figure, give or take a few thousand. The devil, however, is in the detail for there are many other statistics to be factored in. Firstly there are the 58,000 men already in the regular Irish regiments in existence at the outbreak of hostilities, producing a running total to 210,000, though not all by any means were Irish by birth or even background. Much harder to estimate is the number of Irishmen serving in non-Irish units, both in the British and Empire armies. In the north, in particular, many men joined up with other units, often out of frustration at the delay in the formation of the Ulster Division. Scottish regiments were quick to exploit these opportunities. The 1/6th Black Watch already had a territorial battalion in Belfast prior to the war which crossed to Scotland every year for training and the regiment regularly sent recruiting parties to the province. Likewise, the 1/4th Seaforth Highlanders opened up an office in the city and sent over a recruiting sergeant in 1915, who left again with several hundred men. The traffic wasn't all the one way, of course, with several hundred Glasgow Orangemen crossing to Belfast in

September, 1914, to join the 36th (Ulster) Division. Ultimately Belfast was to yield 46,000 of its sons for service, the second best response in the United Kingdom. That there were Irishmen in the Royal Field Artillery is unquestioned, many receiving their initial training at some of the island's coastal defence emplacements, while others ended up in the various corps. The better educated strata of Irish society provided the raw officer material, hundreds of whom were sent to non-Irish regiments. Not insignificantly, many sons followed family traditions in applying to their father's or grandfather's regiments while some battalions appealed to men to join up on the basis of common interests, such as sport or professional affiliations. The likes of the Bantam battalions, created later in the war for men too short in stature to make the 5ft 3ins minimum height applied in 1914, presumably took in its fair share of Irish recruits, as did the soon to be corrupted Church Lads battalion of the King's Royal Rifles, which opened its doors to the God-fearing from the island.

Many exiles served with the Canadian, Australian, South African, New Zealand and American forces. Most served throughout their adopted nation's armed forces though some, particularly in Canada, joined ethnic regiments such as the Irish Canadian Rangers of Montreal, the Irish Regiment of Canada, formed in Toronto, the British Columbia Regiment and the Irish Fusiliers of Canada, from the same area. The man responsible for the raising of Canadian divisions was Orangeman Sam Hughes, the Minister of Militia and Defence, whose father John had emigrated to Ontario from County Tyrone.

Given the difficulties of determining how many Irishmen fought in the war (or, indeed, who truly qualifies as being Irish for such purposes), it is not surprising that there is little agreement on how many lost their lives. Ireland's Memorial Records, published in 1923, list 49,435 "known dead" among those who served in Irish regiments. Not all, particularly in the latter years of the war, would be Irish by birth or even association. Others have estimated the figure of Irish dead, including those who served with Empire forces and the United States, at 35,000, but a definitive figure has yet to be produced and may never be possible.

A look at those who volunteered from among the staff of the Belfast Banking Company serves as a snapshot of recruitment in Ireland and, though not necessarily typical of the overall trend, helps illustrate the difficulties in tracing the Irish contribution. A booklet prepared by the bank, undated but clearly from the latter half of the war, lists a total of 80 staff that had joined the armed forces from its branches in Belfast, Armagh, Ballyshannon, Bangor, Buncrana, Castleblayney, Coleraine, Derry, Donegal, Drogheda, Dublin, Dunfanaghy, Dungannon, Enniskillen, Kingstown, Letterkenny, Lurgan, Magherafelt, Navan, Newry, Pettigo, Portadown, Rathfriland, Sligo and Warrenpoint. Of these, 14 had been killed in action; 30 had been wounded, of which six were then receiving hospital treatment; five officers had been awarded the Military Cross (one with bar) and one soldier the Military Medal (the equivalent for "other ranks"). Most were serving with Irish regiments, as might be expected, but 32 out of the 80 (including two with the Officer Training Corps whose destinies were then undecided) had either chosen or subsequently ended up in regiments, corps or services which were not specifically Irish. These included the Highland Light Infantry, Cheshire Regiment, Machine Gun Corps, including two men who were serving in Tanks, the Black Watch, the Indian Army Reserve, Royal Flying Corps, Royal Garrison Artillery, Royal Sussex Regiment, Royal Navy, Manchester Regiment, King's African Rifles, the Royal Fusiliers, including one man described as being in the 26th (Bankers' Battalion), Royal Army Medical Corps, Royal Field Artillery, 16th King's Liverpool Regiment, Royal Engineers and Army Service Corps. The bank regularly published updates on its staff serving with the armed forces and in one document, dated January 20, 1916, lists J. T. Lockhart, of the bank's head office, as being with the Military Mounted Police, 51st Highland Division. In the booklet initially referred to above,

As many of those serving in the Canadian forces were of Irish, and particularly Ulster stock, the decision was taken to lay up their Colours in St. Anne's Cathedral, Belfast, for the duration of the war

despite being of a latter date, he is recorded as a trooper with the North Irish Horse, which was likely the unit with which he went to war. It is a further complication as it raises the possibility that other soldiers on the list may also have subsequently served with non-Irish units. The attrition rate among officers, particularly early in the war, was very high. Perhaps not surprisingly, therefore, given that these were educated men who had, for the most part, been with the Services since 1914, no fewer than 47 out of the 80 were officers (including the two previously mentioned as then with the O.T.C.). Of these, 34 were second lieutenants, the lowest officer rank, with none higher than a captain. One officer, it was noted, was "Late 2nd Lieutenant, 8th Royal Irish Rifles. Resigned his Commission and re-entered the Bank", an extremely rare occurrence as even severely injured officers were generally kept on the books until after the war's end.

Ireland started the war with nine regiments of regular infantry, most of whom had two battalions, one of which served at home and the other overseas. The Royal Irish Regiment was the oldest truly Irish unit, its 1st battalion dating back to 1683-84 when independent companies of foot soldiers were raised by the Dublin administration. It took part in the Irish battles of 1689-90, fighting alongside William of Orange at the Boyne. The regiment made its reputation, however, in 1695

Men of the 16th (Irish) Division at ease as they prepare to leave Ireland for final training in England before crossing to France in 1915 **Courtesy of the Somme Heritage Centre**

when it stormed the defences at Namur. For this it earned the title Royal Regiment of Ireland, and became the first unit of what was ultimately to become the British army to have a battle honour bestowed on it. As a further tribute, it was allowed to wear the Harp and Crown, the start of a tradition which was to be carried on by many Irish units. The regiment was to serve in virtually every major campaign in the 200 years that followed, seeing action in every corner of the world. In 1914 the 1st battalion was stationed in India, but set sail for home in October, being attached to the 27th Division on its arrival. It crossed to France just before Christmas that year, moving straight to the front where it lost its commanding officer, Lieutenant-Colonel G. F. R. Forbes, a descendant of the regiment's first colonel, in one of its earliest engagements at St. Eloi, Belgium. In 1915 the battalion left for the Middle East, serving in Salonika, Egypt and Palestine, and so took no part in the Somme fighting.

The second battalion, however, had been stationed at Devonport in England at the outbreak of war and was to serve on the Western Front from October 1914 through to the Armistice in 1918. It had first been raised in Ireland at the beginning of the 19th century but was disbanded again in 1814. A new 2nd battalion was formed in 1858, tasting its first experience of battle against the Maoris in New Zealand. Within days of landing in France the battalion was thrown into battle at Le Bassee, suffering terrible casualties as it attempted to stall the German advance. Both Royal Irish Regiment battalions recruited principally from Tipperary, Wexford, Waterford and Kilkenny and were among those disbanded in 1922 following the partition of Ireland.

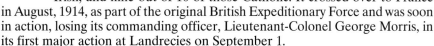

Courtesy of Down County Museum

The Irish Guards, by contrast, was in 1914 the youngest regiment in the army. It was raised in 1900 as a tribute to the courage shown by the other Irish regiments during the Boer War. Queen Victoria, in April of that year, issued an Army Order: "Her Majesty the Queen having deemed it desirable to commemorate the bravery shown by the Irish regiments during the operations in South Africa in the years 1899-1900 has been graciously pleased that an Irish Regiment of Foot Guards be formed to be designated the 'Irish Guards'." Hundreds of Irishmen already serving were allowed to transfer into the new regiment, which had as its colonel the Irish Field Marshal Lord Roberts. In 1914 the Irish Guards, known as the Micks, then only one battalion strong, was stationed at Wellington Barracks. Some 98 per cent of its strength was Irish, and nine out of 10 of those Catholic. It crossed over to France in August, 1914, as part of the original British Expeditionary Force and was soon in action, losing its commanding officer, Lieutenant-Colonel George Morris, in its first major action at Landrecies on September 1.

A second battalion of the Irish Guards was formed in July, 1915. Mobilisation notices had been sent to some 1,322 Irish Guards Reservists in August, 1914, and it was the bulk of these men, who had been quartered at Warley Barracks in England, which formed the 2nd Irish Guards. More than 300 members of the Royal Irish Constabulary served in the new battalion, their time in khaki counting towards their police service and pensions. Among the new officers was John Kipling, the only son of the poet Rudyard Kipling, who had used his influence to have the commission granted. John suffered from poor eyesight and had been refused postings in other regiments. He celebrated his 18th birthday on the day the battalion sailed for France and was reported missing, believed killed, at the Battle of Loos, in September, 1915. He is buried at St. Mary's A.D.S. Cemetery, Haisnes, between Lens and La Bassee, Pas de Calais. With the formation of the Guards Division, the two battalions of the regiment came briefly under the divisional command of Frederick Rudolf Lambart, 10th Earl of Cavan, before his further elevation to head of XIV Corps.

Unlike the other Irish regiments, which had specific counties from which they drew their volunteers, the Irish Guards, with its depot at Chelsea Barracks in London, recruited from the entire island. Throughout the course of the war some 9,633 men served in the Irish Guards, with 7,488 casualties sustained of which 2,349 were fatalities. Four Victoria Crosses (including that of Lt-Col Neville Marshall, serving with the 16th Lancashire Fusiliers) were won and more than 400 medals for distinguished service and bravery awarded.

The Royal Inniskilling Fusiliers, known as the Skins, traced its lineage back to 1689 when the townsfolk of Enniskillen and the surrounding areas organised themselves as Tiffin's Inniskilling Regiment to resist the armies of the Catholic James II and later accompanied William of Orange to the Battle of the Boyne. A second battalion was raised and disbanded twice in the early 1800s, with even a third battalion existing for a period. In 1881, when the 27th Regiment of Foot became the 1st Royal Inniskilling Fusiliers, the regiment's recruiting area was designated as Omagh, Fermanagh, Donegal and Londonderry. On the outbreak of war, the 1st Inniskillings found itself in Trimulgherrey, India. The battalion only returned to Britain in January, 1915, being attached to the 29th Division, part of the Mediterranean Expeditionary Force. It landed at Gallipoli in April, 1915, where it was to serve until January the following year. After two months to regroup, spent in Egypt, the 1st Inniskillings arrived with the division at Marseilles in France in time to take part in the preparations for the Battle of the Somme. In the four-and-a-half years of the war the battalion lost 94 officers and 2,013 other ranks.

It was also in 1881 that yet another second battalion of the regiment was formed. Unlike the previous holders of the title, the 2nd Royal Inniskilling Fusiliers had a separate history. Formerly the 108th Regiment of Foot, it was formed in India in 1853 as the 3rd Madras European Regiment with one of its first actions the suppression of the Indian Mutiny. Even at this stage it had many Irishmen in its ranks. It remained in India for a number of years after transferring to the Crown in 1861, and did not set foot in Ireland until 1882 as the newly named 2nd Inniskillings. The battalion was stationed at Dover in 1914 and was one of the first units to arrive in France in August that year. During its first winter in the trenches Sergeant H. H. Kendrick became the first man from the ranks to be commissioned as an officer during the war. In less than two years he had risen from a Second Lieutenant to a Lieutenant-Colonel in temporary command of a battalion of a Suffolk regiment, an incredible feat by a man who was obviously a remarkable soldier.

The Royal Irish Rifles, by virtue of a recruiting area which included Belfast, Down, Antrim and Tyrone, was destined to be the largest Irish regiment during the First World War with 21 battalions in total. In August 1914, however, it had only the two battalions. The 1st Rifles evolved from the 83rd Regiment of Foot, which had been established in Dublin in 1793 by Colonel William Finch, who was to die two years later at the head of his regiment as it fought its first campaign in Jamaica. Queen Victoria was so pleased with the regiment's performance she granted it a new title in 1859, the County of Dublin Regiment. By 1881, however, the regimental depot had been established at Queen Street Barracks in Belfast, with its Dublin designation disappearing at the same time under its new title, the 1st Royal Irish Rifles. At the outbreak of the war in 1914 the battalion was stationed in Aden, having spent the previous 17 years overseas. It arrived in Liverpool on October 22, 1914, and by November 5 the battalion was in France. It was to spend the next four years on the Western Front, initially with the 8th Division and later as part of the 36th (Ulster) Division. On March 28, 1916, it arrived on the Somme front in preparation for the "Big Push".

Lieutenant-Colonel George Brenton Laurie, who led the 1st Royal Irish Rifles to war, was killed in action in March, 1915

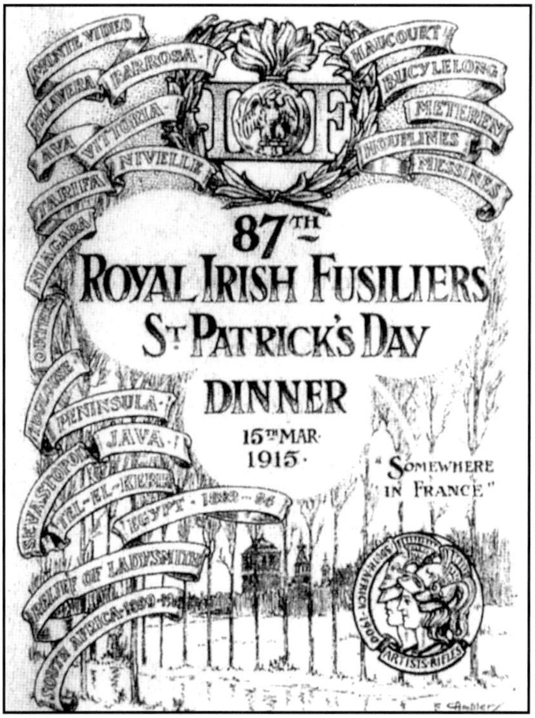

Royal Irish Fusiliers still celebrated St. Patrick's Day in style despite being "Somewhere in France"

Courtesy of the Royal Irish Fusiliers Museum

The 2nd Royal Irish Rifles' origins were in England, where the 86th Regiment of Foot was established in 1793 as General Cuyler's Shropshire Volunteers. The new regiment's first posting was to Ireland where, one assumes, it recruited locally during its two-year stay. By 1806 it was known as the Leinster Regiment of Foot before being titled the Royal County Down Regiment six years later. It finally became the 2nd Royal Irish Rifles in 1881. The battalion, which had fought throughout the Boer War, was stationed at Tidworth in August, 1914, and so was rapidly deployed to Flanders. The battalion marched its way from Belgium to the Somme in June, 1916, only coming up into reserve on the 30th. Throughout the war the 2nd Rifles lost more than 100 officers and 2,000 other ranks killed in action, and its men were awarded close to 400 honours.

The Royal Irish Fusiliers, known as the Faughs (their motto was Faugh-a-Ballagh, or Clear the Way), had been soldiering since 1793 when both the 87th and 89th regiments of Foot, which were to become respectively the 1st and 2nd Royal Irish Fusiliers, were raised in Ireland in the face of the threat from Napoleon. The 87th were no strangers to the French, having earned their reputation for blood and thunder at their expense. At the Battle of Barrosa in 1811 the Faughs had routed the French army, with Sergeant Masterson capturing the Imperial Eagle standard with the immortal words "Be Jabers, boys, I have the cuckoo!" (His great-nephew, Lieutenant James Edward Ignatius Masterson, won a Victoria Cross almost 90 years later, in 1900, as a member of the 1st Devonshire Regiment serving at Ladysmith during the Boer War.) The Army Order of 1881 linking the two units renamed the regiment Princess Victoria's (Royal Irish Fusiliers) with its depot at Armagh. Its catchment area stretched as far as Monaghan and Cavan as well as its home county. Both battalions saw action in the Boer War. The 1st battalion had been based at Shorncliffe in England in 1914 and landed at Boulogne in August with its entire peacetime strength of 27 officers and 1,008 other ranks. In the next four years it was to suffer 94 officer fatalities, with a further 306 wounded, and the lost of 2,013 other ranks.

Lieutenant-Colonel M. G. Moore, and his officers of the 1st Connaught Rangers, pictured at Mullingar in September, 1904

Courtesy of Lester Morrow

The 2nd Royal Irish Fusiliers were in India at the outbreak of the war. On their arrival back in Britain they were placed with the 28th Division and sent to Belgium, taking part in the fighting around St. Eloi. For soldiers used to the temperatures of the sub-continent, the winter in the trenches took a particularly heavy toll. At the end of 1915, the 2nd battalion was ordered to Salonika and later Macedonia, finally becoming part of the 10th (Irish) Division.

Only a brief history of the regular battalions of the Connaught Rangers is necessary as, though both were to see action on the Western Front during the early months of the war, neither served on the Somme, having sailed for the Middle East in December, 1915. The first of the Rangers' Service battalions, the 5th battalion, was latter sent out to serve in the same theatre of war. (Another battalion, the 6th Connaught Rangers, served with the 16th (Irish) Division and its story will be told later.) The Connaught Rangers did leave behind in France and Belgium a legacy which even today is associated with the war as its troops, marching to the front, introduced what until then was the virtually unknown song "Tipperary". Uniquely among the older Irish regiments, the 88th Regiment of Foot, which was to become the 1st battalion, was known from its formation in 1793 as the Connaught Rangers. The 2nd battalion, so designated in the reforms of 1881, was descended from the 94th Regiment of Foot, formed in Glasgow in 1823. The regiment was disbanded in 1922 at partition.

The Leinster Regiment, another of those which was destined to be disbanded following the political upheavals in Ireland, started off in India and Canada. During the Indian Mutiny, Canada volunteered to raise a regiment. This was designated the 100th (Prince of Wales's Royal Canadian) and duly arrived in England in 1858. It was posted to Gibraltar and Malta, and even briefly visited Canada again before returning to England in 1868. For three years, between 1874 and 1877, the regiment was based in Dublin before being sent to India. It was while there, in 1881, that it became the 1st Prince of Wales's Leinster Regiment (Royal Canadians) with its depot in Birr. The battalion was again in India on the outbreak of war in 1914. It left Bombay in October, arriving in England the following month, and was in France by Christmas as part of the 27th Division. Exactly 12 months

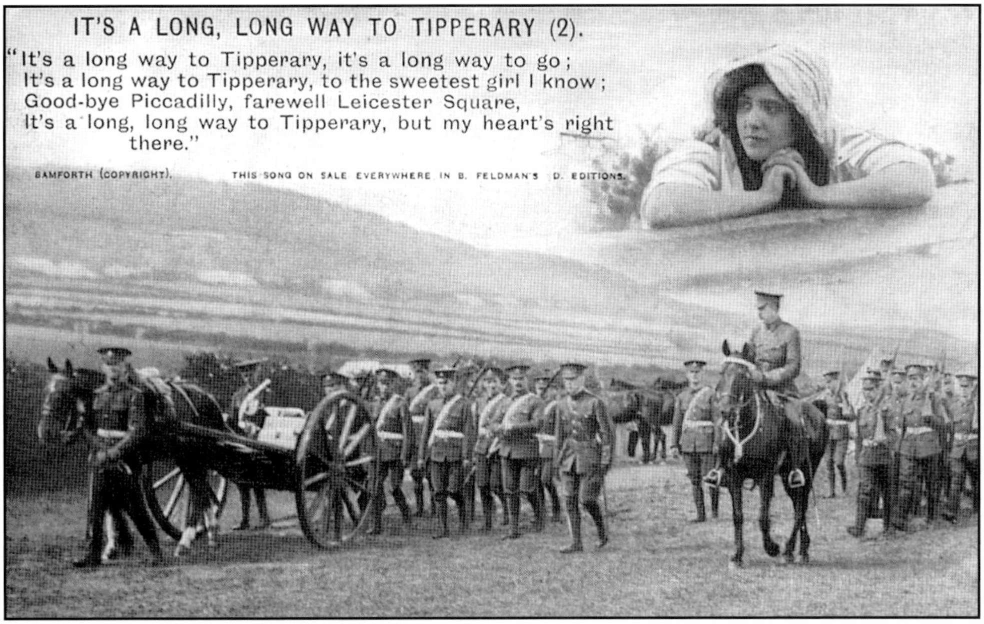

A First World War postcard illustrates the Connaught Rangers' legacy

Courtesy of the Somme Heritage Centre

later it left the Western Front for Egypt and was ultimately to become part of the 10th (Irish) Division.

The 2nd Leinster Regiment had been stationed in Cork in 1914, and at once prepared to cross over to England for reassignment. It landed at St. Nazaire, on the west coast of France, in September, 1914, as part of the 24th Division and was to remain on the Western Front for the next four years. The battalion, known prior to 1881 as the 109th Regiment of Foot, was descended from an Honourable East India Company unit, the 3rd Bombay European Infantry, formed in 1853. It could reasonably be assumed, given the high proportion of Irishmen who had volunteered to serve on the sub-continent, that the regiment would have had a green tinge to it from the outset. In the early 1860s, however, it took on a very different hue with the arrival of 500 recruits from the Jagers regiment, formerly men of the British German Legion. Both the 1st and 2nd battalions, which had fought in South Africa during the Boer War, recruited from Offaly, Meath, Louth and Laois.

India played a huge part in the histories of many of the Irish regiments, as has already been seen, and this was particularly the case with the final two regiments disbanded in 1922. The origins of the 1st and 2nd battalions of the Royal Munster Fusiliers lay with the Bengal European Regiments established from 1756 under the famous Clive of India. The 101st Regiment of Foot was the first to be posted to England, landing in 1869, with the 104th Regiment of Foot doing likewise two years later. The two regiments had been linked by their common past but the connection was made official in 1873, with a common depot set up at Tralee and the counties of Cork, Kerry, Limerick and Clare being their official recruiting areas. In the 1881 reforms they became the 1st and 2nd battalions respectively of the Royal Munster Fusiliers. In 1914 the 1st battalion was at Rangoon, in India. It returned to England to join the 29th Division in its ill-fated landing at Helles at the outset of the Gallipoli campaign. It was so badly depleted by the fighting that it had to be temporarily amalgamated with the Royal Dublin Fusiliers (see below). On being sent to France it became part of the 16th (Irish) Division. The 2nd battalion, meanwhile, had been stationed at Aldershot at the outbreak of hostilities and crossed to France as part of the 1st Division, with which it remained until transferring later in the war to join the 1st battalion in the 16th Division.

Likewise, the Royal Dublin Fusiliers traced its history back to 17th century India. The Honourable East India Company set up its own armed force to protect its interests at Fort St. George, and recruited heavily from Ireland. The 1st battalion was descended from the 1st Madras European Regiment, formed in 1741. The term Fusiliers was later added to the title so that in 1861, when the Crown took over the Indian army, it became the 102nd (Royal Madras) Fusiliers. It was not until 1887, some six years after being designated the 1st Royal Dublin Fusiliers, that the battalion actually moved to Ireland, with its depot established at Naas and its new recruitment area taking in Dublin, Kildare, Wicklow and Carlow. In Madras in 1914, the battalion was the first of the overseas units to come under enemy fire when the German raiding cruiser Emden bombarded the Indian port, though there were no casualties. The Dubliners returned to Britain four days before Christmas to join the 29th Division. At Gallipoli it took such a mauling that it briefly merged with the 1st Royal Munster Fusiliers to form what was termed the Dubsters. The 1st battalion did not arrive on the Western Front until 1917, joining the 16th (Irish) Division.

The 2nd Royal Dublin Fusiliers in France

Courtesy of the Royal Dublin Fusiliers Association

The 2nd Royal Dublin Fusiliers' history goes even further back, to a European corps established in 1661 at Bombay with no known Irish connections. In 1861 the regiment became the 103rd Royal Bombay Fusiliers and left India for the first time after more than 200 years of service. It landed in England in 1871 and was still there when converted to the 2nd Royal Dublin Fusiliers. Again being on home service at the outbreak of the war, it crossed to France in August, 1914. Towards the end of the war it joined the 1st battalion in the 16th Division.

The remainder of the Irish infantry battalions fall into three categories. There were Garrison battalions, often made up of older ex-soldiers recalled to the Colours or men severely wounded in earlier actions. These were often sent to "hold the fort" across the Empire, releasing the regular battalions for war duties. There were also Reserve units which, in the case of the regular regiments, were normally numbered as the 3rd and 4th and sometime 5th battalions and based on the pre-war militias. Their role was to remain at home to train the raw civilian recruits that were despatched to one or other of the parent battalions. A similar system to provide recruits existed among the newly formed Service battalions, so termed as they were temporary units whose "service" would be terminated as soon as the war ended. These units, formed out of civilian volunteers, (and later, though not in Ireland, replenished by conscripts) were the new fighting men and each battalion was adopted by one of the existing regiments. In Ireland, three new divisions were created from Service battalions, the first being the 10th (Irish) Division, whose story is told in the next chapter.

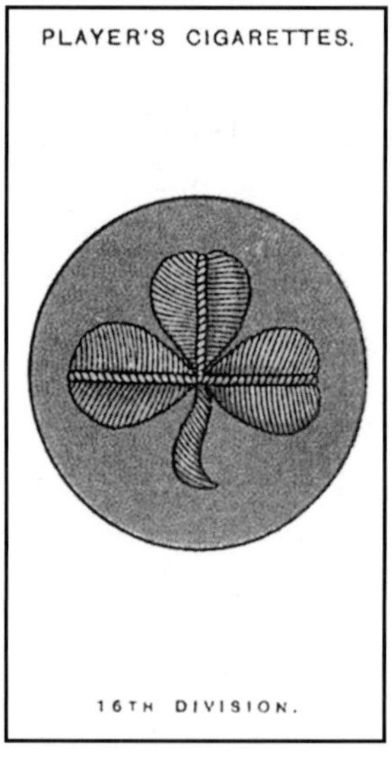

The 16th (Irish) Division was formed as part of the second wave of 100,000 volunteers, known as K2, with the call issued on September 11, 1914. As early as August, John Redmond, leader of the Irish parliamentary party in the House of Commons, had offered the Irish Volunteers as a home defence force to protect against a German invasion of Ireland, so allowing the entire British military garrison to be withdrawn. The suggestion was rejected and Redmond finally gave his approval to service overseas, earning him scorn in some quarters as a "recruiting sergeant for the British army". The Volunteers split, the majority

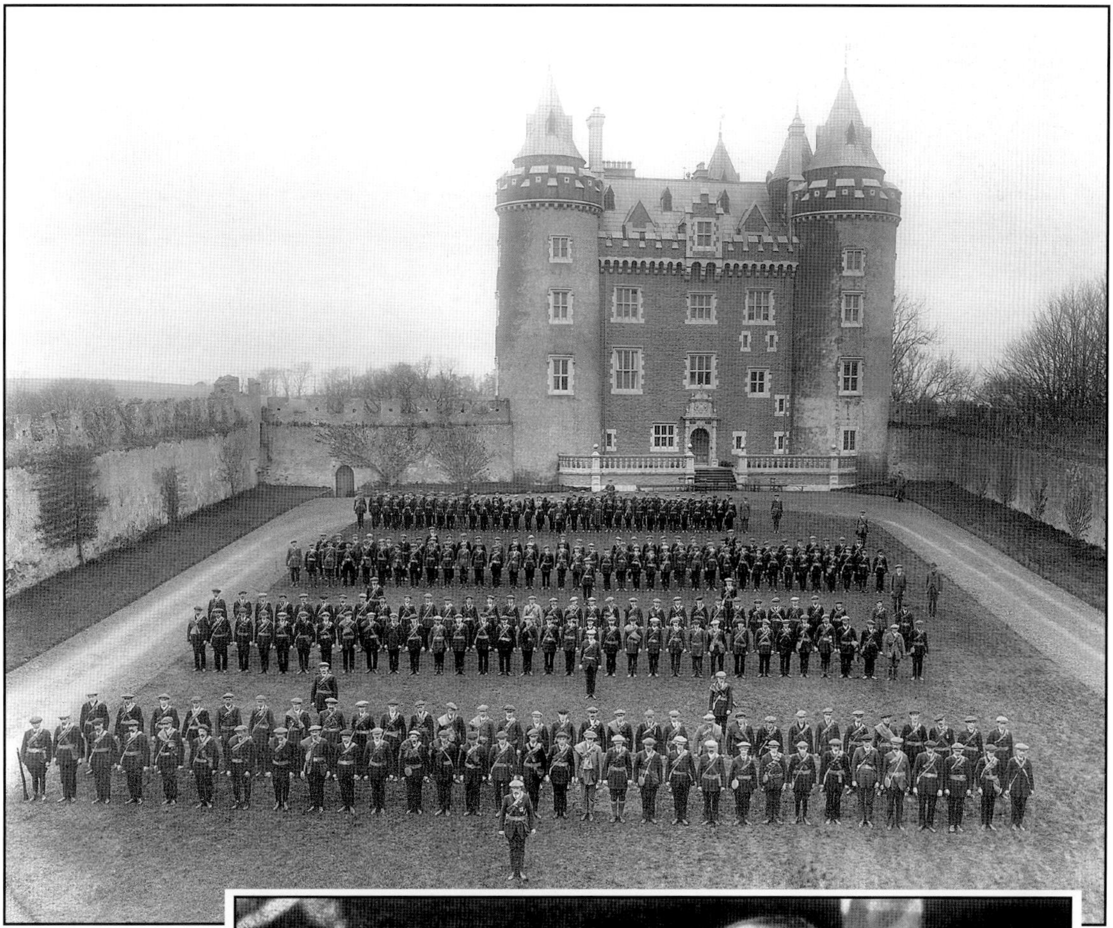

The Ulster Volunteer Force, seen above on parade outside Killyleagh Castle, County Down, was already a well-disciplined and arms-trained organisation prior to the outbreak of war. It had been raised by Sir Edward Carson, right, to resist Home Rule

Courtesy of Lester Morrow

The 36th (Ulster) Division leaves Clandeboye Camp, County Down, for the last time

Courtesy of the Somme Heritage Centre

remaining loyal to Redmond who believed nationalist participation in the war would earn them the right to self-determination afterwards. In 1916 the extent of their differences were shown to the full when some of those who had remained behind played leading roles in the Easter Rising in Dublin, while five months later their former colleagues faced the slaughter on the Somme. The likes of Professor Tom Kettle, a leading nationalist, M.P. for East Tyrone, and an officer in the 9th Royal Dublin Fusiliers, died at Ginchy in 1916 "not for England, but small nations". His body was never found and he is remembered on the Thiepval Memorial to the Missing.

The 16th divisional headquarters was set up in Dublin initially, though later transferred to Mallow then Fermoy. Its first commanding officer was Lieutenant General

Sir Lawrence Parsons, who was called up again at the age of 64 after five years in retirement. From Birr, King's County, he was opposed to Home Rule though kept politics out of his military dealings. He was later replaced, in December, 1915, by Major General William Bernard Hickie, a Catholic from Tipperary, who was to command the division for virtually the entire war.

The brigades were established at Fermoy, Buttevant and Tipperary. Many of the volunteers were Catholics from the north who would never have considered joining the overwhelmingly Protestant 36th (Ulster) Division. The 49th Brigade, consisting of the 7th and 8th Royal Inniskilling Fusiliers and 7th and 8th Royal Irish Fusiliers, was primarily made up of volunteers from Ulster, as was the Belfast-formed 7th Royal Irish Rifles in the 48th Brigade, which also included some 230 men from Jersey. The 6th Connaught Rangers, the only representative of that regiment on the Western Front by 1916, had some 600 volunteers from the Falls Road in Belfast in its ranks and was led by Lieutenant-Colonel J. S. Lenox Conyngham, whose family hailed from Springhill near Moneymore, County Tyrone. Likewise, several hundred volunteers from Derry and Tyrone served in the 6th Royal Irish Regiment. West Belfast M.P. Joe Devlin was the man chiefly responsible for the northern influence. He toured Ulster imploring nationalists to enlist, with an estimated 7,000 having taken the King's shilling by February, 1915. The division transferred to England in September that year, completing its training at Aldershot, with the first two brigades sailing for Le Havre in France just days before Christmas. The third brigade, the 49th, rejoined the rest in February, 1916. The division's first true baptism of fire came two months later when serving in the trenches in the Vermelles sector, Pas-de-Calais. On April 27, and again on the 29th, the Germans unleashed one of their heaviest gas attacks up to that stage of the war on the 16th Division lines, combined with artillery bombardments and trench raids, which were repulsed at a heavy cost.

The 36th (Ulster) Division, the last of the Irish divisions to be officially formed, was ironically the most advanced of the three. Born out of the Ulster Volunteer Force, which had been armed and in training for two years before the outbreak of war in preparation to resist the introduction of Home Rule to Ireland, it already had its own administrative and military structures. By 1914 the situation in Ireland had reached crisis point, with the Home Rule Bill passing through Parliament and the country on the verge of civil war. The declaration of war with Germany sharply altered the focus of all concerned, though one eye remained on the Irish issue. Sir James Craig and Lord Edward Carson, the Unionist leaders, offered the U.V.F. to the Government on the understanding that the implementation of the Home Rule Bill would be delayed and that the new unit would include the designation "Ulster" in its title, both of which were finally granted. Unionists believed that by showing their loyalty to the Crown in this way they would earn the right to remain British. As a result of the delays, authorisation for the formation of the 36th did not come through until October 28, 1914. Its headquarters was established in Belfast, at 29 Wellington Place, with the 107th Brigade (8th, 9th, 10th and 15th battalions of the Royal Irish Rifles), consisting largely of the younger men from the Belfast U.V.F. battalions, undergoing their training at Ballykinlar, County Down; the 108th (11th, 12th and 13th Royal Irish Rifles and 9th Royal Irish Fusiliers) at Clandeboye estate between Bangor and Newtownards, also County Down, and the 109th (9th, 10th and 11th Royal Irish Fusiliers and 14th

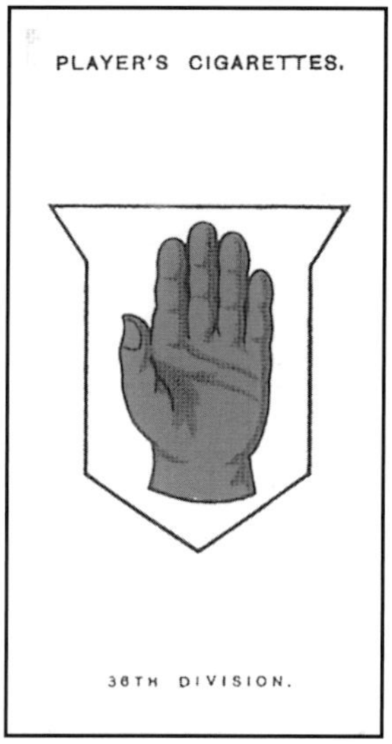

Royal Irish Rifles) at Finner Camp, Ballyshannon, County Donegal. Thirteen battalions made up the division, each taking the title of an established regiment, with the artillery formed in London. After initial training in Ulster, the division, initially under the command of Major-General Sir C. H. Powell, was despatched by train to Dublin in July, 1915, then on to Seaford in southern England, where they were inspected by Earl Kitchener on the 20th of the month. After short spells at Bordon and Bramshott, an advance party crossed to France in late September and the remainder the following month after an inspection by the King. The division spent the rest of the year and all of 1916 up until July on the Somme front.

Three English-raised units with Irish links are mentioned to varying degrees in the pages that follow. Two are individual battalions, the 8th Kings (Liverpool) Regiment and the 18th London Irish Rifles, both of which contained substantial numbers of Irishmen, often second or third generation. The same can be said of the Tyneside Irish Brigade of the 34th Division. Attempts to have it transferred to the 16th Division were frustrated by red tape and objections from both sides. Instead, four battalions of the Northumberland Fusiliers were created. A second brigade was made up of the Tyneside Scottish, and a friendly rivalry between the two groups developed as to which would be the first to raise the numbers needed. In the event, both claimed victory though a careful look at the composition indicated that neither brigade had restricted itself to its own ethnic groupings, with the Scots in particular having at least 75 per cent of their number made up of pure Geordies with no Scottish blood. The Tyneside Irish crossed to France in January, 1916, moving to the Somme sector in May.

The 34th Division's Christmas card of 1916 featured Albert's 'Leaning Virgin'

Courtesy of the Somme Heritage Centre

THE EARLIEST POSSIBLE MOMENT

It is of the utmost importance in the present emergency that every regular reservist shall join at the earliest possible moment, and his Majesty's Government rely with confidence upon the railway and other transport companies, employers, and the reservists themselves to do all in their power to facilitate rapid mobilisation

Secretary of the War Office notice, August 4, 1914

One of the first casualties of the Great War in Ireland was breakfast. Hard-pressed ticket collectors on the daily excursion trains which ferried the "townies" of Belfast to the seaside at Portrush, on the County Antrim coast, braved the wrath of Sunday school excursionists and works outings when they announced during the first few days of August, 1914, that neither luncheon nor breakfast would be served in the dining cars. The reason, they explained, was that many of the staff in the Midland Railway hotels, which prepared the meals, were foreigners and had been forced to leave the country in a hurry after receiving their military call-up papers. Some of the ladies on board would have already been aware of the problem, as a similar crisis had hit hairdressing salons in the city hard, forcing some to close entirely or cancel appointments. The foreign nationals crossed over to England but, with the suspension of the cross-channel sailings, it is unlikely they got much further that month. Certainly the Germans didn't, many being rounded up by the police as aliens and potential spies.

It was exactly one month after the assassination of Archduke Franz Ferdinand at Sarajevo, on June 28, 1914, that the Austro-Hungarian Empire declared war on Serbia. Within weeks the nations of Europe were dragged into conflict, honour-bound to fight by international treaties and understandings with their respective allies and all motivated by self-interest. On August 1, Germany declared war on Russia; the following day it invaded Luxembourg and demanded

Two unidentified members of the Ulster Volunteer Force

Courtesy of the Somme Heritage Centre

that Belgium gave it free access across its borders; the Kaiser declared war on France on August 3, and the German army crossed the Belgian frontier the next day, leading to a declaration of war by Britain, which had undertaken to protect its neutrality.

The swiftness of developments came as a shock to Britons more concerned with ice cream and holidays than what their politicians were up to. War of sorts had never been far from the minds of people in Ireland, however, in that unusually hot summer of 1914. The country was on the brink of its own conflict, with two civilian armies standing ready to defend their fundamentally opposing views, with only those same British soldiers who were shortly to be despatched to France standing between them.

The stand-off came at the end of almost 30 years of political manoeuvrings by the British Liberal Party to return a form of limited self-government to Ireland. Its first two attempts, by the Gladstone administration, were defeated by parliamentary means. The third Home Rule Bill, brought forward in 1912, seemed assured of becoming law, given Prime Minister Herbert Asquith's Westminster majority and determination to force it through the House of Lords. Unionists, who had formed their own party in 1885 to oppose the first Bill, were equally determined to retain the Union with Great Britain. In Parliament they combined with the Conservatives to oppose Home Rule while at home they raised their own army, the Ulster Volunteer Force. Some 90,000 strong by 1914, it openly trained with dummy rifles until the real thing, in the form of 25,000 rifles and three million rounds of ammunition, were smuggled from Germany to Larne in April of that year and distributed across the north. In the south, the Irish parliamentary party, after initial reluctance, embraced the Irish National Volunteers, established in November, 1913, in direct response to the Ulster Volunteer Force (and partially armed in 1914 with the landing of 900 guns and close to 30,000 rounds of ammunition at Howth, Co. Dublin).

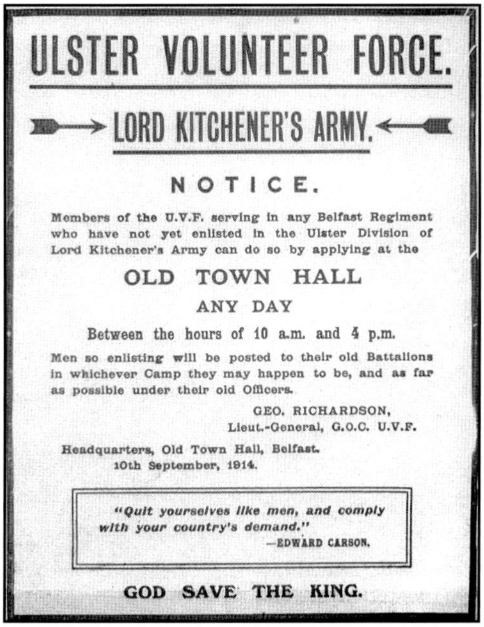

ULSTER VOLUNTEER FORCE.

LORD KITCHENER'S ARMY.

NOTICE.

Members of the U.V.F. serving in any Belfast Regiment who have not yet enlisted in the Ulster Division of Lord Kitchener's Army can do so by applying at the

OLD TOWN HALL

ANY DAY

Between the hours of 10 a.m. and 4 p.m.

Men so enlisting will be posted to their old Battalions in whichever Camp they may happen to be, and as far as possible under their old Officers.

GEO. RICHARDSON,
Lieut.-General, G.O.C. U.V.F.

Headquarters, Old Town Hall, Belfast.
10th September, 1914.

"Quit yourselves like men, and comply with your country's demand."
—EDWARD CARSON.

GOD SAVE THE KING.

An attempt in March that year to subdue unionist resistance by force of arms failed when almost 60 army officers tendered their resignations rather than take action to coerce Ulster. The Curragh Mutiny, as it became known, meant the government faced the setting up of a Provisional Government in Belfast, with Sir Edward Carson and Sir James Craig at its head and supported by thousands of armed men, unsure of how the army would respond to further confrontation. In August, 1914, the Third Home Rule Bill was nearing the completion of its passage through parliament and the government and the Ulster Unionists appeared to be on a collision course.

The declaration of war not only transformed the situation overnight, but made unlikely bedfellows of former enemies. The News Letter reported on August 6:

> *Yesterday afternoon unprecedented scenes were witnessed in Dungannon, when some thousand Nationalists escorted to the railway station a number of Irish National Volunteers who had been called on to rejoin the Colours. The local Nationalist flute band, playing the "Marseillaise," headed the procession, and a large party of the Irish National Volunteers, wearing bandoliers, marched behind. On arriving at the railway station the band and Volunteers assembled on the platform, and as the afternoon mail train steamed off loud cheers were raised for the departing reservists, the band playing "The girl I left behind me" and "Auld Lang Syne." All the leading*

officers of the Dungannon Battalion Ulster Volunteer Force have also been called up, including Viscount Northland, Major Alexander, CMG; Major E. Milnes-Gaskell, and Mr Percy Mallet, battalion instructor.
A large number of Unionist Volunteer, assembled on the railway platform to bid farewell to Mr Mallet, battalion instructor, and Mr David Williamson, and Mr Stevenson, second in command, presented Mr Mallet with a purse of sovereigns.

It was a similar story across Ireland, with thousands of reservists on the move to their depots, and large crowds gathered at barracks, railway stations and docks to cheer them on. At Belfast's Great Northern Railway terminal the train to Dublin, packed with men returning to the Colours, set off at 2.30pm to a roar of approval, though not before a woman who had fallen onto the lines had been pulled to safety. On the same day a young man from Oxford in England appeared in court at Queenstown accused of being a spy. He had been caught two days earlier with a sketch pad and pencil in hand executing a drawing of Queenstown harbour and military fort. Pleading his innocence, he insisted he was merely sketching for pleasure as part of a holiday in Ireland. Over the coming weeks many more "spies" of a similar ilk appeared in courtrooms the length and breadth of Ireland. At sea, the Belfast steamer Carrigan Head, belonging to Messrs G. Heyn and Sons of Waring Street, was requisitioned and ordered to Devonport. (Another Headline ship, the Bengore Head, missed the call-up, having already left for Montreal in Canada. Pressed into service on its return, it was torpedoed and sunk in 1917, one of 11 vessels lost by the Belfast shipping company.)

The bulk of the civilian armies remained uncommitted, however, though neither unionists nor nationalists wanted to be seen as disloyal with the inherent dangers of losing popular support for their cause. A compromise which all hoped would

Irish Volunteers cheer the arrival of guns and ammunition at Howth, County Dublin.

Courtesy of the Somme Heritage Centre

ultimately be settled in their favour was quickly agreed, including the passing into law of the Home Rule Bill (which received the Royal assent on September 18) but with its operation suspended until the end of the conflict. Both sides declared their backing for the war effort – after receiving reassurances and concessions from the government– urging their supporters to join up. The Irish Volunteers, initially offered as a home defence force, were encouraged to enlist by John Redmond, leader of the Irish parliamentary party, in a speech at Woodenbridge, County Wicklow, on September 20, when he declared they should defend freedom and religion "wherever the firing line extends". The membership split, the greater number remaining loyal to Redmond, many of whom enlisted in the 16th (Irish) Division. The remainder continued to recruit dissidents and formed the bulk of those who took part in the Easter Rising two years later.

The U.V.F. formed the nucleus of the 36th (Ulster) Division, its pre-war units being absorbed en masse to form the largest of the "pal" units in the army. At a meeting of the Ulster Unionist Council in the Ulster Hall on September 3, Sir Edward Carson outlined the plans for the formation of an Ulster division: "I say to men, so far as they have confidence and trust in me, I advise them to go and do their duty to the country and we will take care of politics hereafter." Earlier in the day he had addressed the North Belfast Regiment of the U.V.F., which paraded at Dunmore House on the Antrim Road. He told them: "You may have many difficulties – you will have many difficulties – you will have plenty of suffering and sacrifice before you, but from what I know of you I am confident that you will acquit yourselves as Irishmen in the field, and above all, as Ulstermen, proud of your British connection." They then marched to the Old Town Hall to enlist. "The first man to pass the medical examination and to reach the attestation room was William Hanna, aged 44 years, of 42, Brussels Street, a member of the Special Service Battalion, North Belfast Regiment," noted the News Letter. "Hanna, who served in the South African war with the Royal Irish Rifles, wore the ribbons of the Queen's and King's medals for that campaign, and he smiled cheerfully as his papers were completed, securing for him the distinction of being the first member of the Ulster Volunteer Force to be accepted as such by the military authorities."

Even as the talking over Ireland's political future began, other Irishmen were making more pressing arrangements for the war with Germany. The rush of volunteers in 1914, though less so in Ireland where particular circumstances existed, owed much to the efforts of Horatio Herbert Kitchener. Born in June, 1850, just a year after the family had bought a bankrupt estate at Ballygoghlan, astride the county border between Kerry and Limerick on the banks of the Shannon estuary, he was Irish by birth if not blood. He started the war already a national hero of long standing, so that his appointment as Secretary of State for War on August 5 seemed inevitable. He accepted the post on a non-party, non-political basis, commenting the following morning: "May God preserve me from the politicians." Kitchener shocked his cabinet colleagues by dismissing the commonly held belief that the war would be short or, as the expression widely circulating at the time put it, "would be all over by Christmas". He warned it would last at least three years, though stopped short of telling them his opinion, often expressed privately, that a war between Britain and Germany could only end in stalemate. He insisted that to win the war he would need a million men, and on August 11 issued an appeal for the first 100,000 volunteers, which were to be formed into six new divisions. For the first time Britain was to raise a national army rather than depending on its small professional force. The citizen soldiers were to become known as the New Army, though many of those who signed up in those early days would always consider themselves as simply "Kitchener's men". In the event, Earl Kitchener did not live to see his army put to the test on the Somme. In June, 1916, as he set out in atrocious weather on a trip to Russia to encourage that country to continue in the war, his ship, the H.M.S. Hampshire, hit a mine off

Recruits of the 9th Royal Irish Fusiliers undergoing training at Clandeboye Camp, County Down

Courtesy of the Somme Heritage Centre

Orkney and sank within 10 minutes. He was last seen walking the deck in serious conversation, apparently unperturbed by the situation, and made no attempt to find a lifeboat. His body was never recovered.

While the first of the fresh-faced volunteers queued in Ireland's cities and towns to take the King's shilling, it was the professionals who took the field. The army which marched off to war in 1914 was much changed from that which had struggled to defeat the Boers during the South African campaign a decade-and-a-half earlier. The man responsible for implementing those reforms was Field Marshal Lord Roberts, the most senior of the Irish generals and the last commander-in-chief of the British Army. His Irish credentials were the opposite of Kitchener's. Born at Cawnpore, India, in September 1832, he was sent to be educated in England by his Irish father, General Sir Abraham Roberts, attending Eton before passing out of Sandhurst. He returned to India where he was to serve for the next 41 years in the region (including securing a resounding victory during the second Afghan War), the last eight as overall commander. He was put in charge of the forces in Ireland from 1895, the same year he received his Field Marshal's baton, and was despatched to South Africa in January, 1900, following the disastrous start to the campaign which had claimed the life of his son. He quickly turned the army's fortunes round and returned to England exactly a year later, leaving Kitchener to continue the war against the Boers. Lord Roberts had long retired from the active service list by the outbreak of the First World War but happily donned his uniform again to pay a visit to his Indian troops on the Western Front. On November 13, 1914, he retired to bed with a chill which rapidly evolved into pneumonia and at 8pm the following evening he passed away with his daughter and Sir Henry Wilson by his bedside. Three days later, his coffin was borne on a gun carriage from the house in which he had died, 50 Avenue Carnot, St. Omer, to the town's Hotel de Ville, where a funeral service attended by senior British and French generals was held. Then, accompanied by Indian troops, his body was taken to Boulogne and transported home for burial at St. Paul's Cathedral in London in the presence of King George.

Sir Henry Wilson was the man whose preparations and planning were to ensure the prompt and efficient arrival of the British Expeditionary Force in France. From County Longford, he was both an unashamed Francophile, who did much to maintain good relations between the British and French armies, and a staunch unionist, his latter disposition making him something of an outcast among his fellow staff officers. His support for the officers who took part in the Curragh Mutiny earned him political enemies, particularly in the Liberal Party, and prevented his appointment as chief of staff in 1914. Wilson had been Director of Military Operations since 1910 and soon after the outbreak of war was appointed liaison officer to the French headquarters. He commanded the IV Corps on the Western Front for a spell in 1915 but was a better administrator than commander and subsequently held a number of posts until made commander-in-chief in February, 1918. His friendship with Marshal Foch, who was made supreme Allied commander the following month in response to the threatened German breakthrough on the Somme, was instrumental in ensuring the two armies worked in harmony. Sir Henry was Britain's chief military advisor during the subsequent Paris Peace Conference, retiring as a Field Marshal in February, 1922, to enter Parliament as the Unionist MP for North Down. Just four months later, as he returned to his London home after unveiling a war memorial, and dressed in full ceremonial uniform, he was shot dead by two IRA men (who were subsequently hanged for murder), the last British general to die with a sword in his hand as he bravely tried to defend himself.

For Sir Hubert Gough, from Gurteen, County Wexford, the outbreak of war revitalised a career blighted by the Curragh incident. A Boer War veteran who had taken part in the relief of Ladysmith, he was commander of the 3rd Cavalry Brigade at the Curragh and had offered to resign his commission rather than take on the Unionists in Ulster. In 1914 he was made a divisional commander and crossed to France with the British Expeditionary Force. Two years later he was promoted to corps commander and ultimately took command of the Fifth Army. Highly regarded by many as one of the best generals on the Western Front, he was replaced in 1918 following the poor showing of some divisions within his army group in the face of the German attacks of March-April that year. He retired from the army in 1922.

Other Irishmen were to prove influential during the course of the war without leaving the home front. Alfred Charles William Harmsworth, later Alfred Lord Northcliffe, was a publishing tycoon who owned a string of newspapers and magazines including The Times, Daily Mail and Daily Mirror, the latter two of which he founded. He campaigned vigorously from the outset against Kitchener and Prime Minister Herbert Asquith. In 1917 he was made Director of Propaganda by new premier David Lloyd George, resigning from the post on Armistice Day. He died in 1922; Lord Charles Beresford, born at Philipstown, King's County to the 4th Marquess of Waterford, had been leading a bitter campaign of his own for a decade before the conflict. He had joined the Royal Navy in 1859 and had risen to full Admiral by 1906. His best fighting, however, was waged on the floor of the House of Commons. As a Conservative M.P. he campaigned vigorously for an enlarged and better equipped Navy, targeting in particular the policies of Sir John Fisher, as First Sea Lord, during the years up to 1910 when Germany was increasing its fleet; Sir Roger Casement, born in Dublin into a mixed religion marriage and a one-time British Consular member, was of a different persuasion. A committed Irish nationalist who helped form the Irish National Volunteers, he toured America seeking support for his cause. In November, 1914, he travelled to Germany in an unsuccessful attempt to recruit Irish prisoners-of-war to come over to the Axis powers and possibly take part in the planned uprising. Similarly, his bid to persuade the enemy to provide arms and officers for the rebellion yielded little. Having failed on both counts, he returned to Ireland by German submarine in the hope of stalling the rebellion but was arrested in April, 1916. Having had his name blackened by the leaking of his "Black Diary" which recorded many of his homosexual liaisons, he was tried in London for treason

Earl Kitchener and Lord French, featured here on postcards, were national heroes

Courtesy of the Somme Heritage Centre

and executed at Pentonville Prison on August 3, 1916. His remains were returned to Dublin in 1965.

Of the military commanders on the ground, the greatest responsibility lay with Sir John French as commander of the British Expeditionary Force. Although born in Kent, he was descended from a long-established Irish family with roots in Roscommon and Galway, with an ancestor having commanded a troop of Inniskilling Dragoons at the Battle of Aughrim in 1689. The first B.E.F. troops arrived in France on August 7, an average of 144 trains a day, meticulously timetabled, moving it into position. On the same day, the French pushed into German-held Alsace, one of the provinces it had had to cede to its traditional enemy following the war of 1870. It was to be another fortnight before the British fired their first shots in anger. On August 23, the soldiers of the 2nd Royal Irish Regiment, 2nd Royal Irish Rifles and 2nd Connaught Rangers were in action to varying degrees at the Battle of Mons. Despite contributing to the "bloody nose" suffered by the Germans at the hands of the fast-firing and accurate British infantry, they were soon in retreat, passing through a fall-back line held by the Irish Guards. At Le Cateau three days later they were supported by the 2nd Royal Inniskilling Fusiliers, 1st Royal Irish Fusiliers and 2nd Royal Dublin Fusiliers. After another short, sharp engagement, the bulk of the B.E.F. was able to slip away thanks to the heroics of a stubborn rearguard which included elements of the Royal Irish Regiment which, along with the Dubliners, took a mauling at the hands of the enemy. Lance-Corporal John Preston, 2nd Royal Inniskilling Fusiliers, was seriously wounded around this time. From his bed in the First Eastern General Hospital in Cambridge, England, he wrote to his wife in Banbridge:

> *When I landed in France we were pushed right up to the front and had no time to do anything but keep clear of the Germans, which we did all right*

up to Wednesday week last. We encountered the Germans on Sunday at Mons, and fought on till Monday night. It was on the retreat from Mons that I was caught. They had about one hundred guns playing on us all the time we were retiring. We had the 110th Battery of Artillery with us. The whole plain was strewn with dead and wounded. I hope my eyes will never look on anything so horrid again. I am lucky I escaped as I did.

In another letter he wrote:

I am badly broken up. I got very severely wounded. My jaw is dislocated, my right arm broken, and my right shoulder dislocated too, so you may guess I have got my share, but there are others who have lost their arms and legs altogether. The doctor says I will be all right again in a week or so. He says I will not know myself. I was lying wounded and sleeping on the field when an Artillery Major picked me up, and took me to the Artillery camp, and gave me in charge of the Medical Corps. Only for that I never would have seen England again. The Germans would have got me and if you are badly wounded they kill you outright. I was in the trenches from 4am to 6.30 in the evening, when I got hit with a shell, so you can realise what sort of a position I was in. My regiment fought well. They blew the Germans down in hundreds. I would like to march with them again through Berlin on the top of the Kaiser, but I think they have knocked me past going anywhere.[1]

Two other Inniskilling fusiliers wounded in the early fighting returned home to Cookstown, County Tyrone, in September to a heroes' welcome. "As the train steamed into the station the explosion of fog signals announced its arrival to the waiting crowd outside," recorded the News Letter. "A rush was made to the carriage, and almost before the train stopped, the first of the soldiers, Private John Harvey, who had been shot through the leg, was carried shoulder high through the cheering crowd to a motor car. The cheering was renewed as Harvey's two little boys, aged 5 and 4 years, were passed in over the heads of the crowd. The other man, Lance-Corporal Robert Farr, was welcomed by his young wife and baby girl, who were waiting for him, and who were accommodated with seats in the motor, which was accompanied by a crowd of several hundreds singing 'Rule Britannia' and other patriotic songs. Up till a late hour the soldiers were visited at their homes by leading townspeople who welcomed them home on their fortnight's sick furlough."

The Retreat from Mons devastated some of the Irish battalions. The 2nd Royal Munster Fusiliers, part of the rearguard, was cut off at Etreux and suffered the most horrendous casualties, being reduced to just five officers and barely 200 men. A memorial in the cemetery there marks their sacrifice[2]. The Irish Guards had their first major engagement at Landrecies. Commanding officer Lieutenant-Colonel George Morris, rallying his troops amid the confusion of war, told them: "Do you hear that? They are only doing that to frighten you," to which he received the reply from a private "If that's what they're after, Sir, they might as well stop. They succeeded with me hours ago" (recorded in Rudyard Kipling's The Irish Guards in the Great War). At Compiegne the Guards were to be involved in a life-or-death dash for the high ground. A wounded guardsman, interviewed by

[1] Lance Corporal Preston did recover sufficiently to return to duty and win promotion to sergeant. He never got the chance of marching through Berlin, however, as he was killed on the Somme on November 23, 1916. His body was never found and so his name is recorded on the Thiepval Memorial to the Missing.

[2] The same battalion, after being brought up to strength, was again all but destroyed just days before Christmas, 1914, when it was thrown into the line at Festubert to regain ground lost during a German attack on Indian troops near Givenchy.

The live and let live attitude of the first Christmas in the trenches had long passed by the following December

Courtesy of the Somme Heritage Centre

the Evening News in a hospital at Woolwich, England, told the reporter: "It was really a race between the two parties to reach the hill first, but the Germans won easily, owing to their being nearer by half a mile. As soon as their guns and infantry had taken up a position the cavalry came along in a huge mass, with the intention of riding down the Irish Guards, who were nearest to them. When the shock came it seemed terrific to us in the distance. The Irishmen didn't recoil in the least, but flung themselves right across the path of the German horsemen. We could hear the crack of the rifles and see the German horses impaled on the bayonets of the front ranks of the guardsmen. The whole force of infantry and cavalry were mixed up in one confused heap, like so many pieces from a jigsaw puzzle. Shells from the British and German batteries kept dropping close to the tangled mass of fighting men, and then we saw the German horsemen get clear and take to flight as fast as their horses would carry them. Some had no horses, and they were bayoneted where they stood." By the end of 1914 the 1st Irish Guards had suffered close to 1,000 casualties, including Lieutenant-Colonel Morris – buried by the advancing Germans among many of his men at The Guards Grave at Villers-Cotterets, Belgium. He was the first of five commanding officers of the 1st Irish Guards to be lost in the opening 15 months of the war, four being killed and one wounded.

The B.E.F. was forced back to within 20 miles of the French capital, finally halting near Melun on September 5 on land now occupied by Disneyland Paris. The Germans had remained on their heels throughout but the tide of war was about to turn with the arrival of the French Sixth Army, reinforced by the Paris garrison brought up to the line in a stream of Renault taxis and buses. They attacked the exposed German flank, forcing a withdrawal. With the enemy now in retreat, the Irish regiments, along with the rest of the B.E.F., began to advance on September

An early photograph showing two members of the Royal Irish Rifles in a Somme trench. Note the depth of water they had to wade through, often leading to a condition known as trench foot.

Courtesy of Lester Morrow

6 into the gap which had opened between the German armies. A week of hard fighting, in what was to be known as the Battle of the Marne, saw initial gains but German resistance increased as the enemy retired to entrenched positions behind the river Aisne and fed in reinforcements. The Western Front was beginning to take shape and the "Race to the Sea", during which both sides tried to outflank each other to the north, was under way.

The Germans had entered the Somme region in the first month of the war, their armies sweeping through the countryside virtually unhindered by the retreating French and British, the former poorly organised and both too few in number. At Amiens, the only city in the Somme department, the enemy divisions turned south for Paris and what, they hoped, would be the knockout punch of the war. By late September, 1914, however, the Germans left on the Somme had defence, not attack, on their minds. They took up positions on the high ground of Thiepval Ridge, capturing the village of Thiepval on the 27th. The small French force in the area did its best to harass the enemy though, in truth, could do little but watch the old foe dig in. In the final months of 1914, however, the Irish troops' concerns were further north. They were in the thick of it at La Bassee, Le Pilly and Armentieres, where the 2nd Leinster Regiment had its first taste of heavy fighting, and at Ypres and Messines as the year came to a bloody but inconclusive end.

By late autumn a continuous line of trenches and barricades existed from the Belgian coast to the border with Switzerland. The Western Front, of which the Somme formed but a small part, would move comparatively little in the next four years and only then at horrendous cost in human life as the Germans clung on, hoping in vain to force the French to the negotiating table as they had done in the war of 1870. But there was no talk of compromise in Paris or London, only of attack.

The B.E.F., back in Flanders by the end of 1914, contained nine Irish infantry battalions initially – the 2nd Royal Irish Regiment, 2nd Royal Irish Rifles, 2nd Connaught Rangers, 2nd Royal Dublin Fusiliers, 2nd Royal Munster Fusiliers, 1st Irish Guards, 1st Royal Irish Fusiliers, 2nd Leinster Regiment and 2nd Royal Inniskilling Fusiliers. Many of those who had filled the ranks in August that year were already dead or injured, with the battalion strengths being rebuilt time and again from the reserve list. There were also four cavalry units: the 4th Royal Irish Dragoon Guards, the 5th Royal Irish Lancers, B Squadron of the South Irish Horse and A and C Squadrons of the North Irish Horse. With the exception of the Horse squadrons, all were highly-trained career soldiers or recently-retired reservists returned to the Colours though, as the Kaiser pointed out, the British force was as yet a "contemptible little army" compared to the millions of men being mobilised by the other nations. Further regular battalions were back in England, being grouped in divisions, or in transit from their outposts across the world. The drive for the first 100,000 civilian recruits was well under way, though it would take many more months before the advance parties of these arrived in France. After a winter of consolidation, during which the only major engagement was the Battle of Neuve Chapelle in March, with the 1st Royal Irish Rifles playing a pivotal role and the Leinsters and Royal Irish Regiment engaged in bloody hand-to-hand fighting at St. Eloi, the campaign began in earnest again with the German-inspired Second Battle of Ypres. On April 22, 1915, the enemy released a cloud of green chlorine gas which drifted into the Allied lines, sparking panic among the French territorial and Algerian troops who fled their posts. A five-mile gap opened up and the Germans streamed through. In the following days the 1st Royal Irish Regiment, 2nd Royal Dublin Fusiliers, and 1st Royal Irish Fusiliers were thrown in along with other reserves to plug the gap and regain lost ground around St. Julien. Their losses were horrendous, with the Dubliners alone losing more than 500 men. Among the Irish Fusiliers' dead was Private Robert Morrow, from New Mills, County Tyrone, who just two weeks earlier, on April 12, had risked his own life to save those of comrades buried by shellfire, for which he was later awarded the Victoria Cross.[3]

Sergeant Hugh Alexander Wilson was so severely wounded in the leg on the outskirts of St. Julien that he had to be invalided out of the army. He recalled of his 12-hour wait for rescue:

Sergeant Hugh Wilson survived the war but was crippled for life

Courtesy of the Royal Irish Fusiliers Museum

> *There was nothing to dig with only my bayonet, so with bayonet and hands I laboured on, digging it with the bayonet and throwing it out with my hands. At last I had to stop for I had got just under cover and I was getting done up with loss of blood, for when I looked there was a big pool of it by my knee. I got my towel from my haversack and bound it on top, as tight as I could, but it soon came through this and I began to think I would die from loss of blood before night came and I was picked up. I did not expect to get away before, as no one could come near. So I lay that day through, wishing night would come, and all the time shells were bursting all about, so that I began to think I was to have another one.*[4]

[3] Eleven Irishmen won Victoria Crosses up to the end of 1915, though only two, one of them Robert Morrow, were serving with Irish regiments. Irish Guardsman Michael O'Leary, from Inchigeela, County Cork, was the other. On February 1, 1915, he single-handedly killed eight Germans, including the three-man crew of a machinegun holding up his battalion's advance at the La Bassee Canal, and took others prisoner. He was commissioned in September that year and ended the war as a major. He is buried in Belgium at White House Cemetery, north-east of Ieper, then known as Ypres (and referred to throughout this work by its old name).

[4] Quoted in Angels and Heroes, The Story of a Machine Gunner with the Royal Irish Fusiliers, August 1914 to April 1915, by Amanda Moreno and David Truesdale.

In May, the 1st Royal Irish Rifles lost 22 officers and almost 500 men in an attack at Rouges Bancs, while the 2nd Munsters suffered almost as severely. A week later, at the Battle of Festubert, it was the turn of the 2nd Royal Inniskilling Fusiliers and Irish Guards to bear the brunt of the carnage, with the latter's engagement in the 10-day battle costing it almost 480 soldiers in dead, wounded and missing for a gain of barely 600 yards. The Guards' newly-formed 2nd battalion endured its baptism of fire four months later, at the Battle of Loos, suffering 324 casualties of which almost half were dead. The 1st/18th London Irish Rifles, also engaged at Loos, led the way across No-Man's-Land kicking a football and taking the first line of German trenches at the point of a bayonet.

All told, the British Empire had landed some 250,000 troops in France by the autumn of 1915, of which half had been killed or wounded, principally at the battles at Ypres and Loos. A further two million men had rallied to the Colours at home, and were in the final months of their basic training. At the beginning of the year the British army had held small sectors of the line, often with its units separated by French troops. Gradually this was rationalised, the remnants of the Belgian army taking over the left of the line by the coast, then the B.E.F., with the French to the south. Life in the trenches proved difficult from the outset and grew worse over the course of the war. The smell caused by rotting corpses, open latrines and unwashed bodies was overpowering; drainage was poor, with the freezing cold water which gathered in winter causing "trench foot"; clothes rapidly became infested with lice (the origins of the term "lousy") and huge rats abounded, possibly the most irritating of the hardships the soldiers had to endure. Veteran William Calvert, who served with the 11th Royal Irish Rifles in the trenches from late 1915 on, recalled: "The rats were terrible, but like everything else you got used to them. There were hoards of them, especially when we were using

The 10th (Irish) Division band, photographed in Egypt in 1915

Courtesy of the Somme Heritage Centre

the farmers' barns as billets. They ran all over you, and they were big, because of the dead bodies, they fed on them. You couldn't keep food, no matter where you put it they got into it somehow. They were terrible things."

Lieutenant-General Bryan Mahon commanded the 'forgotten soldiers' of the 10th (Irish) Division

Courtesy of the Somme Heritage Centre

The greatest Irish contribution to the war in 1915, however, had arguably not been on the Western Front at all but in Turkey. The 10th (Irish) Division was the first raised in Ireland and the earliest to see action. As part of the ill-fated Gallipoli expedition its members, more than any others, have become the forgotten soldiers of Ireland. The least political of the three Irish divisions raised, its formation followed directly Earl Kitchener's appeal for the first 100,000 volunteers. Men from throughout Ireland, keen to get to the front as quickly as possible, were the first recruits. They included all creeds, classes and political opinions, Protestant and Catholic alike, and officially came into existence on August 21, just 10 days after the call to arms. Lieutenant-General Bryan Mahon, a 52-year-old Protestant and Unionist from County Galway, was its commander. He had made his reputation at the relief of Mafeking during the Boer War and was a personal friend of Kitchener. Initial training was undertaken by individual battalions, such was the spread of recruitment across the entire island. It was eight months before the first divisional exercise could be organised at the Curragh, in April, 1915. After crossing to England the division was based at Hackwood Park, near Basingstroke, in Hampshire, the home of Lord Curzon, a future member of the War Cabinet and a Conservative peer who the previous year had been actively encouraging Unionists to resist Home Rule by force of arms if necessary. King George inspected the division there at the end of May, 1915, with Earl Kitchener visiting the camp on June 1. In addition to the Irish volunteers, some of the excess English recruits were taken into the 10th Division, most of them Roman Catholics in accordance with a tradition dating back to Napoleonic times. Later, men from the 16th Division were transferred to the 10th to bring it up to strength, while some of the Protestant recruits were allowed to move to the 36th (Ulster) Division. The order for deployment to Gallipoli came at the end of June. When the 10th Division gathered on the island of Lemnos in preparation for the battle ahead it consisted of the 29th Brigade, made up of the 6th Royal Irish Rifles, 5th Connaught Rangers, 6th Leinster Regiment and 10th Hampshire Regiment; the 30th Brigade of 6th and 7th Royal Dublin Fusiliers and 6th and 7th Royal Munster Fusiliers; and the 31st Brigade, consisting of 5th and 6th Royal Irish Fusiliers and 5th and 6th Royal Inniskilling Fusiliers. The 5th Royal Irish Regiment was the divisional pioneer battalion. The landing at Suvla Bay, on the Gallipoli peninsula, on August 7, 1915, was one of confusion and, had the stakes not been so

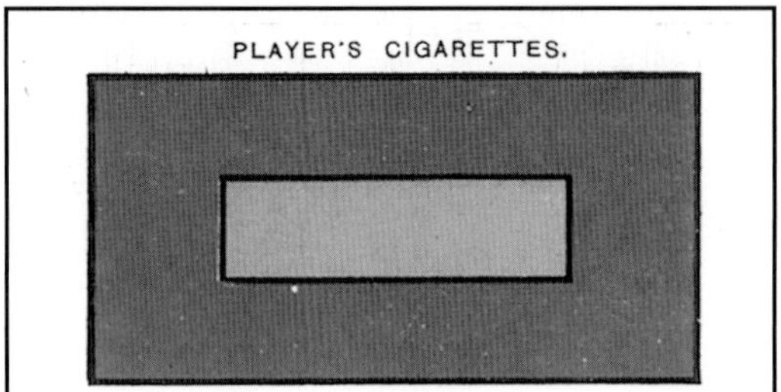

Soldiers from various regiments, injured early in the war, convalesce in Dublin

high, even farce with elements of the attacking force coming ashore miles from their intended destinations. The 10th Division ended up split in two, with three battalions and the pioneers finding themselves on the bare slopes of Kiretch Tepe ridge while the bulk of the division was involved in the successful attack on Chocolate Hill, some four miles away. After a week of baking heat and little water, Mahon was ordered to attack along the ridge on August 15, sustaining 2,000 casualties for little gain.

Lance Corporal Norman Brown, of the 7th Royal Dublin Fusiliers, was the nephew of County Court judge W. H. Brown and grandson of former Presbyterian Moderator the Rev N. M. Brown of Limavady. Writing from his hospital bed in Alexandria after being wounded, he recalled:

> *The order to land was given. Lighters and little boats were manned, and we made for the shore. Two of our boats were hit by shells, and before the whole battalion had disembarked wounded were being carried back on board on stretchers. We formed up under cover of a hill, and then the order was given to advance. We carried our full kit – pack, a blanket, a waterproof sheet, two days' iron rations, a water bottle (respirators and rations in haversack), our rifle and 220 rounds of ammunition – a heavy weight to carry in the heat. Advancing by short rushes we went on for about two miles, all the time under heavy shrapnel fire, and then took a rest under cover, and took off our packs. Then on we went with our haversacks strapped on our backs in lieu of the pack, over hills and then along a sandy beach. Horrible sights we passed – men dead and mangled wounded groaning piteously, men lying dead as they fell in the charge, rifle and bayonet fixed in their hands."*

As at Anzac, where the Allies had first landed, Suvla soon became bogged down in tit-for-tat minor skirmishes with the Turkish defenders. With no prospect

Captain Edward Graham Mylne, left, of the Irish Guards, was the eldest son of the former Bishop of Bombay, while Captain Eustace George Walter Bourke, son of the future Earl of Mayo, had been A.D.C. to the Lord Lieutenant of Ireland

of breaking the deadlock, the decision was taken to evacuate both Suvla and Anzac. Mahon, who had all but become isolated on the ridge, led his small force back to the safety of the main lines and all the Allied troops were withdrawn without loss by December 20 in what was, ironically, the most successful operation of the campaign. After its mauling at the hands of the Turks, the 10th spent the rest of its war with the Mediterranean Expeditionary Force, with spells in Macedonia and Palestine.

As always, it had been the ordinary soldier who had suffered most in the opening two years of the war, with many well-known names, almost inevitably officers, among the casualties. These included Captain Gerald Hugh Fitzgerald, of the 4th Royal Irish Dragoon Guards, a son of Lord Maurice Fitzgerald of Johnstown Castle, Wexford, who was killed in September, 1914; Captain Arthur Edward Bruce O'Neill, of the 2nd Life Guards, the son of the second Baron O'Neill of Shanes Castle, Antrim, and the first Member of Parliament to die in the First World War when he was killed in November, 1914; the Hon. Andrew Edmund Somerset Mulholland, a captain in the 1st Irish Guards, who also died in November, 1914. He was the son of the second Baron Dunleath of Ballywalter Park, County Down; Robert Bernard, a Lieutenant in the 1st Royal Dublin Fusiliers and son Dr J. H. Bernard, a former Archbishop of Dublin, was killed in April, 1915, at V Beach in Gallipoli; and Captain Eustace George Walter Bourke, Adjutant of the 9th King's Royal Rifle Corps, who was a son of the future 8th Earl of Mayo. Killed in June, 1915, he had formerly been A.D.C. to the Lord Lieutenant of Ireland; Captain Edward Graham Mylne, 32, of the 1st Irish Guards, was killed in June, 1915. His father had been Bishop of Bombay and he himself had been born in India. He is buried at St. Sever Cemetery, Rouen, France; Lieutenant Arthur McLaughlin, whose father was a principal of McLaughlin and Harvey builders, with offices in Belfast and Dublin, died in action in May, 1915. Another brother, Trooper George McLaughlin, had been killed during the Boer War; and Lieutenant Edward Workman, the son of the founder of Belfast shipyard Workman, Clark and Co. Ltd., a former High Sheriff of the city, died in hospital in January, 1916, from a blow to the head received during a raid on a German trench.

SUCH SIGHTS YOU NEVER SAW

It was proper hell; nobody can imagine what it was like only those who were in it. We could hardly get over the dead and wounded and such sights you never saw in all your life as the poor chaps lying there with legs, and arms and heads off, some with their body blown out of them.

Ulster Division private Robert Stewart, wounded July 1, 1916

It had fallen to the French *poilus* to initially man the trenches of the Somme, which they did with their usual attitude of live and let live, making this sector one of the quietest on the Western Front during the latter part of 1914 and into 1915. The B.E.F., sufficiently reinforced, extended its frontage further south and in August that year the troops of the newly-formed Third Army filed into trenches running almost up to the banks of the River Somme. Among their number was the 4th Division, which at that time had the 1st Royal Irish Fusiliers, 2nd Royal Dublin Fusiliers and 2nd Royal Irish Regiment in their ranks, the first Irish units to be posted to the trenches on the Somme front since the stabilising of the line.[1] The first two battalions were still with the division on July 1, 1916, though the 2nd Royal Irish had by then transferred to the 7th Division. In March, 1916, the Fourth Army, again a new formation under General Sir Henry Rawlinson, took over the Somme sector. The British now held close to 80 miles of front line; the French, by comparison, manned 400 miles (including a short stretch running through

[1] They were not, however, the first Irish soldiers to serve or die in the Somme sector, as the B.E.F. briefly fought here early in the war. In Ham British Cemetery, for instance, lie the remains of Private Thomas Duffy, of the 1st Royal Irish Fusiliers, who died in August, 1914 (noted in The Somme Battlefields, by Martin and Mary Middlebrook). It was also at Ham that the 2nd Royal Irish Rifles crossed the Somme on its retreat in 1914. It crossed again at almost the same point some three-and-a-half years later, on its way to Cugny where it made a desperate last stand as the Germans again advanced in March 1918.

The Empire's defenders, including Irishmen Field Marshal Sir John French, Lord Kitchener and Earl Roberts, feature on a postcard of the day.

Courtesy of the Somme Heritage Centre

Germany next to the Swiss border), though large sectors were to see little action throughout the war.

The seeds of the Battle of the Somme had been planted as the troops had prepared to mark their second Christmas in the trenches. The plan, conceived during the inter-Allied conference in Chantilly in December, 1915, was simple enough in essence, if over ambitious given the state of the war on the Eastern Front: to stretch the German army to breaking point by launching simultaneous attacks by the Russian, Italian, French and British forces. On February 18, 1916, the French and British commanders, General Joseph Joffre and Sir Douglas Haig (the latter having replaced Field Marshal French as head of the B.E.F. in December, 1915), met to confirm the joint offensive in the Somme region that summer. The choice of location was not only politically expedient, but also coincided with the traditional invasion path between the hills of Artois and Noyon. Joffre, in his memoirs, recorded:

The strategic aim I intended to carry out was to direct a mobile mass at the enemy's communication network, stretching from Cambrai to Le Cateau to Maubeuge. The road from Bapaume to Cambrai thus defined the initial line of attack. The objective was marked out by Miraumont, Le Sars, Ginchy, Guillemont, Maruepas, Hem, the Flaucourt plateau.

The British Official History of the war takes a very different view, suggesting the Somme, which "might be considered the strongest" in terms of German resistance, had been chosen "solely because the British would be bound to take part in it". Haig's desire had been to mount an offensive in Belgium, where the enemy was at that juncture less well prepared. The Germans had used the two years they had spent on the Somme front converting every hilltop into a defensive redoubt, woods into strongholds and the ruins of the frontline villages into fortresses, often with interconnecting underground corridors. Whereas the British and French refused to construct anything but rudimentary trench systems on the principle that they were merely temporary positions until such times as they threw the enemy out of France and Flanders, the Germans on the Somme were largely content to hold the line. Elsewhere, however, they had other plans and just days after the Joffre-Haig meeting, on February 21, the Germans attacked at Verdun, the intention being, according to General Erich von Falkenhayn, German Chief of the General Staff, to "bleed to death" the French army. The historical significance of this fortified city was such that the French were prepared to defend it to the last man. Before the year was out, more than 300,000 French had become casualties, with German losses only marginally less severe.

The original Allied plan of attack on the Somme had envisaged 39 French and 28 British divisions taking part. Following the start of the Verdun campaign it was scaled back to just 14 French and 26 British and the emphasis now was as much on forcing the Germans to withdraw forces from Verdun as securing a breakthrough. In the former, if nothing else, the battle succeeded, as the German army withdrew some 23 divisions from other sectors of the front to the Somme in the first month of the battle alone.

The Germans, realising their vulnerability on the Somme, had prepared the ground meticulously. Two principle lines of trench systems existed, several hundred yards deep in places and reinforced by natural strong points and man-made redoubts. A third was under construction in June, 1916, and in between were fall-back trenches, where an enemy could be held up while reinforcements manned the next line. Elaborate subterranean barracks, complete with electric lighting and a light railway system, were dug out of the chalk and earth. In these the men slept and ate, were treated in field hospitals or relaxed when off-duty, immune to the dangers above ground. Passageways connected the living accommodation to a network of machinegun nests and artillery observation posts.

The strength of the German resistance on the Somme was well known to the British. It had been probed time and again in trench raids; night patrols had crept to within feet of the enemy trenches in search of information; and countless photographs had been taken from the air. Nonetheless, the generals were confident that nothing could survive the massive artillery barrage planned to precede the battle. The guns opened up along the 18-mile British front on June 24. Employed were 1,537 artillery pieces, of which 467 were heavy calibre guns, effectively providing one gun for every 20 yards of front. It was the heaviest concentration of guns gathered for an offensive up to that point in the war, but was undermined by the poor quality of the shells supplied, a third of which failed to explode. The French, by comparison, had 900 heavy guns in operation on a much smaller front and did considerably more damage. Bad weather made observation, particularly from the air, difficult and threatened to turn No-Man's-Land into a quagmire. June 29, the date set for the opening of the campaign, came and went with the

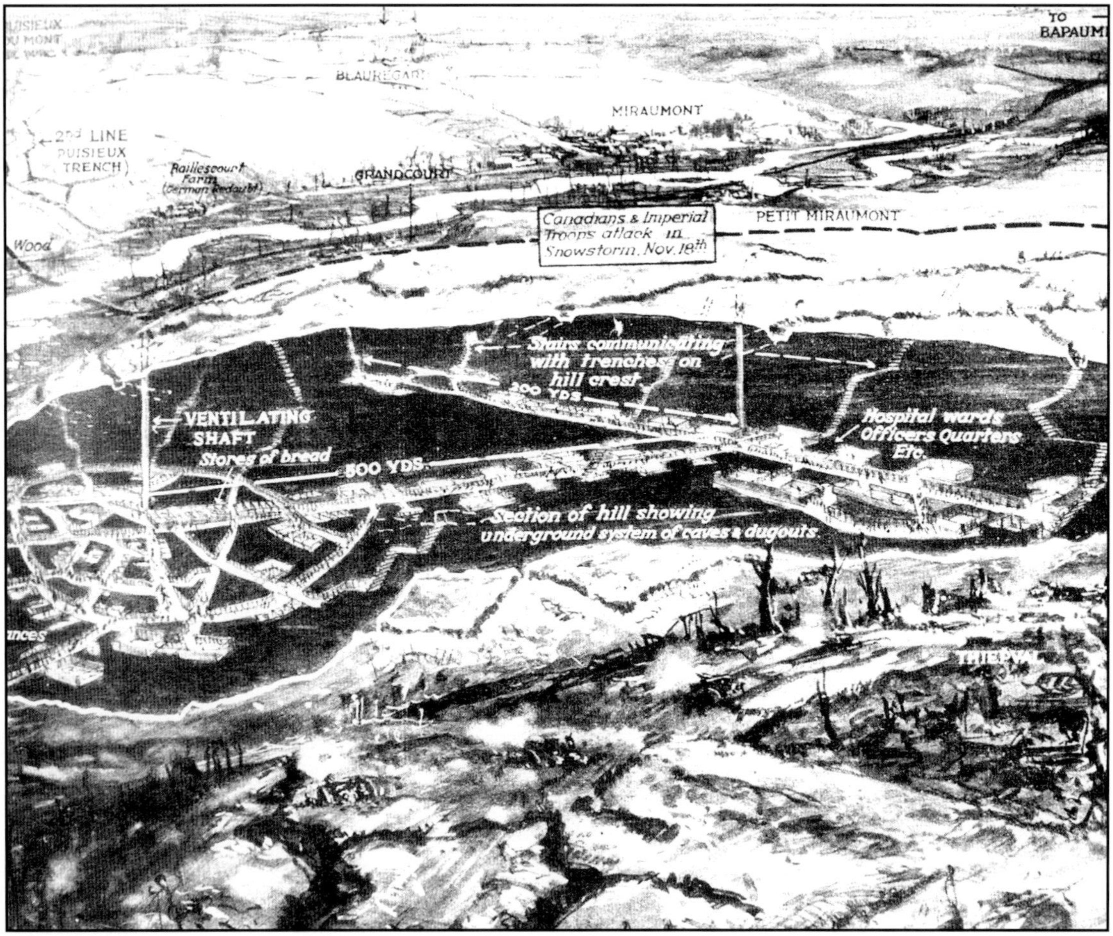

This artist's impression of the Schwaben Redoubt, although not entirely accurate, gives some idea of the extent of the German underground fortifications

troops still sheltering in their trenches, a two-day postponement having been forced upon the planners by the adverse weather conditions. The change of date meant another 48 hours of torment for the waiting troops, though for the men of the 36th (Ulster) Division it seemed a good omen. The divisional official history records:

> *The extra strain of waiting was more than counterbalanced by the coincidence of the date. For it was upon July the 1st, the anniversary of the Boyne, that the sons of the victors in that battle, after eight generations, fought this great fight. To them, it had a very special significance. A stirring in their blood bore witness to the silent call of their ancestors. There seemed to them a predestination in the affair. They spoke of it as they waited, during the final intensive bombardment, while the German counter-barrage rained upon their trenches.*

At 7.30am on July 1 the whistles finally blew. The first waves of troops clambered up roughshod wooden ladders, filed through the gaps cut in their own barbed wire defences for the purpose, and began forming up in orderly lines for the slow trudge across No-Man's-Land. Each soldier was weighed down by some 66lbs of equipment, more than half the body weight of the average Tommy. Just moments before going over the top a series of mines, the access tunnels having been laboriously prepared in the months previous, were detonated under the

The 'iron harvest' turned up by the plough each year on the Somme bears testimony to the intensity of the bombardment and poor quality of the shells

German positions. The British Fourth Army, with its centre at Thiepval, bore the brunt of the fighting, with elements of the Fifth Army involved to the north. To the south the French Sixth Army, under General Fayolle, enjoyed early success.

The failure of the artillery to sufficiently cut the barbed wire in front of the German lines or to make any significant impact on the deep German dugouts was quickly evident. The troops were caught in No-Man's Land by the German gunners returning to their weapons after the lifting of the artillery barrage, leading to thousands dying as they bunched up to get through the few gaps in the barbed wire.

The attack, which involved 13 British divisions on the first day, failed to achieve the hoped for breakthrough along a front which stretched from north of Gommecourt to Maricourt. The little gains made were rarely supported on the flanks and largely had to be given up again within hours. By the end of the day, the British had suffered 57,000 casualties, of which approximately a third were fatalities.

By mid-July all attempts at mass attacks on broad fronts had been abandoned and instead a series of smaller offensives, fiercely resisted by the Germans, made small gains. September witnessed an escalation in the ferocity of the attacks but from the following month through to November 18, when the battle officially ended, the fighting was restricted to comparatively minor actions. The British army had paid with its blood for the capture of Fricourt, La Boisselle, Bazentin, Ovillers, Guillemont, Guichy, Longueval, Thiepval, Delville and High woods.

Despite its failure to produce a decisive victory, the Battle of the Somme did mark the first genuine Anglo-French initiative of the war. It saw the introduction of the tank into battle, used by the British in the Pozieres-Courcelette sector on September 15, though of the 49 tanks employed, only 32 managed to leave the start line and many of those broke down within a few miles. It also confirmed the airplane as an effective weapon of war and not merely a tool for observation. The New Armies had been "blooded", in some cases virtually annihilated, by the fighting. The Somme, in the words of historian Liddell Hart, had "proved both the glory and the graveyard of Kitchener's Army". And, although it may not have been appreciated at the time, the German army had lost the core of its experienced men and was never to be the same again.

Of the 56 British and Imperial divisions on the Western Front in 1916, 53 took part in the Somme fighting between July 1 and its conclusion in mid-November, 1916. The front line moved forward less than seven miles at the centre in the four-and-a-half months of slaughter. Estimates of the overall casualties vary greatly but even conservative figures put it at more than 200,000 French, in excess of 600,000 Germans and 400,000-plus British, of which approximately 125,000 were dead, including troops from Australia, South Africa, New Zealand, Canada, India and, as the next chapter shows, Ireland.

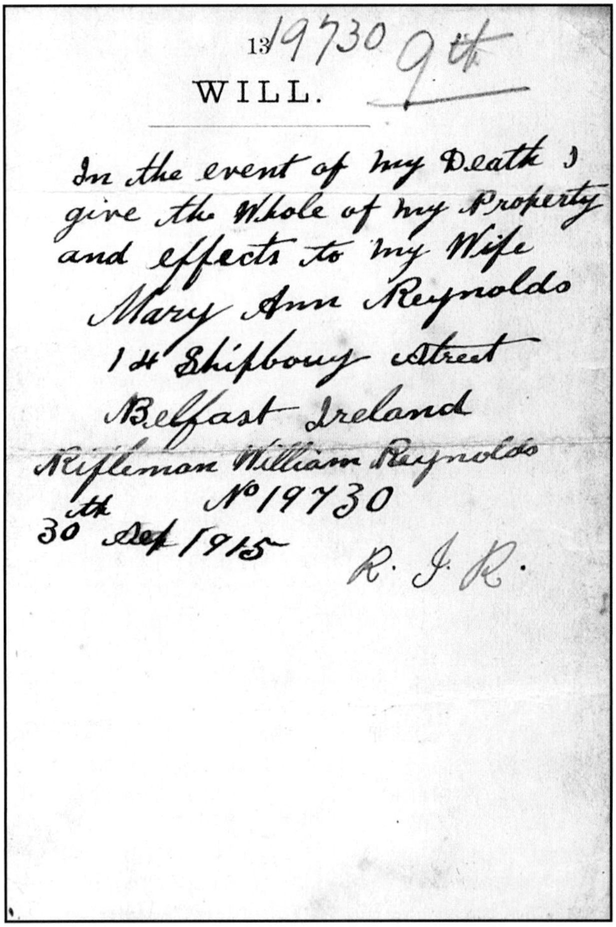

13 19730 9th

WILL.

In the event of my Death I give the Whole of my Property and effects to my Wife Mary Ann Reynolds 14 Shipbouy Street Belfast Ireland

Rifleman William Reynolds No 19730

30th Sept 1915

R. I. R.

Every soldier had to ensure his Will was in order before going into battle

Courtesy of the Somme Heritage Centre

IT WAS GLORIOUS

We went in and attacked but failed to advance. We reorganised, and in a few hours made a second attack, which also failed. Our CO was in despair, and we asked for relief. The latter was sent for, but meantime we made a third attack, and carried the position. It was glorious. I could see Huns actually running away from our bayonets.

Lieutenant G. Leybourne Murphy, RAMC, attached Royal Irish Rifles, July, 1916

Every Irish infantry battalion on the Western Front in 1916 took its turn in the trenches during the Battle of the Somme. For some it was just the once, the slaughter rendering them incapable of further action. Others, spared the crippling casualties of the bigger set battles, returned time and again until they, too, needed to be withdrawn, with fresh drafts of men taking the place of the dead and wounded. These units were a mix of the regular pre-war battalions, many of which had been in France since August 1914, and the partially-trained citizen volunteers who were largely untried in battle. Including English-raised units, there were some 42 battalions which were expressly Irish or sufficiently Irish to warrant the term in either their formal or popular titles. Of these, 24 took part in the first phase of the battle and it is their story which we look at first. On occasion, where a battalion's subsequent part in the battle is limited, it is concluded before moving on to the next unit in the line. The battalions operating to the north, or left, of the line are dealt with first before moving south, in much the same direction as most visitors are likely to arrive at the battlefields. The Irish battalions which took part in the later fighting are taken chronologically, according to when they first became heavily involved, rather than geographically.

Most people know a little of what went on at Beaumont Hamel on the morning of July 1, 1916, even if they aren't aware of the village by name. It was made famous by the exploding of a mine under the German trench system 10 minutes

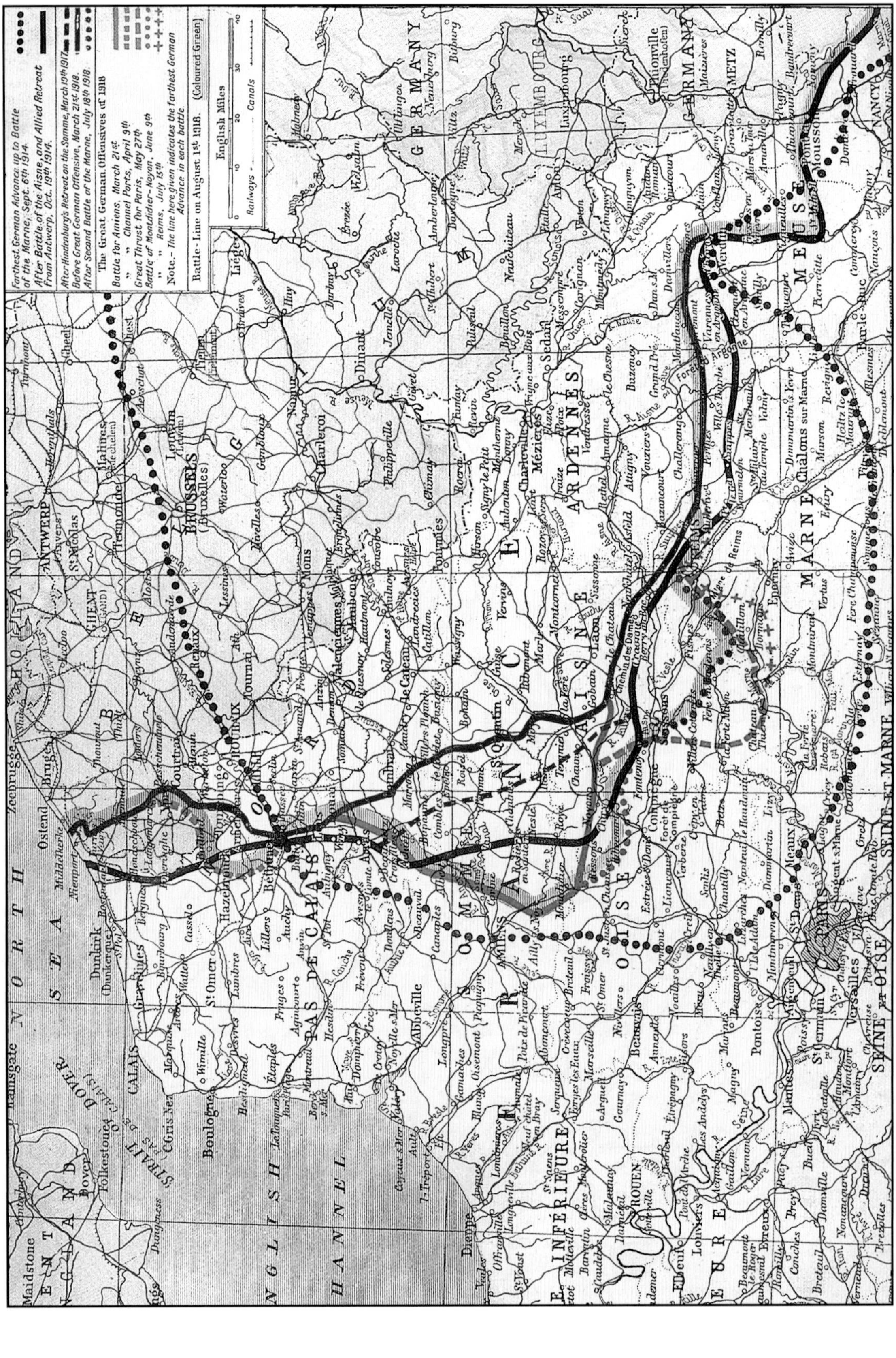

Farthest German Advance up to Battle of the Marne, Sept. 6th 1914.
After Battle of the Aisne, and Allied Retreat from Antwerp, Oct. 19th 1914.
After Hindenburg's Retreat on the Somme, March 19th 1917.
Before Great German Offensive, March 21st 1918.
After Second Battle of the Marne, July 18th 1918.
The Great German Offensives of 1918
Battle for Amiens, March 21st
" " Channel Ports, April 9th
Great Thrust for Paris, May 27th
Battle of Montdidier-Noyon, June 9th
" " Reims, July 15th
Note.- The line here given indicates the farthest German Advance in each battle.
Battle-Line on August 1st 1918. (Coloured Green)
English Miles
0 10 20 30 40
Railways
Canals

before the zero hour of 7.30am so that it could be filmed for posterity. It was arguably a worthwhile exercise, assuming you can forgive the thousands of lives lost as a result of the Germans being given such precise advance notice of the impending attack, as it is probably the television footage most often used to illustrate the First World War. It is here that the Irish troops of the VIII Corps awaited the start of battle. Their objectives were the northern fringes of the village and the formidable Hawthorne Redoubt fortress. The corps included four Irish battalions, divided between two divisions. The 1st Royal Irish Fusiliers and 2nd Royal Dublin Fusiliers, pre-war regular battalions, were both in the 10th Brigade of the 4th Division, along with the 1st Royal Warwickshire Regiment and 2nd Seaforth Highlanders. The remainder of the division consisted in 1916 of the 11th Brigade (1st Somerset Light Infantry; 1st East Lancashire Regiment; 1st Hampshire Regiment; 1st Rifle Brigade) and 12th Brigade (1st King's Own Regiment, 2nd Lancashire Fusiliers; 2nd Essex Regiment; 2nd Duke of Wellington's Regiment) with the 21st West Yorkshire Regiment acting as its pioneers.

The Old Toughs, as the Dubliners were nicknamed, found themselves on the right of the 4th Division line. The battalion was in the second wave which moved forward at 9am and the men immediately came under intense fire from Ridge Redoubt and Beaumont Hamel. With the German line to their front untaken, and elements of the East Lancashires and Royal Hampshires, the leading battalions, still in No-Man's-Land, many of the Dubliners were instructed to remain in the trenches. Those that did go over the top paid the price the minute they emerged above ground.

The 1st Royal Irish Fusiliers had been on the Western Front since August, 1914, and had played a role in all the major campaigns in Flanders. Like many of the Dubliners, they were to be spared the mad dash across No-Man's-Land on the first day of the Somme. As part of the second wave, they had been waiting to pass through the first to consolidate any gains when they received the order to stay where they were. At 1.20pm, the Fusiliers were ordered to send up a company to the captured strong point known as the Quadrilateral, to help hold it against German counterattacks. (The enemy, realising the difficulty in defending this position, had mined it themselves. The explosives, presumably accidentally while final preparations were being made, were detonated at 7.30am, killing the German engineers and machine gunners, and delaying their own troops from reaching the site.) C. Company was despatched, but was held up in No-Man's-Land, but a later attempt by D. Company succeeded. Due to confusion over orders, the rest of the units holding the Quadrilateral withdrew, leaving the Fusiliers alone. At one point it was feared they had been overwhelmed but, after a night of fending off enemy counterattacks, during which Second Lieutenant Ralph Le Mare was said to have thrown hundreds of hand grenades, or bombs as they were then referred to, the company withdrew in good order. The battalion had suffered barely 100 casualties, of which 10 were killed and three officers wounded.

Next to the 4th Division, on its right flank, was the highly respected 29th Division, which had made its reputation at Gallipoli the year before, earning the title the "Incomparable Division". Its objectives included Beaumont Hamel. Following the mine blast under the Hawthorne Redoubt, the Germans had succeeded after hand-to-hand fighting in gaining control of the crater. The division's Irish battalions, both pre-war regulars, were the 1st Royal Dublin Fusiliers, part of its 86th Brigade (which also included the 2nd Royal Fusiliers, 1st Lancashire Fusiliers and 16th Middlesex Fusiliers), and the 1st Royal Inniskilling Fusiliers in the 87th Brigade (made up of the 2nd South Wales Borders, 1st King's Own Scottish Borders and 1st Border Regiment). The division was completed by the 88th Brigade of the 4th Worcestershire Regiment, 1st Essex Regiment, 2nd Hampshire Regiment and the Royal Newfoundland Regiment.

The 1st Inniskillings were in the first wave of the attack, on the right of their divisional front, and next to their fellow countrymen of the 36th (Ulster) Division attacking north of the River Ancre. They found the wire in front of the German lines virtually uncut and only a handful made it to the enemy lines, where they made a valiant but vain attempt to push on without support. Bunched up at the few gaps cut in the German wire, the men made easy targets for the machineguns and the casualties rapidly mounted. Forced back to their own lines, the roll call revealed they had suffered 568 casualties, including 20 officers.

The 1st Dubliners, reinstated after their loses at Gallipoli, were in the second wave of the attack, but their advance was delayed by the failure of the leading battalions to make any headway. By the time they were able to climb over the parapets the German machine-gunners were in complete control of the battleground, their weapons trained on the gaps in the British wire. Some 230 officers and men of the battalion rapidly became casualties without any gain and it finished the morning back in the same frontline trenches from which so many had gone to their deaths hours before.

The X Corps contained the largest force of Irishmen in its ranks thanks to the inclusion of the 36th (Ulster) Division and, on its right, the 2nd Royal Inniskilling

The Germans had a good opinion of the Irish regiments but never shirked a fight

Courtesy of the Somme Heritage Centre

Fusiliers, part of the 96th Brigade of the 32nd Division. On their front lay two of arguably the most difficult German fortifications on the entire front: the Schwaben Redoubt and the fortified Thiepval village. The front line here ran along a ridge opposite the Ulster Division, before turning sharply right in front of Thiepval. This meant the Germans in the village could look down their gun sights on the flanks of the advancing troops in No-Man's-Land and pour fire into the occupied trenches.

The Ulster Division's front was split unequally by the River Ancre. To the north of this natural obstacle was the 108th Brigade, consisting of the 11th (South Antrim), 12th (Central Antrim), and 13th (County Down) Royal Irish Rifles and the 9th Royal Irish Fusiliers (County Armagh, Monaghan and Cavan). Despite being hindered by poorly cut wire, sufficient numbers of the first wave of troops made it into the German frontline trenches to make their presence felt but far too few to hold the position. Armed with maps on which the division's objectives on both sides of the Ancre had been labelled with Ulster town names, such as Lisburn, Cavan, Moy, Dungannon, Omagh, Strabane, Bundoran, Portadown, Lurgan, Clones, Derry and Enniskillen, they advanced on an ever-decreasing front, attempting to reach Beaucourt station and coming within, perhaps, 100 yards of it. But they now found themselves attacked from all sides. With the failure of the 29th Division attack to their left, the German guns in Beaumont Hamel were able to turn south on the Ulstermen, while the withering artillery and machinegun fire now being unleashed on No-Man's-Land was savaging the later waves and preventing further reinforcements. The Germans retook their front line, virtually cutting off any hope of retreat by the forward troops, though some did escape by crossing the railway lines and making their way down the banks of the river.

Colonel Ambrose Ricardo, who used a loud hailer to encourage his men forward

Courtesy of the Somme Heritage Centre

South of the river the opposition was every bit as great, though the division did manage to gain a better foothold. The 107th Brigade, made up of the 8th (East Belfast), 9th (West Belfast), 10th (South Belfast), and 15th (North Belfast) Royal Irish Rifles, and the 109th Brigade, formed by the 9th (County Tyrone), 10th (County Derry), and 11th (Donegal and Fermanagh) Royal Inniskilling Fusiliers, and 14th (Young Citizen Volunteers) Royal Irish Rifles were involved here with the leading troops rapidly overrunning part of the German front line.

Colonel Ambrose Ricardo, standing on the parapet of the assembly trench with a loud hailer, encouraged his men forward. He recalled later: "They got going without delay; no fuss, no shouting, no running, everything solid and thorough – just like the men themselves. Here and there a boy would wave his hand to me as I shouted 'Good Luck' to them through my megaphone. And all had a cheery face. Most were carrying loads. Fancy advancing against heavy fire with a big roll of barbed wire on your shoulder!"

Frank Percy Crozier, who later became a brigadier-general but who in 1916 was leading the west Belfast men of the 9th Royal Irish Rifles, spoke of the air "rent with deafening thunder; never has such man-made noise been heard before". Looking to his right, he realised Thiepval village was still in German hands and that his men would face a withering fire from their flanks as they moved forward:

Again I look southward from a different angle and perceive heaped up masses of British corpses suspended on the German wire in front of the

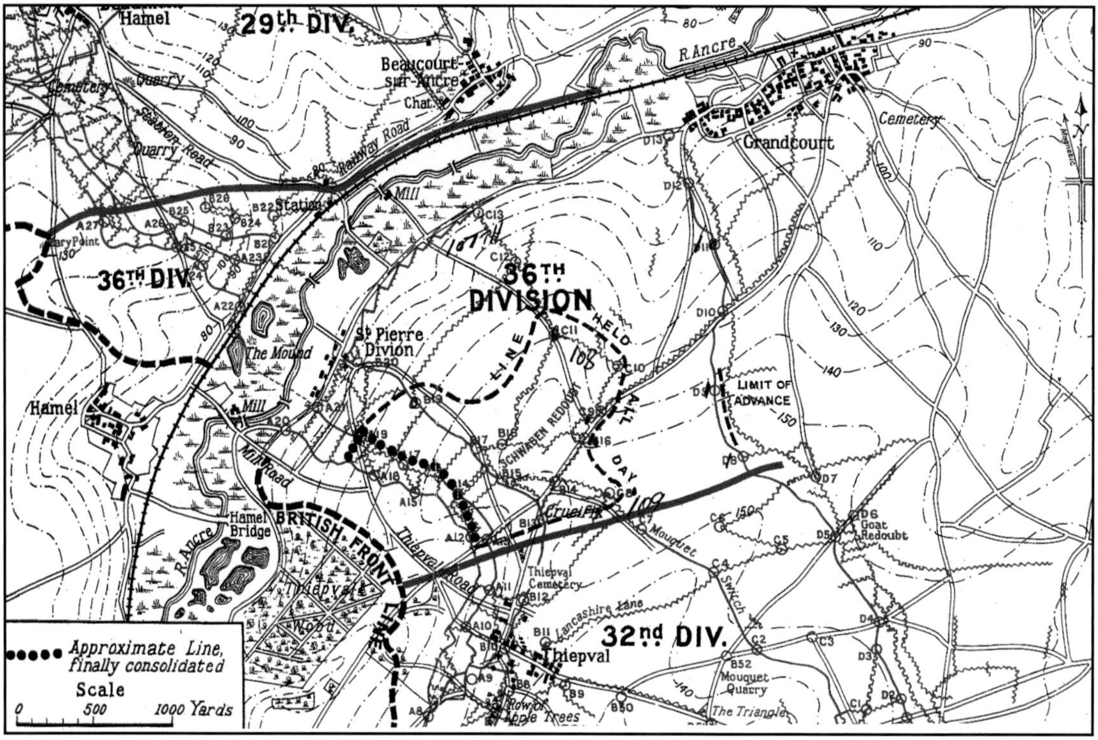

The 36th (Ulster) Division attacked out of Thiepval Wood but came under fire from both flanks

Thiepval stronghold, while live men rush forward in orderly procession to swell the weight of numbers in the spider's web. Will the last available and previously detailed man soon appear to do his futile duty unto death on the altar of sacrifice? We march on – I lose sight of the 10th Rifles and the human corn-stalks, falling before the Reaper.

The division's official history recorded how "flanking machine-gun fire burst out from the dominating position of Thiepval cemetery. The 11th Inniskillings and 14th Rifles, as they emerged from the wood, were literally mown down, and 'No-Man's-Land' became a ghastly spectacle of dead and wounded".

Pausing just long enough to toss grenades into dugouts and tunnel entrances, the first wave of Ulster soldiers had pressed on, attempting to stay on a timetable which required them to be at the German third line by 7.48am. The men swept across the Schwaben Redoubt, only for those Germans deep inside to emerge later in their rear. They pushed ahead, their front shrinking all the time, to take the second, third and fourth lines of trenches. An order to postpone the final push was too late in arriving and, in a last desperate effort, the Belfastmen of the 107th Brigade briefly attacked a short segment of the last German trench system after bitter hand-to-hand fighting. It meant that the Ulster Division was the only one in the Somme sector to partially achieve all its objectives. By this time the contest on either flank had long been settled in the Germans' favour and the encroachment of the Ulstermen was getting their full attention. Bullets filled the air from the machineguns firing from Thiepval village to the right and the high ground of Beaumont Hamel on the left. The Germans were reinforcing, with fresh troops arriving at Grandcourt by train. The enemy counterattacked, pushing down from St. Pierre Divion. Inch by inch the division was forced back, giving up its hard-won gains. The survivors found themselves pinned down in a segment of the German front line trenches. The 16th Royal Irish Rifles (2nd

The old mill at St. Pierre Divion, from which the Ulster Division was attacked on July 1

Courtesy of the Somme Heritage Centre

County Down), the division's Pioneers, attempted to cut a trench across No-Man's-Land but were forced to give up the task because of the weight of enemy fire. When they were relieved on July 2-3, the Ulster Division had suffered some 5,500 casualties in dead, wounded and missing, including more than 200 officers – the 8th and 9th Royal Irish Rifles lost 20 each and none of the remaining battalions, with the exception of the Pioneers, suffered less than a dozen officer casualties.

Divisional commander Major-General Oliver Nugent, from a long-established County Cavan family, in his Special Order of the Day of July 3, 1916, recorded that, in his opinion, "nothing finer has been done in the war than the attack by the Ulster Division on the 1st July". He added:

> *The advance across the open to the German line was carried out with the steadiness of a parade movement, under a fire both from front and flanks, which could only have been faced by troops of the highest quality.*

That July 12, instead of the traditional Orange Order parades, all traffic across Ulster came to a halt at noon for five minutes of silence.

It had fallen to the 32nd Division to take the village of Thiepval and their failure to dislodge the enemy, as noted above, had a disastrous impact on the Ulster Division's fate. Composed of the 14th Brigade (19th Lancashire Fusiliers, 1st Dorset Regiment, 2nd Manchester Regiment and 15th Highland Light Infantry), 96th Brigade (which included the Inniskillings along with the 16th Northumberland Fusiliers, 15th Lancashire Fusiliers and 16th Lancashire Fusiliers), and 97th Brigade (11th Border Regiment, 2nd King's Own Yorkshire Light Infantry, 16th Highland Light Infantry and 17th Highland Light Infantry) with 17th Northumberland Fusiliers as its Pioneers, the division's forward troops were driven back under a hail of artillery and machinegun fire. Only to the right of its line, where the 17th Highland Light Infantry had crept forward to within 40 yards of

Major-General Oliver Nugent expressed pride in the way his Ulster troops had advanced

Courtesy of the Somme Heritage Centre

the German lines before the artillery barrage lifted, had ground been taken. The Scots had been able to rush the Leipzig Redoubt which, with later reinforcements, they held throughout the day.

The 2nd Inniskillings had only been with the 32nd Division since Christmas Eve, 1915, having previously served short stints with the 2nd, 4th, and 5th Divisions and as unattached army troops. The battalion was in reserve on July 1, waiting in trenches just south of Thiepval Wood. The 16th Northumberland Fusiliers and 15th Lancashire Fusiliers, who attacked from the frontline trenches in their sector, were beaten back, with only a handful of the latter reaching the German lines. Finding themselves trapped, they made their way north to join the Ulstermen at the Crucifix. Shortly after 9am, the Inniskillings were called into action. Along with two companies of the 16th Lancashire Fusiliers, they launched a fresh attack on the village in a bid to forge a link with the 36th Division. Again the machineguns in and around the fortified remains of Thiepval Chateau drove the advancing troops back to their starting line. At 1.30pm they were ordered to try again, two companies of Inniskillings being among the mixed force which launched the fresh attack from the edge of Thiepval Wood. Again they were stopped in No-Man's-Land.

The Inniskillings remained on the Somme, taking part in a number of minor operations. On July 10, they were back in action north-west of Ovillers, gaining a small foothold after desperate hand-to-hand fighting, and subsequently repulsing two counterattacks, before being withdrawn. (The 32nd Division was back on the Somme in time for the end of the campaign, with both the 14th and 97th Brigades taking part in the final attack of the battle near Serre on November 18.)

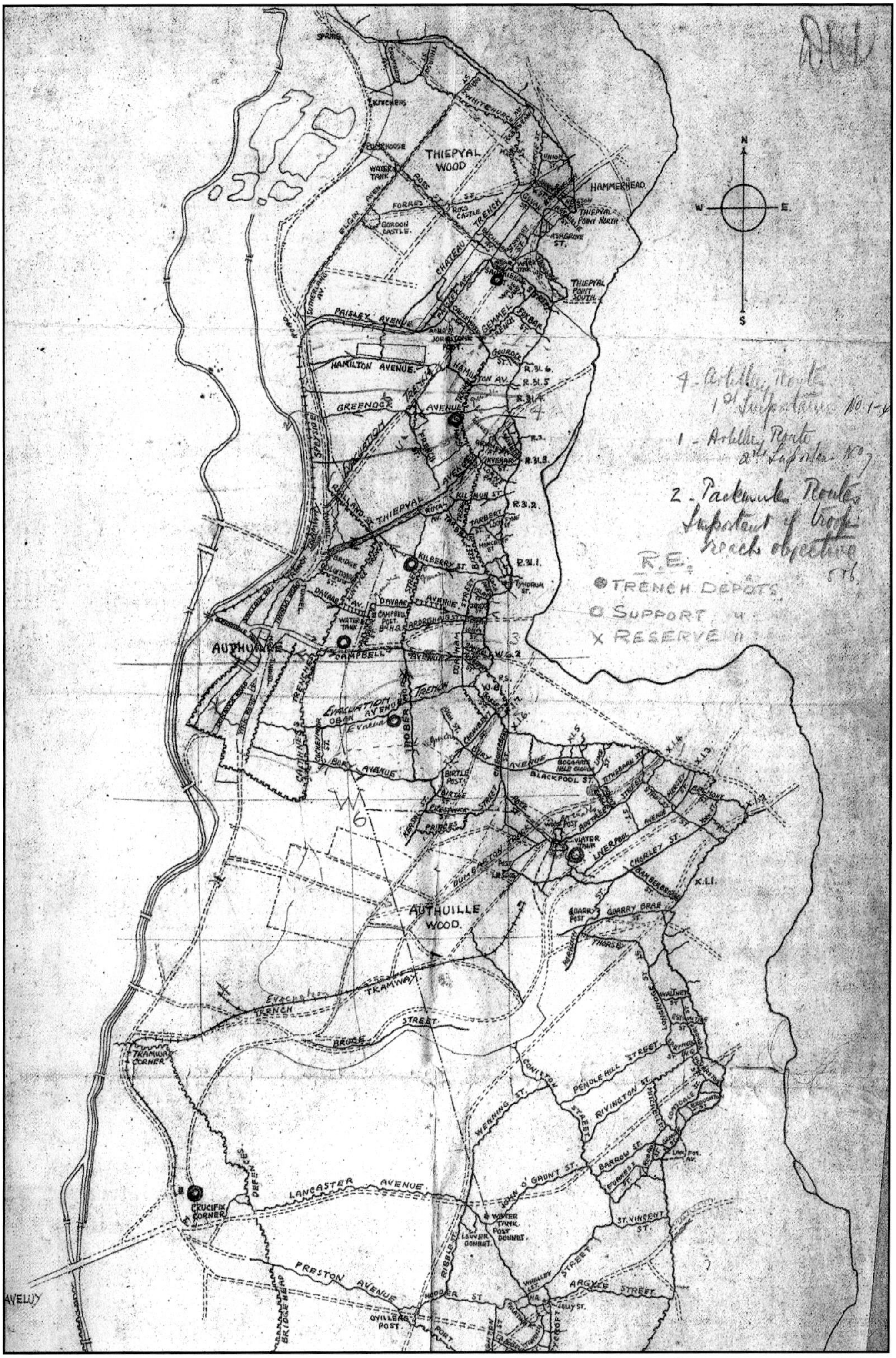

A Royal Engineers map of the British trench system around Thiepval and Authuille woods prior to July 1, 1916, showing strong points and the communication trenches to the support lines

German prisoners taken by the Ulster Division are ushered through the British lines

Courtesy of Lester Morrow

The III Corps was also particularly rich in Irish interest, with the regulars of the 1st Royal Irish Rifles serving in the 8th Division, and the four battalions of the 103rd (Tyneside Irish Brigade) of the 34th Division, consisting of the 24th Northumberland Fusiliers (1st Tyneside Irish), 25th Northumberland Fusiliers (2nd Tyneside Irish), 26th Northumberland Fusiliers (3rd Tyneside Irish), and 27th Northumberland Fusiliers (4th Tyneside Irish) manning the trenches on its flank.

The 8th Division's three brigades were the 23rd (2nd Devonshire Regiment, 2nd West Yorkshire Regiment, 2nd Middlesex Regiment, 2nd Scottish Rifles), 24th (1st Worcestershire Regiment, 1st Sherwood Foresters, 2nd Northamptonshire Regiment, 2nd East Lancashire Regiment) and 25th (the 1st Rifles along with the 2nd Lincolnshire Regiment, 2nd Royal Berkshire Regiment and 2nd Rifle Brigade), with the 22nd Durham Light Infantry as its Pioneers.

The 1st Rifles had been on the Somme since the end of March, 1916, and had barely settled into its new sector opposite La Boisselle when, on April 11, the Germans unleashed a merciless bombardment, including gas shells, upon them. A sizeable trench raid followed, which left 10 dead, 39 wounded and 28 taken prisoner. Lieutenant G.H.P. Whitfeld, who later served as the battalion Adjutant for 16 months, recorded:

The battalion was severely criticised by the General Staff for what was seen as a poor showing, with little allowance made for the intensity of the bombardment or the fact the men were defending a position they were unfamiliar with while wearing sack type gas masks.

Ironically, a German official report of the raid took a more positive view than their British counterparts: "The regiment of Royal Irish Rifles created a

The impressive Thiepval Chateau, on the edge of the village, was reduced to rubble during the fighting

Courtesy of the Somme Heritage Centre

most favourable impression both by their physique and their mode of repelling an assault."

On July 1, 1916, the Rifles found themselves in support in the middle of their divisional front, opposite the fortified village of Ovillers. Their objectives, laid out in a General Instruction issued on the eve of battle, used town names such as Belfast and Holywood to mark points to be consolidated, the battle having been played out countless times on open ground at Bazieux with the German trenches represented by a series of flags. In the event, few were ever to reach the real thing. One officer watched in horror as the first wave of troops climbed out of the trenches: "The men simply got up and fell back into the trench, either killed outright or badly wounded. Those who did get further were never seen or heard of again, as far as I know." The accuracy of the German artillery on the support and communication lines was such that many died or were wounded before ever reaching their own front line and the survivors were cut down in No-man's-Land as they tried to renew the attack. Within an hour the battalion had suffered 65 per cent casualties, amounting to more than 400 men and including their commanding officer Lieutenant-Colonel C. C. MacNamara, who had only taken up his post on June 12. Despite his terrible injuries, which included the loss of an eye and a shattered leg, he refused to allow the stretcher-bearers to take him away until he had properly handed over command. Small segments of German trench were taken, up to the second line in isolated places, but had to be given up again. The division was relieved on July 2 and put on a train further north, but was to return to the Somme front in October.

The Tyneside Irish were in action further south at La Boisselle. Unlike other divisions that day, the 34th Division had decided to commit all its forces at once, hoping to overwhelm the German defenders by numbers alone. The division consisted of the 101st Brigade made up of the 15th Royal Scots, 16th Royal Scots, 10th Lincolnshire Regiment and 11th Suffolk Regiment; the 102th (Tyneside Scottish) Brigade of the 20th, 21st, 22nd and 23rd Northumberland Fusiliers; and the 103rd (Tyneside Irish) Brigade. The latter was officially the 24th, 25th, 26th and 27th Northumberland Fusiliers but was commonly referred to by their "Pals" numbering of 1st, 2nd, 3rd and 4th Tyneside Irish, a tradition continued in the passage below.

Attacking astride the road to Pozieres, with the 2nd battalion to its north and the 3rd, 1st and 4th in that order to the south, the Tyneside Irish's orders were to follow the rest of the division in, passing through their own lines to take Contalmaison. Their starting point was the Tara-Usna trench line, a mile behind the front line. The German machine-gunners could hardly believe their eyes as the Tynesiders climbed out into the open to begin their advance. From their vantage points on the high ground, the gunners simply raised their sights onto the perfect rows of slow-moving soldiers. The 2nd and 3rd battalions were destroyed as a fighting force long before they reached their own lines. The 1st and 4th made it to the British front lines despite taking almost 20 minutes of sustained fire, but just kept going, through the wall of artillery fire tearing up the 500 yards of No-Man's-Land and into the German front line captured by the leading ranks of their division. Still they didn't stop but pushed on, the remnants of the two battalions linking up as they carried on to the German second line and beyond, aiming for Contalmaison despite being down to barely 50 fighting men. Two-thirds of the 3,000 soldiers who had set off became casualties, with the 1st Tyneside Irish alone suffering 620 dead, wounded and missing. Tyneside Irish bombardier Edward Dyke was wounded. In a letter home he said: "The gates of hell were opened and we accepted the invitation. The coolness and courage of the Tyneside Irish was marvellous. Not a man wavered." The division was taken out of the line on July 3, being relieved by the 23rd Division, but elements of it returned briefly on the last day of the month, taking over from the 19th Division, without being involved in any major engagements.

The 2nd Royal Irish Regiment took part in one of the few genuine successes of the day. It attacked on the XV Corps front facing Fricourt and Mametz as part of the 7th Division. The division consisted of the 20th Brigade's 8th Devonshire Regiment, 9th Devonshire Regiment, 2nd Border Regiment and 2nd Gordon Highlanders; the 22nd Brigade of 2nd Royal Warwickshire Regiment, 1st Royal Welsh Fusiliers, 20th Manchester Regiment as well as the 2nd Royal Irish; and the 91st Brigade made up of the 2nd Queen's Royal Regiment, 1st South Staffordshire Regiment, 21st Manchester Regiment and 22nd Manchester Regiment.

Aided by the narrowness of No-Man's-Land, which in places was barely 100 yards wide, the 22nd Manchesters and 1st South Staffordshires penetrated 700 yards, reaching Mametz before having to fall back. After receiving reinforcements, they advanced on the village ruins again.

The Royal Irish played a supporting role on July 1, but after nightfall on July 2 was sent, along with the 1st Royal Welsh Fusiliers, to strengthen the division's grip south of Mametz Wood, but became disorientated and failed to take up position. Shortly after midnight on July 5, the same two battalions, along with the 9th Northumberland Fusiliers and 10th Lancashire Fusiliers from the 17th Division, overran the Quadrangle Trench strong point and Shelter Alley. The Royal Irish, on the right of the line, was counterattacked by the Germans and forced to withdraw. Despite regrouping and attempting twice more to regain the land, the element of surprise had been lost and they were beaten back. The 7th Division was withdrawn from the line to regroup but was soon to return to the fray. In a renewed attack on July 14 in the same sector, it again made ground with the Royal Irish, in reserve, leading a later assault on Bazentin-le-Petit. It reached the southern edges of the village at 6.30am and, after a brief pause, pushed on with assistance from the 6th Leicestershire Regiment to clear the German defenders from the ruins. Despite being counterattacked and having to temporary give up some of its gains, the Royal Irish consolidated the ground won, resisting all further attempts to dislodge them. The division's 91st and 20th brigades took part in the early attempts to take the notorious High Wood on July 15 and 20 respectively while the 22nd Brigade, with the Royal Irish, regrouped away from the front.

The 25th Division entered the battle in early July, improving positions around the Leipzig Salient captured by the 32nd Division on July 1. Almost a week later, on July 7, the 2nd Royal Irish Rifles, part of the 25th's 74th Brigade (along with the 11th Lancashire Fusiliers, 13th Cheshire Regiment, and 9th Loyal North Lancashire Regiment) took part in an attack on trenches some 700 yards south of Ovillers, another July 1 objective, sustaining close to 160 casualties. The following evening they advanced again, but missed their objective and instead took a trench line some 600 yards beyond it. Through the rest of the night and early morning they resisted German attempts to shift them while also having to endure their own artillery shelling the position. That afternoon, realising they were in danger of being cut off, the men withdrew to their original objective, a trench line along the Albert-Bapaume road about 1,000 yards due east of Ovillers. After a couple of days out of the line, the 2nd Rifles were back again in the trenches at Ovillers on July 14, leading their brigade's attack on the village and spearheading an attempt to link up with another unit which had been cut off to their left. On July 16, Ovillers finally fell, opening the way for an attack on Thiepval from the rear. The Rifles, now reduced to half its normal fighting strength, was withdrawn from the line to Bouzincourt, where they received drafts of fresh troops. Cyril Falls, in his Regimental History of the Royal Irish Rifles, records:

> *The men were so weary that they could scarcely set one foot before another, but delighted with their triumph. One in two of them wore German helmets, these being still the days of the peace-time pickelhaube, a very pretty trophy.*

The 25th Division, which included the 7th and 75th brigades (consisting of the 10 Cheshire Regiment, 3rd Worcestershire Regiment, 8th Loyal North Lancashire Regiment and 1st Wiltshire Regiment; and 11th Cheshire Regiment, 8th Border Regiment, 2nd South Lancashire Regiment and 8th South Lancashire Regiment respectively), remained on the Somme front throughout most of the campaign. The under-strength Rifles' role was primarily as a relieving force in the quieter parts of the line until they were finally withdrawn at the end of October and sent north to Belgium.

By mid-July the 2nd Royal Munster Fusiliers, which had arrived in France with the original B.E.F., was in action on the Somme with the 3rd Brigade of the 1st Division, its fellow battalions being the 1st South Wales Borders, 1st Gloucestershire Regiment and 2nd Welsh Regiment. (The remainder of the division was made up of the 1st Brigade's 10th Gloucestershire Regiment, 1st Black Watch, 8th Royal Berkshire Regiment and 1st Cameron Highlanders; and the 2nd Royal Sussex Regiment, 1st Loyal North Lancashire Regiment, 1st Northamptonshire Regiment and 2nd King's Royal Rifle Corps of the 2nd Brigade.)

The Munsters and 1st Gloucesters made a frontal attack on the German lines on July 16 west of Bazentin-le-Petit Wood, while the 2nd Welsh Regiment assaulted from the flank. All objectives were taken comfortably. Two days later the Munsters, having named a captured trench in their honour, snatched a section of the old

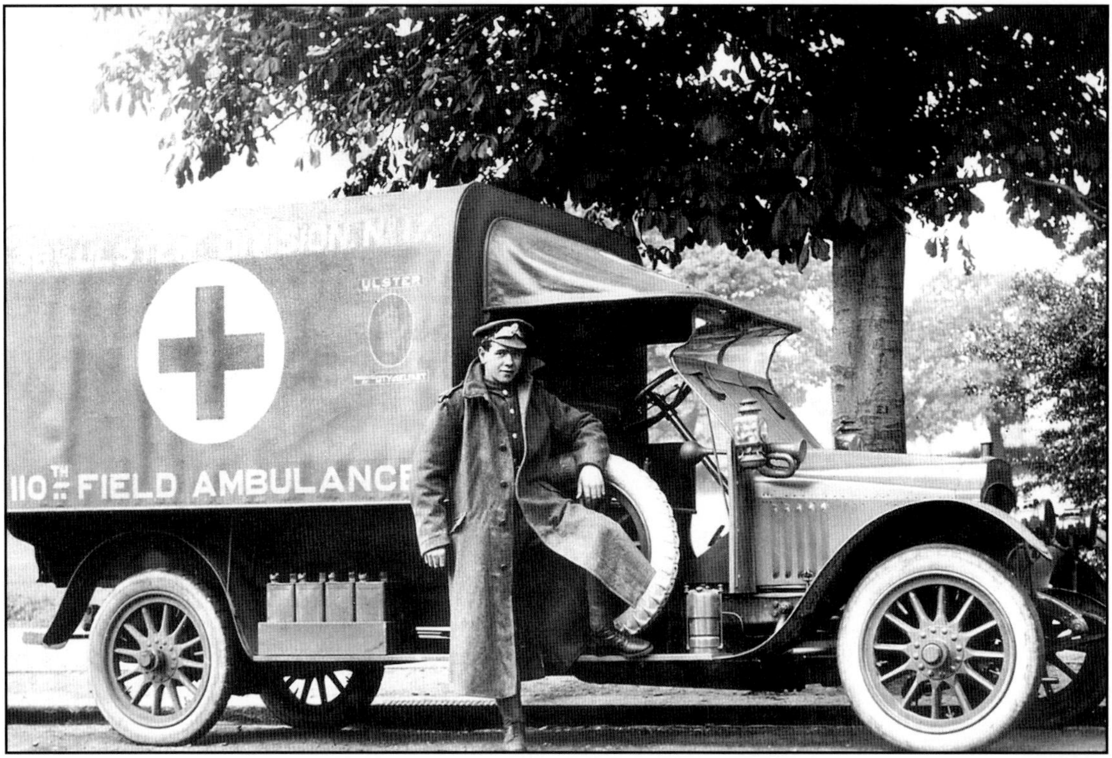

The ambulances of the 110th Brigade, part of the 36th (Ulster) Division, were worked non-stop throughout the opening days of the battle

Courtesy of Lester Morrow

German support line south of Pozieres, holding it long enough to allow a line of strongpoints to be constructed on Pozieres Ridge. The division later took part in the opening day of the Battle of Pozieres, which raged from July 23-September 3, and remained in the fighting zone until September 27, taking part in a number of limited actions.

September 1 saw the first major assault by the 2nd Leinster Regiment. The battalion was part of the 73rd Brigade of the 24th Division, which also contained the 9th Royal Sussex Regiment, 7th Northamptonshire Regiment and 13th Middlesex Regiment. The other brigades were the 17th (8th Buffs, 1st Royal Fusiliers, 12th Royal Fusiliers and 3rd Rifle Brigade) and 72nd (8th Queen's Royal Regiment, 9th East Surrey Regiment, 8th Royal West Kent Regiment and 1st North Staffordshire Regiment). The division, which had relieved the 14th Division the day before, took part in limited actions to win back lost territory east of Deville Wood following German counterattacks. The 2nd Leinsters, which had been brought up the previous evening to contain enemy assaults, bombed their way along two trenches, forcing the Germans to abandon one of them entirely.

The 2nd Royal Irish Regiment's 22nd Brigade of the 7th Division had been back in the forward trenches since early August but it wasn't until September 2-3 that they were involved in a major action along the Longueval-Ginchy road. The Royal Irish attempted to take Ginchy in a late afternoon assault after other elements of the division had been forced to give up gains on the edge of the village, but were beaten back.

It was the 16th Irish Division, however, which was to come into its own early that month. Its 47th Brigade, consisting of the 6th Royal Irish Regiment, 6th Connaught Rangers, 7th Leinster Regiment, and the 8th Royal Munster Fusiliers, joined the 20th Division in the taking of Guillemont. This village, which had been attacked time and again without success, had already earned its own little ditty. To the tune of Moonlight Bay, and with the usual disrespect the Tommies paid to the proper French pronunciation or spelling, it went:

I was strolling along
In Gillymong,
With the Minnywerfers singing
Their old sweet song . . .

The division's finest hour was yet to come, however. On September 9 it stormed Ginchy with such enthusiasm that neither the heavy German artillery barrage or machinegun fire, while inflicting horrendous casualties, could hold up the attack. Indeed, some of the Irishmen had to be stopped from pursuing the fleeing enemy from the village so that they could dig in and consolidate the gain. In addition to the 47th Brigade, the men of the 48th Brigade, consisting of the 7th Royal Irish Rifles, 1st Royal Munster Fusiliers (which had replaced the disbanded 9th Royal Munsters), 8th Royal Dublin Fusiliers, and 9th Royal Dublin Fusiliers, and the 49th Brigade, made up of the 7th Royal Inniskilling Fusiliers, 8th Royal Inniskilling Fusiliers, 7th Royal Irish Fusiliers, and 8th Royal Irish Fusiliers, were all involved in the fighting. The 16th Division's losses, after more than a week of continuous fighting, were very high. Willie Redmond, MP, brother of the nationalist leader John, and an officer in the 6th Royal Irish Regiment, wrote:

For two years the Germans had been entrenched there, and they had, as well they know how, made the position very strong. Barbed-wire entanglements of the most intricate kind, machinegun emplacements where the guns, by cunningly contrived lifts, could disappear during bombardment and reappear at once afterwards. Everything that could be contrived to ward off attacks had been contrived, and quite openly the enemy boasted that the place was impregnable.

The battle had been hard won. The German lines, which had repeatedly resisted previous attacks, had fallen to the dash and heart-on-sleeve courage of the Irish troops. A contemporary account of the battle, compiled mostly by newspaper journalists and published shortly after the actual events in the eight-volume History of the Great War, makes up for its historical inaccuracies with its reflection of the euphoria felt by the division at proving itself in battle. It records:

When the Irish brigades marched back towards camp in the afternoon of September 10th, the worn shrunken battalions, mechanically keeping step with a piper at their head, were a sight to stir anybody with Irish blood in them. For more than a week the men had been fighting and little sleep had they had. Their eyes were bloodshot and ringed with shadows, their seamed faces were grey with dust. The mud was caked on them and their bodies huddled forward in the weakness of utter fatigue. Yet a spirit of triumph shone from them. They had made Ginchy and Guillemont monuments to the valour of their race.

The Guards Division, which included both the 1st and 2nd Irish Guards battalions in the 1st Guards Brigade and 2nd Guards Brigade respectively (with the 2nd Grenadier Guards, 2nd Coldstream Guards, 3rd Coldstream Guards completing the first and 3rd Grenadier Guards, 1st Coldstream Guards, and 1st Scots Guards the second), were next to move into the front lines. On September 12 they had suffered heavy losses during attacks on German machinegun posts on the Morval Road. In the early hours of September 15, the men, both Protestant and Catholic, gathered to pray under the stewardship of Fr. Brown. Kneeling in the mud, their steel helmets in one hand and their rifles with fixed bayonets

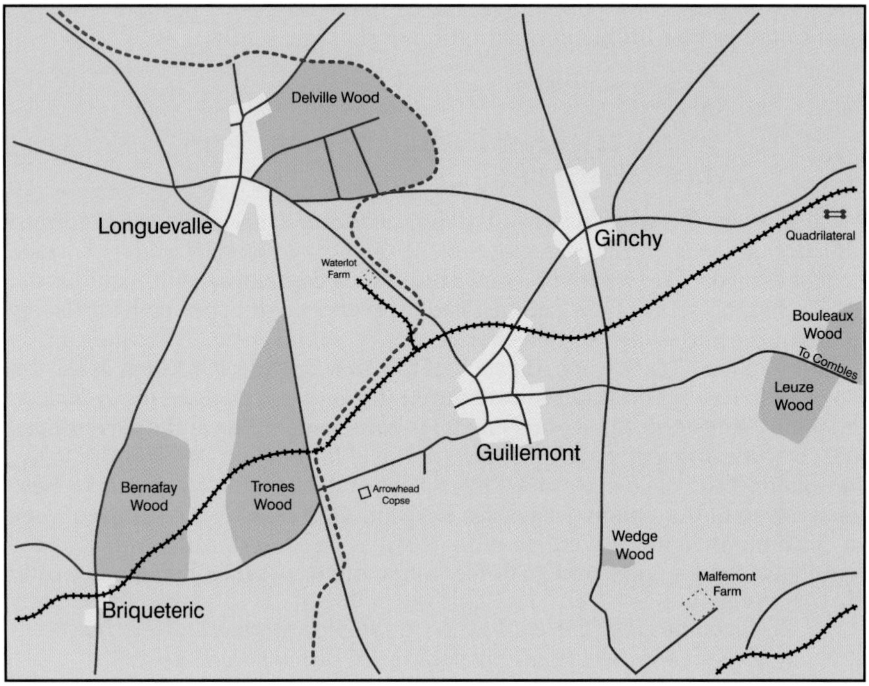

The 16th (Irish) Division sustained terrible losses in the taking of Guillemont and Ginchy in September 1916

in the other, they sought a moment's solitude amid the roar of the guns and the chaos of war to ready themselves for the battle ahead.

The men then moved into line preparing for what was to be the first wide-front offensive mounted since July. There was a new element in the mix this time, however: the tank was about to rumble into the history books, with the Guards Division accompanying them into a wall of machinegun fire around Bouleaux Wood. Ten days later, the 1st Irish Guards and 2nd Scots Guards attacked at Lesboeufs, helping to take the village by bombing dugouts on the sunken road while the 4th Grenadiers protected their left flank. The Guards Division continued to make small gains throughout September, with their casualties on the Somme mounting to in excess of 1,000.

Also in action on September 15 had been the 1/18 (County of London) The London Regiment, also known as the London Irish Rifles. Described as being made up of "men connected with Ireland by birth, marriage, or property", it was serving with the 141st (5th London) Brigade of the 47th (2nd London) Division. The objective was the infamous High Wood which they helped to secure with the aid of four tanks in a bloody contest with the heavily dug-in Germans. The London Irish also played a part in the struggle for Eaucourt l'Abbaye, during the October fighting.

Another division with an Irish interest, the 55th (West Lancashire), took part in battles at Guillemont, Ginchy, Flers-Courcelette and later Morval. Among this territorial division's infantry units was the 1/8th (Irish) The King's Regiment (Liverpool), which served in the 164th Brigade. A second battalion, the 2/8th, served with the 57th (2nd West Lancashire) Division, but did not arrive in France until 1917 and was merged with the 1/8th in January, 1918.

The 4th Division, which had taken part in the July 1 attacks north of Beaumont Hamel, returned to the fray in October, fighting alongside the French at the Battle of Transloy Ridge. By this stage in the campaign the mass attacks had been replaced by small and often bitter engagements in which every yard of land was fiercely contested. The 1st Royal Irish Fusiliers was the first of the division's two Irish battalions in action when it attacked trenches north-east of Lesboeufs on October 12. They had the aid of a creeping artillery barrage keeping the German heads down in front of them, but halfway across the few hundred yards of open ground to their objectives they came under heavy machinegun fire from their flanks. The battalion fell back with heavy casualties. Between the four companies taking part in the attack there were only five officers and barely 209 men who remained unwounded by nightfall and not an inch of ground had been taken.

On October 22 it was the turn of the 2nd Royal Dublin Fusiliers in the same sector. Along with the 1st Hampshire Regiment, they had been due to attack at 11.30am, but a heavy mist delayed the operation until 2.30pm. The Hampshires and the French, on their flank, were all but stopped in their tracks by the German heavy fire, though the Dubliners managed to establish a foothold in the enemy line, taking a gun pit and a strongpoint beyond. They were later reinforced by the 1st Rifle Brigade. During this action Sergeant Robert Downie, of the 2nd Dubliners, won the Victoria Cross. Despite being wounded early on, he charged the German line alone, calling out 'Come on, the Dubs', his rallying call being answered by his comrades who followed him into action.

The 1st Royal Irish Rifles were also back in the Somme fighting in October, taking part in actions on the Le Boeufs-Morval line on the 23rd of the month in terrible weather conditions. By this stage its fighting strength stood at just 250 men. Along with the 2nd Royal Berkshires, the Rifles attacked behind a creeping barrage but were stopped by intensive machinegun fire after advancing 70 yards.

The 10th Royal Dublin Fusiliers, part of the 63rd Royal Naval Division, brought the Irish contribution to the Battle of the Somme to a close. On November 13 it was involved in the divisional assault on Beaucourt and Beaumont Hamel, both of which rapidly fell. The Dubliners, after an uneasy night in the German frontlines, pushed on the following day, supported by a couple of tanks, making further gains and capturing hundreds of prisoners.

"Everywhere and Always Faithful"

The Irish Brigade

5621 Sgt. J. Crowe
2nd Royal Irish Regt

I HAVE · READ · WITH · MUCH PLEASURE · THE · REPORTS OF · YOUR · REGIMENTAL COMMANDER · AND BRIGADE · COMMANDER REGARDING · YOUR · GALLANT · CONDUCT · AND · DEVOTION · TO DUTY · IN · THE · FIELD · ON

Aug 1st to 16th 1917

AND · HAVE · ORDERED · YOUR · NAME AND · DEED · TO · BE · ENTERED · IN · THE RECORD · OF · THE · IRISH · DIVISION

W.B. Hickie.

Major-General
Commanding 16th Irish Division

A gallantry certificate awarded to Sergeant James Crowe by 16th (Irish) Division commander Major-General Hickie. Sergeant Crowe survived the war and later enjoyed a long career in the Royal Ulster Constabulary. He volunteered to come out of retirement to serve with the R.U.C. during the Second World War

Courtesy of the Somme Heritage Centre

XVI

LONDON INVICTA

With the Compliments of the
FSA

WO2 (SQMS) SS Jardine AGC (SPS)
16th Regiment Royal Artillery
RA Barracks
Woolwich
SE18 4BB

Sorry I didn't have time to wrap it. Stephen found this book on the internet & thought you would like it.

Love Sara.

Military Network:	(9)4691 3838
Fax:	(9)4691 3815
Civil Network:	0208 781 3838
Fax:	0208 781 3815

HANGING ON THE OLD BARBED WIRE

If you want the old battalion
I know where it is,
I know where it is,
I know where it is.
If you want the old battalion
I know where it is,
It's hanging on the old barbed wire.

I saw them, I saw them,
Hanging on the old barbed wire.
I saw them, I saw them,
Hanging on the old barbed wire.

A popular army song during the First World War

The generals' focus shifted north in 1917, a year which began with hope and ended in despair. The winter months had been spent consolidating and rebuilding an army left devastated by the Somme. Fresh drafts of men were taken in, new officers initiated in the art of trench warfare and fresh plans drawn up for further offensives. What appeared to be a good omen came at Vimy Ridge, north of Arras, where the Canadians succeed in April where so many others had failed when they pushed the Germans off the high ground. The British, for the first time, now had dominating views over the plateau below. Any hopes that the war had turned in the Allies' favour quickly evaporated, however, when that same month the French army was thrown into disarray. Its attack at Chemin des Dames had promised much but delivered only small gains at a huge cost. It was the final straw for the war-weary conscripts. What began as one unit refusing orders rapidly evolved into a full-scale mutiny in which the French soldiers refused to attack, though remained on the defensive in their trenches. It was to be many months before discipline and confidence could be restored, leaving it to the British to take the war to the enemy.

Two major offensives were launched in Belgium that summer. The first, in June, was the textbook success of the Battle of Messines, in which the Catholic 16th and Protestant 36th divisions fought side-by-side. For more than a year the sappers had been working on a series of 21 tunnels, some thousands of yards in

Major Willie Redmond was killed after insisting he be allowed to accompany his men into battle

Courtesy of the Somme Heritage Centre

length, running under the German lines. A million pounds of ammonal explosive was packed in the end chambers and, at 3.10am on June 7, 1917, they were detonated. (Two failed to explode – one erupted in 1955 during a lightening storm and the other, its exact position unknown, still exists). The Ulster Division soldiers, already on the move, were showered with debris. As some 2,266 artillery guns opened up on the enemy's positions, the British infantry advanced and within hours had taken the majority of their objectives. German counter-attacks the following day were beaten off and further gains made. The success, however, wasn't exploited to the full, with the troops ordered to consolidate rather than push on through a disorientated enemy. The 1st Munsters, in the second wave of the attack, led the charge into Wytschaete, where they linked up with the 9th Inniskillings to their south. Major Willie Redmond, of the 6th Royal Irish Regiment, led his men into battle at the age of 56. He was wounded twice, the second time leaving him unable to walk. John Meeke,[1] a stretcher bearer with the Ulster Division, bandaged his injuries, being wounded himself in the process, and arranged

[1] Meeke, who was awarded a Military Medal for his courage, survived the war only to die in 1923. He lay in an unmarked grave at the Old Derrykeighan Burial Ground, north Antrim, until recently when, following a campaign by author Robert Thompson, a headstone was erected.

for him to be carried from the field of battle. Despite medical attention, Major Redmond died at the dressing station.

In comparison to the carefully prepared plans at Messines, the Third Battle of Ypres, which saw the introduction of a new weapon, flesh-burning mustard gas, was decidedly ad hoc. It opened on July 31, 1917, with initial gains which included a sector of line taken by the 2nd Royal Leinster Regiment at considerable cost and the loss of the 2nd Irish Guards commanding officer, Lieutenant-Colonel Eric Beresford Greer, during its attack on the Yser Canal. A holder of the Military Cross, he is buried nearby at Canada Farm Cemetery. That evening the skies opened and the unseasonable rain continued almost without let up for weeks, turning the battlefield into a quagmire and bringing the attack to a virtual halt. On August 14, the 2nd Royal Irish Rifles succeeded in taking the fortified village of Westhoek, but the gain was wiped out by strong German counter-attacks. The 16th and 36th divisions were to take part in the second wave of assaults on August 4, but these were postponed because of the weather. For a further 12 days they remained in frontline trenches, their positions continuously shelled by the Germans. On August 16 the two divisions left their trenches and advanced side-by-side, the 36th to the left of the line. They had approximately a mile of open ground to cover to their objectives, much of it uphill, under a hail of machine-gun fire from well-constructed German strongpoints and pillboxes and incessant artillery fire. Thousands of men fell, with the few survivors who made it to the enemy lines rapidly forced out again. By the time they were withdrawn from the line two days later, the 16th and 36th divisions had sustained more than 8,800 casualties between them. Among the losses was Father Willie Doyle, chaplain to the Dubliners, whose courage in attending the wounded during battle had earned him the respect of all, while the Ulstermen had two battalion commanders killed outright, Lieutenant-Colonel A. C. Pratt, of the 11th Inniskillings and Lieutenant-Colonel Somerville, of the 9th Royal Irish Fusiliers. The Irish Guards, which had been in reserve at Messines though hadn't been needed, were in action at Ypres, winning two Victoria Crosses. Lance Sergeant John Moyney, his section isolated in No-Man's-Land for four days, fought off a concerted German attack before manoeuvring his unit, under heavy fire, across

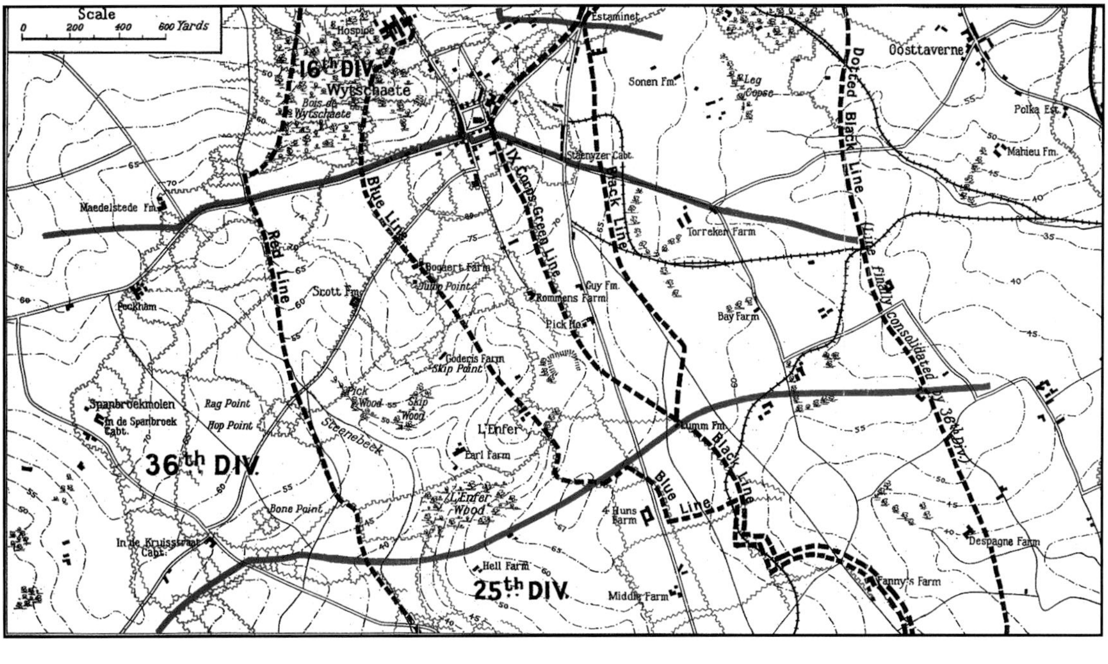

The 16th and 36th divisions fought side-by-side at the Battle of Messines

Poppy wreaths at the entrance to Langemarck German Cemetery in Belgium

the Broembeek stream and back to his own lines. (From Rathdowney, County Laois, he survived the war to return to Ireland where he worked for the Great Southern Railway Company, spending many years as station master at Roscrea, County Tipperary. He died in 1980 at the age of 85.) Lance Corporal Thomas Woodcock took part in the same action, risking his own life to cross back over the stream under fire to rescue a comrade. (He was subsequently killed during the German advance of 1918 and is buried in Achiet Le Petit Cemetery, some 14 miles south of Arras.) In October, the 1st Royal Dublin Fusiliers, in its last action with the 29th Division prior to joining the 16th, stormed the German lines at Langemarck, where Sergeant Ockenden earned himself the Victoria Cross for single-handedly taking a machinegun emplacement and leading the assault on a fortified farm. The battle came to a close in November, but not before the 1st Royal Munster Fusiliers had helped secure Passchendaele Ridge. They enjoyed initial success but were then counter-attacked, and shelled by their own artillery, suffering losses of 400, the majority taken prisoner. On the 16th of the month the 2nd Leinsters where back in the front lines, losing their commanding officer, Lieutenant-Colonel Alfred Murphy, to a chance shell as he visited the wounded.

November, 1917, saw the opening of the Battle of Cambrai, though not before the 16th (Irish) Division had taken the notorious Tunnel Trench at Fontaine les Croiselles in a subsidiary action. Only on the flanks was their serious action, with the 6th Connaught Rangers contesting the ground for several days before it could be consolidated. The 36th (Ulster) Division, sent to the Somme for a rest after Ypres, was given the task of "rolling up" the German line either side of the Canal du Nord after the initial success at Cambrai. The attack was led by the Inniskillings of the 109th Brigade who managed to take a substantial part of their objective, the ruined village of Moeuvres, but could not hold it. The 1st and 2nd Irish Guards, coming into the line on November 23, attacked Fontaine and Bourlon Wood but were forced to withdraw with the loss of 300 men. To the north of the canal, the 1st Royal Inniskilling Fusiliers, with the 29th Division, were led into battle by their South African-born commander Lieutenant-Colonel Sherwood-Kelly, who won a Victoria Cross for his courage in action. On November 30 the Germans launched a major pincer movement on the British bulge in their lines. To the south they were repulsed by the 29th Division but managed to make headway to the north. The Irish Guards were moved up from the reserve to restore the line, even winning back some of the lost ground. The enemy attacks persisted, however, and the decision was taken on December 5 to evacuate much of the territory taken on the first day of battle. The 36th Division, meanwhile, had been recalled to Cambrai from Arras at the start of the German counter-offensive and arrived just in the nick of time to save the day. The 9th Inniskillings went straight into the line, halting an attack on the 61st Division front then later, supported by the 14th Royal Irish Rifles, pushed the enemy back in places. County Louth-born Lieutenant James Samuel Emerson, badly wounded in the head and cut off with just eight men from his battalion, fought off repeated efforts over several hours to dislodge him until killed leading an assault. He was awarded the Victoria Cross for his sacrifice.

On the Somme, though never truly quiet, the war had settled back to what passed as normality. Efforts continued to iron out the odd kink in the line that the fighting of 1916 had left. The 1st Royal Inniskilling Fusiliers, for example, were involved in another major attack on Le Transloy in January, 1917. Moving into a line of broken trenches on the main Bapaume to Peronne road, near the former village, the Skins attacked at dawn on a front of two-thirds of a mile, taking the German first and second lines and capturing 200 prisoners. For the most part, however, the Somme returned to its routine of stand-to at dawn and dusk, the "morning hate" artillery barrages which greeted each and every day, and the constant battle to dominate No-Man's-Land, spiced up by the occasional trench raid.

As early as September, 1916, while the battle was still raging, the Germans had begun work on a new strategy for the Somme front. Their solution was to construct new defensive positions, to be known as the Hindenburg Line, further to the east. There were a number of advantages to the scheme. Firstly, the Allies had taken, at great cost to both sides, many of the carefully fortified villages and redoubts constructed over the previous two years, and captured in places the prized higher ground. Rebuilding such formidable defences, the Germans realised, would take considerable time and have to be completed while facing an increasingly aggressive enemy. Further, by building a defensive line at their leisure, out of reach of enemy eyes and guns, they were free to incorporate every geographical advantage (such as the St. Quentin canal with its underground passages) and devise a new system which employed the lessons learnt in the past. And finally, but not insignificantly, the new line was considerably shorter than the bulging front line it replaced, and so required fewer troops to man it – an important element to an army already aware of the manpower shortages which would ultimately be its downfall. In March, 1917, the British troops stood at the ready at their parapets unaware that the trenches opposite were empty. As suspicions grew, patrols were sent out all along the line, returning with the news that the enemy had gone. The 1st Royal Irish Rifles, who had returned to the Somme in January 1917 to take over trenches at Rancourt, discovered the Germans had withdrawn on St. Patrick's Day, March 17, when a patrol found the enemy trenches to their front unoccupied. The British cautiously moved forward through what historian Captain Cyril Falls described as an "abomination of desolation". In their wake, the Germans had cut down trees, pulled up rail tracks, destroyed roads, blown up buildings which might be of use to the Allied troops, poisoned wells, and left booby traps to catch out unsuspecting Tommies. A cordon of snipers and machinegun teams covered the retreat, punishing any British troops who threatened to catch the withdrawing columns. When they finally arrived at the new front line, the British and French discovered it had changed out of all recognition. A new "Forward Zone" was effectively the front line and consisted of concrete strongpoints, each covering the next in the line by mutually-supporting fire, linked by thinly-manned trench systems stretching back many hundreds of yards and protected by layer upon layer of barbed wire. This was intended to be a killing zone where a small number of defenders, supported by artillery gunners who had zeroed their weapons on every conceivable approach with pin-point accuracy, could inflict severe losses on an advancing enemy Two to three miles further back was the "Battle Zone" where any soldiers who made it through the forward lines were to be met by elite storm troopers armed with machineguns, flamethrowers and grenades. A third line of resistance, the "Reserve Line", was manned by the bulk of the forces in the area and lay several miles to the rear. Overall, it was, by far, the most formidable defensive system constructed throughout the war. The British, who were to extend their line further south in 1917, set about creating a similar, though weaker, version with fewer strongpoints and less troops. As always, the Allied emphasis was not on defence but on preparing another attempt at a breakthrough. It was the Germans, however, who were to make the first move on the Somme in 1918.

ONE GREAT CRASH

With one great crash there opened a tremendous bombardment, of trench mortars by the hundred and every calibre of artillery save the 77mm field gun. Its continuous roar was punctuated, to those a little distance from the line, by the explosions of huge single shells upon objectives in rear.

Cyril Falls, History of the 36th (Ulster) Division

While the Germans were the masters of defence, they were also more than capable of doing the arithmetic which told them that they would ultimately lose the war of attrition. The Americans had entered the conflict in 1917 and their might, both sides knew, would prove the decisive factor. By the middle of 1918, the United States had managed to deliver a million troops to France, and the total would top two million by the end of the year. At the end of 1917, however, the Americans were largely still in training and, following the defeat of Russia in the east, the Germans realised they had a numerical superiority for the first time. If they were to snatch victory on the Western Front it had to be sooner rather than later.

At 4.40am on March 21, 1918, the German artillery opened up with 6,608 guns and more than 3,500 trench mortars on a front of about 50 miles. Operation Michael, alternatively known as Kaiserschlacht or Kaiser's Battle to the Germans, and the March Retreat to the British, had begun. Some 74 German divisions, with the backing of 700 airplanes, moved forward in the first stage of a plan to knock Britain out of the war. It took four weeks, and an agreement at long last to appoint an overall Allied commander, French Marshal Foch, to bring the German advance to an end just short of Amiens. The British suffered 38,500 casualties, of which 21,000 were prisoners and some 7,000 dead, while more than 500 artillery guns were lost on the first day alone.

The British had taken a decision late in 1917 to reorganise their divisions,

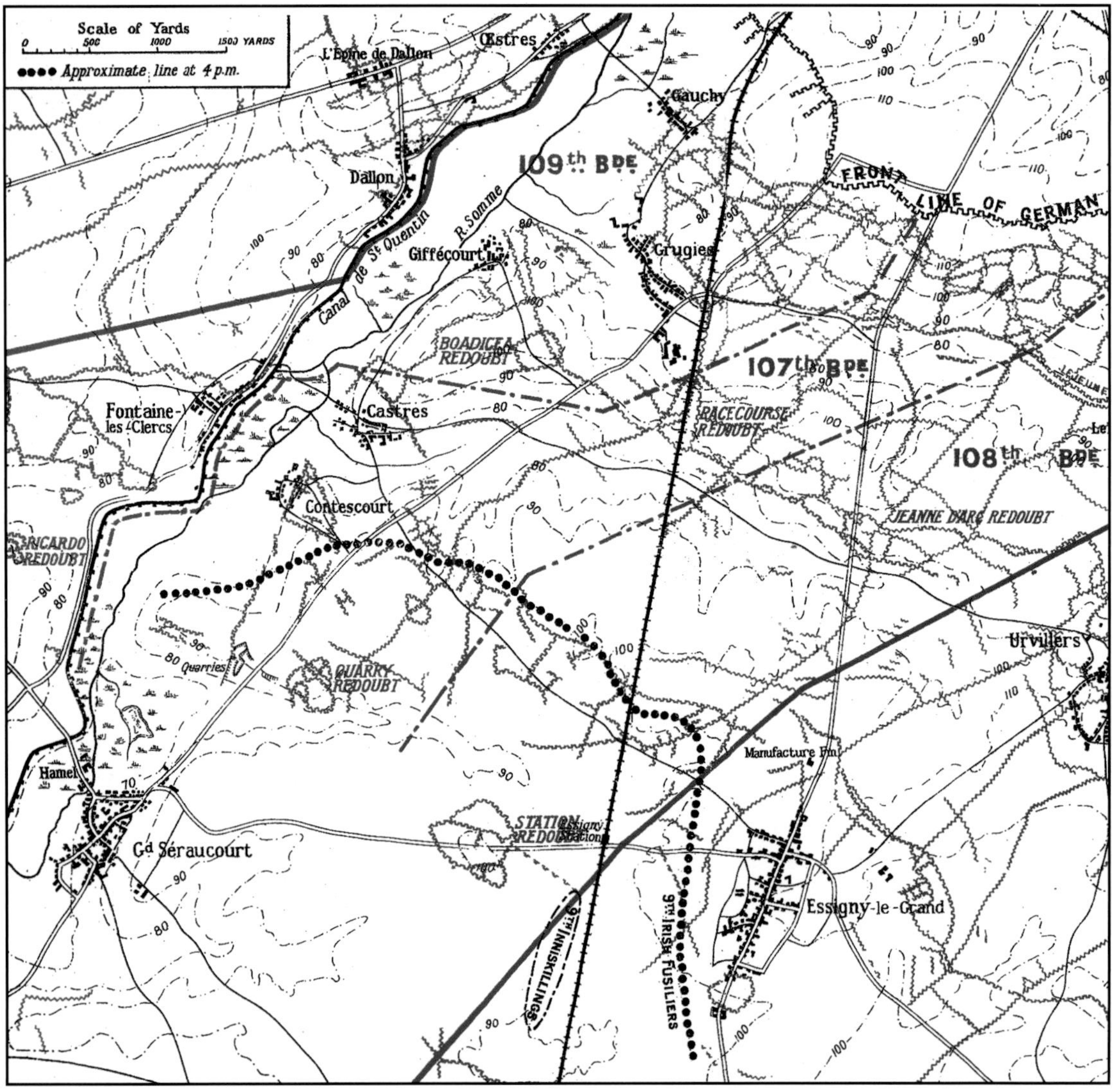

The positions held by the 36th (Ulster) Division on the eve of the German attack launched on March 21, 1918

reducing them from 12 to nine infantry battalions and disbanding more than 140 Service battalions. As a result, virtually all the pre-war Irish infantry battalions which had fought on the Somme in 1916 (with the notable exception of the Irish Guards, the 1st remaining with the Guards Division and the 2nd transferring to the 31st Division) had been transferred to either the 16th or 36th divisions. It is also worth noting that, by this stage in the war, the Irish element of these units had been greatly reduced by a system of allocating men according to need rather than any ethnic or political considerations. The story of the Irish battalions in the 1918 battle is, therefore, simpler to tell than the 1916 campaign.

The 16th (Irish) Division had been radically altered from the force which had taken Guillemont and Ginchy two years earlier. Even before the rationalisations of 1918, the fall in the numbers of fresh recruits from Ireland had resulted in some of the original battalions being merged and others disbanded, the shortfall made up by drafting in recruits from Great Britain. Of the nine battalions making up the division in March 1918, six were pre-war regular battalions, leaving the 16th consisting of the 6th Connaught Rangers, 2nd Leinster

Regiment and 1st Royal Munster Fusiliers in the 47th Brigade; the 2nd Royal Munster Fusiliers, 1st Royal Dublin Fusiliers and 2nd Royal Dublin Fusiliers in the 48th Brigade; and the 2nd Royal Irish Regiment, 7th (South Irish Horse) Royal Irish Regiment and 7th/8th Royal Inniskilling Fusiliers in the 49th Brigade.

On the opening day of the battle the division was on the right of the VII Corps line, east of Peronne on the high ground north of Ronssoy. At 9am they were attacked by 10 German divisions, with two companies of the 7th Royal Irish Regiment in the forward zone overrun in minutes without any chance of escape. The 1st Royal Dublin Fusiliers held off the first assault but by 11.30am had been forced to withdraw to the support lines, while the 49th Brigade was struggling to retreat in order, such was the speed of the enemy advance. The 7th/8th Inniskillings, holding Ronssoy, were surrounded, the few survivors continuing to put up resistance until forced to surrender that evening. The 6th Connaught Rangers counterattacked near Ronssoy Wood without support, the order to hold their ground having failed to reach them, and were cut to ribbons by the German machine-gunners. They fell back to Tincourt where, with the 1st Royal Munster Fusiliers, they held out for several hours until, surrounded and short of ammunition, they attempted a breakout across open ground only to be rapidly cut down and the survivors taken prisoner. At Lempire, the 2nd Royal Irish Regiment was cut off, with virtually the entire battalion killed or taken prisoner. Only the 1st Royal Dublin Fusiliers had managed to retire in good order to Peronne, where it covered the withdrawal of other units across the Somme.

The 48th and 49th brigades were by this time so depleted that they were combined to form makeshift battalions, with HQ staff, artillery members and signallers all pulled into the line as infantry men to help cover the retirement on March 23. Two days later what was left of the division was again the butt of the German attack, but managed to hold the line, withdrawing on the night of the 25th to Mericourt, where it could at last rest.

The composition of the 36th Division had likewise been radically altered by 1918. Many of the original battalions had been disbanded and the personnel drafted into other battalions of their own regiments. The 107th Brigade now consisted of the 1st Royal Irish Rifles, 2nd Royal Irish Rifles and 15th Royal Irish Rifles; the 108th Brigade of the 12th Royal Irish Rifles, 1st Royal Irish Fusiliers and 9th Royal Irish Fusiliers; and the 109th was made up of 1st Royal Inniskilling Fusiliers, 2nd Royal Inniskilling Fusiliers and 9th Royal Inniskilling Fusiliers.

The division had moved back to the Somme front in January, 1918, initially working on improving the defences in the Battle Zone after relieving the French who had formerly manned the St. Quentin front. The following month they were relieved of this task, moving into the line proper. On St. Patrick's Day, March 17, 1918, the Catholics of the 1st and 2nd battalions of the Royal Irish Rifles held Mass together for the first time since 1854. Four days later, on March 21, the three battalions holding a 6,000-yard front to a depth of 1,200 yards in the Forward Zone at St. Quentin were subjected to a five-hour bombardment followed by an attack by three German Divisions. The zone was overwhelmed, though pockets of troops held out. Some 24 hours after the initial assault, members of the 12th Royal Irish Rifles swam and waded down the canal at night to report that the battalion was still holding out at the Racecourse Redoubt. The Battle Zone held firm initially, only giving ground at Contescourt. At Essigny, however, to the divisional right, the line was turned with the reserves of the 36th deployed in an attempt to stabilise it. The 1st Inniskillings at Fontaine-les-Clercs, despite driving off numerous German assaults, finally had to pull back for want of support. On the evening of March 22, the division withdrew, falling back in subsequent days as it continuously fought rearguard actions. The 2nd Rifles were trapped

A British pill box on the Somme today clearly shows the scars of war

at Cugny on the 24th, and effectively wiped out. Cyril Falls records: "There cannot be many instances, even in the late war, of a battalion being blotted out so completely as this. Only the transport, a handful employed with it, a few officers kept back, and those on leave were left." At Velleselves, the 9th Royal Irish Fusiliers along with the Royal Dragoons recaptured Erches. With the British retiring due west, and the French towards Paris, a gap opened in the line. The 36th and 30th divisions were thrown forward to plug it on March 26, which they did successfully. By the time the German assaults ground to a halt, the division had lost more than 5,000 men, the vast majority of them having been taken prisoner. A letter home to Dungannon, County Tyrone, by a non-commissioned officer in the 36th (Ulster) Division was published in the News Letter on April 17, 1918, without the writer being identified. It read:

> *At first the Hun had all in his favour, as for the first five days you could not see 50 yards ahead owing to the mist, and we always found on retiring that the enemy had gone four or five miles past us. Some of our best lads have fallen but all played the game, and when the Huns surrounded them, and shouted 'Ulster Division surrender' they cut them down in hundreds and got away. We brought the rations up to the lads each night, and once we went five miles past the Germans to reach our battalion and safely returned. Another night a mounted patrol surrounded us when we were unloading the rations but we drove them off with rifle fire and rescued from them two of the Inniskillings whom they had made prisoners. On the second day of the offensive we held the Haig line, although the Germans were five miles past us. On our fourth day of retirement we were relieved late at night, but at five o'clock the next morning we had to rush into the line at the double. We stopped one night in a village, but next morning the Hun was on top of us, so it was a case of fighting again. It was very sad to see the women and children flying for their lives and leaving everything behind.*

The 36th Division was withdrawn from the line and moved north to Flanders, where it remained until the end of the war, taking part in a number of the final actions as the Germans were pushed back towards Mons.

The Guards Division, including the 1st Irish Guards, had been withdrawn from the line facing Arras on the night of March 20 to retire to a rest sector. Following the German breakthrough the following day, however, it was rapidly moved south, joining the line at the junction of the Third and Fifth armies to ensure no gap appeared as the British forces withdrew. By March 27, its sector had been stabilised. The 2nd Irish Guards, along with the 3rd Coldstream Guards and 4th Grenadier Guards, who together made up the recently-formed Guards Division's 4th (Guards) Brigade, had been attached to the 31st Division in February, 1918. It was on the Third Army front, to the north of the line, on March 21, and subsequently took part in the battles of St. Quentin, Bapaume and Arras all within a week. Such was its casualties, the brigade effectively ceased to exist. (Among its dead was Private Harry Robertshaw, in whose memory the regiment still raises a glass each year thanks to a bequest left by his sister, who he told to "please buy my friends a drink" as he set off for the front.) The 2nd Irish Guards were withdrawn from operational duties, being based at Criel Plage on the coast where it acted as a training battalion for new officers until the end of the war.

The Tyneside Irish had been greatly reduced prior to the 1918 battle. The 1st and 4th battalions (the 24th and 27th Northumberland Fusiliers respectively) were amalgamated in August, 1917, to form the 24/27th Northumberland Fusiliers. The new battalion, in turn, was disbanded on February 26, 1918. The following day the 3rd Tyneside Irish, or 26th Fusiliers, was disbanded also. The remaining battalion, the 2nd Tyneside Irish (25th Fusiliers) was transferred to the 102nd Brigade of the 34th Division. The Tynesiders took part in the Battle of St. Quentin, in the opening days of the Somme offensive. It was to the north of the line attacked, with the 59th Division to its front at Hirondelle, Noreuil and Buillecourt, and wasn't in action until 11.30am. It held its positions well into the afternoon, and was able to adjust its line in good order. The division was later withdrawn and moved north, where, in June, 1918, the remaining Tynesiders were reduced to cadre strength.

The London Irish Rifles, by contrast, was in the thick of the defensive action

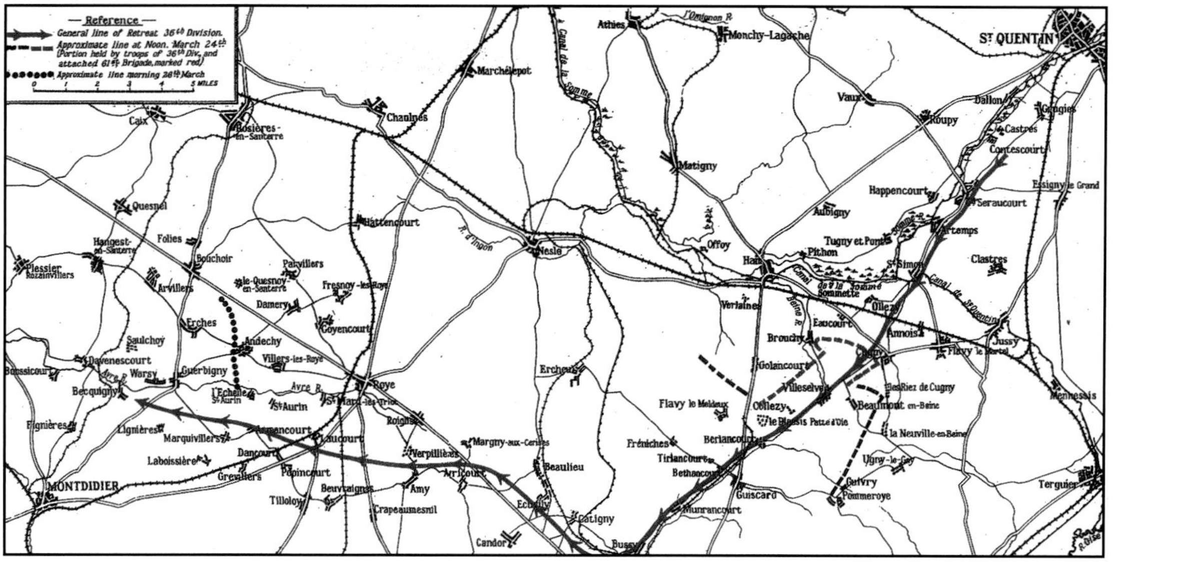

The Ulster Division was forced to fight a series of rearguard actions as it was pushed west by the German onslaught

from March 24, when its 47th (2nd London) Division was deployed to defend the line near Bapaume and again in April on the Ancre. The division took part in the Allied offensives of August and September, and the final push to victory.

The Liverpool Irish took no part in the 1918 fighting on the Somme. It had been transferred to the 57th (2nd West Lancashire) Division in January, 1918, and was engaged further north for the rest of the war.

Not all those who died in the German onslaught of March-April, 1918, were military. One of the best known characters to lose his life was Hugh Malcolmson, a well-known horse breeder, who had volunteered in 1917 to serve with the French Red Cross motor ambulances. He owned the Loughlinstown Stud, County Meath, and his horse, the appropriately named War Duke, had won the National Hunt Steeplechase at Cheltenham as well as a number of races in Ireland, including the Ward Hunt Cup. Mr Malcolmson, described as a driver with the French Red Cross section of Sanitaire, British Ambulance Committee, was killed on April 14, 1918, and buried at Perreuse Chateau Franco-British National Cemetery, some 40 miles east of Paris.

BITTERNESS AND RANCOUR

Would that all those who still may harbour bitterness and rancour against any of their own countrymen in Ireland might stand for even the moment and read the cross inscriptions in the cemeteries of France.

MP Willie Redmond, killed at Messines, 1917

The end of what Prime Minister David Lloyd George termed the "great Armageddon" came suddenly and with little warning to those on the front line. Men who had been biting at the heels of the retreating Germans for months were ordered to hold their positions. Commanding officers rode up and down marching columns giving out the news that the war had ended. Some cheered; others remained silent; and most just waited to see what came next. Before 1918 was out Irish troops would be on German soil as an army of occupation.

To these men, and the hundreds of thousands of others who were patiently waiting to return home, the Battle of the Somme was already a distant memory. Yet today, some 90 years on, it defines many people's perceptions of the First World War. It is an image of uncaring generals, surrounded by pen-pushing staff officers, sitting miles behind the lines in the comfort of fine chateaux with little or no idea of what was really happening on the ground; of pointless attacks repeated again and again; and the useless slaughter of tens of thousands of naive young men who formed up, as ordered, in straight lines in No-Man's-Land on July 1, 1916, and slowly walked into the face of merciless machinegun and artillery fire.

As with all perceptions, there are elements of truth. Even for those observing from their own front lines the battle was confused and the messages sent back from the forward troops a few hundred yards ahead of them contradictory. With the battle running to a predestined timetable which assumed victory and

A group of officers of the 9th Royal Irish Fusiliers, along with a member of the Royal Irish Rifles on attachment, photographed on November 11, 1918, at Moyscoyne, France, on the day the guns fell silent

Courtesy of the Royal Irish Fusiliers Museum

left little room for amendment, the old adage of reinforcing success was equally and unwittingly applied with devastating effect to the points of failure as well. Communications were, at best, difficult and often impossible even between those in sight of the action: telephone lines were more often than not cut by artillery shelling; both the British and German frontline troops fired flares, their colours meant to indicate their position and circumstances to their respective supporting arms but only served to add to the overall confusion of battle; divisional signs appeared above enemy trenches only to disappear again, leaving observers unsure whether they were held by friend or foe; and runners darted back and forth across No-Man's-Land, often dying or being wounded in their efforts to carry messages that were likely to be no longer relevant by the time they reached the right hands.

The generals, always hoping against hope for the big breakthrough, realised in 1915 that a "breach" in the enemy's lines by one assault was unlikely. Their strategy on the first day of the Somme, therefore, relied on the "limited objective" in which a battalion was given a target of its own, with fresh troops designated to pass through to take its own stretch of trench. It, too, failed miserably on the day, with few reaching their objectives. As Cyril Falls records: "It is absurd to suggest, as is sometimes done today, that the attack went according to plan, or that the limited success achieved on the right represented anything approaching what had been hoped. We had learnt new lessons, but at a terrible price."

Some of the papers issued to soldiers as they prepared to go back to civilian life

These lessons came from experience and were developed to such an extent over the remaining two-and-a-half years of the war that historian Richard Holmes suggests that the warfare of 1918 bore more of a resemblance to that of 1940 than it did to 1914. The artillery was the first to evolve new methods of operating

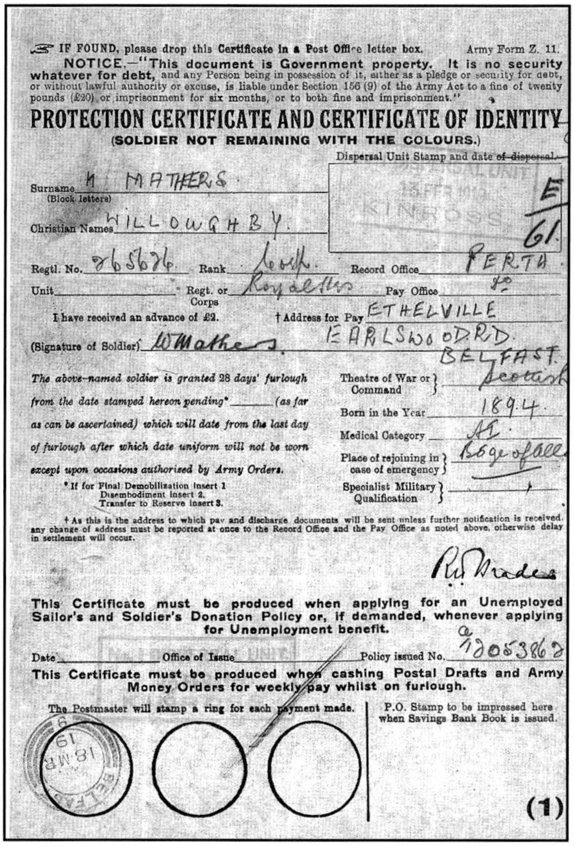

IF FOUND, please drop this Certificate in a Post Office letter box. Army Form Z. 11.

NOTICE.—"This document is Government property. It is no security whatever for debt, and any Person being in possession of it, either as a pledge or security for debt, or without lawful authority or excuse, is liable under Section 156 (9) of the Army Act to a fine of twenty pounds (£20) or imprisonment for six months, or to both fine and imprisonment."

PROTECTION CERTIFICATE AND CERTIFICATE OF IDENTITY

(SOLDIER NOT REMAINING WITH THE COLOURS.)

Dispersal Unit Stamp and date of dispersal.

Surname (Block letters) MATHERS

Christian Names WILLOUGHBY

Regtl. No. 265626 Rank Corpl. Record Office PERTH

Unit ___ Regt. or Corps ___ Pay Office ___

I have received an advance of £2. † Address for Pay ETHELVILLE EARLSWOOD RD. BELFAST.

(Signature of Soldier) W Mathers

The above-named soldier is granted 28 days' furlough from the date stamped hereon pending ___ (as far as can be ascertained) which will date from the last day of furlough after which date uniform will not be worn except upon occasions authorized by Army Orders.*

* If for Final Demobilization insert 1
Disembodiment insert 2.
Transfer to Reserve insert 3.

Theatre of War or Command Scottish

Born in the Year 1894.

Medical Category A1.

Place of rejoining in case of emergency ___

Specialist Military Qualification ___

† As this is the address to which pay and discharge documents will be sent unless further notification is received, any change of address must be reported at once to the Record Office and the Pay Office as noted above, otherwise delay in settlement will occur.

This Certificate must be produced when applying for an Unemployed Sailor's and Soldier's Donation Policy or, if demanded, whenever applying for Unemployment benefit.

Date ___ Office of Issue ___ Policy issued No. ___

This Certificate must be produced when cashing Postal Drafts and Army Money Orders for weekly pay whilst on furlough.

The Postmaster will stamp a ring for each payment made.

P.O. Stamp to be impressed here when Savings Bank Book is issued.

(1)

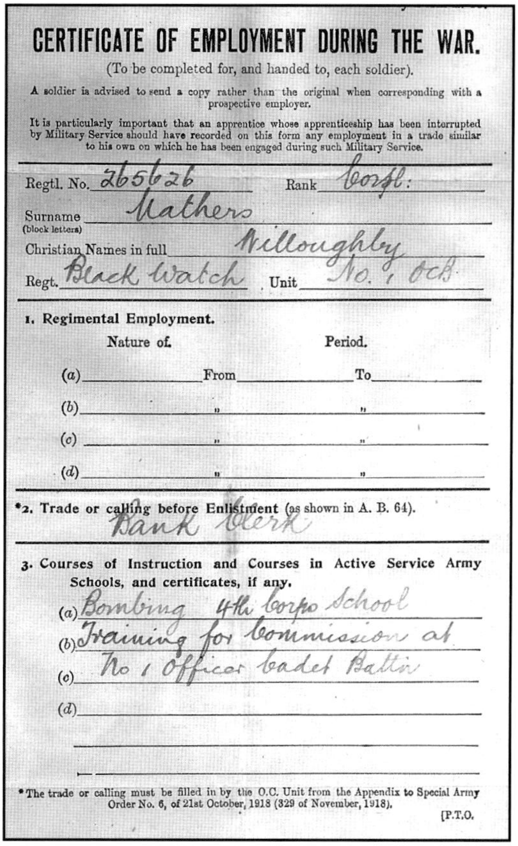

CERTIFICATE OF EMPLOYMENT DURING THE WAR.

(To be completed for, and handed to, each soldier).

A soldier is advised to send a copy rather than the original when corresponding with a prospective employer.

It is particularly important that an apprentice whose apprenticeship has been interrupted by Military Service should have recorded on this form any employment in a trade similar to his own on which he has been engaged during such Military Service.

Regtl. No. 265626 Rank Corpl.

Surname (block letters) Mathers

Christian Names in full Willoughby

Regt. Black Watch Unit No. 1 OCB

1. Regimental Employment.

Nature of.	Period.	
(a)	From	To
(b)	"	"
(c)	"	"
(d)	"	"

***2. Trade or calling before Enlistment** (as shown in A. B. 64).

Bank Clerk

3. Courses of Instruction and Courses in Active Service Army Schools, and certificates, if any.

(a) Bombing 4th Corps School
(b) Training for Commission at
(c) No 1 Officer Cadet Battn
(d)

* The trade or calling must be filled in by the O.C. Unit from the Appendix to Special Army Order No. 6, of 21st October, 1918 (329 of November, 1918).

[P.T.O.

The End in Sight as portrayed by the 36th (Ulster) Division's Christmas card of 1918

Courtesy of the Somme Heritage Centre

which gave better protection to the advancing troops: the creeping barrage, which replaced the timed lifting of fire from line to line used on July 1, 1916, provided a wall of shell fire which moved steadily forward keeping the enemy pinned down while allowing the infantry to follow in its wake. It was later further improved by the inclusion of flanking fire, giving protection on three sides. The use of surveys to pinpoint enemy guns so they could be engaged immediately without the need by the gunners to "zero" greatly hampered the German response to attacks, while gas, first introduced by the Germans, was used to good effect to hinder the troops in the trenches being assaulted.

The tank was first used in limited numbers and thinly spread out during the Battle of the Somme. It was used in massed ranks at Cambrai in November, 1917, and by the following year thousands of these machines were in action on the Western Front. The latest versions in 1918, chiefly Mark IVs and Mark Vs, were faster, more reliable, better armoured, with greater versatility and were

The tank, which played a crucial role in the Allied victory, is commemorated at Pozieres

Below right: An invitation to a welcome home banquet for the men of the Royal Irish Fusiliers

Courtesy of the Royal Irish Fusiliers Museum

used in increasingly large numbers as shock weapons to hammer holes in the enemy's defences. The Germans, who failed to develop an effective tank force of their own during the Great War, exploited armour to the full in the Second World War, when their massed panzers spearheaded the Blitzkrieg on Poland, France and Russia.

Likewise the airplane, barely a decade old by the start of hostilities, came into its own as a weapon of war. Some were equipped to attack artillery emplacements; others to drop supplies and ammunition to forward troops; some squadrons concentrated on clearing the skies of enemy planes, ensuring as little intelligence as possible of the Allied movements reached the German high command, while yet others acted as the eyes of the battle planners by photographing and reporting on movements and strongpoints beyond the range of ground observers. By 1918 they were being used in campaigns by the hundreds to ensure air superiority, another glimpse of what was to follow during the Second World War.

The "poor bloody infantry" benefited little from mechanical innovations, though attempts were made to improve protection with the use of body armour to supplement the introduction of steel helmets in late 1915. The arrival of the Mills bomb in the autumn of the same year replaced the primitive stick grenade which, in its turn, had substituted for the "homemade" jam tin grenades created by the men in the trenches. They still had to negotiate No-Man's-Land, of course, and while objectives were still being determined by the generals, it was the battle

Orangemen, members of the 8th Royal Irish Rifles, meet in the Rhineland in October, 1919, under the military warrant LOL 862

Courtesy of the Somme Heritage Centre

hardened troops who were literally calling the shots on the ground. The machinegun, utilised to great affect by the Germans, grew increasingly important to the British, who developed a tactic of using them en masse to fire over the heads of their own advancing troops to keep the enemy under cover. And instead of the extended lines of July 1916, the infantry would move forward in small groups which took cover where they could find it, and pushed on regardless of the progress to their left or right. In response, the Germans created storm troopers, lightly equipped but heavily armed, to lead the counterattacks. In essence, and more out of necessity than design, both sides were preparing armies which had grown accustomed to static trench warfare for the open battles which were finally to bring the war to a conclusion in 1918.

The world had changed during the four-and-a-half years of fighting and, in the months and years that followed the Armistice, empires were dissolved, new states created and old ones given back their independence. To the east Communism had come to the fore and with it the seeds of a new superpower; to the west America, reluctant to enter the war in the first place, retreated back to its policy of isolation. Words alone failed to resolve the "Irish problem", left hanging at the outbreak of war. The bloody violence of what was known to one side as the Anglo-Irish War and to the other the War of Independence ended in partition. Separate governments were set up in Belfast and Dublin, with their first tasks to deal with the violence of the "Troubles" and civil war respectively.

On June 12, 1922, as a result of the founding of the Irish Free State, the Colours of the Royal Irish Regiment, the Royal Dublin Fusiliers, the Royal Munster Fusiliers, the Connaught Rangers, the Leinster Regiment and South Irish Horse – each emblazoned with battle honours won in the First World War – were handed over to King George V at Windsor Castle for safekeeping prior to the regiments disbanding. Today they are still on show at the castle's State Apartments as testimony to the courage, sacrifice and service of generations of Irishmen.

SUPERIORITY OF OUR CAVALRY

The Brigadier desires to congratulate the 4th Dragoon Guards on the spirited action of two troops of the squadron on reconnaissance which resulted in establishing the moral superiority of our cavalry from the first over the Germany cavalry.

Regimental history of the 4th (Royal Irish) Dragoon Guards on first contact with the enemy

The cavalry regiments of 1914-18 were the heroes in waiting, though their day was never to truly come. Outside of the short war of movement which characterised the early months of the war, and the final 100 days' push to victory, they largely remained backroom boys, keeping their sabres sharpened and their horses well shod for that elusive big breakthrough. During the Big Pushes they were held in reserve, ready at a moment's notice to charge their mounts through the gaps in the German lines created by the infantry so they could harass the enemy in the rear. But the lines never broke. In between they served in a variety of roles: at times in the trenches as dismounted cavalry; acting as stretcher bearers or burial parties during major engagements; as escorts for senior officers; mounting ceremonial guards outside headquarters; or as a last line of defence when the Germans threatened to drive a wedge between units. Their casualties were, generally, less than for the infantry as the flow of battle rarely allowed the cavalry more than bit parts during the major campaigns.

There were four Irish cavalry regiments in 1914, though such was the nature of this arm that many of the troopers came from outside Ireland. The 4th (Royal Irish) Dragoon Guards was the oldest of the cavalry regiments, dating back to 1685, when it was raised in the north of England. It only became an Irish regiment in 1746 with the title of the Blue Irish Horse. In 1788 its title was altered to the 4th Dragoon Guards, with the Royal Irish added as testimony to its time spent in Ireland. The regiment, which had been stationed at Tidworth in England at the declaration of war, was the first to encounter the Germans, firing the first shots and drawing the first blood by sword. It was also the first regiment to cross into Germany as the British Army of Occupation. Throughout the war it served as part of the 2nd Cavalry Brigade of the 1st Cavalry Division. Its primary contribution to the 1916 battles was as reserve during the Flers-Courcelette push of September 15, 1916, though it was actively engaged during the retreat on the Somme from March 1918, and the battles of Amiens and Albert in August that year.

The 5th Royal Irish Lancers had a chequered past. Raised initially in 1689 at Enniskillen, it fought at the Battle of the Boyne and later under Marlborough in Europe. However, on its return to Ireland it was used essentially as a garrison force and ultimately disbanded in 1799. Re-raised in 1858, it earned a reputation for professionalism and bravery, not least during the Boer War. It was based in Dublin in 1914, and was caught up in the so-called Curragh Mutiny, during which 18 of its 20 officers declared themselves prepared to resign rather than engage the Ulster Volunteer Force in the north. The regiment was initially sent to the 1st Cavalry Division, serving with the 3rd Cavalry Brigade which, from September 1914, became part of the 2nd Cavalry Division. The Lancers were engaged on the Somme throughout much of 1918 from March through to October, including the battles at St. Quentin, Amiens, Albert, Bapaume, the Canal de Nord and the crossing of the St. Quentin Canal, before being transferred to Flanders. The 5th Royal Irish Lancers were the first troops into Mons in 1918.

The 5th Royal Irish Lancers in Dublin

Courtesy of the Royal Dublin Fusiliers Association

The 6th Dragoons (Inniskillings), as the name implies, was another regiment which owes its formation to the Protestant resistance at Enniskillen in 1689-90 and again fought at the Battle of the Boyne. In 1914 the regiment was in India, arriving in France in the middle of December as part of the 2nd Indian Cavalry Division. The Dragoons were subsequently transferred to the 2nd British Cavalry Division, becoming part of the 4th Cavalry Brigade where they remained until the end of the war. Its battle honours, therefore, have much in common with the 5th Lancers which served in the same division. The Dragoons lost nine officers and 185 men throughout the war.

The 8th King's Royal Irish Hussars were raised in 1693, with its first Colonel being Henry Conyngham, whose father had raised the 6th Inniskillings Dragoons. It, too, had been in India at the outbreak of the war, arriving in France in October with the Ambala Cavalry Brigade of the 2nd Indian Cavalry Division, which in turn was renamed the 5th Cavalry Division in November, 1916. The Hussars remained with the division until March, 1918, often serving in the trenches as dismounted cavalry. Its 1916 engagements on the Somme include the Battle of Bazentin from July 14-17, and the Battle of Flers-Courcelette, September 15-22 and, the following year, the advance to the Hindenburg Line. It joined the 9th Cavalry Brigade of the 1st British Cavalry Division less than two weeks before Germany launched its huge Somme campaign of 1918, and so again found itself engaged on this sector (in common with the 4th Dragoons) through to August, 1918, including the battles of St. Quentin, Bapaume, Rosieres, Amiens and Albert. It lost more than 100 men during the war.

The territorial soldiers of the North Irish Horse and its sister regiment, the South Irish Horse, were the first non-regular units to land in France when they sailed from Dublin onboard the SS Architect to land at Le Harve on August 19, 1914, and were soon in the thick of the action. Frank Percy Crozier, soon to be commanding officer of the 8th Royal Irish Rifles but then waiting for the formation

The plaque marking the 4th (Royal Irish) Dragoon Guards' first action

Courtesy of the Royal Irish Fusiliers Museum

of the Ulster Division, recalled meeting a group of the former unit as they killed time in Belfast waiting to set off:

> *In the little room on the ground floor of the Ulster Club – that holy of holies – big, muscular, horsy men sit and sip and smoke, in the uniform of the North Irish Horse. Their blood is up and they are proud. Why not? Are they not to accompany the British Expeditionary Force to France? They are not regular soldiers – though many of them have been – yet they are chosen, on account of merit, to accompany the greatest, hardest, best trained, most gentlemanly little army the world has ever seen, on the greatest adventure the world has ever known. The gay careless fox-hunters of the north finish their drinks with a clink of glasses and rise to depart to their horses and ships . . .*

The N.I.H. was also the first reserve force unit to see action during the retreat, losing its first casualty on September 15 when Trooper William Moore was killed during the Battle of Aisne.

Over the course of the war four more squadrons of the N.I.H., comprising 70 officers and 1,931 men recruited from across the nine counties of Ulster, were sent out to the Western Front from the regimental depot in Belfast. Their duties were largely confined to the ceremonial and the mounting of guards, though on occasion, such as the opening days of the Battle of the Somme, they acted as prisoner escorts, stretcher bearers and burial parties for the 36th (Ulster) Division.

The frustration of waiting for the breakthrough which would have seen the cavalry come into its own was such that many men transferred into other units. In August 1917, this movement of troops became more wholesale with the 2nd N.I.H. jointly forming the 9th (N.I.H.) Royal Irish Fusiliers as infantry, with 50

Private Thomas David Bratty joined the North Irish Horse in 1915. He was one of 300 who transferred to the 9th (N.I.H) Royal Irish Fusiliers in 1917 and was captured during the retreat of March the following year. As a prisoner-of-war Private Bratty was, according to information passed down through the family, made to work in the salt mines of Silesia, in the Oder valley of what today is Poland. Following his release he settled in New Zealand, where he married and had five children. He died in 1971 at the age of 77

Courtesy of the Royal Irish Fusiliers Museum

of the 300 who transferred losing their lives subsequently. All told, 150 officers and men of the North Irish Horse died during the war.

It was a similar story for the Clonmel-based South Irish Horse, which had earned itself the nickname Lord French's Body Guard within days of its arrival at the front as it helped cover his retreat following Mons. Many of its men, recruited from the remaining three provinces, transferred to the infantry, a large segment serving with the 7th (S.I.H.) Royal Irish Regiment in 1918. The regiment also holds the distinction of actually having seen mounted action during the Battle of the Somme when it advanced from Hametz on September 26 towards Flers, scene of the first tank action 11 days previously, along with the mounted troops of the 19th (Indian) Lancers. One can only imagine the surprise of the British soldiers as these horsemen crossed over their lines and rode across the open ground towards the enemy. After being shelled, the Horse retired to Gueudecourt, where they attacked enemy positions with Hotchkiss guns and rifles. The Germans counterattacked in force but were held at bay long enough for the infantry to come up several hours later to relieve the cavalry.

Private William Coates, 25, went to war with the South Irish Horse but was killed in March 1918 after his transfer to the 7th (S.I.H.) Royal Irish Regiment. From Foxrock, County Dublin, he is buried at Villers-Bretonneux Military Cemetary

The Victoria Cross presented to Private William McFadzean and held at the Royal Irish Rifles Museum in Belfast.
Gavan Caldwell, News Letter

SOLDIER BOY OF THE McFADZEANS

You people at home make me feel quite proud when you tell me 'I am the Soldier Boy of the McFadzeans'. I hope to play the game and if I don't add much lustre to it I will certainly not tarnish it.

Private William Frederick McFadzean, V.C.,
14th Royal Irish Rifles

There were 51 Victoria Crosses awarded during the Battle of the Somme in 1916, of which 10 were won by men of Irish blood. Four went to the 36th (Ulster) Division for its actions on July 1; two to the 16th (Irish) Division for the capture of Guillemont on September 3; and one to a soldier of the 2nd Royal Dublin Fusiliers. The remaining three medals were awarded to men serving in non-Irish units. The names and actions of a further four Irish V.C. winners who either won their awards on the Somme, are buried there or whose names appear on memorials in the French department, but whose actions took place outside July 1-November 18, 1916 (in one case in a different war), are given at the end according to the date of the award. Descriptions of their actions are based on the original citations from the London Gazette.

Captain Eric Norman Frankland Bell, 9th Royal Inniskilling Fusiliers, came from a military family. His father was formerly the Quartermaster at the Inniskillings' Depot in Omagh and in 1916 was adjutant of the 1st Garrison battalion of the Royal Irish Regiment. Captain Bell was 20 years old and attached to the 109th Light Trench Mortar Battery at Thiepval on July 1, 1916, and was advancing with the infantry when killed. His body was never found and his name is among those recorded on Pier and Face 4D and 5B of the Thiepval Memorial. The medal citation reads:

Lieutenant Cather brought four wounded men to safety before being killed taking water to others in No-Man's-Land

Courtesy of the Royal Irish Fusiliers Museum

The Victoria Cross memorial stone was placed in the grounds of the Ulster Tower by the Royal Irish Rangers

> *For most conspicuous bravery, when the front line was hung up by enfilading machine gun fire, Captain Bell crept forward and shot the machine gunner. Later, on no less than three occasions, when our bombing parties, which were clearing the enemies' trenches, were unable to advance, he went forward alone and threw trench mortar bombs among the enemy. When he had no more bombs available he stood on the parapet, under intense fire, and used a rifle with great coolness and effect on the enemy advancing to counter-attack. Finally he was killed rallying and reorganising infantry parties which had lost their officers. All this was outside the scope of his normal duties with his battery. He gave his life in his supreme devotion to duty.*

Lieutenant Geoffrey St. George Shillington Cather, the 9th Royal Irish Fusiliers, was a son of the cloth, his father being the Belfast clergyman the Rev. Robert Cather. The family also had connections to Portadown, County Armagh, where his grandfather, Thomas Shillington, lived at Tavanagh House. His name is recorded on the Thiepval Memorial, Pier and Face 15A. His citation records how the 25-year-old Lieutenant Cather had spent five hours on the evening of July 1, up until midnight, searching for wounded men in the No-Man's-Land north of the Ancre. During that time he rescued three men, dragging them to safety. His medal citation continues:

> *Next morning, at 8am, he continued his search, brought in another wounded man, and gave water to others, arranging for their rescue later. Finally, at 10.30am, he took out water to another man, and was proceeding further on when he was himself killed. All this was carried out in full view of the enemy, and under direct machine gun fire and intermittent artillery fire. He set a splendid example of courage and self-sacrifice.*

Captain Bell used his mortar bombs then his rifle to clear the enemy trenches

Lieutenant-Colonel Carton de Wiart was wounded eight times during the war

Sergeant Robert Downie rallied his comrades to press home his battalion's assault

Lieutenant Holland ran the gauntlet of his own artillery to attack the enemy

All photographs courtesy of the Somme Heritage Centre

Private Frederick Jeremiah Edwards with his mother during home leave granted after winning his V.C.

Courtesy of the Somme Heritage Centre

Lieutenant-Colonel Carton de Wiart, commanding officer of the 8th Gloucestershire Regiment, had an Irish grandmother and so may not be considered sufficiently Irish by some to warrant the description. His bravery, however, is unquestioned. Born in Belgium, he had served during the Boer War (in which he was wounded twice) and sustained injuries on no fewer than eight occasions during the First World War, the most serious of which cost him a hand and an eye. His V.C. was won on the night of July 2-3, 1916, when he rallied the troops of three battalions, as well as his own, to hold off enemy counterattacks. He retired to County Cork, but enlisted again during the Second World War, ending up as a prisoner of war.

Sergeant Robert Downie, of the 2nd Royal Dublin Fusiliers, was born in Glasgow where his father, originally from Dublin, had taken the family in search of work. He had joined up in February, 1912, at the age of 18, and survived the war, dying in Glasgow in 1968 at the age of 74. On October 23, 1916, his battalion was in action near Lesboeufs, where it had captured a line of enemy gunpits. With most of the officers dead or wounded, Downie rallied his comrades to press home the assault. His medal citation recorded:

> *When most of the officers had become casualties, this non-commissioned officer, utterly regardless of personal danger, moved about under heavy fire and reorganised the attack, which had been temporarily checked. At the critical moment he rushed forward alone, shouting: 'Come on, the Dubs!'; this stirring appeal met with immediate response, and the line rushed forward at his call.*

Private Frederick Jeremiah Edwards, of the 12th Middlesex Regiment, was born at Queenstown (now Cobh), County Cork. He was 21 in 1916 when on September

Private Thomas Hughes being presented with his medal by the King

Courtesy of the Somme Heritage Centre

26 he single-handedly attacked a machinegun post at Thiepval which was holding up his battalion's advance. All the officers had become casualties and the men, sensing the confusion, were starting to withdraw when Edwards leapt into action, tossing grenades as he ran at the gun. His comrades rallied and pressed home the attack to take more ground. He later rose to the rank of Corporal and survived the war to die in an old people's home at Richmond, England, in 1964 at the age of 79. His Victoria Cross is on display at the National Army Museum.

Lieutenant John Vincent Holland, from Model Farm, Athy, County Kildare, was 27 when he won his Victoria Cross. He had been in America at the outbreak of war and had initially joined the 2nd Life Guards as a trooper before being commissioned into the 3rd Leinster Regiment. Holland was wounded at the Second Battle of Ypres in May, 1915, while attached to the 2nd Royal Dublin Fusiliers, and was transferred to the 7th Leinsters, part of the 16th (Irish) Division, on his recovery. On September 3, 1916, he was leading a party of bombers at Guillemont. While others dealt with the enemy dugouts in the area already taken, he pressed on, running the gauntlet of his own artillery to attack the Germans still in the village. The London Gazette noted: "He started out with 26 bombers and finished with only five after capturing some 50 prisoners. By this gallant action he undoubtedly broke the spirit of the enemy and saved many casualties. He was far from well at the time and later had to go to hospital." Two Distinguished Conduct Medals and six Military Medals were awarded to other members of his platoon and one of his men, Private John Ford, was given a battlefield commission. Holland stayed in the army after the war, joining the 9th Lancers in India before taking up employment in the Colonial Services in Kenya. Following the Second World War, during which he again briefly served, he emigrated to Australia. He died in 1975.

Private Thomas Hughes, 6th Connaught Rangers, was from Castleblayney, County Monaghan, but had been working at the Curragh before enlisting. He was 31 at the time he won his V.C. at Guillemont on September 3, 1916. Despite being wounded he refused to leave the firing line. Hughes rushed a machinegun, killing the gunner and capturing the weapon and a number of prisoners. He was wounded a second time during this action, and was later promoted to corporal. He died in 1942 and is buried at Larough, Castleblaney.

Rifleman William Frederick McFadzean, 14th Royal Irish Rifles, was born in Lurgan, County Armagh, but had been living in the Cregagh area of east Belfast when he enlisted. In the early hours of July 1, 1916, he was in a concentration trench in Thiepval Wood preparing grenades for distribution. A box of bombs slipped into the crowded trench, with two of the safety pins falling out. Instantly realising the danger, "with heroic courage threw himself on the top of the bombs. The bombs exploded, blowing him to pieces, but only one other man was injured. He well knew his danger, being himself a bomber, but without a moment's hesitation he gave his life for his comrades". Some accounts indicate that two men, rather than the one, were injured. His name is on the Thiepval Memorial to the Missing (Pier and Face 15A and 15B) as his body, believed to have been buried in the woods to the rear of Connaught Cemetery, could not later be found.

Private Martin O'Meara was born at Lorrha, County Tipperary, but moved to Australia as a youth. He joined the Australian Expeditionary Force in 1915 and a year later was serving as a stretch-bearer at the Somme. Over four days of fighting around the Pozieres Heights from August 9, 1916, he carried arms and water to the front line and repeatedly went out into No-Man's-Land in search of the wounded, displaying what his medal citation described as an "utter contempt of danger". He was the only Irish-born winner of a Victoria Cross in the Australian forces during the First World War. O'Meara survived the war, despite being wounded on three occasions, and returned to Australia in 1918, but suffered a mental breakdown and spent the rest of his life in the psychiatric wing of Claremont Military Hospital, Perth. He died on December 20, 1935, and was buried with full military honours, with three other Australian V.C. winners the chief mourners.

Rifleman Robert Quigg, 12th Royal Irish Rifles, was from Carnkirk, Bushmills, County Antrim. He had been employed on the estate of Sir Harry Macnaghten at Dundarave, Bushmills, before the war and followed his master into the army, serving in Sir Harry's platoon. He was 31 in 1916 and, according to his medal citation, took part in three assaults on July 1. It goes on

> *Early next morning, hearing a rumour that his platoon officer was lying out wounded, he went out seven times to look for him under heavy shell and machine gun fire, each time bringing back a wounded man. The last man he dragged in on a waterproof sheet from within a few yards of the enemy's wire. He was seven hours engaged in this most gallant work, and finally was so exhausted that he had to give it up.*

Quigg remained in the army until 1934, retiring as a sergeant. He died in 1955 and is buried at Billy Parish Churchyard, close to his Bushmills home.

Other Irish Victoria Cross winners on the Somme

Lieutenant Alexander Young, of the 4th South African Infantry Regiment, though killed on the Somme, had earned his medal in an earlier war. On August 13, 1901, the then Sergeant-Major Young rushed a Boer defensive position at Ruiter's Kraal in South Africa. Spotting the enemy leader further on, he galloped ahead of his comrades to shoot one man dead and take captive Commandant Erasmus,

Private Martin O'Meara suffered a mental breakdown at the end of the war

Rifleman William McFadzean threw himself on grenades to save the lives of others

Rifleman Robert Quigg brought seven wounded men in from No-Man's-Land

Lieutenant Alexander Young earned his V.C. in 1901 during the Boer War

All photographs courtesy of the Somme Heritage Centre

Second Lieutenant Dunville was mortally wounded shielding a working party. He is buried at Villers-Faucon Communal Cemetery

Courtesy of the Somme Heritage Centre

"the latter firing at him three times at point blank range before being taken prisoner". Young, from Ballinamana, County Galway, died on October 19, 1916, aged 44. His body was never found with his name recorded on Pier and Face 4C of the Thiepval Memorial.

Second Lieutenant John Spencer Dunville, 1st Royal Dragoons, was 21 years old when killed. He had lived at Redburn, Holywood, County Down and is buried at Villers-Faucon Communal Cemetery, eight miles north-east of Peronne. He was in charge of a wire demolition party of scouts and Royal Engineers at Epehy on June 24-25, 1917, when they came under enemy fire. Displaying "great gallantry and disregard of all personal danger", Lieutenant Dunville used his body as a shield to protect his men and allow them to complete their task. His citation read: "Second Lieutenant Dunville, although severely wounded, continued to direct his men in the wire cutting and general operations until the raid was successfully completed, thereby setting a magnificent example of courage, determination, and devotion to duty to all ranks under his command. The gallant officer has since succumbed to his wounds."

Second Lieutenant Edmund de Wind, 15th Royal Irish Rifles, originally from Comber, County Down, had been working as a bank clerk in Cavan before moving to Canada. He returned in 1914 to join up. For seven hours after the launch of the German assaults of March 21, 1918, and despite being wounded twice, he fought on against overwhelming odds to hold his position at Groagie. His citation adds:

> *On two occasions, with two NCOs only, he got out on top under heavy machine-gun and rifle fire and cleared the enemy out of the trench, killing many. He continued to repel attack after attack until he was mortally*

Second Lieutenant Edmund de Wind, above, was determined to hold his position.

Above right: Lieutenant Harvey went on to become a brigadier in the Canadian armed forces

Courtesy of the Somme Heritage Centre

wounded and collapsed. His valour, self-sacrifice, and example were of the highest order.

The 34-year-old's body was never found and his name appears on Panel 74-76 of the Pozieres Memorial.

Lieutenant Frederick Maurice Watson Harvey immigrated to Canada and was the first of that country's cavalrymen to win a Victoria Cross. He was born at Athboy, County Meath, to a Dublin clergyman and was educated at Portora Royal School in Enniskillen, County Fermanagh. On March 27, 1917, he single-handedly assaulted a machinegun which was holding up his men, leaping the barbed wire to kill the gunner with a pistol and drive off his comrades. Lieutenant Harvey, who won the Military Cross in 1918, eventually reached the rank of brigadier and returned home to Canada, where he died at Calgary, Alberta, in 1980.

LEAVING THE TRENCHES

I was feeling very ill, with pains all over me. I do not remember what I did. I was dazed. I do not remember being warned for any duty. I cannot remember leaving the trenches even.

Rifleman James Crozier, 9th Royal Irish Rifles, executed February 27, 1916

During the First World War 346 officers and men were executed by their fellow soldiers-in-arms. In some cases the offences committed, such as murder, would have merited capital punishment under the civil court system. Most, however, were shot after falling foul of military laws, such as striking an officer, refusing a direct order, falling asleep at their post, cowardice, disobedience, or casting away their rifle. The vast majority were shot for desertion. In recent years a campaign for a blanket pardon has been denied by the British government, despite a number of celebrated cases having highlighted the shortcomings of the military court system. Three senior officers acted as judges with the accused often offered little assistance with his defence and, until late in the war, denied the benefit of legal representation. Of those shot at dawn, recent research has indicated that as many as 26 may have been Irish, though the evidence in some cases is far from conclusive while further Irish connections may yet come to light.

At least seven of these men were executed on the Somme front, with the case of Rifleman James Crozier, of the 9th Royal Irish Rifles, probably receiving the most attention. Executed for desertion, he was shot at dawn on Sunday, February 27, 1916, by a firing party made up of his battalion comrades. He is buried at Sucrerie Military Cemetery, three miles north-west of the Ulster Tower. It is widely believed that Crozier, from Battenberg Street, in the Shankill area of Belfast, was suffering from shell-shock at the time of his desertion and subsequent arrest.

The headstone of James Crozier lies among his comrades in Sucrerie Military Cemetery. His namesake and commanding officer, Frank Percy Crozier, right, described his execution in great detail

His trial was presided over by Major H. G. Barnard, of the 8th Royal Irish Rifles, with Lieutenant H. T. Blackwood, also of the 8th Rifles, and Captain G. H. Gaffikin, of Crozier's own 9th Rifles, making up the panel. A summary of proceedings is still on record and shows that the evidence for the defence was solely his own statement:

> *On 31 January 1916 I went into the front line trenches with my platoon. I was feeling very ill, with pains all over me. I do not remember what I did. I was dazed. I do not remember being warned for any duty. I cannot remember leaving the trenches even.*

Under cross-examination he admitted that at the time of his desertion "there were some rifle grenades bursting about a few yards from me", and claimed he had been ill before entering the line but "got worse when I began to get cold". A corporal with the 7th Ammunition Supply Park told the court how he had spotted Crozier a week after he had gone missing: "I saw the accused walking aimlessly about. He had no numerals, cap badge, pay book or rifle. I asked him his name and particulars of his regiment and he told me he was a deserter." The military policeman sent to collect the runaway reported that his "bevaviour was peculiar" and that Crozier had been unable to tell him where he had been in the previous seven days.

The court found Crozier guilty and sentenced him to death. The verdict was passed further up the rank structure for confirmation. The 107th Brigade commander approved the execution "as a deterrent to a repetition of offences of this nature", adding: "The discipline of the 9th R.I. Rifles is good for a Service battalion." The XVIIth Corps commander wrote: "I consider that, in the interests of discipline, the sentence, as awarded, should be carried out." The most interesting comment, however, came from Lieutenant Colonel Frank Percy Crozier, who commanded the 9th Royal Irish Rifles. In 1916 he wrote:

This photograph, according to the scrapbook which holds it, is a mock execution by the Royal Irish Fusiliers with the "victim" being the battalion cook

Courtesy of the Royal Irish Fusiliers Museum

> *(1) From a fighting point of view this soldier is of no value. His behaviour has been that of a "shirker" for the past three months. He has been with the Expeditionary Force since 3/10/15.*
>
> *(2) I am firmly of the opinion that the crime was deliberately committed with the intention of avoiding duty in the trenches, more particularly as he absented himself shortly after the case of another soldier had been promulgated for a similar crime. The officer commanding the man's company is of the same opinion. Sentence was remitted in the case mentioned to two years, one hard labour.*

Crozier, who retired from the army with the rank of brigadier-general, talks of his namesake's execution (though refers to him as "Crocker") in his book A Brass Hat in No-Man's-Land, published in 1930. He writes:

> *I am asked my opinion as to whether sentence of death should be carried out on Crocker. In view of certain circumstances I recommend the shooting be carried out. At last I receive the orders and documents relative to the execution. We leave the line for four days' rest at Mailly-Maillet. In the afternoon of the first day out we parade in hollow square. The prisoner – Crocker – is produced. Cap off he is marched by the sergeant-major to the centre. The adjutant reads the name, number, charge, finding, sentence and confirmation by Sir Douglas Haig. Crocker stands erect. He does not flinch. Perhaps he is dazed; who would not be? The prisoner is marched away by the regimental police while I, placing myself at the head of the battalion, behind the band, march back to billets. The drums strike up, the men catch step. We all feel bad but we carry out our war-time pose. Crocker didn't flinch, why should we?*

That night, Crozier arranged for the rifleman to be given plenty of drink and briefed the junior officer commanding the execution squad on what he had to do. He goes on:

> *In the morning, at dawn, the snow being on the ground, the battalion forms up on the public road. Inside the little garden on the other side of the wall, not ten yards distant from the centre of the line, the victim is carried to the stake. He is far too drunk to walk. He is out of view save from myself, as I stand on a mound near the wall. As he is produced I see he is practically lifeless and quite unconscious. He has already been bound with ropes. There are hooks on the post; we always do things thoroughly in the Rifles. He is hooked on like dead meat in a butcher's shop. His eyes are bandaged – not that it really matters, for he is already blind. The men of the firing party pick up their rifles, one of which is unloaded, on a given sign. On another sign they come to the Present and, on the lowering of a handkerchief by the officer, they fire – a volley rings out – a nervous ragged volley it is true, yet a volley. Before the fatal shots are fired I had called the battalion to attention. There is a pause, I wait. I see the medical officer examining the victim. He makes a sign, the subaltern strides forward, a single shot rings out. Life is now extinct. We march back to breakfast while the men of a certain company pay the last tribute at the graveside of an unfortunate comrade. This is war.*

Crozier adds a final line which could be equally applied to the men whose stories follow: "War is all pot-luck, some get a hero's halo, others a coward's cross. But this man volunteered in '14. His heart was in the right place then, even if his feet are cold in '16."

The first double execution of Irishmen on the Somme also involved members of the Royal Irish Rifles. Rifleman James Templeton, who lived at 12 Enfield Street in Belfast, was serving with the 15th battalion when he, along with comrade Rifleman J. F. McCracken, deserted their posts in early 1916. Arrested

Riflemen James Templeton and J. F. McCracken were shot together and still lie side-by-side in Mailly-Maillet Communal Cemetery

behind the lines they were tried, found guilty and subsequently executed on Sunday, March 19, 1916. They are buried side-by-side in Mailly-Maillet Communal Cemetery Extension, six miles north of Albert, facing towards the quarry where their executions are believed to have been carried out.

While the slaughter which was the Battle of the Somme raged a few miles away, the next Irishman to die at the hands of his comrades was awaiting execution. James Cassidy, of the 1st Royal Inniskilling Fusiliers, was shot on Sunday, July 23, 1916, after being found guilty of desertion. His remains lie in Englebelmer Communal Cemetery Extension, six miles north-west of Albert. Another fusilier, Joseph Carey, of the 7th Royal Irish Fusiliers, was shot at dawn on Friday, September 25, 1916, for deserting his post while on active duty. He had lived at 4 Julian's Place, Mayor Street, at Dublin's Northwall. He was buried at Corbie Communal Cemetery Extension, 10 miles east of Amiens.

Driver James Mullany, of the 72nd Battery of the Royal Field Artillery, was the only Irishman executed on the Somme for an offence other than desertion. On September 16 he was ordered by his sergeant major to harness up his horse team but maintained that he should be allowed to have his tea first. An argument developed during which Mullany knocked over the sergeant major then attacked him again as he got to his feet. He was charged with striking a superior officer and sentenced to death, the verdict being confirmed by his Corps commander, Lieutenant-General Lord Cavan. Mullany, who had a reputation for insolence, was executed on Tuesday, October 3, 1916, alongside another driver from his unit who had also been found guilty of striking a superior officer in a separate incident. He is buried at Ribemont Communal Cemetery Extension, five miles south-west of Albert.

The last of the Irish Somme executions took place in 1917. Fusilier Thomas Hogan, who had enlisted under the name of Murphy, was serving in the 2nd Royal Inniskilling Fusiliers when accused of desertion. The 31-year-old, from Tralee, County Kerry, was shot on Monday, May 14, 1917, and is buried at Ham British Cemetery, Muille-Villettes, 14 miles south-west of St. Quentin.

The quarry, taken from the cemetery wall, where the double execution of Templeton and McCracken is believed to have taken place

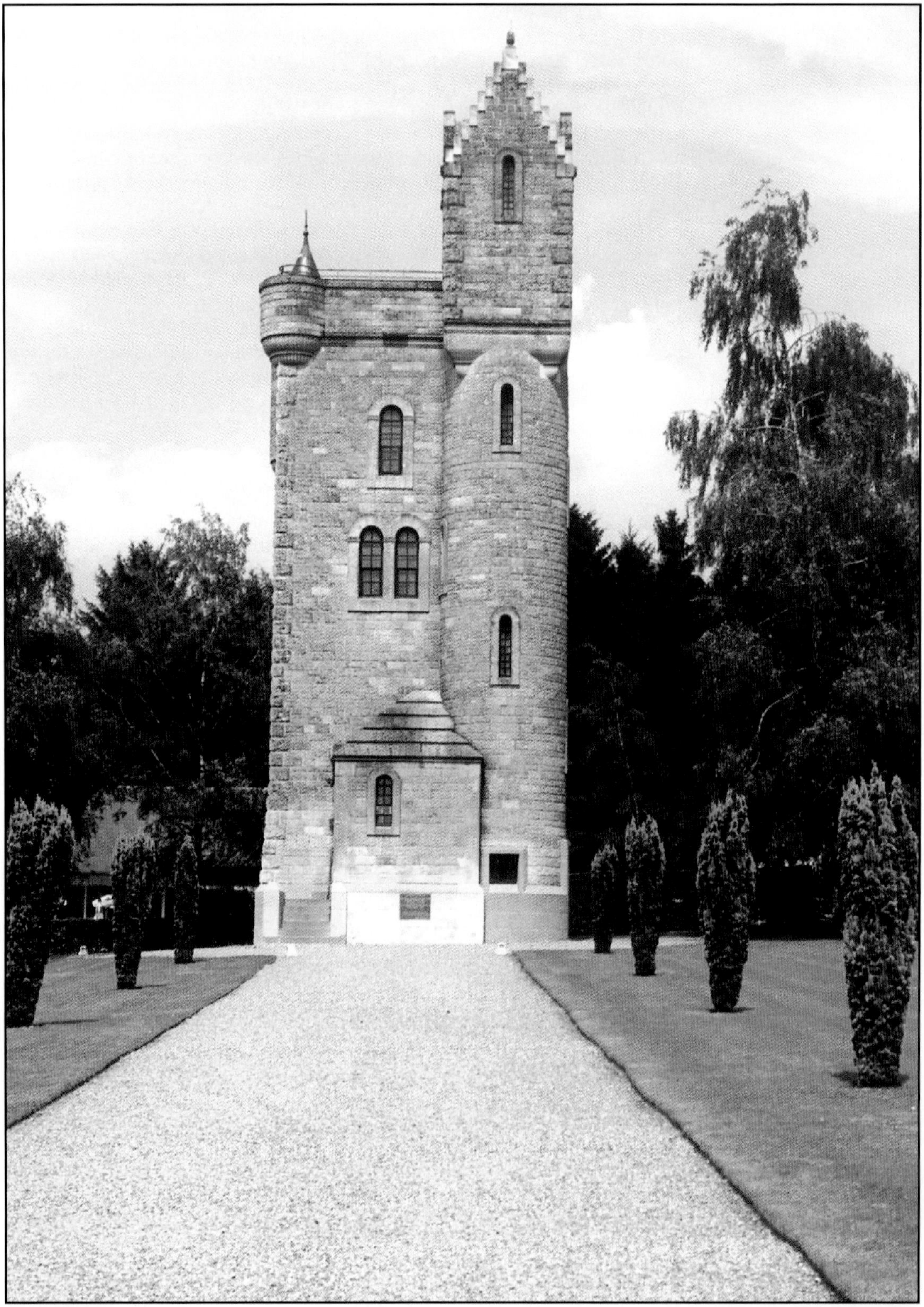

The Ulster Memorial Tower was the first, and remains one of the most impressive, of the Western Front memorials

THE SUPREME SACRIFICE

On sea, on land, and in the air you have fought for your King and country, and you have helped to secure the freedom of the world! Let us not in this hour of victory forget those of your comrades who have made the supreme sacrifice.

Sir Edward Carson, Ulster Unionist leader

The First World War, more than any conflict before and arguably since, struck a common chord with the public. For the first time Britain, its pre-war professional force insufficient for the task ahead, had been forced to form a civilian army. Millions of men volunteered or, in the latter half of the war (though not in Ireland), were conscripted for service. On the home front, thousands of women went to work in the munitions factories or as stand-ins for the serving soldiers in what had previously been exclusively male areas of employment. Most women were left behind to fret and worry, living in dread of the black-rimmed telegram from the War Office which would carry word of a loved one's death or injury.

Ireland had been embroiled in its own political conflict prior to the outbreak of war and the Easter Rising in Dublin in 1916 had only served to remind people that the end of hostilities abroad would not bring peace to their own country. It was against such a backdrop that the Irish soldiers returned to their homes and civilian life. Those in the north were greeted as conquering heroes, while in the south they sometimes faced ridicule for having "fought for the British". The differing attitudes affected how the war was remembered and commemorated both at home and on the Somme.

Following the Armistice in November, 1918, a fund was opened in Ulster with the aim of providing a suitably grand memorial on the Western Front. A proposal put forward by Sir James Craig, the future first Prime Minister of Northern

Ireland, that it be based on a prominent Ulster landmark was accepted at a meeting held in the Old Town Hall in Belfast on November 17, 1919. After some debate, the decision was taken to construct a replica of Helen's Tower, which today still stands proudly on the Clandeboye estate, between Bangor and Newtownards, County Down. The reasoning was that units of the division had undergone their basic training in the shadow of the tower before transfer to England, and ultimately France. The site chosen was at Thiepval, on the old German front line captured by the division on July 1, and which, just 24 hours later, was virtually all it was left with as a reward for so much valour and suffering. London architects Bowden and Abbot oversaw the work, which was carried out by another English firm, Fenning and Company Limited, of Hammersmith, in conjunction with the Societe de Construction et Travaux Publics d'Arras. The building, known as the Ulster Memorial Tower, was speedily erected amid the devastation of the surrounding countryside. Standing 70ft at its highest point, it was the first official memorial to be completed on the Western Front and proudly dedicated on November 19, 1921, by Field Marshal Sir Henry Wilson, Chief of the Imperial General Staff and himself an Irishman.

On the ground floor of the tower is the memorial chamber, measuring 16ft by 16ft, and faced in stone. Its marble inscription tablet reads:

> *This Tower is dedicated to the Glory of God, in grateful memory of the officers, non-commissioned officers and men of the 36th (Ulster) Division and of the sons of Ulster in other Forces who laid down their lives in the Great War, and of all their comrades-in-arms, who, by divine grace, were spared to testify to their glorious deeds.*

Also inscribed on the walls, in gold lettering, are the slightly amended words of Alfred Lord Tennyson (the word 'Ulster' replacing the original 'Mother') of the poem engraved on the walls of Helen's Tower at Clandeboye. The Ulster Tower version reads:

Helen's Tower here I stand
Dominant over sea and land
Son's love built me and I hold
Ulster's love in letter'd gold

The Germans used the tower as a sentry post during their occupation of France during the Second World War, with a bored guard leaving his own mark by cutting a Swastika into the stonework at the top.

A resident caretaker lived in the upper floors of the building up until the early 1970s. Then, for more than a decade, it was left virtually abandoned with a local woman providing a key, on request, to visitors. A community project started by the Farset group in Belfast began raising public awareness of the growing state of disrepair of the tower and lobbied the British government to take action. On July 1, 1991, the 75th anniversary of the opening day of the battle, the tower was rededicated in the presence of H.R.H. Princess Alice, Duchess of Gloucester. The Somme Association, which grew out of the Farset project, now manages the tower. It built a visitors' centre to its rear in 1994 and employs full-time caretakers on site who guarantee the visitor a genuine Ulster welcome and a cup of tea.

Within the gardens of the tower are two further memorials. One is a marble stone to the left of the entrance which commemorates the 36th Division's nine Victoria Cross winners. The other remembers the members of the Orange Order who died in the First World War. The inscription reads: "This memorial is dedicated to the men and women of the Orange Institution worldwide who at the call of

Above: the memorial chamber on the ground floor of the Ulster Memorial Tower; bottom right: the Orange Order monument prior to being relocated to the back of the tower; and, bottom left, Helen's Tower, Conlig, which provided the inspiration for the Ulster Tower

The machinegun post to the left of the Ulster Tower gives the visitor an understanding of the advantages enjoyed by the German gunners

King and country left all that was dear to them, endured hardness and faced danger, and finally passed out of the sight of man by the path of duty and self sacrifice, giving up their own lives that others might live in freedom. Let those who come after see to it that their names be not forgotten." It stands within a gated enclosure to the rear of the tower and was moved there from its original position on the roadway, to the left of the main entrance, as it was considered a traffic hazard, a point proved in practice by a Frenchman who crashed into its surrounding wall.

The tower stands on the extreme left of the trenches captured by the 36th Division. About 60 paces along the small track to the left of the entrance is the remains of a concrete machinegun post (to the right-hand side) which is surrounded by crops in the summer months but exposed the rest of the year. It was part of a German cluster of strongpoints known to the Ulster troops as the Pope's Nose. The Ulstermen had intended to "bloody" it in the first hours of battle but it remained in German hands that day and inflicted terrible casualties on those attempting to cross No-Man's-Land. If you crouch down behind the emplacement, looking towards Thiepval Wood from which the Ulstermen launched their attack, you get a good impression of the advantage granted the German gunners.

The Pope's Nose was also linked to the Schwaben Redoubt complex, a vast fortress built beneath the Somme chalk. To the rear of the tower, just beyond its boundary and officially out-of-bounds to the public, is another entrance to the underground tunnels. It is concealed in the undergrowth of a copse of trees which, at one time, boasted preserved trenches and which today still bears the scars of war. The redoubt was believed by many to be the most formidable obstacle facing the Allied forces on July 1, not least because of its many exit points. The Ulster troops swept over it in the first hour of the battle only for German soldiers, who had been sheltering in the bomb-proof chambers, to re-emerge to their rear. A whole German division could live, eat and sleep in the Schwaben Redoubt in comparative safety. Officers lived in what were, compared to the Allied trenches, lavish quarters, fitted out with the best of furniture taken from abandoned French homes and Thiepval Chateau, once sited close to the open land in front of the present village church until destroyed during the war. Less sophisticated, but more than adequate, was the soldiers' accommodation. The redoubt was self-sufficient, with its own food stores, underground field hospital, ventilation, heating and sanitary systems. A network of tunnels, which linked the chateau's cellars to the Pope's Nose, allowed men to move around the front line without exposing themselves to hostile fire. Many of the headstones in Mill Road Cemetery, which stands between the Ulster Tower and the village and, like Connaught Cemetery on the road opposite, contains many Irish graves – had to be laid flat because of subsidence caused by the passages running beneath it.

Following the war, the tunnels were used by those clearing the battlefield of debris as a dumping ground for explosives and munitions. In the 1960s the French farmers, frustrated at the stream of souvenir hunters tramping across their land to plunder the redoubt, buried the entrances, though the more determined still find ways underground even today.

Between the cemeteries is the roadway which replaced the heavily-banked original "sunken road". Situated in No-Man's-Land, it provided a place of refuge for the wounded on July 1, acting like a broad trench amid the exploding shells and flying bullets. So many injured and dying soldiers were gathered here, waiting to be evacuated to the medical stations further back, that it was said their blood flowed down its slopes. The official history notes it was thereafter "known as Bloody Road, owing to the mass of dead heaped up on it at the end of the day".

The entrance to Crozier's bunker, to the rear of Connaught Cemetery. It was filled with the dead and dying on July 1

It was from the trenches dug within Thiepval Wood, or to give it its proper name, Bois d' Authvile, that the Ulster Division attacked. The woodland had once been part of the chateau's estate. The land was sold after the war and again changed hands following the 1939-45 conflict and has only recently, with the help of a British government grant, come into the hands of the Somme Association, which plans to provide public access to it for the first time. The wood still bears the scars of war with the outline of trenches, despite natural erosion, still clearly visible along with the deep recesses caused by shell fire. The entrances to dugouts, which provided the troops with shelter and often housed command centres, can still be found. Frank Percy Crozier returned from No-Man's-Land after seeing his troops off to discover his dugout H.Q. full of the dead and wounded. He recorded:

> *None of the wounded can walk. There are no stretchers. Most are in agony. They have seen no doctor. Some have been there for days. They have simply been pushed down the steep thirty-feet-deep entrance out of further harm's way and left – perhaps forgotten. As I enter the dugout I am greeted with the most awful cries from these dreadfully wounded men. Their removal is a Herculean task, for it was never intended that the dying and the helpless should have to use the deep stairway. After a time, the last sufferer and the last corpse are removed.*

The trees, severely damaged by the constant

artillery fire, have regenerated themselves to an extent that forestry has again been possible, though in fact comparatively little has been carried out over the years. Despite the warnings against trespassing, many people have explored the woods (myself included, it has to be admitted) and unexploded artillery shells and small arms are regularly discovered. Some are even foolish enough to carry the munitions to the wall of the nearby cemetery or to the Ulster Tower a short distance away, much to the alarm of the caretakers. The wood has by no means given up all its dead, with many of those listed on the nearby Thiepval Memorial having their last resting place here.

Although the 36th Division had the first official war memorial erected in its honour, the 16th (Irish) Division staked its claim as early as 1917. A Celtic cross, designed by commanding officer William Bernard Hickie, was made out of oak beams salvaged from a ruined house in Flanders and erected on the churned up ground between the villages of Guillemont and Ginchy, both of which had cost so many Irish lives to capture. During the fighting of 1918 the land was lost and regained, the cross surviving the onslaught largely intact. In 1923 it was removed, at the request of the landowner, and is currently housed at the National Memorial Park in Dublin. Major-General Hickie then formed an Irish Battlefield Memorial Committee which raised funds for the purchase of land and the construction of three stone crosses, similar in design to the original. The 16th (Irish) Division Cross was erected on the roadside at Guillemont, next to the newly-built church, on August 23, 1926. French Marshal Foch was the main guest of honour and did the unveiling in front of several hundred former officers and men of the division. The other crosses were placed at Wytschaete, in Belgium, and at Salonika, the latter in memory of the 10th (Irish) Division. The cross bears

The unveiling of the 16th (Irish) Cross at Guillemont in August, 1926, a decade after the division had taken the village and nearby Ginchy

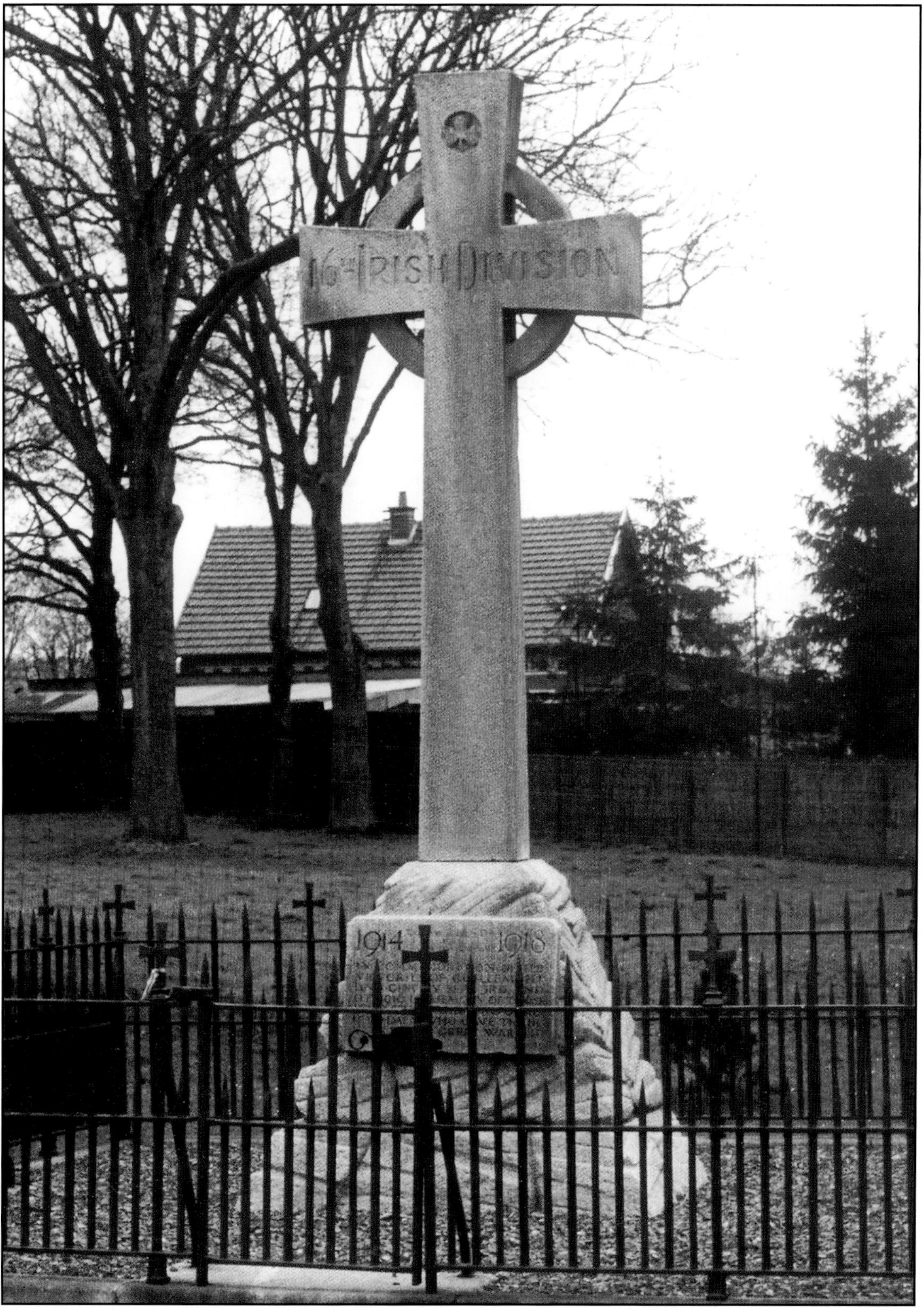

The 16th (Irish) Cross, for the 'honour of Ireland', stands next to Guillemont church in the centre of the village

the words *Do cum Gloire De agus Onora na hEireann*. It translates as "For the glory of God and the honour of Ireland". Guillemont fell to the 20th Division and a brigade of the 16th Irish on September 3, 1916. It could be argued, however, that Ginchy, taken in a tremendous divisional effort six days later, might have been the proper place to site it, though French restrictions on the placing of religious symbols other than on church property may have been a deciding factor. Fr. William Doyle, who was to die at the Battle of Langemarck in Belgium in 1917, was assigned to the division. In a letter home he spoke of going up to the battlefield after the fighting at Ginchy:

> *The wounded, at least I hope so, had all been removed, but the dead lay there stiff and stark with open staring eyes, just as they had fallen. Good God, such a sight! I had tried to prepare myself for this, but all I had read or pictured gave me little idea of the reality. Some lay as if they were sleeping quietly, others had died in agony or had had the life crushed out of them by mortal fear, while the whole ground, every foot, was littered with heads, or limbs, or pieces of torn human bodies.*

The 29th Division, formed in early 1915 from regular army battalions arriving from overseas garrisons, included the 1st Royal Munster Fusiliers, 1st Royal Dublin Fusiliers and 1st Royal Inniskilling Fusiliers. The division landed at Gallipoli in

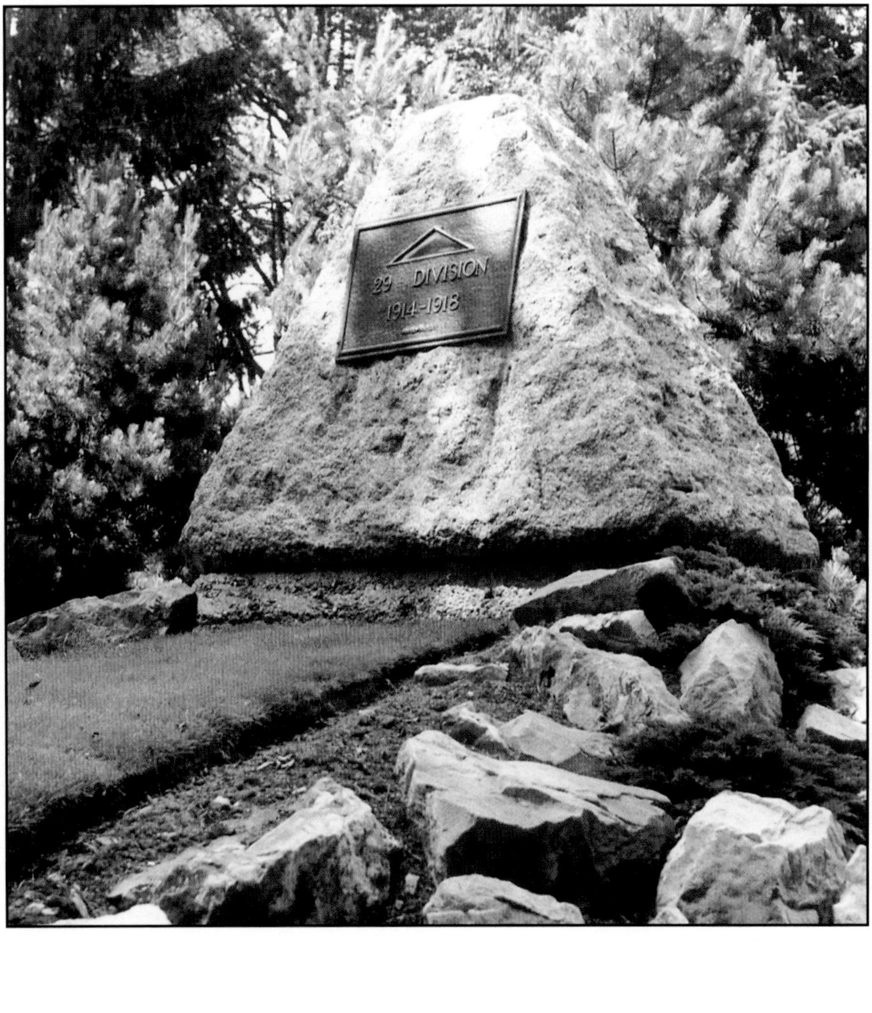

The 29th Division Memorial is one of the most visited as it is situated at the entrance to Newfoundland Park

April 1915, where it earned a high reputation and the title of the "Incomparable Division". It was evacuated in January of the following year, its troops being the last off the peninsula. After a spell in Egypt it was transferred in March to the Western Front. It was in the thick of the action on the Somme on July 1 and returned in October. The 29th Division Memorial is one of the most visited as it stands at the entrance to Newfoundland Park at Beaumont Hamel. The ill-fated Newfoundland Regiment had joined the division before its move to Gallipoli, replacing an under-strength Scottish territorial battalion. On July 1 it received orders to attack. With the communication trenches congested, and the battalion in a reserve trench some 300 yards from the British front line, the execution of the command in time would have been impossible. The decision was made to attack from where they were, across the open ground, in full view of the German machine-gunners. Of the 752 Newfoundlanders who began the attack, all 26 officers and 658 men became casualties. Nothing was gained and, as historian Martin Middlebrook points out in his book The First Day On The Somme, it is probable that not a single German soldier was killed or wounded.

The village of La Boisselle, lying to the south on the Albert-Bapaume road, was attacked by the 34th Division on July 1, 1916, including the four battalions of the Tyneside Irish which made up the 103rd Brigade. A bronze figure of Victory, paid for by a mixture of divisional funds and public subscription, was erected on the eastern edge of the village in 1923 as the 34th Division Memorial. It is reached by a pathway off the road to Pozieres. The monument stands beyond the German forward trenches attacked that day and, though the ground to either side was captured briefly by the Tyneside Scottish and Tyneside Irish before they were forced back, few are likely to have reached this spot. With the memorial at your back you can look along the direction of the old German front line, which ran due north. The famous Mash Valley is to the right, its title chosen to compliment Sausage Valley, as in "sausage and mash". Sausage Valley, so-named because the Germans constantly flew sausage-shaped observation balloons from here, lies behind the monument and was the path taken by the Tyneside Irish. To appreciate the task facing the 103rd Brigade you need to drive through La Boisselle (following the German trench line which ran along the left-hand side of the road before turning left beyond the village) and out to Bapaume Post Military Cemetery (which contains the graves of many who fell that day), approximately a mile away. From this spot, looking back along the route you have just travelled, the 2nd Tyneside Irish would have been just in front of you to the left of the road, with the remaining three battalions in trenches to the right. The open land from there to the village had to be crossed in the face of fierce German fire. The 34th Division had been expected to advance 2.5 miles that first day, but the frontline troops barely made it to the German trenches. In total, it suffered 6,380 casualties, more than any other division on July 1. The Tyneside Irish were supposed to be in reserve but, so confident of success were the top brass, they were ordered to leave their trenches and advance, in the open, with the rest of the division at zero hour. Their task had been to exploit the gap expected to be made by the leading troops. The reserve army and cavalry were waiting nearby ready to move should a pathway be cleared, and advance into the open countryside beyond. The plan started to unravel within minutes. The Tyneside Irish had to cross a mile of barren land, with the German machineguns, once they had run out of targets in No-Man's-Land, able to raise their sights and concentrate on the exposed Irish. Despite horrendous casualties, the Tyneside Irish made it to the German lines, where they regrouped before carrying on, their front growing ever narrower and all hope of success long gone. The remnants, down to fewer than 50 fit men and some 700 metres behind the German lines, even attempted to storm Contalmaison, a fortified village, and their objective that day. This strongpoint, a mile behind the German front, didn't fall for another 10 days when the Green

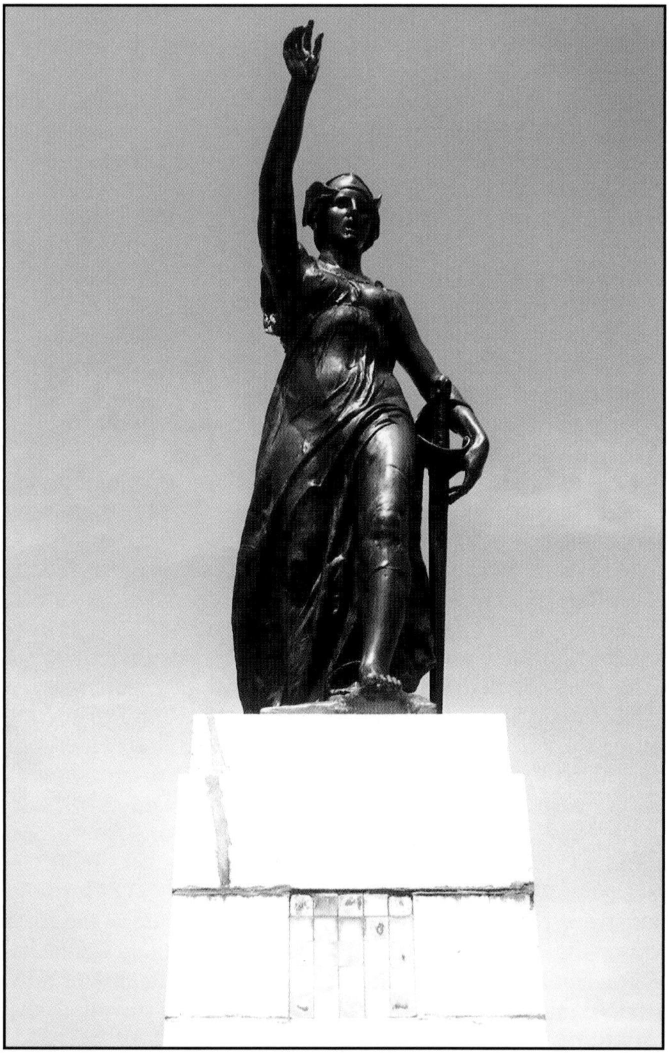

The figure of Victory stands atop the 34th Division Memorial at La Boisselle, which also sports the divisional chequered emblem

Howards of the 23rd Division took it. By the end of the day on July 1, only one in four of the Tyneside Irish had escaped injury. The brigade had suffered 2,139 casualties – more than 70 per cent of its total. Among the wounded was the brigade commander and three of his battalion COs. A Tyneside Scottish and Irish Memorial Seat, on the edge of the village by the road to Albert, is an ideal place to contemplate such statistics.

Another casualty of note was the 34th Division's commander, General E. C. Ingouville-Williams, known to his troops as Inky Bill, who was killed later in the month, on July 22, near Mametz by a stray shell. The official history says he was checking out the lie of the land. The rumour among his men had it, however, that he was souvenir hunting. The 54-year-old son of General Sir J. McWilliams was laid to rest in Warloy-Baillon Communal Cemetery Extension.

The London Irish Rifles, properly known as the 1/18 (County of London) London Regiment, is commemorated as part of the 47th (2nd London) Division Memorial. It stands next to the notorious High Wood, between Martinpuich and Longueval, which it helped to take in an attack launched on September 15, 1916, with the support of a number of tanks. This was the date on which this new weapon was used for the first time and it enjoyed success at Flers, a short distance away.

The Tyneside Scottish and Irish Memorial Seat, on the edge of La Boisselle, and, right, the 47th (2nd London) Division Memorial Gateway at Martinpuich

At High Wood, however, the war-ravaged terrain with its blasted tree stumps made the manoeuvring of such vehicles virtually impossible. The wood, which had resisted numerous assaults in the previous weeks, did fall though to the infantry's bayonets and guns. In Martinpuich itself, next to the school, is the 47th Division Memorial Gateway. The division was back in action on the Somme the following month, taking part in what was known as the Battle of le Transloy, which included the capture of Eaucourt l'Abbaye, Le Sars and, nearby, the assault on the Butte de Warencourt, a man-made mound on the right-hand side of the Albert to Bapaume road. In 1918 the 47th Division was again on the Somme, resisting the German assaults in March and April, and being particularly heavily engaged in the counterattacks in August, including the second Battle of Albert.

The 63rd (Royal Naval) Division Memorial stands on the edge of Beaucourt village. The division, which included the 10th Royal Dublin Fusiliers, fought here in November, 1916. The monument is actually close to one-and-a-half miles away from the division's starting point, with the village falling on November 14. The division was made up largely of naval reservists and Royal Marines, who were excess to the Royal Navy's requirements, and one-third army battalions. It was one of the first units sent to Belgium in 1914, and then went to Gallipoli the following year. It arrived in France in May, 1916, with the 10th Royal Dublin Fusiliers joining its only non-naval brigade, the 190th, in August that year. Its participation in the attacks around Beaumont Hamel during the fighting of

The 10th Royal Dublin Fusiliers' sacrifice on the Somme is marked by the 63rd (Royal Naval) Division Memorial at Beaucourt

November 13-18 was the division's only engagement during the Battle of the Somme. However, it did return to the region in 1918 – by which time the Dubliners had moved to the 16th (Irish) Division – and took part in a number of actions between March and September. The 2nd Royal Irish Regiment joined the division in April, 1918, and remained with it throughout the final months of the war.

Both the 1st and 2nd Irish Guards are remembered by the Guards Division Memorial, which was placed in open countryside between Ginchy and Lesboeufs. It is a lonely spot, wind-swept and desolate, and not a place the visitor is likely to linger. The division attacked from Ginchy, which had fallen to the 16th (Irish) on September 15, towards Lesboeufs and Morval, with the German fortress known as the Triangle in their path. The attack was to have been supported by nine tanks, a third of which had been allocated to subdue the obstacle, but few actually made it as far as the jumping-off point. The memorial lies at roughly the point reached by the forward assaulting troops. Further along the same road towards Lesboeufs is the Guards Cemetery (passing on the way a personal memorial to a member of the Coldstream Guards), which holds 3,096 graves representing many of the regiments which fought in this area from 1916-18. Another Guards Cemetery stands on the edge of Combles, about six miles to the south.

The site of Brock's Benefit, a series of observation trenches built overlooking the battlefield from Mesnil Ridge, still gives the visitor a panoramic view today. It was created by the 36th (Ulster) Division's London-raised artillery and named after their commander, Brigadier-General H. J. Brock. It was subsequently used by countless other artillery observers long after the 36th had left the region. After two-and-a-half years in charge of the divisional artillery, Brigadier-General Brock saw out the war at the head of infantry after being appointed commander of the 107th Brigade in September, 1918. There is no trace of the trenches of Brock's

The site of the Guards Division Memorial, between Ginchy and Lesboeufs, is in wide-open countryside

Benefit today but you can still stand on the same ground for a good view of the battlefield. It lies to the east of Mesnil village, the road to Hamel on your left and the road to Authuille on the right. In the valley below is Thiepval Wood, with the Ulster Tower just beyond. The hilltop to the right, beyond Mill Road Cemetery, is where the Germans built the Schwaben Redoubt.

One of the most unusual "memorials" is in the village of Mesnil. The story goes that Ulster troops, heavily shelled each time they entered and left the lines, concluded a spy was at work. The 14th Royal Irish Rifles, in particular, became suspicious that the clock in the still-standing church tower at Mesnil, a little behind the British line but easily in view of the Germans, was being used to signal troop movements by being deliberately set at the wrong time. In frustration the soldiers removed the clock hands, bringing them back to Belfast with them. In 1927, in what must have been an odd ceremony by any standards, a delegation of old soldiers returned the "liberated" clock hands to the village mayor. Today they take pride of place, still mounted on the crest on which they were returned, in Mesnil *Mairie*. The church in Mesnil didn't survive the war but has since been rebuilt. The hall is on the opposite side of the street and the office holding the clock hands is at the top of the stairs at the side of the building and can be viewed out of hours, if you wish, through the glass panelled door.

In Auchonvillers is Avril Williams' guesthouse and tearooms, named after the term used by the troops for the village, Ocean Villas. Although the house itself was rebuilt following the First World War, its cellars are original and are believed to have once served as an advanced dressing station, where the most elementary first-aid was carried out before a casualty was passed further back for proper attention. The entrance to the trench system still exists and an excavated stretch of trench, as true to the original as possible, has been created in the adjacent gardens. The cellars boast carvings in the soft chalk walls, including several apparently from Irish soldiers. One wall bears the legend "J M'Kay, YCV, 14th RIR" while another shows the initials "J.C." intertwined along with the date 1916 and the abbreviations R.I.P. and U.V.F. in what the owner believes is a reference to James Crozier, the 18-year-old soldier of the 9th Royal Irish Rifles shot for desertion in 1916. Ms Williams, an Englishwoman, is always happy to show visitors the trenches and cellars, and her tearoom provides a welcome break during a day on the battlefields. On the road between Epehy and Ronssoy stands the 12th (Eastern) Division Memorial, which serves as a good signpost for the original Malassise Farm, which was sited at this point on the opposite side of the road. The 2nd Royal Dublin Fusiliers were holding the remains of the farm buildings as part of the British forward line on March 21, 1918, when the Germans launched their attack. It was quickly overrun in the mist.

In October, 2003, one of the latest in a long line of Irish monuments was inaugurated at Longueval as an addition

The crests on the surrounding wall at the Pipers Memorial include Irish regiments

to the Pipers Memorial, a tribute to pipers killed during the First World War. It takes the form of a remembrance wall to which has been added the crests of the Irish Guards, Royal Irish Regiment, Royal Inniskilling Fusiliers, Royal Irish Rifles, Royal Irish Fusiliers, Connaught Rangers, Leinster Regiment, Royal Munster Fusiliers, London Irish Rifles, Liverpool Irish, Tyneside Irish and Royal Dublin Fusiliers. A memorial, sculpted by Birmingham artist Andy de Comyn and taking the form of a piper in full battle dress emerging from a trench, was unveiled in July, 2002. Longueval was selected as the site as the men of the 9th (Scottish) Division fought there in July, 1916.

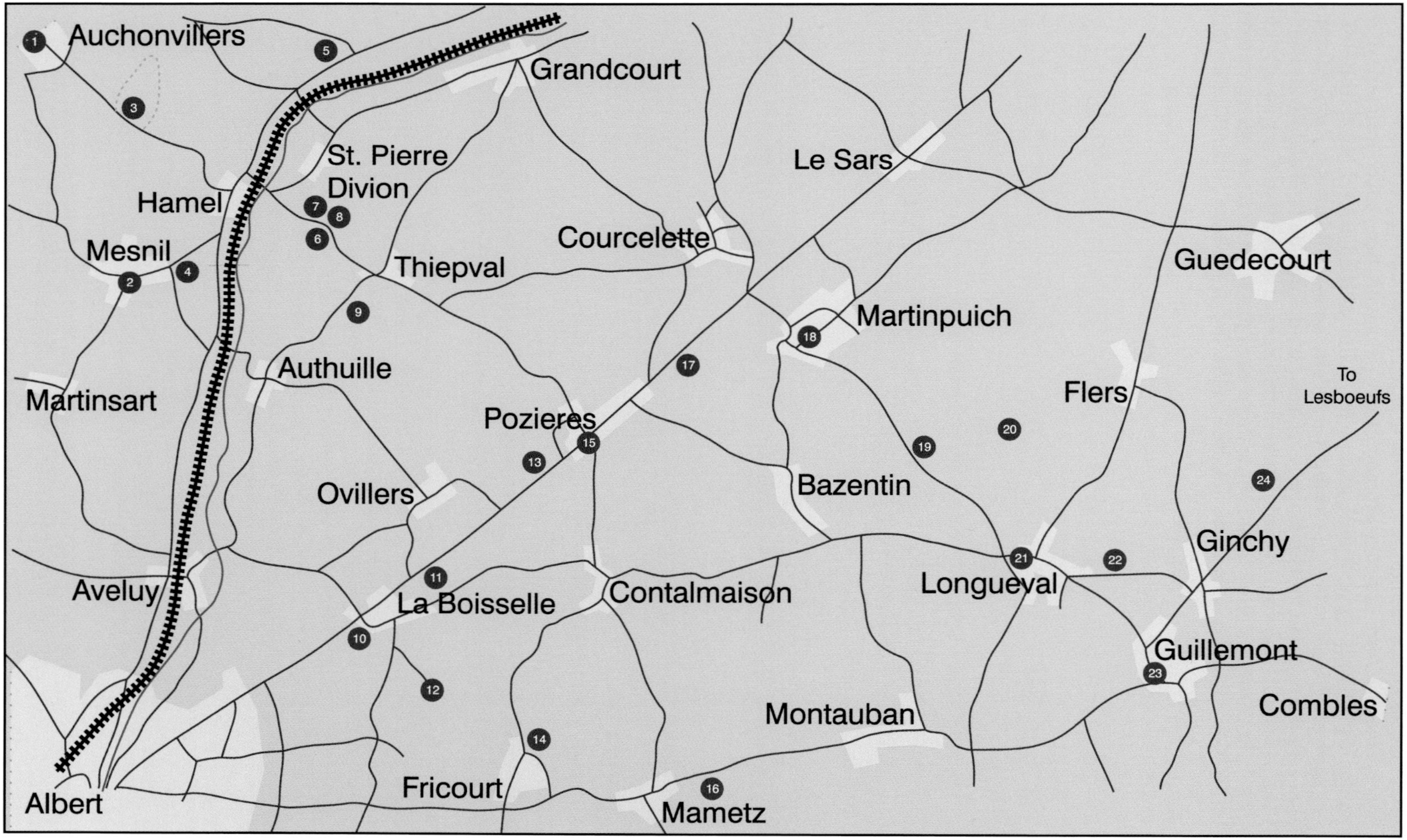

1. Avril Williams trenches and carvings
2. Mesnil church clock hands
3. Newfoundland Park
4. Site of Brock's Benefit
5. 63rd Division Memorial
6. Thiepval Wood
7. German machinegun post
8. Ulster Tower
9. Thiepval Memorial to the Missing
10. Tyneside Scottish and Irish Memorial Seat
11. 34th Division Memorial
12. Lochnagar crater
13. Pozieres Memorial to the Missing
14. Fricourt German Cemetery
15. Le Tommy restaurant and bar
16. Devonshires Cemetery
17. Tank Memorial
18. 47th Division Memorial Arch
19. 47th Division Memorial
20. New Zealand Memorial
21. Pipers Memorial
22. South African Memorial
23. 16th (Irish) Division Cross
24. Guards Memorial

IN ORDER NOT TO DIE

History will celebrate the tenacity and proud energy displayed during these four years by our country, which had to continue in order not to die. . . I refer with emotion to our dead, whose sacrifice has given us victory. I sent greetings full of sad affection to the fathers and to the mothers, to the widows and to the orphans of France, who are ceasing to weep for a brief moment in these days of national joy to applaud the triumph of our arms. I bow myself before your magnificent flags. Vive le France!

Marshal Petain, November, 1918

This book is designed to help the visitor to the Somme battlefields understand and appreciate the part played by Irish soldiers. It is important, however, to place their contribution within the context of the overall war effort. What follows is a short and personal selection of sites which help illustrate the immensity and diversity of the armies which shed blood on this battlefield. All are worth visiting and represent a cross-section of national memorials and the more unusual. They are, it has to be stressed, but a tiny portion of all there is to see and experience on the Somme so exploration and the purchase of a general guide are recommended.

Rancourt is the site of the most prestigious and largest of the French cemeteries on the Somme. Deliberately situated on the main road south to Peronne (once a busy thoroughfare before the creation of the nearby motorways), the **Rancourt French National Cemetery** is on a gently sloping hill just short of the furthest point reached by the French in the 1916 fighting. The cemetery, which lacks the more personal character of Commonwealth War Graves Commission cemeteries, holds the bodies of 8,567 French soldiers. On the roadside is the Rancourt Memorial Chapel, privately built by the du Bos family, whose son was killed on September 25, 1916, during the 32nd French infantry corps assault on the village. It is dedicated to the memory of all French soldiers killed during the Somme offensive and also carries a number of plaques in memory of other soldiers, some of whom were British. The chapel contains a small display of documents and battlefield items.

Rancourt French National Cemetery, above, was deliberately placed on a then busy highway to attract visitors

Fricourt German Cemetery holds the bodies of 17,026 men, most in mass graves to the rear

The doors were often locked in previous years but on all my visits recently I have found the chapel open to view. A small British plot, Rancourt Military Cemetery, is situated on the opposite side of the road and contains just 92 graves, while a short distance away is the Rancourt German Cemetery holding 11,422 bodies, many in mass graves. German cemeteries are few and far between on the Somme, due in large measure to France's reluctance to give up any more of its soil than was absolutely necessary to its traditional enemy. I normally try to find the time to visit **Fricourt German Cemetery** on my visits to the Somme. It holds 17,026 graves, again mostly in mass burials to the rear. It is both peaceful and forlorn and I cannot walk among the metal crosses and the surprisingly large numbers of Stars of David, marking the Jewish dead who fought for the Kaiser, without thinking of the sorrow felt by German mothers and fathers who, just like those in Ireland and across the world, had their hopes and dreams devastated by the slaughter on the Somme. Fricourt temporarily held the body of the German air ace Manfred von Richthofen until it was removed after the war and taken home to a hero's grave in Germany.

Delville Wood was one of the most costly pieces of French soil. Six divisions fought for the wood and village of Longueval, with the sacrifice of the South African Brigade, part of the 9th (Scottish) Division, particularly remembered here. The German bombardment of the wood was of such intensity that up to 400 rounds a minute were exploding among the trees. The South Africans, with

A French postcard featuring the impressive entrance archway to the South African Memorial and Museum

Courtesy of the Somme Heritage Centre

The Newfoundland Caribou looks over the now restricted battlefield at Beaumont Hamel, with the recently built interpretative centre

An early French postcard illustrates how Newfoundland Park, preserved as it was after the war, has been changed by natural erosion and man's interference

Courtesy of the Somme Heritage Centre

no chance of retreat, hastily dug shallow trenches and endured the worst the enemy could throw at them for five days. Of more than 3,000 men who entered the battle on July 14, 1916, only 143 emerged unscathed. The wood today is owned by the South African government and is the site of the **South African Memorial and Museum**. A car park located on the edge of Delville Wood, near Longueval, comprises a shop and cafe, and offers visitors the chance to purchase war souvenirs. From here you walk along a roadway which runs between the wood and cemetery before reaching the path on the left which leads to the memorial and museum. The whole setting is suitably impressive, with the original trench positions signposted by stone markers and, in many cases, still easily distinguishable. The trees surrounding the memorial were seeded with South African acorns. The triumphal arch includes a bronze sculpture of Castor and Pollux, sworn enemies who were reconciled – a clear reference to the Boer War. Beyond the arch is the museum which commemorates the South African contribution in both world wars.

The popularity of the **Newfoundland Memorial Park**, a short drive north of the Ulster Tower toward Beaumont Hamel, has resulted in it being transformed from one of the most open and interesting sites on the Western Front to one of the most restricted. The British and German trench systems in place throughout the Battle of the Somme were left intact in the park, which also contains three cemeteries and three memorials (one of which, the 29th Division Memorial, is detailed in the previous chapter). The park is named after the sacrifice of the Newfoundland Regiment, also previously described, with the Newfoundland Caribou and Memorial to the Missing the most impressive of the monuments here. The third memorial commemorates the 51st (Highland) Division and stands on the German front line taken by the division on November 13, 1916. Up until

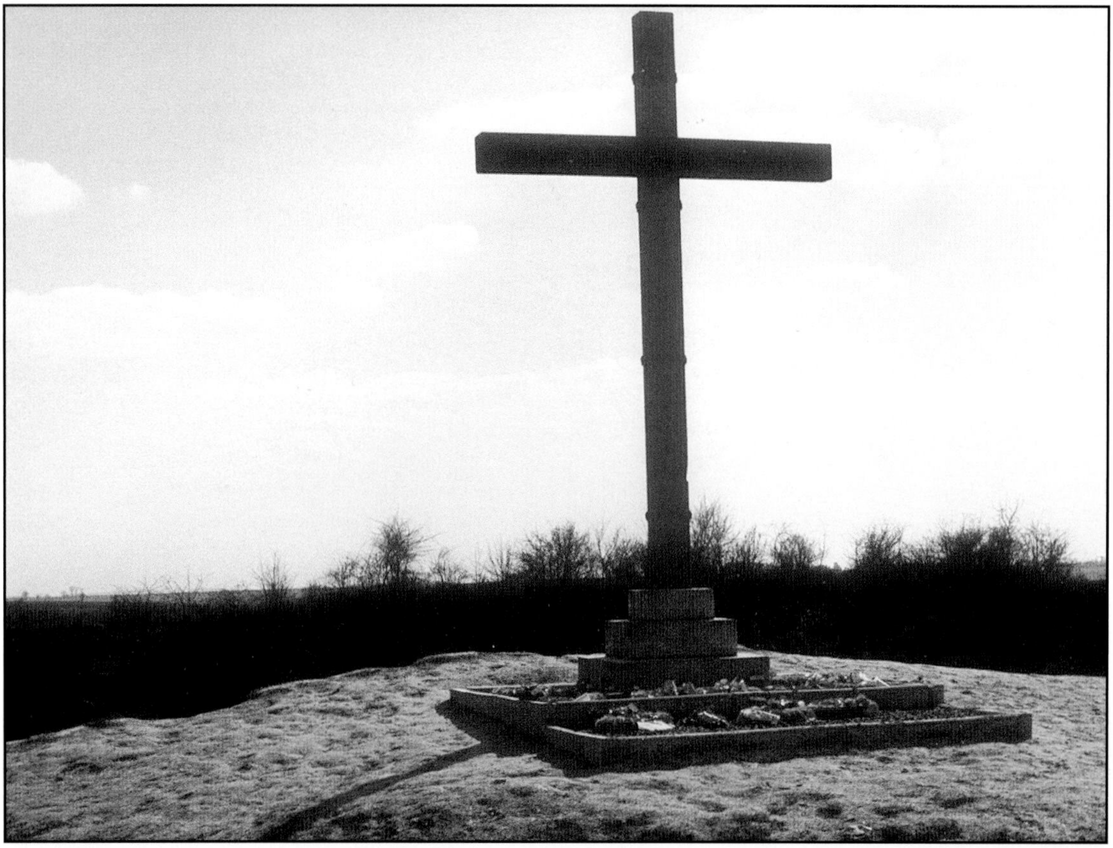

The wooden cross on the edge of the Lochnagar Mine Crater is the focus of a ceremony of remembrance every July 1. The crater was created when 26 tons of ammonal explosives were detonated in a mine under a German strongpoint
Courtesy of the Somme Heritage Centre

recent years access to the park had been unrestricted, with visitors free to walk the trenches, crossing the old No-Man's-Land at will and enjoying a site which more than any other provided the best understanding of the battle fought at this crucial part of the line. Now, and admittedly with the best of intentions in mind, access to the park has been greatly restricted for fear that the ever-increasing numbers of visitors will accelerate the natural erosion already evident. Much of it has been cordoned off by tape, with limited paths provided to the memorials and cemeteries. Guided tours can be arranged at a recently built and impressive museum/interpretative centre to the right of the entrance. To some extent the loss of freedom to explore the park independently has removed that emotive link with the past that only solitude can provide. Another comparatively recent addition is much more welcome – a car/bus park is now available on the opposite side of the road from the entrance.

Close to the village of La Boisselle is one of the most impressive of the First World War memorials. The **Lochnagar Mine Crater** was created on July 1, 1916, when more than 26 tons of ammonal explosives were detonated beneath a German strongpoint, the Schwaben Hohe, just two minutes before the British troops went over the top. The Germans were naturally stunned by the severity of the explosion and the British troops, including the Tyneside Scottish, took control of the crater rim though no further progress was possible that day. The tunnel dug from the

The Australian War Memorial at Villers-Bretonneux marks a major turning point in the war

British trenches to plant the explosives was later opened up again to allow reinforcements to cross No-Man's-Land in safety. The crater measures some 300ft across and is 90ft deep. A pathway runs round its circumference, with seats provided for those who may wish to sit and contemplate the horror enacted here. Making your way down to the bottom of the crater is strongly advised against, though many still do, judging by the well-worn paths leading to the crater floor. Each July 1, at 7.30am, a ceremony of remembrance is held at the crater, which is privately owned after being purchased by Englishman Richard Dunning in the 1970s to prevent the French farmers from filling it in.

The village of Villers-Bretonneux, lying astride the main road between Amiens and St. Quentin, arguably marks the most significant turning point in the war. During the German offensive of March-April, 1918, it marked the closest point reached by the enemy in their bid to take Amiens. The village fell during a determined push on April 24 supported by 13 German tanks. A similar number of British tanks, seven of which were the new light "whippet" models, took part in the defence and the first tank-on-tank battle in history was enacted here, with the British Mark IV emerging the victor. (A **Tank Memorial** is situated further east at Pozieres. It was from here that three of the first tanks ever deployed in war set off on September 15, 1916, though nearby Flers is generally accepted as the true starting point of tank warfare.) Less than 24 hours after the German attack, Villers-Bretonneux was back in Allied hands following a joint British-Australian night assault. On August 8, 1918, the Allies attacked along a 24-mile front, aided by a massive artillery barrage and more than 400 tanks, with Villers-Bretonneux at its centre. In what the Germans described as their "Black Day", they were pushed back more than six miles and sustained losses of 75,000, close to half of whom were taken prisoner. The Australian and Canadian divisions were at the centre of the line and secured the greatest gains that day and it is here that the former choose as the site to remember its dead on the Western Front. The **Australian War Memorial** forms the centrepiece of Villers-Bretonneux Military Cemetery, the largest of the 1918 cemeteries on the Somme front. It holds 2,141 bodies, more than a third of whom are Australian and 607 others unknown. The Australian memorial, unveiled by King George VI in July 1938, stands on the highest ground to the rear of the cemetery, its central tower providing a tremendous advantage point from which to view the battlefield and surrounding area. The names of close to 11,000 Australian soldiers with no known graves are inscribed on the walls of the memorial. Each April 25 a ceremony is held here, the date marking the Australian landings at Gallipoli in 1915 and commemorating the Aussie attack which took back Villers-Bretonneux in 1918.

Irish graves at Villers-Bretonneux Military Cemetery

In 1940, the memorial tower was strafed by a Messerschmitt 109 and fired on by a German tank which crashed through the right-hand cemetery boundary wall to fire on Senegalese machine-gunners using the memorial as a defensive position. If you look carefully you can still spot where the cemetery wall was repaired after the war, while a number of the bullet holes on the Cross of Sacrifice,

The American Somme Cemetery, above, is immaculately maintained, with the Stars and Stripes ceremonially raised and lowered each morning and evening. The nearby Bellicourt American Memorial provides a map and explanation of the battlefield at this point

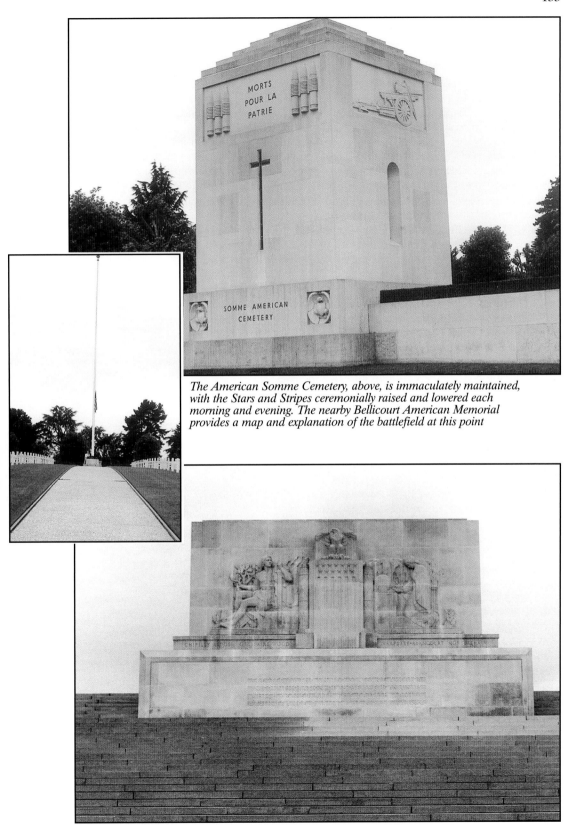

headstones and the memorial building itself have been deliberately left as a reminder of the incident. New Zealand's war effort has, to some extent, been overshadowed by that of Australia. The **New Zealand Memorial** on the Somme stands to the north of Longueval and commemorates the New Zealand Division's success at Flers on September 15, 1916.

The American forces were late arrivals on the Western Front and, for the most part, served with the French further south. They are represented on the Somme, however, where they fought alongside both the British and French during the advances of 1918. At Bony, just behind the old Hindenburg Line, is the **American Somme Cemetery**, which holds 1,844 graves, with the names of a further 333 U.S. troops with no known grave recorded on the walls of a chapel. It is immaculately maintained throughout, to the extent of almost feeling sanitised. Sadly, I sometimes feel I could be visiting a film set and have to remind myself of the reality of the tragedy represented here.

Nearby, the **Bellicourt American Memorial** commemorates the part played by United States forces in the Somme battles. In keeping with standard U.S. practice, a map on the back of the memorial outlines the actions in which the "Doughboys" took part.

The overwhelming majority of cemeteries on the Somme are British, and few of the larger ones are without Irish dead. There is one very English cemetery which draws me back time and again, however. Situated on a hillside, next to a small copse of trees, at a turn in the old British front line just south of Mametz, the **Devonshire Cemetery** used to be awkward to get at, though the recent addition of a small parking area has helped greatly. A German machinegun post, dug in under a large cross in the village cemetery, decimated the 9th Devons as they left the trench on July 1. Captain D. L. Martin, one of the regiment's officers, had warned what would happen if the post wasn't destroyed by the bombardment. He is among the dead buried here in a mass grave in part of the old trenches. Their colleagues erected a wooden sign: "The Devonshires Held This Trench; The Devonshires Hold It Still." Today a stone monument next to the pathway to the cemetery bears the same words.

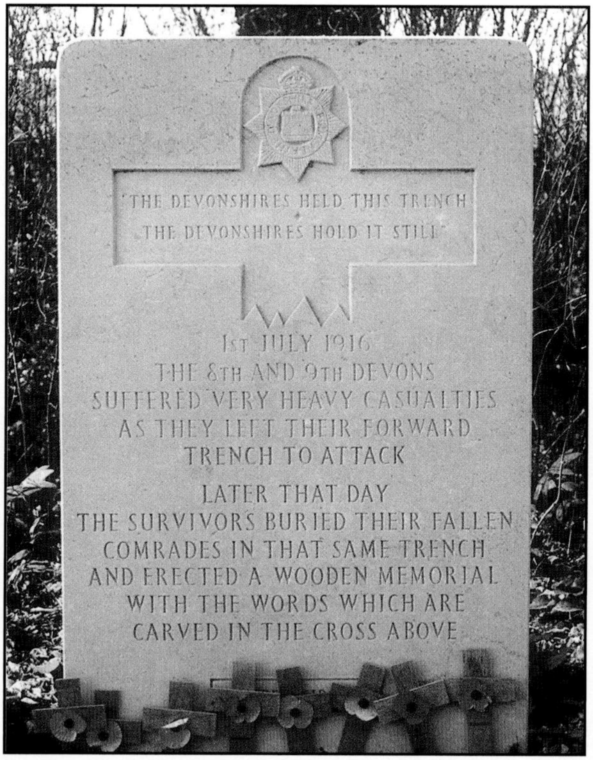

The Devonshires are still holding the line today

An unusual feature which played a significant part in the German defences at the Hindenburg Line was the **St. Quentin Canal**. The canal was constructed over an eight-year period, from 1802-10, on the orders of Napoleon. Much of it runs through tunnels, on average some 16 metres underground, making it totally impervious to Allied artillery. The canal was connected to the main German defensive lines by shafts, and used for offices, stores and field hospitals, with electric lines running along its length. Barges were used as billets and wooden rafters laid across the ledges above the water at other points for the same purpose. The southern entrance of the canal emerges at Riqueval, some two miles south of Bellicourt. At the side of the road, next to a sign for the canal entrance, is a **Memorial to the American soldiers of Tennessee** killed in the battles to cross the waterway. The route to the canal entrance lies behind this but, be warned, it is a long, twisting dirt path which takes you down

Some of the displays and items on show at the rear of Le Tommy, on Pozieres main street. The inside of the cafe and bar are similiarly bedecked in First World War photographs and flags

to the water level, and, of course, has to be renegotiated on the way back. It is, however, well worth the effort.

A very different attraction is **Le Tommy**, a restaurant/Café du Souvenir, on the main street of Pozieres. In the back garden is a mock-up of both Allied and German trench systems along with a varied assortment of battlefield items and debris ranging from grave markers to artillery pieces, and including more shell casings than can be counted.

St. George's Church in Ypres, Belgium, was built as a place of pilgrimage for families who lost a loved one in the First World War. Virtually everything inside the building is a memorial

HIS NAME BE NOT FORGOTTEN

He whom this scroll commemorates was numbered among those who, at the call of King and Country, left all that was dear to them, endured hardness, faced danger, and finally passed out of the sight of men by the path of duty and self-sacrifice, giving up their own lives that others might live in freedom.

Let those who come after see to it that his name be not forgotten.

From the Next of Kin Memorial Scroll sent to Irish families

Irish soldiers fought all along the British sector of the Western Front, from north of Ypres in Belgium to, by 1918, south of the River Somme. They played major roles in all the campaigns from the Mons retreat to the final push. After the war many divisional, regimental and battalion memorials were erected, often financed by surviving members of the units involved, to mark the sacrifice of colleagues. A number of these with Irish connections are detailed below, along with cemeteries of particular interest. Anyone planning a trip to France, and travelling by way of the short sea routes, might wish to consider breaking their journey to take in some of these sites.

The Belgium town of Ypres, now commonly known by its Flemish spelling Ieper, was surrounded on three sides by the enemy and reduced to rubble. Holding the "Salient" became a matter of intense pride and countless thousands lost their lives in the immediate vicinity. Poelcapelle British Cemetery (1) lies seven miles north-east of Ypres on the road to Brugge. It holds 7,478 graves, of which 6,321 are not known by name. Among those who were identified is Private John Condon, of the 2nd Royal Irish Regiment, who died on May 24, 1915, at the age of just 14 – the youngest authenticated battle casualty of the First World War. It was only when a letter arrived at his Waterford home telling his family he was missing in action that his real age came to light. His remains were found in the mid-1920s by a farmer.

The First World War spawned a generation of war poets and among Ireland's most famous is Francis Ledwidge. Born in Slane, County Meath, in 1887, he was 29 years old when killed in Flanders on the last day of July, 1917, during the Third Battle of Ypres. His best-known poem, a tribute to his friend Thomas McDonagh, one of those executed following the Easter Rising in Dublin in 1916, was written in a Manchester hospital in 1916 as he recovered from wounds. The 1st Royal Inniskilling Fusiliers lance-corporal is buried in Artillery Wood Cemetery (2) at Boezinge, north of Ypres.

A memorial to the 7th Division, in which the 2nd Royal Irish Regiment served for five months from May, 1916, until joining the 16th (Irish) Division, stands at Broodseinde (3). The division was involved in the fighting here in 1914, and is credited with digging, on October 16-20, the first trenches in the Ypres Salient.

In Ypres town centre (4), to the rear of the cathedral, is a Celtic cross in memory of the Royal Munster Fusiliers. A short distance away is St. George's Church, built as a place of pilgrimage at the bequest of Sir John French for the relatives of those killed in the area to visit. Virtually everything inside is dedicated to the memory of either individuals or military units, from the plaques which adorn its walls to the prayer cushions and pews. Many of these have Irish

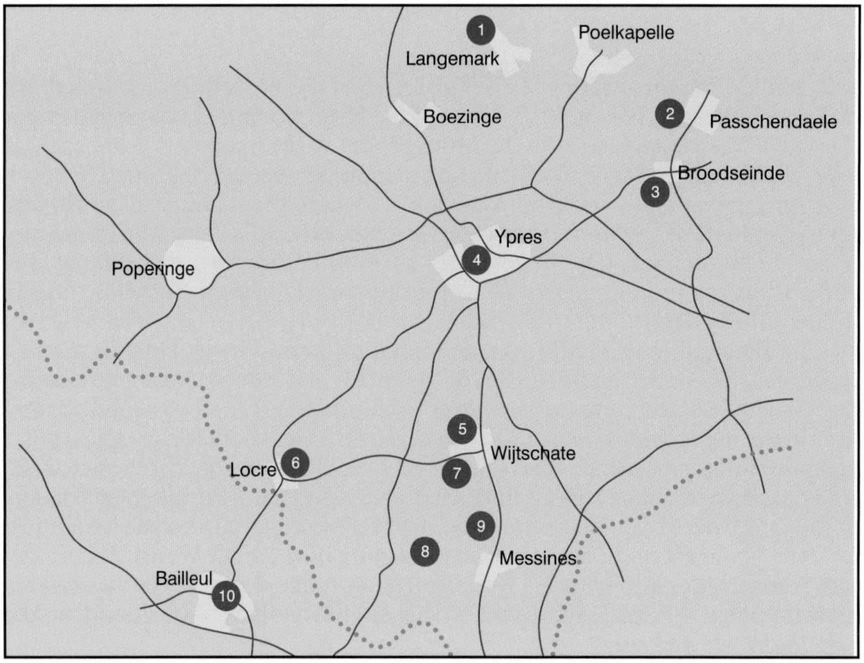

The Munster Cross to the rear of Ypres cathedral as it is today and, right, in 1926 surrounded by 16th (Irish) Division veterans

connections and it is worth taking the time to read the inscriptions. There is, sadly, also a large representation of Irishmen listed at the Menin Gate in the town, which lists on its walls almost 55,000 soldiers with no known grave. Each evening at 8pm the Last Post is sounded by members of the local fire brigade. The tradition dates to the 1920s and has continued uninterrupted with the exception of the four years of German occupation during the Second World War. (The Last Post was instead sounded at Brookwood Military Cemetery in England and reinstated on the evening Ypres was liberated.) Travelling through the gate and along the Menin road, passing along the way the famous Hellfire Corner, you will come across Birr Crossroads and cemetery. The name honours the Leinster Regiment which served here in April, 1915. Visitors to Ypres should try to visit the In Flanders Fields Museum. It is situated in the Cloth Hall, which was meticulously reconstructed from 1934-58 to resemble the original 14th century building destroyed by German artillery fire.

Head south out of Ypres and you come across a cluster of sites of particular Irish interest. The 16th (Irish) Division had three Celtic crosses constructed, with one placed at Wytschacte (5). It marks the dividing line between the 16th and 36th (Ulster) Divisions at the Battle of Messines, during which both made great advances. A little further to the west is the final resting place of William Redmond, an MP and brother of the nationalist leader John. He was serving as a major in the 6th Royal Irish Regiment when wounded at Messines. He was carried from the battlefield by men of the 36th Division, but died later in a field hospital even

The unveiling of the 16th (Irish) Division Memorial Cross in 1926. General Hickie, who commanded the 16th throughout most of the war, can be seen to the left without a hat. Below: The Menin Gate on which is carved the names of almost 55,000 soldiers who died in the Salient but who have no known grave

Courtesy of the Somme Heritage Centre

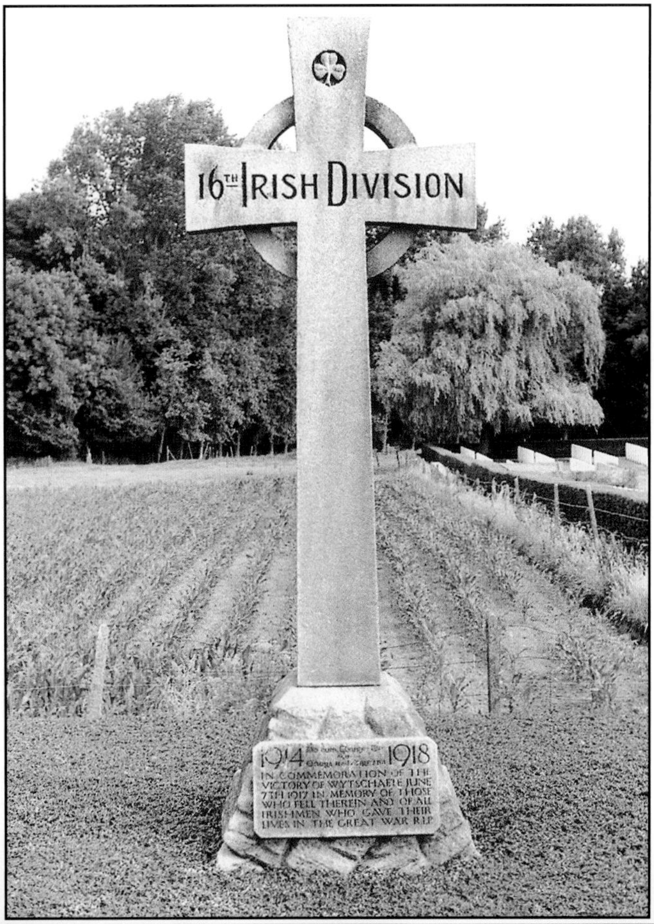

The 16th Irish Cross at Wytschacte as it is today, with the railings having been replaced with a low hedge surround

Below: The beautiful interior of St George's Church, Ypres

The funeral of Willie Redmond at Locre was attended by the nuns from the hospice.

Below: A later photograph of the grave with the C.W.G.C. cemetery in the background

Courtesy of the Somme Heritage Centre

though his wounds were not initially thought to be life-threatening. The 56-year-old was buried in the grounds of a hospice at Locre (6), then being used as the divisional headquarters. While other graves there were later moved into the nearby military cemetery, his remained after family objections to its disinterment and promises from the hospice nuns to maintain it. The nuns have long since moved out and the building replaced, but the Redmond grave, close to the path leading to Locre Hospice Cemetery, still remains separated from his comrades.

Spanbroekmolen crater (7), measuring 129 metres across and 27 metres deep, was created by 91,000lbs of explosives being detonated underground in June, 1917, as a prelude to the beginning of the Battle of Messines. It was here that the 36th (Ulster) Division attacked and a delay in the detonation meant the Ulstermen were already in No-Man's-Land when it exploded. Nearby are the Spanbroekmolen and Lone Tree cemeteries (8), both holding many of the division's dead. Some of those buried here are said to have been killed by falling debris from the crater blast, a claim not backed up by official accounts. The crater itself is a man-made lake now called the Pool of Peace. Its tranquillity today contrasts sharply with the vision of hell it must have been in 1917.

On November 11, 1998, the Island of Ireland Peace Park (9) was opened a short distance from Messines. A round Irish tower, built by young people representing both communities in Ireland using stone exported from Tipperary, forms the centre piece. The gardens are laid out to represent the four provinces of Ireland. The park is in memory of the Irishmen of the 16th (Irish) and 36th (Ulster) divisions who fought side-by-side during the successful Battle of Messines. Some, however, might view it more as a political statement for today than a memorial to the sacrifices of 1917. After some initial difficulties regarding maintenance of the site, the Commonwealth War Graves Commission stepped in to oversee its upkeep.

An impressive obelisk in the centre of Bailleul marks the sacrifice of the 25th Division (10), which captured the ruins of the town in August, 1917, an achievement shared by the 2nd Royal Irish Rifles which was part of this division from October 1915 up until November 1917, when it transferred to the 36th (Ulster) Division.

The Island of Ireland Peace Park is dedicated to the memory of the 16th and 36th divisions.

Mons lies much further east and so for most it will involve a conscious decision to visit rather than a casual detour. La Bascule crossroads (11) was the scene of a tremendous rearguard action by the 2nd Royal Irish Regiment on August 23, 1914, when a group of cooks and clerks under the direction of the regimental sergeant-major held back – with the help of a hastily repaired machinegun – a German attempt to cut off the British Expeditionary Force. A memorial, in the form of a Celtic cross, was later erected here and it is now the site of the B.E.F. memorial which was formerly situated in the centre of Mons.

An Irishman fired the first shots of the war. Corporal Thomas, of the 4th Royal Irish Dragoon Guards, opened up on German Cuirassiers at Maisieres, outside Mons, on August 22, 1914.

At the same time two troops of the Royal Irish Dragoons charged the enemy, with Captain Hornby becoming the first officer to draw blood with his sword and capturing some 30 prisoners in the same action. He was later awarded the D.S.O. for his courage. A plaque (12) at Maisieres records this first action of the war.

St. Symphorien Military Cemetery (13) was started by the Germans following the Battle of Mons in August,

1914, and remained in their hands up until the last month of the war. The Germans built a seven-metre high granite obelisk as a memorial to the dead of the battle, both German and British. They also erected a number of memorials to individual units, including the Royal Irish Regiment. Among the bodies buried here is that of Maurice James Dease, from Gaulstown, County Westmeath, who was one of the earliest British officer battle casualties and the first recipient of a Victoria Cross in the war. The London Gazette of November 16, 1914, recorded of the 24-year-old lieutenant, who was serving with the 4th Royal Fusiliers, "though two or three times badly wounded he continued to control the fire of his machineguns at Mons on 23rd August, until all his men were shot. He died of his wounds". He is commemorated at Nimy Bridge, where the action took place. (A second V.C. winner with Irish connections, Major Ernest Wright Alexander, of the Royal Field Artillery, won his award for saving his guns at Elouges the following day. He survived the war.) Also buried at St. Symphorien is Private George Edwin Ellison, of the 5th (Royal Irish) Lancers, believed to be the last battle casualty of the war. Another soldier, for whom the same claim is made, Private George Lawrence Price, of the Canadian Saskatchewan Regiment, is buried nearby. A bronze plaque at the gateway to the Hotel de Ville marks the last death before 11am on November 11, 1918. Many others, of course, died of their wounds in the hours, weeks, months and even years that followed.

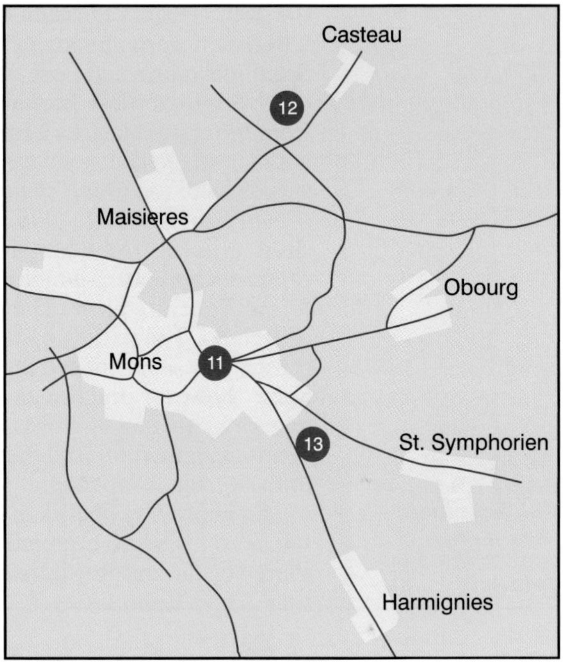

A member of a fascinating Irish family of Victoria Cross winners lies in Estaires Communal Cemetery, seven miles west of Armentieres in France. Brigadier General Sir John Edmond Gough, of the Rifle Brigade, was also A.D.C. to the King and Chief of Staff to the First Army. The 43-year-old, who was killed on February 22, 1915, held a K.C.B. and C.M.G. as well as a V.C. won in Somaliland in 1903. He was the son of General Sir Charles Gough and nephew of Hugh Henry Gough, both of whom won Victoria Crosses in separate actions during the Indian Mutiny of 1857.

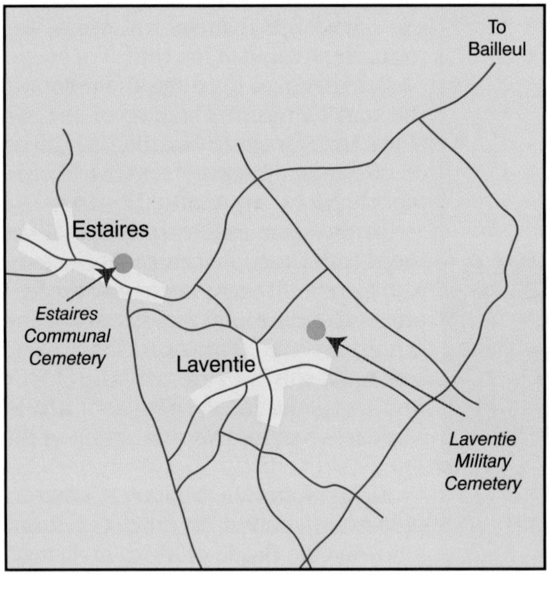

Ireland's highest-scoring air ace of the war was George Edward Henry "McIrish" McElroy, who lies buried at Laventie Military Cemetery, La Gorgue, in the Nord department of France. From Donnybrook, Dublin, he had 47 confirmed "kills" to his name when shot down by anti-aircraft fire on July 31, 1918. He was 25 years old and the holder of the Distinguished Flying Cross and bar, and the Military Cross and two bars,

Lieutenant Maurice James Dease, from Gaulstown, County Westmeath, was the first man to win a Victoria Cross in the Great War

Courtesy of the Somme Heritage Centre

all gazetted in 1918. Captain McElroy, who served with the 24th and 40th Royal Flying Corps and later Royal Air Force squadrons, had enlisted with the Royal Irish Regiment in August, 1914. He was badly injured in a mustard gas attack at Ypres and sent home to recover. He transferred to the R.F.C. and accumulated his victories in just 40 weeks of flying.

The Guards Division, of which the 1st and 2nd Irish Guards were part, has a memorial (14) at Cuinchy, south of the La Bassee Canal and east of Bethune. The division was in the thick of the 1914 fighting around Ypres and the subsequent battles in the salient. It was at Cuinchy, on February 1, 1915, that Lance Corporal Michael O'Leary, of the 1st Irish Guards, won the Victoria Cross, killing eight Germans and taking an enemy barricade and machinegun post single-handedly.

Major General Louis James Lipsett holds two claims to fame. One is as the last British general to command a Canadian division and the other, unfortunately, is being the last of the 59 British generals to be killed in the First World War. Born in Ballyshannon, County Donegal, he had already served in India and South Africa when posted to Canada in 1911 as part of a policy of standardising training in Britain and its Dominions. At the outbreak of war he was given command of a Canadian unit of riflemen and later became a brigade, then divisional, commander. He transferred back to the British army in September, 1918, as head of the 4th Division but was killed by a machinegun bullet wound to the face the following month. The 44-year-old lies buried at Queant Communal Cemetery British Extension (15), some 16 miles south-east of Arras on the outskirts of Riencourt-les-Cagnicourt, Pas-de-Calais.

The 2nd Royal Munster Fusiliers were part of the 1st Division on July 1. A divisional memorial (16) stands at La Groise/Chapeau Rouge crossroads, to the south-east of Le Cateau, where it held up the German advance in August, 1914, and to which it returned in the closing months of the war. Nearby is Etreux where a cross and plaque honour the Royal Munsters who fought virtually to the last man in an heroic rearguard action. Both are within the walls of Etreux British Cemetery, surrounded by the battalion's dead.

Neither the 8th Division nor the 1st Royal Irish Rifles, which fought with this unit from October 1914 until February 1918, have specific memorials on the Western Front that I'm aware of. It is the same story with the 2nd Royal Inniskilling Fusiliers, which spent most of its war with the 32nd Division. The 4th Division had strong Irish connections throughout the war. Both the 1st Royal Irish Fusiliers and 2nd Royal Dublin Fusiliers were with it at the Battle of the Somme, while the 2nd Royal Irish Regiment, 2nd Royal Irish Fusiliers and 2nd Royal Inniskilling Fusiliers were, for varying spells, within its ranks at other times. A detachment of the 36th (Ulster) Division spent a three-month spell with the 4th Division as part of its training, from November 1915-February 1916. There is, however, no memorial on the Somme to the division, to the best of my knowledge, or anywhere else on the Western Front apart from a monument at La Ferte, south-west of Chateau-Thierry and to the east of Paris, to the divisional engineers who built a bridge there under tremendous fire in September, 1914.

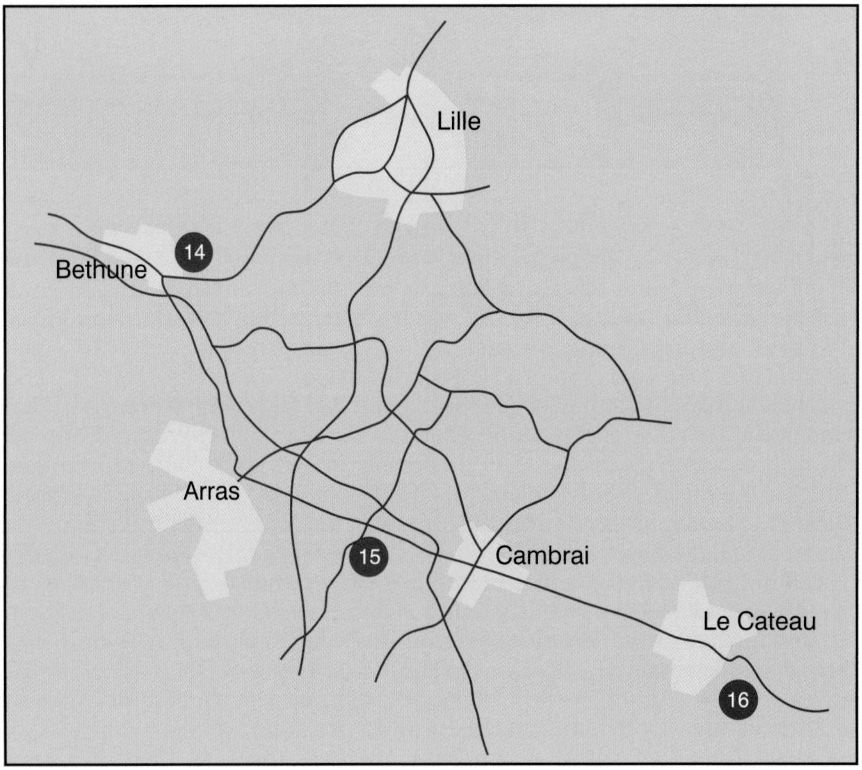

THOUGHTS OF THE FUTURE

When peace came we had many thoughts of the future. A year has passed. In a measure those thoughts and ideals have been fulfilled as yet but little. Therefore, we need to pray for the future in the present.

The Rt. Rev C. T. P. Grierson, Bishop of Down and Connor, November 11, 1919

A conscious and deliberate attempt was made to turn the battlefields of the Somme back to the farmland and small village communes they had been before 1914. The French brought in labourers to clear away the debris and begin the reconstruction. Some of these came from the Far East and later returned home wealthy men by the standards of their own communities; others arrived from the likes of Belgium and often stayed on to make new lives for themselves in France, creating a source of friction with the local community for years to come. Attempts were made to recreate the glory of some of the finest buildings lost, such as the Basilica in Albert, though for the most part the need to provide accommodation for the families keen to return necessitated the emphasis be on the practical rather than the beautiful. Villages were recreated, roads rebuilt, communities re-established and, with the return of the plough, the landscape began again to resemble what it had been before the war.

The cemeteries dotted along the length of the line, and literally to the coast behind it, remain the most potent reminders of the slaughter enacted on this now peaceful landscape. Still to be found among the rolling hills and pastures are concrete pillboxes, often half-hidden in the undergrowth having defied all attempts to remove them, or sitting forlornly by the side of a road like a forgotten relic. Among the places to find the scars of the violence is in the little coppices of trees or acres of woodland, still very common in this area, untouched by the farmer. Here on

The Historial de la Grande Guerre in Peronne is housed in a high-tech building incorporating restored sections of the chateau

occasion you will find the craters caused by artillery shells and mortars, the outlines of trenches, or even the remains of dugouts. Such areas are generally privately owned, can conceal unexploded ordnance and, without little doubt, hold the remains of some of the many thousands of bodies never recovered. For all these reasons, the land needs to be treated with the respect it deserves.

Ceremonies connected with the First World War are held on a number of dates throughout the year, some on an annual basis, others when the need arises, such as the burial of the war dead the land still gives up virtually every year. On the Somme, July 1 remains the main day of remembrance. The first event of the day is at the Lochnagar Crater at 7.30am, the exact moment the battle began. The largest takes place at the Thiepval Memorial to the Missing at 11am; and there is another at Newfoundland Park in the afternoon. It is also the day on which the Irish soldiers of the 36th (Ulster) and 16th (Irish) divisions are honoured in ceremonies at the Ulster Tower at Thiepval and Celtic Cross at Guillemont respectively, both organised by the Somme Association.

Seven out of 10 visitors to the battlefields of the Somme are British or Irish, followed by the Australians, New Zealanders, Canadians, Americans and Germans. The French, who view Verdun to the south as the most sacred place of remembrance, make up only 20 per cent of the total. The French authorities are represented, however, at all the ceremonies of remembrance and have funded on the Somme one of the most prestigious museums on the whole Western Front. The *Historial de la Grande Guerre* was opened in 1992 within the remains of the centuries-old chateau in the town of Peronne which, for much of the war, was in German hands. It first fell to the enemy in August, 1914, and was a major medical and troop concentration area before and during the Battle of the Somme.

A cleverly created hedge "soldier" welcomes visitors to Peronne. The French have become increasingly aware of the tourist potential of the First World War

Despite eight months of French bombardment throughout the 1916 campaign, it was only in March, 1917, when the town was abandoned during the fall back to the Hindenburg Line, that it returned to Allied hands. A year later it was recaptured in the German offensive of 1918. It was the Australians who took back Peronne once again in September that year. The chateau itself sustained considerable damage during this period with little more than a restored façade remaining. The museum is modern, bright and designed as an international research centre and educational resource. It presents a balanced view of the war from the British, French and German perspectives.

There are five main halls, featuring the uniforms, weapons, souvenirs and artefacts of the period. Documentaries, often highlighting the British contribution to the war, are shown constantly in a 120-seat auditorium. Despite the ultra clean and airy atmosphere, there is no attempt to give a sanitised version of events. If anything the candid presentation of the reality of war in such modern surroundings only serves to reinforce the horrors. Modern technology plays a major part, with 60 small monitors, dotted throughout the museum, constantly showing "real time" footage of the many aspects of the conflict: from the funeral of Archduke Franz Ferdinand to the celebrations marking the end of the war, or the suffering of the injured and shell-shocked to life behind the lines for both troops and civilians. The wall displays are on three levels - German exhibits at the top, French in the middle and British on the bottom tier. Each is given equal space while other combatants, including the Americans, South Africans, and Australians are also remembered. All items and documents are original. The museum remains open all year, though is generally closed on Mondays out of the main summer season.

Two views of the same postcard, dating from the war years. Above is the Basilica in Albert before the war and, on the right, well on its way to destruction in 1915. The "Leaning Virgin" was wired in place by French engineers after being struck by a German shell.

Underneath the church is the Musee Des Abris, or Shelters Museum, with one of the exhibits illustrated, left. The tunnels which house the displays were built as a precaution against the expected German air raids in the Second World War

The *Musee Des Abris*, or Shelters Museum, is based in the underground tunnels which were to have provided the residents of Albert with refuge in the event of a second world war. It has a large Irish, and particularly Ulster, content to its exhibits. Occupied by the Germans between August 29 and September 14, 1914, until they withdrew following the Battle of the Marne, the town was under heavy bombardment throughout much of the war. Its peacetime population of 7,343 was rapidly reduced to just 120 by the end of 1917. On January 15, 1915, the figure of the Virgin, on top of the Basilica, was partially dislodged by a large- calibre German shell. The "Leaning Virgin", as it was known to the British, became a symbol of the war when they took over the Somme front in July, 1915. Held up by cables fixed by French engineers, the myth grew that the war would only end when the Madonna finally fell. Albert became a British rear-line base and was a hive of activity in the lead up to the Battle of the Somme. It was a staff headquarters, billet to countless men and a major staging post for trains bringing in men and supplies. The flow of troops and vehicles passing through its streets never stopped, day or night, with men heading to or from the front lines. Lost again during the German offensives of March, 1918, British artillery targeted the Basilica to prevent the enemy using it as an observation post, finally bringing down the Virgin. Albert was recaptured in August of that year.

During the rebuilding of the town after the war, no expense was spared in recreating the beautiful Basilica, complete with a replica of the Madonna. The original is believed to have been shipped back to Germany, where it was melted down for its metal value. In the late 1930s, the people of Albert feared again for their town as the war clouds began to gather. With an aircraft factory only two miles away, it was felt the whole area was likely to come under aerial attack. Air raid shelters were required and, out of the Somme chalk, they dug several miles of underground tunnels, with the entrance below the Basilica. In the event, it was not the bombers but the panzers which swept through the Somme in 1940 and the town fell after little more than a skirmish.

The steep stone steps, now enclosed within a glass frontage added to the side of the church, lead from the museum entrance down into the atmospheric cellars. A short video display in one of the chambers sets the tone for the visit, telling the story of the Battle of the Somme, again with the part of the Irish soldiers receiving particular mention. In recesses along the corridors are the main exhibits, many consisting of scenes of trench life, complete with rats and insect-covered severed limbs. One exhibit features an officer and soldier wearing Orange Order sashes in a frontline trench dugout. While Lodge meetings did take place in France, they were generally held when the troops were out of the line. The tour through the cellars concludes at a modern shop selling items found on the battlefield (and some less glamorous modern pieces), most of which are in good condition and reasonably priced. Once you pass through its doors you will discover just how far you have walked – for the tunnels re-emerge in a park several hundred yards from the church. Worth noting, as you head back to the town centre by way of the steps immediately adjacent to the shop exit, is a mural on a wall by the park gates. It features three soldiers walking past the damaged Basilica, the right-hand one of which is Irish. Of the 20,000 visitors to the museum annually, approximately one third are from the British Isles. The museum is generally open from March through to November, but closes for lunch outside of July and August.

Amiens is the only city in the Somme region, and was briefly occupied by the Germans in 1914, from August 31-September 10. For the most part, however, it provided a safe haven and source of entertainment for the Allied troops, mostly officers, when they were out of the line. Comfortably within ear-shot of the big guns, Amiens was the temporary home to a wide variety of combatants – Australians, Americans, Canadians, Indians, Senegalese, Madagascans, British and, of course, French. Many of the top showbusiness names from Paris made the journey to the city to entertain the troops; the well-to-do holidayed there for the excitement of being nearer the war without encountering the dangers; and it proved a good base for the posse of war correspondents. It provided, in a sense, the link between the civilian and military populations. Physically, the city, which suffered considerably during the Second World War, retains little evidence of its wartime role outside of its impressive cathedral, which houses a number of commemorative plaques.

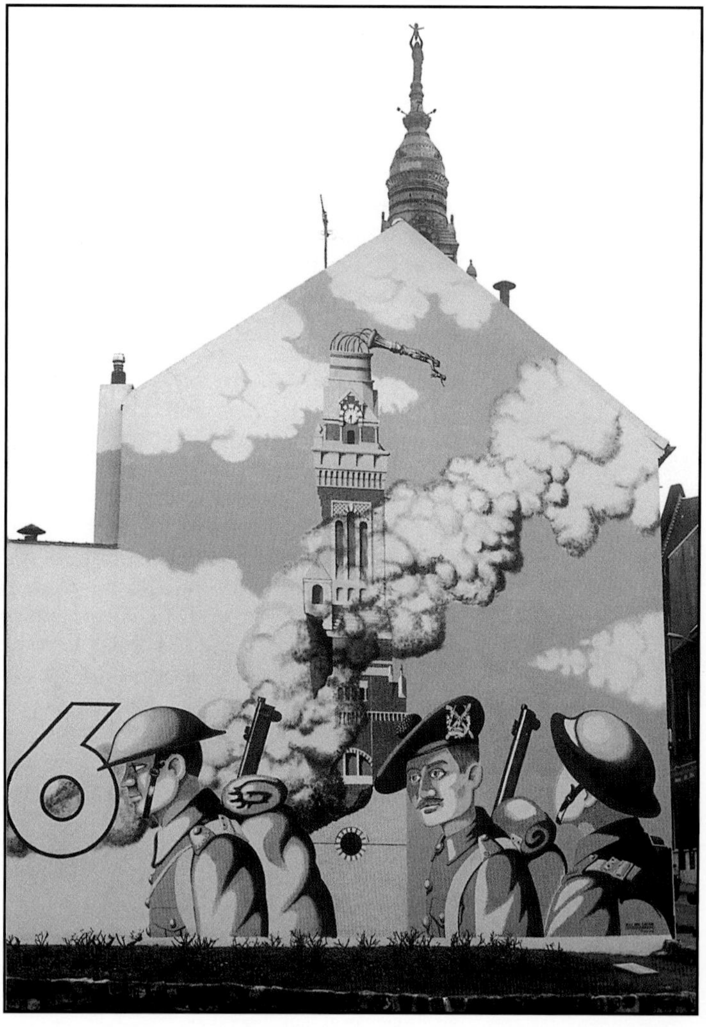

The mural, close to the park in which the Albert museum tunnels exit, features a soldier of the Royal Inniskilling Fusiliers. In the background, above the image of the "Leaning Virgin", can be seen the restored Madonna

SLEEP THAT KNOWS NO BREAKING

Soldier, rest, thy warfare o'er,
Sleep the sleep that knows no breaking;
Dream of fighting field no more,
Day of toil and night of waiting

Tribute on the cross placed at the grave of teenage soldier John Clay, Forceville

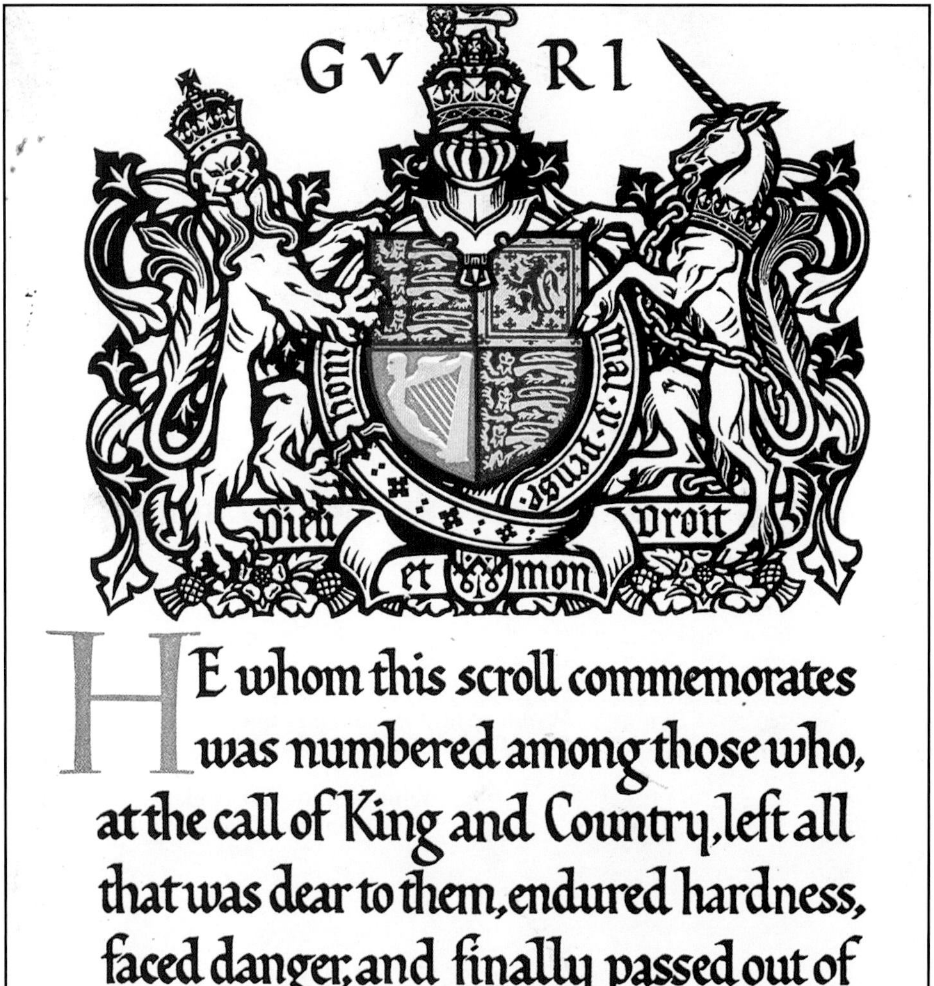

HE whom this scroll commemorates was numbered among those who, at the call of King and Country, left all that was dear to them, endured hardness, faced danger, and finally passed out of the sight of men by the path of duty and self-sacrifice, giving up their own lives that others might live in freedom.
Let those who come after see to it that his name be not forgotten.

Pte. Thomas Joyce
Royal Irish Fusiliers

A scroll and a letter from the King were sent to all families who lost loved ones during the war

Courtesy of the Somme Heritage Centre

THIEPVAL MEMORIAL TO THE MISSING

Tell my father and all at home that I died as an Irishman ought to die, and that I was prepared to go.

Final words of Private Samuel Annett Foster

The Thiepval Memorial to the Missing is the scene each July 1 of a commemorative service remembering the sacrifices on the Somme. A place of peace and tranquillity, its massive multi-arched structure never fails to impress with its magnificence and significance. Its panels contain the names of some 72,357 soldiers who died on the Somme front between 1915 and 1917, the majority during the battles of 1916, who have no known graves. Work began on the memorial in 1929 to a design by Sir Edwin Lutyens and it was officially unveiled by the Prince of Wales in 1932, the last and largest of the official British memorials to be completed. It stands 45 metres tall and is sited on one of the few high points in the Somme region, making it visible from miles around and comfortably within walking distance of the Ulster Tower. A joint French/British cemetery was added almost as an afterthought as a symbol of the joint sacrifice of the two nations on this sector of the front. Details of it are recorded in the cemeteries section, Buried In A Distant Grave.

Thousands of the dead commemorated here were Irishmen, including Private James Gamble. In mid-August, 1916, a package reportedly arrived at the home of the Gamble family in Ebrington Street, Londonderry. Inside was a battered hymn book which had belonged to their son, James, of the 10th West Yorkshire Regiment. Severely wounded on July 1, he had inscribed on the cover his final words: “From Jim. Dear father and mother, I have done my best, and I hope to meet you in heaven. God bless you." The hymn book was said to have been found with his body at the bottom of a trench and must have been picked up by a comrade. Jim Gamble's remains were never recovered for burial and today his name is inscribed on the Thiepval Memorial *(Pier and Face 2A, 2C and 2D)*. For Private Gamble's family, his hymn book served as a tangible battlefield memorial in its own right but for most with lost loved ones whose remains were never found, the Thiepval Memorial was, and remains, a pivotal point for remembrance and pilgrimage.

The memorial was built on land which was once part of the 300-year-old Thiepval chateau, a fine pre-war building totally obliterated along with the rest of the village during the fighting of 1916. Prior to 1914 Thiepval had been a thriving

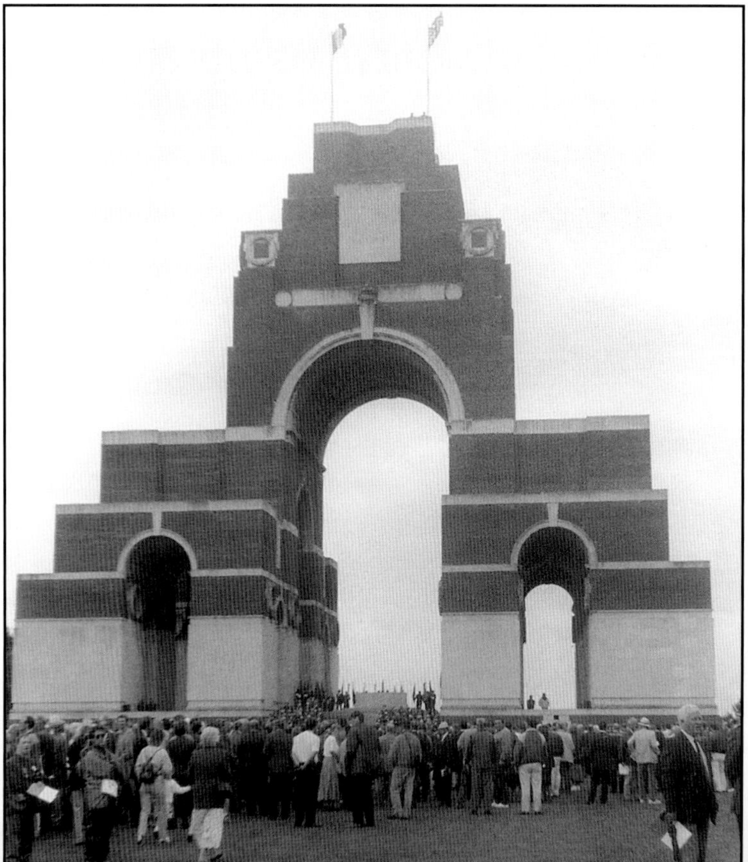

The Thiepval Memorial to the Missing is the scene each year of a service of remembrance on July 1

Courtesy of the Somme Heritage Centre

Below: The recently built visitors' centre

community of 60 houses, shops and a church. The Germans fortified the village to such an extent that they were able to comfortably fend off the July 1 assaults. Its garrison did not lack courage and fought virtually to the last man before it finally fell on September 27, 1916. Hardly a stone was left standing one upon another, with little more than the foundations of the former buildings even traceable amid the rubble and churned earth. Only the bodies of German and British soldiers alike, some of which had been lying in the open for almost three months, littered the ground in various states of decay and mutilation. For a number of years it appeared that no attempt would be made to revive the commune at Thiepval, with only the memorials and cemeteries bearing testimony to its existence, but today a small, generally modern, village has developed a little further up the hillside than the original.

The most recent addition to the village is the Thiepval Visitors' Centre, opened on September 27, 2004, by the Duke of Kent. It aims to present what is described as a "whole of the British Isles Great War history exhibition" and is a joint Anglo-French initiative. English, German and French is used to describe the exhibits and put the battles fought on the Somme into an historical context. During excavation of the site the remains of six German soldiers were uncovered.

The Thiepval memorial is much more than merely symbolic stone and what follows is an attempt to add that all important human element. It can only be, given the immensity of the carnage represented here, a snap shot of the Irishmen whose deaths are recorded on its walls. The list is a cross-section of rank, social standing and creed, though contains a proportionately higher number of officers. The reason for this is twofold: officers generally came from wealthy and influential families, many of whom would still be remembered today; and secondly, such was the class system during the First World War, the death of an ordinary rank-and-file soldier or non-commissioned officer merited barely a mention in the newspapers, regimental files or history books whereas the demise, or even wounding, of an officer inevitably prompted an obituary or tribute of some description.

The names are in alphabetical order with the panel reference number for the Thiepval Memorial at the end of each entry to ease the path for those visiting the monument.

Rifleman Robert William Abbott enlisted in the 11th Royal Irish Rifles with his two brothers, James and William, the three having formerly been members of the South Antrim battalion of the Ulster Volunteer Force. William, the youngest of the trio, was killed on July 1, 1916, with the 108th Company Machine Gun Corps. Before the war the boys had lived with their parents, Thomas and Maggie, at McKeown Street in Lisburn, County Antrim. *(Face and Pier 5C and 12C)*

Rifleman Joseph McCann Agnew, a 19-year-old with the 10th Royal Irish Rifles, was killed on July 1, 1916. A month later his brother, **Private William Agnew**, of the 5th Seaforth Highlanders, was killed on the Somme. Their parents lived at Ravenscroft Street, Belfast. *(Pier and Face 15A and 15B; Pier and Face 15C)*

Second Lieutenant John Alexander, of the 8th Leicestershire Regiment, had been an invoice clerk in the head office of the Belfast Co-Operative Society and had only been at the front a few days when killed on July 15, 1916. Two weeks earlier, on July 1, his 19-year-old brother, **Rifleman Robert Alexander** of the 13th Royal Irish Rifles, had been killed on the Somme. Tragically for their parents, who lived at Drumbeg, Dunmurry, on the outskirts of Belfast, neither body was ever found. *(Pier and Face 2C and 3A; Pier and Face 15A and 15B)*

Rifleman Thomas Joseph Allen, 8th Royal Irish Rifles, was killed shortly after fending off a German counterattack on captured trenches. The 38-year-old, who

Angus brothers Blair, Robert and James were killed within three months of each other

Courtesy of the North Down Heritage Centre

won the Military Medal, single-handedly drove back the enemy by tossing grenade after grenade. He was fatally injured a few minutes after returning to his comrades and died on July 2, 1916. He left a widow, Margaret, at home in Spring Street, Belfast. *(Pier and Face 15A and 15B)*

Rifleman Blair Angus, of the 13th Royal Irish Rifles, was one of three brothers killed in as many months in 1916. The youngest of the three, he died on July 1. The middle brother, **Lance Corporal Robert Angus**, 23, was killed on July 9 while serving with the 2nd Royal Scots and his name is also recorded on the Thiepval Memorial. The last of the sons, **Private James Angus**, 29, was killed at Vimy Ridge with the 29th Canadian Infantry on September 11 and his name carved on a memorial there. It was almost a year, to June, 1917, before their parents, living in Albert Street, Bangor, County Down, were given confirmation of youngest son Blair's death, he having been initially reported as missing. *(Pier and Face 15A and 15B; Pier and Face 3C)*

Second Lieutenant Claude Ashley, of the 15th Northumberland Fusiliers, was on attachment to the 22nd battalion (Tyneside Scottish) when killed on July 1, 1916. He was 21 and the only son of Frederick Ashley, of Westland Road, Belfast. He was commissioned from Queen's University O.T.C. *(Pier and Face 10B, 11B and 12B)*

Captain Armar Leslie Auchinleck, 4th Cameronians attached to the 123rd Company Machine Gun Corps, had formerly been an assistant resident magistrate in northern Nigeria. Killed on September 17, 1916, he was the younger son of the late Lieutenant Colonel Claude Auchinleck and brother to Captain Claude Auchinleck, who was then serving in Mesopotamia with the Indian Army but who would go on to become a Field Marshal credited with bringing Rommel to a halt in North Africa during the Second World War. The head of this long-established County Tyrone family had been 37-year-old **Captain Daniel George Harold Auchinleck**, of the 2nd Royal Inniskilling Fusiliers, until he was killed in October, 1914. He is buried at Strand Military Cemetery, Belgium. *(Pier and Face 4D)*

Captain Henry Parker Beggs, 26, of the 8th Royal Irish Rifles, had been prominent in athletics in Belfast and Lisburn, County Antrim. He had played cricket for both Cliftonville and Lisburn and was a member of Cliftonville Hockey Club.

Captain Beggs, from Dunmurry, on the outskirts of Belfast, had worked for Richardson Sons and Owden Ltd. *(Pier and Face 15A and 15B)*

Company Sergeant Major John H. Bell, of the 11th Royal Irish Rifles, had served in the Boer War and volunteered again in 1914, leaving his farm at Carnaghliss, in the Parish of Killend, County Antrim, to others to run in his absence. A member of Ballyhill Loyal Orange Lodge, he had written to his wife with a premonition of his death. Quartermaster Sergeant Waring, a personal friend, wrote home: "That on Sergeant Bell being wounded and although asked by his captain to retire, he refused to do so and fought on until he was killed by a German shell." *(Pier and Face 15A and 15B)*

Gunner John Bell, of the 119th Battery, 27th Brigade of the Royal Field Artillery, was killed on July 24, 1916. He had formerly worked at the Sandy Row Tramway Depot in Belfast. *(Pier and Face 1A and 8A)*

Second Lieutenant Ernest George Boas, still formerly with the 5th Royal Irish Rifles, had been attached to the 13th battalion for just three weeks before the opening of the Somme offensive. The 19-year-old, killed on July 1, 1916, had been in business with his father at the Loopbridge Weaving Factory in Belfast. The family home was at College Gardens, Belfast. *(Pier and Face 15A and 15B)*

Private Samuel Boston, 2nd South Lancashire Regiment, had lived at Bromley Street, Belfast. He was killed, on July 15, 1916, a year after his brother, **Private Joseph Boston**, 6th Loyal North Lancashire Regiment, had died in the Dardanelles. Joseph is remembered on the Helles Memorial. *(Pier and Face 7A and 7B)*

Lance Corporal James S. Boyd, 6th Black Watch, was from Harcourt Street in Belfast. He was with a machinegun section when killed on July 30, 1916. *(Pier and Face 10A)*

Sergeant Samuel Bond, 23, from Belfast, served with A Company of the 14th Rifles. The son of a Royal Navy member, his death is recorded on Pier and Face 15A and 15A

Courtesy of the Somme Heritage Centre

Sergeant George Wesley Jackson, left, of the 9th Royal Irish Fusilliers, was 21 when he died on July 1, 1916. His family were from Stranmillis Gardens in Belfast (Pier and Face 15A)

Courtesy of the Somme Heritage Centre

Second Lieutenant Brown was a member of the Leinster Regiment but attached to the Munsters at the time of his death

Courtesy of the North Down Heritage Centre

Second Lieutenant William Hatchell Boyd, 29, of the 9th Royal Dublin Fusiliers, was the elder son of the Rev. Samuel Boyd, a native of Belfast who, in 1916, was minister of Blackhall Place Methodist Church, Dublin, and a former Vice-President and Secretary of the Methodist Conference. Second Lieutenant Boyd, who was killed on September 9, 1916, had been working as an accountant in Londonderry before the war and had only been at the front from the end of July, 1916. *(Pier and Face 16C)*

Second Lieutenant Francis Alfred Joseph Brown, 6th Leinster Regiment attached to the 8th Royal Munster Fusiliers, was 22 when killed on September 9, 1916. He was the youngest son of retired Royal Navy Chief Officer William Henry Brown, Ballyholme Esplanade, Bangor, County Down. *(Pier and Face 16C)*

Captain Dominick Augustus Browne, of the 1st Royal Irish Rifles, had an address in Dublin though was from a County Wicklow family. He was commissioned in 1908 and served for a spell as Adjutant in 1915 until injured in a riding accident. Said to have had a "tongue like a razor", he was unpopular among the rank-and-file. He was reportedly hit while crossing No-Man's-Land and bleed to death from a wound to his femoral artery. Although his body was reportedly recovered, its final resting place was subsequently lost. *(Pier and Face 15A and 15B)*

Lieutenant The Honourable Brian Danvers Butler, 13th King's Royal Rifle Corps, attached to the 7th battalion, was the youngest son of the sixth Earl of Lanesborough, of Lanesborough Lodge, Belturbet, a former Lord Lieutenant for County Cavan for 24 years and an Irish peer for 27 years. The 40-year-old lieutenant was an uncle of the Duchess of Sutherland. He was killed on August 18, 1916. *(Pier and Face 13A and 13B)*

Lieutenant Lawford Burne Campbell, from Coolgreany, Fortwilliam Park, Belfast, was 20 when killed on July 1, 1916, serving with the 12th Royal Irish Rifles. The

Wellington College student, a nephew of Major-General Walter Campbell who had helped organise the withdrawal of British troops from Gallipoli, had previously worked for his father's spinning mill. *(Pier and Face 15A and 15B)*

Second Lieutenant Matthew Carruth, 26, of the 4th Royal Irish Regiment attached 6th Connaught Rangers, lived at Hilltown, Mallusk, on the outskirts of Belfast. A teacher at the Model School, Londonderry prior to the war, he had only been at the front for four weeks when killed on September 9, 1916. His brother, **Lieutenant John Carruth**, of the 6th Royal Dublin Fusiliers, died of wounds while on attachment to the Royal Irish Rifles. From Stewartstown, County Tyrone, he passed away in October, 1918, and is buried in Tincourt British Cemetery, some 12 miles east of Peronne. *(Pier and Face 3A)*

Second Lieutenant William John White Carson was educated at Dungannon Royal School and took a degree in surveying at a London college before joining his father's estate agency in Rosemary Street, Belfast. He was commissioned into the 14th Royal Irish Rifles. *(Pier and Face 15A and 15B)*

Quartermaster Sergeant Hugh Carton, 1st Irish Guards, died on September 15, 1916. The 29-year-old had sailed with the British Expeditionary Force in August, 1914, and spent two years at the front without serious injury, earning several mentions in despatches. His commanding officer, writing to the family at Kirkhills, Ballymoney, County Antrim, said had he not been killed he would have recommended him for the Distinguished Conduct Medal. In the event, he was awarded the Military Medal for his bravery. *(Pier and Face 7D)*

Second Lieutenant Sinclair Baxter Coghill, 5th Royal Inniskilling Fusiliers attached 8th battalion, was from Marlborough Road, Donnybrook, Dublin. Educated at St. Andrew's College, Dublin, and London University, he was working for the Civil Service when the war started. *(Pier and Face 4D and 5B)*

Lieutenant Edward William Costello, 3rd Royal Inniskilling Fusiliers, was 19 when killed. He was attached to the 87th Coy Machine Gun Corps. His family was from Pembroke Road, Ballsbridge, Dublin. *(Pier and Face 4D and 5B)*

Captain Philip Cruickshank, of the 9th Royal Inniskilling Fusiliers, had been editor of the Tyrone Constitution from 1905, having previously worked on the Derry Standard after his arrival from his native Aberdeen. The 34-year-old member of the Ulster Unionist Council had been active in the Unionist Club movement and had commanded the U.V.F. battalion in Mid-Tyrone. He enlisted as a private on the outbreak of war, bringing with him many of his Ulster Volunteers to the Omagh Depot. Captain Cruickshank was commissioned in September, 1914, and had been wounded twice in the spring of 1916. He was killed on July 1 alongside many of those with whom he had joined. *(Pier and Face 4D and 5B)*

Privates John and James Cumberland, 9th Royal Irish Fusiliers, both died on July 1, 1916. The brothers had been members of the Derrygortreavy Company of the Dungannon U.V.F. and belonged to their local Kilnacart Orange Lodge No. 295, near Eglish, Dungannon, County Tyrone. *(Pier and Face 4D and 5B)*

Private William Cunningham, 1st Irish Guards, had formerly served with the Royal Irish Constabulary in Lisburn, County Antrim, and had been previously wounded. His parents, Mitchell and Maggie, lived at Terrawee, Gleneely, County Donegal. He was 24 when he died on September 12, 1916. *(Pier and Face 7D)*

Second Lieutenant Arthur Denman Deane, 1st Royal Irish Regiment attached 2nd battalion, was killed on July 14, 1916. Educated at the Royal Belfast Academical Institution, and a member of Knock Rugby Club, he had been serving an engineering apprenticeship at the Workman Clark and Company shipyard in

Brothers Arthur and James Hollywood were both killed on July 1, 1916. Their bodies were never found. The telegrams reporting their loss arrived at the home of their parents, James and Elizabeth, at Helen's Bay, County Down, a day apart.

Arthur, 24, right, had worked with his father in his Albertbridge Road business in east Belfast. The lieutenant with the 9th Royal Irish Fusiliers had been wounded early in 1916 and had only recently returned to duty. James, a year younger at 23, had left his employment with Ross Brothers in Belfast's Linenhall Street to take a commission in the Royal Irish Rifles. He was attached to the 12th battalion as a second lieutenant.

At the July meeting of the Belfast City and District Water Commissioners, of which their father had been a member, the chairman resolved: "That the deep and heartfelt sympathy of the members of the board be respectively tendered to Mr. and Mrs. Hollywood in the great sorrow that has fallen upon them by the death in action in France of their two sons, who, in response to their country's call, entered his Majesty's army, and have yielded up their lives in defence of the Empire."

Arthur's name is on Pier and Face 15A and James, as the picture above shows, is recorded among his comrades on Face and Pier 15A and 15B

Courtesy of the North Down Heritage Centre

Belfast when the war started. He enlisted and spent several months as a motor despatch rider before being commissioned. His parents, who lived at Knockdene Park, Belfast, received a letter from him just hours before the War Office telegram arrived telling of his death. A fellow officer later wrote to them to say that Second Lieutenant Deane had died in a German counterattack on a captured trench. His body was found and identified when the trench was retaken, but subsequently lost. *(Pier and Face 3A)*

Sergeant Patrick Devine had been an employee of Guinness before the war, working in the Vathouse of the Dublin brewery. He was killed on August 18, 1916, while serving with the 1st Northumberland Fusiliers. *(Pier and Face 10B, 11B and 12B)*

Rifleman John Doherty, of the 13th Royal Irish Rifles, had been a footman on Major Perceval Maxwell's staff at Finnebrogue House, Downpatrick, County Down, before the war. The 21-year-old, whose parents lived at Limavady, had been a member of the Inch Company of the Ulster Volunteer Force. The Major's butler, Rifleman Henry Walker, was wounded on July 1, 1916, but appears to have survived the war. *(Pier and Face 15A and 15B)*

Lieutenant Robert Joseph Dougal, of the 21st Northumberland Fusiliers (Tyneside Scottish), was a member of his late father's carting company in Belfast. The 21-year-old had been commissioned in October, 1914, and promoted the following year. His widowed mother lived in May Street, Belfast. *(Pier and Face 10B, 11B and 12B)*

Second Lieutenant James Downing, 3rd Royal Irish Regiment but attached to the 6th battalion, was the fifth son of John Downing, Hill Hall, Lisburn, County Antrim. The 32-year-old had been working in Dublin for the Belfast-based firm of Robert Watson and Company. *(Pier and Face 3A)*

Captain Guy Wellesley Eaton, of the 8th Royal Irish Fusiliers, was killed on September 6, 1916. He had been wounded the previous May and had only just returned to his unit. From Blackrock, County Dublin, he was educated at St. Andrew's College, Dublin, and Cowbridge Grammar School, south Wales, and was about to graduate in Science from a London university when the war broke out. A man of great courage, he was rapidly promoted to captain after leaving the Dublin University Officer Training Corps. Major-General William Hickie sent him a certificate on vellum just weeks before his death which recorded: "I have read with much pleasure the reports of your Regimental Commander and Brigade Commander regarding your gallant conduct and devotion to duty in the field on July 11th, 1916, and have ordered your name and deed to be entered in the record of the Irish Division." A short time later he was awarded the Military Medal. A letter sent by a fellow officer to his mother said: "You will probably have received news from the War Office of the great loss not only you, but the battalion, has sustained in the death of your son. He was hit about 7 o'clock on the evening of the 6th September, and died about 3 o'clock this morning at battalion headquarters. His end was quite peaceful, I believe, and he was unconscious when brought to headquarters. I saw him when he was first brought in. I cannot tell you what a splendid soldier he was. He was most popular with officers and men alike, and his chief thoughts were for the welfare of his men and the regiment. When he was brought in he kept on saying: 'Hold on, boys, remember the left flank is exposed.' At the time he received his wound he was holding a very difficult part of the line against a German attack, and he succeeded in preventing the enemy making any appreciable advance." *(Pier and Face 15A)*

Second Lieutenant Thomas Brignall Elliott, 10th Royal Irish Rifles, was from Knockdene Park in Belfast. The former Royal Academical Institution student, who was 29 when killed in action, enlisted as a private before being commissioned in November, 1914. Chaplain the Rev. James Quinn, writing to the family after they had initially been told he was "missing", informed them: "He fell leading his men on the morning of the 1st inst. It is hardly possible for him to have been left lying where he fell if the wound had not been mortal, as the ground has been frequently and fully searched." *(Pier and Face 15A and 15B)*

Lance Corporal George Farr, of the 9th Inniskilling Fusiliers, had followed a family tradition when he left his home at Claggan, Mulnagore, Dungannon, County Tyrone, to go to war. A brother had been killed in the South African campaign more than 15 years previously. Lance Corporal Farr suffered the same fate on July 1, 1916. When the news reached home that George was "missing believed killed" a third brother, Robert Farr, immediately volunteered for the same battalion. On August 7, 1917, he too was killed and is buried at Ypres Reservoir Cemetery in Belgium. *(Pier 4A and 5D)*

Private James H. Ferguson, 8th Royal Irish Fusiliers, was a member of the Orange Order and Ulster Volunteer Force. From Harbour Road, Kilkeel, he had been chauffeur to Robert Nicholson, Kilkeel, before the war. *(Pier and Face 15A)*

Rifleman Samuel Ferguson, 13th Royal Irish Rifles, killed on July 1, 1916, was from Holywood, County Down. He had been a member of Holywood Purple Star L.O.L No. 785 and had worked for William Heron, a former High Sheriff for County Down, who lived at Maryfield, next to Palace Barracks, Holywood. His brother James, a regular soldier with the Royal Irish Fusiliers, had been in India at the outbreak of war and came through the landing at Suvla Bay only to be severely wounded at Ypres, Belgium. *(Pier and Face 15A and 15B)*

Private Samuel Annett Foster was carried from the battlefield by his wounded brother, Private Matthew Foster, both men serving in the 4th Regiment South African Infantry (South African Scottish). From his bed in the Red Cross Hospital in London, Matthew told his father Joseph, from Church Street, Rathfriland, County Down, how Samuel, who died of his wounds, had been struck down by a shell which killed another comrade instantly. As the brothers waited to be taken to a field hospital, Samuel passed on a last message: "Tell my father and all at home that I died as an Irishman ought to die, and that I was prepared to go." *(Pier and Face 4C)*

Second Lieutenant John Stewart-Moore Gage, 23, of the 9th Royal Inniskilling Fusiliers, was the son of Dr. Francis Gage and grandson of General Ezekiel Gage, of Rathlin Island. His mother was a daughter of Captain Stewart-Moore of Moyargot, Ballycastle, County Antrim. Second Lieutenant Gage had been wounded in the head in April, 1916, and had only just rejoined his battalion when killed on July 1, 1916. *(Pier and Face 4D and 5B)*

Second Lieutenant Albert Henry Gibson, of the 12th Inniskilling Fusiliers, was attached to the 9th battalion when killed. His father Robert was the Grand Secretary of the County Grand Orange Lodge of Belfast. A Methodist College student, he had worked for a chartered accountant and flax merchant before enlisting in the Black Watch. He was commissioned into the fusiliers and only drafted to France on June 15, 1916 – two weeks before his death – on his 19th birthday. Writing to his father at Devonshire Villas, North Parade, Belfast, Lieutenant-Colonel A. St. Q. Ricardo said: "Your boy led his platoon over our parapet across No-Man's-Land in the most gallant way, and there our information stops. The survivors of the company uninjured are few, and none of them can throw any light on what happened to him." He added: "Your lad was brought in the day before the advance to replace an officer wounded during the preliminary

Rifleman Samuel Hoy, of the 11th Royal Irish Rifles, was killed on July 1, 1916 (Pier and Face 15A and 15B)

Courtesy of Eileen Lewis

bombardment. He was the senior of his company in waiting, and was so delighted at getting his chance." *(Pier and Face 4D and 5B)*

Second Lieutenant William Henry Gregg, 5th Royal Irish Rifles attached to the 1st battalion, was reportedly shot in the head between the first and second German lines. He was a member of a well-known Belfast family and had worked for his father, a Justice of the Peace who lived in Chichester Gardens, Belfast, in Gregg Sons and Phoenix. A member of the North of Ireland cricket and football clubs, he had been rejected for service on five separate occasions because of his poor eyesight before securing a commission. In a cruel irony, his brother, Lieutenant A. L. Gregg, of the Royal Irish Fusiliers, lost an eye at the Dardanelles in 1915. *(Pier and Face 15A and 15B)*

Second Lieutenant Frank Douglas Gunning had enlisted with the Royal Dublin Fusiliers initially, but was invalided home after being wounded in the Dardanelles. He managed to obtain a commission in the 6th Royal Inniskilling Fusiliers and was attached to the 1st battalion when killed on July 1, 1916. The 22-year-old, from Willoughby Place, Enniskillen, County Fermanagh, had been educated at Portora Royal School and worked for the Ulster Bank pre-war. *(Pier and Face 4D and 5B)*

Rifleman Jack Hamilton, 13th Royal Irish Rifles, was killed on July 1, 1916. It was the second tragedy for the family as his brother, **Bombardier Thomas Hamilton**, 58th Battery, Royal Field Artillery, had been killed in May, 1915, and buried in Rue-du-Bois Military Cemetery, Fleurbaix, Pas-de-Calais. Their parents, Robert and Maggie Hamilton, ran the Scriptural Schools on the Downshire Road, Newry, County Down. *(Pier and Face 15A and 15B)*

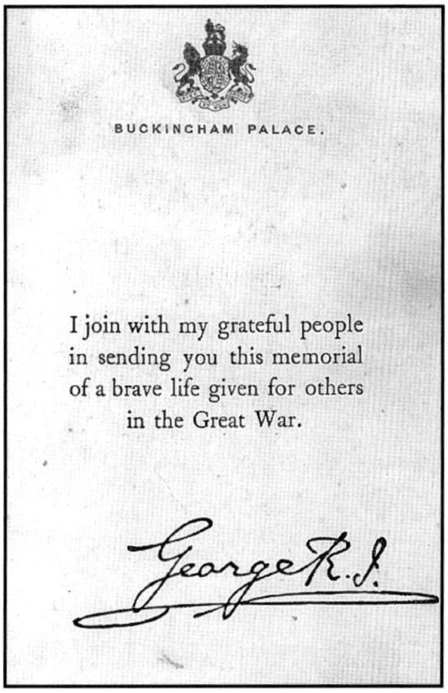
BUCKINGHAM PALACE.

I join with my grateful people in sending you this memorial of a brave life given for others in the Great War.

George R.I.

Courtesy of the Somme Heritage Centre

Second Lieutenant John Hamilton was a clerk in the Coleraine branch of the Belfast Bank and a son of John Hamilton, Woodview, Stranocum, north Antrim. He was killed on July 1 while serving with the 11th Royal Inniskilling Fusiliers. *(Pier and Face 4D and 5B)*

Second Lieutenant Robert Victor Hamilton was the 24-year-old son of James and Matilda Hamilton, of Glendarra, Charnwood Avenue, Belfast. After attending the Royal Belfast Academical Institution, he entered the Civil Service and was working for the Treasury Department in Dublin Castle at the start of the war. He was commissioned into the 17th Royal Irish Rifles in August, 1915, and had only been in France three months when killed on July 1, 1916. *(Pier and Face 15A and 15B)*

Lieutenant E. H. Harper, 8th South Staffordshire Regiment, was the eldest son of Henry Harper, of Northland Place, Dungannon, County Tyrone. The lieutenant had attended Dungannon Royal School, Queen's University, Belfast and Dublin's Trinity College, and had played rugby for both his home town club and Queen's. He had been a lecturer at Bangor University, Wales, and Professor of Mathematics at Cork University. Commissioned into the Royal Munster Fusiliers, he later transferred to the Staffordshires. His brother, **Lieutenant Ernest Harper**, was killed at the Dardanelles in August, 1915, while serving with the Munsters. *(Pier and Face 7B)*

Second Lieutenant Hind, left, was waiting to join the Royal Flying Corps when killed

Captain Elliott Johnston won the Military Cross for his daring during a trench raid on June 26, 1916, but was killed five days later in the German second line

Courtesy of the Somme Heritage Centre

Captain Barry Hill, of the 10th Royal Irish Rifles, was 30 years old when killed on July 1, 1916. A son of Squire and Sarah Hill, Ballyclare, County Antrim, he had worked as a dentist in a practice in University Street, Belfast, prior to the war. *(Pier and Face 15A and 15B)*

Lieutenant Walter James Hill, 2nd Regiment, South African Infantry, was a son of Hewson Hill, Bruce Hall, County Cavan. The 32-year-old had immigrated as a young man to Natal where he had seen active service with the Natal Carabineers facing down a native rebellion in 1906 and fought under General Botha in German South West Africa. *(Pier and Face 4C)*

Second Lieutenant Ernest William Gayles Hind was serving with the 15th Royal Irish Rifles while waiting to begin training as a pilot with the Royal Flying Corps when killed. From Holywood, County Down, he was one of four brothers serving and had worked for Graham and Company accountants based at the Scottish Temperance Buildings in Belfast. *(Pier and Face 15A and 15B)*

Robert, Andrew and **David Hobbs** were all killed on July 1, 1916, serving with the 9th Royal Irish Fusiliers. The brothers' widowed mother lived in Union Street, Armagh, where she shared a home with Andrew's wife Elizabeth. A fourth brother, Herbert, served in the same battalion. He was wounded but appears to have survived the war. *(Pier and Face 15A)*

Captain Elliott Johnston won the Military Cross for his daring raid on the enemy trenches on June 26, 1916, during which his party captured 13 German soldiers. The former North Down U.V.F. company commander, serving with the 13th Royal

Irish Rifles, did not live long enough to see it, however, as he was killed just days later on July 1 when struck in the upper body by machinegun fire close to the German second-line trenches. The 28-year-old was the son of Samuel Johnston of Deramore Park, Belfast. *(Pier and Face 15A and 15B)*

Lieutenant John Ernest Johnston, attached to the 10th South Staffordshire regiment from the 4th battalion, was the eldest of three soldier sons of David Johnston, JP, of Grace Hall, Lurgan. In Australia at the start of the war, he returned home to enlist, serving as a private before being awarded a commission. *(Pier and Face 7B)*

Rifleman Frank Keenan, 14th Royal Irish Rifles, was the second son of Colour Sergeant W. Keenan, of the 5th Rifles, to die in the war. A brother, **Lance Corporal Patrick Joseph Keenan**, 21, also of the 1st Rifles, had been killed in March, 1915, and is buried at the Royal Irish Rifles Graveyard, Laventie. Both men had been born at Fermoy, County Cork, though the family was then living at Sussex Place, Belfast. *(Pier and Face 15A and 15B)*

Private James Kelly was just 15 when he enlisted in 1914. From Mill Street in Midleton, County Cork, he joined the 6th Connaught Rangers. He was one of seven members of his battalion killed by artillery fire on September 8, 1916, as they moved forward in preparation for the attack on Ginchy the following day. His cousin, **Bill Cahill**, just a year older and with whom he had joined up, had been wounded on September 3 during the assault on Guillemont and died within hours of James. He is buried at Corbie Communal Cemetery Extension, some 10 miles east of Albert. *(Pier and Face 15A)*

Lieutenant Thomas James Kennedy, 8th Royal Inniskilling Fusiliers, was the eldest son of Samuel Kennedy, Cookstown, County Tyrone. He had trained as a journalist with the Mid-Ulster Mail and was Editor of the Monaghan Standard before joining the army. Lieutenant Kennedy was killed on September 9, 1916. *(Pier and Face 4D and 5B)*

Lieutenant Thomas Michael Kettle, of the 9th Royal Dublin Fusiliers, is one of the most significant, and certainly best remembered, of the 16th (Irish) Division casualties on the Somme. The 36-year-old, from Rathmines, Dublin, was killed on September 9, 1916. A leading nationalist figure in the push for Home Rule, he had been the Member of Parliament for East Tyrone and a professor of National Economics at University College, Dublin. Under additional information on his entry in the Commonwealth War Graves Commission booklet he is described as “poet, journalist, essayist and idealist”. He wrote a number of war poems, some published after his death. Lieutenant Kettle, never comfortable in the uniform of a British officer, recorded how he had joined up after the German invasion of Belgium to fight “not for England, but for small nations”. *(Pier and Face 16C)*

Second Lieutenant John Lecky, of the 18th Royal Irish Rifles attached to the 2nd battalion, died on July 10, 1916. He was the son of the Rev. Alexander Gourley Lecky, Presbyterian Minister at Ballylennon, Feddyglass, Raphoe, County Donegal. He was 25. *(Pier and Face 15A and 15B)*

Lieutenant A. D. Lemon, from Edgcumbe House, Strandtown, Belfast, was a member of the 12th Royal Irish Rifles. Educated at Methodist College, he had managed Barn Mill in Carrickfergus before the war and had been a member of the Royal North of Ireland Yacht Club. He was reportedly “shot by a German officer at close range” in the enemy trenches on July 1, 1916. *(Pier and Face 15A and 15B)*

Private Peter Loughan, 8th Black Watch, was killed in action on July 14, 1916. The Belfastman’s brother, **Private Charles Loughan**, of the 1st Leinster Regiment, died in January, 1915. His body was never found either and his name is recorded on the Menin Gate Memorial to the Missing in Ypres, Belgium. *(Pier and Face 10A)*

Sergeant S. Lowry, 8th Royal Irish Rifles, died on July 2, 1916. He had formerly been a member of East Belfast U.V.F. and had worked for the Belfast Cooperative Society at Ravenhill Avenue in the city. A married man who left a widow, Harriet, at Bankmore Street, Belfast, he had played soccer for Willowfield United before the war. Mentioned previously in despatches by Sir Douglas Haig, he was award the D.C.M. shortly before his death. *(Pier and Face 15A and 15B)*

Captain William Thomas Lyons was a graduate of Queen's University Officers Training Corps in Belfast. From Rosetta Park in the city, he was posted to the King's Own (Royal Lancaster Regiment), in which one of his brothers was also serving. Made a lieutenant in July, 1915, he was awarded the Military Cross in March the following year for "conspicuous gallantry during operations when leading his company after the commander was wounded, and in consolidating the position won". A month later he was promoted to captain. The 24-year-old was killed on July 18, 1916. *(Pier and Face 5D and 12B)*

Lieutenant William Felix MacCarthy-O'Leary was 22 when killed at Ginchy on September 7, 1916, with the 1st Royal Munster Fusiliers. He was a member of a family with a proud military tradition. His father, Lieutenant Colonel William MacCarthy-O'Leary, of Coomlagane, Millstreet, County Cork, was killed at the head of the 1st South Lancashire Regiment in the assault on Pieter's Hill during the Boer War, while his older brother, Heffernan William Denis MacCarthy-O'Leary commanded both Royal Irish Rifles and Royal Irish Fusilier battalions during the First World War and retired from the Army in 1937 as a full Colonel. *(Pier and Face 16C)*

Second Lieutenant Sir Edward Harry Macnaghten was serving in the 12th Royal Irish Rifles on attachment from the 1st Black Watch (Royal Highlanders) when killed on July 1, 1916. According to a Private Galloway, on home leave to Ballycastle a month after the 20-year-old was reported missing, Sir Harry was badly wounded on the parapet of an enemy trench. Three Germans climbed out to take the officer a prisoner, fighting off and killing a soldier who attempted to thwart them. He was last seen being carried towards the rear by his captors. Rumours that he was lying injured in No-Man's-Land inspired Rifleman Robert Quigg to leave his own trenches seven times, returning on each occasion with a wounded man, an act which earned him the Victoria Cross. The Eton-educated Sir Harry, son of the late Hon Sir Edward Charles Macnaghten of Dundarave, Bushmills, County Antrim, had been the 6th Bart. The title would have passed to **Second Lieutenant Sir Arthur Douglas Macnaghten**, of the 8th Rifle Brigade, but the 19-year-old former Wellington College student was himself killed on September 15, 1916, before the fate of Sir Harry had been confirmed. He lies in Caterpillar Valley Cemetery on the Somme. *(Pier and Face 10A)*

Second Lieutenant Thomas George Mahony, 15th King's (Liverpool) Regiment, was on attachment to the 19th Lancashire Fusiliers when killed on July 13, 1916. The 21-year-old was the second son of Royal Irish Constabulary District Inspector Owen Mahoney, of Holywood, County Down. A well-known rugby player, he had been educated at Lurgan College and before the war had been working in the land agency business. *(Pier and Face 3C and 3D)*

Lieutenant Douglas Slade Maunsell had been a member of the 4th Royal Dublin Fusiliers since 1911 and was later commissioned into the 2nd Royal Muster Fusiliers, to which his father, Major Arthur Munro Maunsell, had formerly belonged.

Rifleman Herbert George Holohan, on the left holding the flag with a friend,was serving with the 9th Royal Irish Rifles when killed on July 1, 1916 (Pier and Face 15A and 15B)

Courtesy of the Somme Heritage Centre

Although born in Belfast and educated at the Royal School, Armagh, he had strong family connections in Limerick and Wicklow. He had returned to France in September, 1916, after recovering from an earlier wound and was killed, between Guillemont and Ginchy, on the 5th – just five hours after rejoining his regiment. *(Pier and Face 16C)*

Second Lieutenant G. C. Martin, Royal Dublin Fusiliers, was killed on August 3, 1916. He was the youngest son of Captain R. W. Martin, of Longford Terrace, Monkstown, and had been educated at Campbell College in Belfast before taking up an appointment with the Eastern Telegraph Company's Training School for Submarine Telegraphy. *(Pier and Face 4D and 5B)*

Second Lieutenant Allan John McClellan, attached to the 15th Royal Irish Rifles, was 21. He had lived at Ballyboley, Ballynure, County Antrim, and had been an assistant master at Larne Grammar School before receiving his commission. *(Pier and Face 15A and 15B)*

Captain John Stuart McClinton was one of three brothers serving, he in the 7th South Lancashire Regiment and the others in the Royal Irish Rifles. Before the war he had worked in his father's business, McClinton and Co., seed merchants, in Victoria Street, Belfast. Educated at Royal Belfast Academical Institution, he was a member of the North of Ireland Football Club. *(Pier and Face 7A and 7B)*

Lieutenant William Clark McConnell, attached to the 2nd Royal Irish Rifles from the 3rd battalion, was killed on July 8, 1916. The youngest son of Sir Robert McConnell, of Glen Dhu, Strandtown, Belfast, he was in charge of a machine-gun section. In a letter home, Lieutenant G. L. Murphy, from Rathmines, County Dublin, wrote: "Our machine gun officer, Lt. W. C. McConnell, of Belfast, was wounded in the leg and face, and I went up to the first trench to dress him. When I had finished dressing him, I turned to go back and bid him good luck. Alas! I had only gone about ten yards when one of the shells got him fair and square in the back, and poor McConnell was no more, blown to bits! Nice chap, he was, and very decent to me. He had explained to me the mysteries of the machine gun and altogether was a pretty decent chap." *(Pier and Face 15A and 15B)*

Second Lieutenant John W. McVicker was from Craignamaddy, Stranocum, Mosside, County Antrim. He had joined the North Irish Horse as a trooper but was later commissioned into the 13th King's (Liverpool) Regiment. The 21-year-old had attended Coleraine Academical Institution and had just completed his first year of medical school at Edinburgh University when the war started. He was killed on July 14, 1916. Two of his brothers were also serving, while a cousin, **Lieutenant D. Kerr**, had been killed in action at Gallipoli in 1915. *(Pier and Face 1D, 8B and 8C)*

Second Lieutenant Thomas George Moore was the son of Head-Constable G. Moore of York Road R.I.C. Barracks. Educated at Skegoniel School, the Model School and the Royal Belfast Academical Institution, he was in the linen business before joining the 17th Royal Irish Rifles. He went to the Western Front in February, 1916, being attached to the 8th Rifles. *(Pier and Face 15A and 15B)*

Second Lieutenant John Ross Moore, 3rd Connaught Rangers attached to the 7th Royal Inniskilling Fusiliers, was the eldest son of Samuel and Anne Moore, of Ulster Bank House, Ballina, County Mayo. He had joined the Honourable Artillery Company and was wounded in Flanders in August, 1915. He received his commission in January, 1916, and was posted to the Inniskillings in July that year, just weeks before being killed on September 9. He was just 20 years old. *(Pier and Face 15A)*

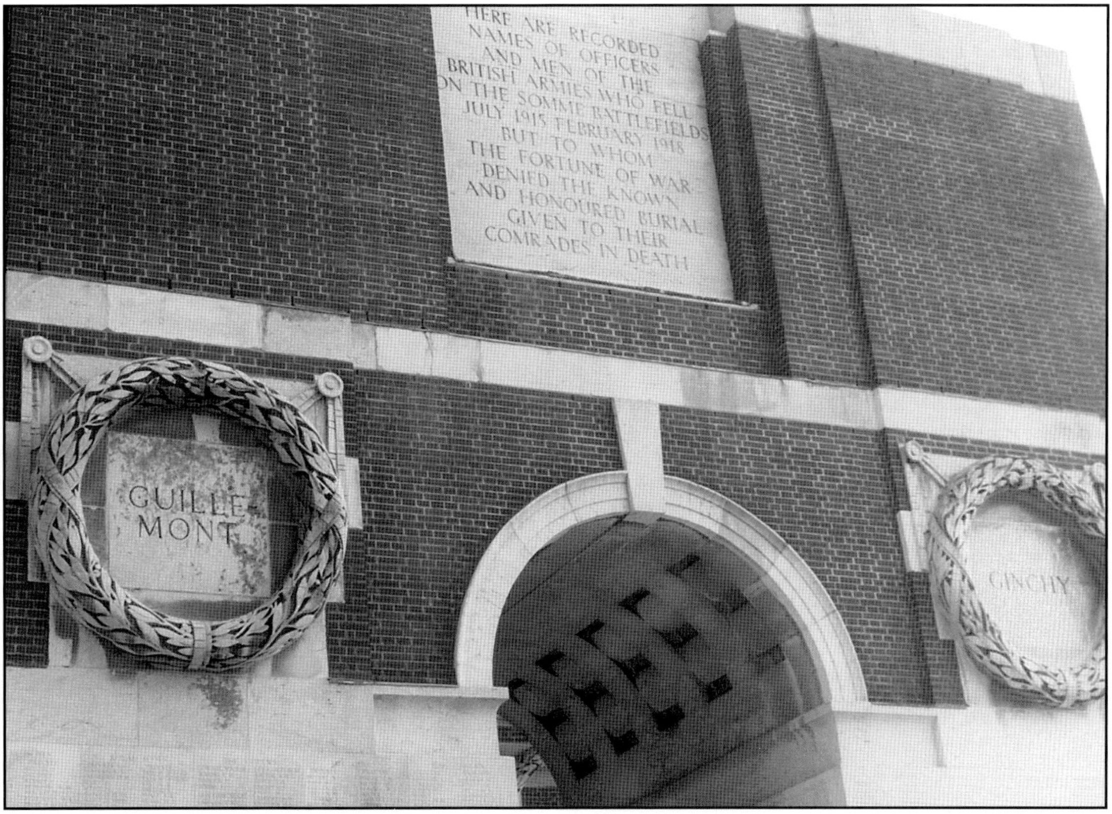

Guillemont and Ginchy, where so many men of the 16th (Irish) Division died in September, 1916, are enshrined on the memorial

Lieutenant Francis Campion Mulcahy-Morgan, 7th Royal Irish Rifles, died on September 9, 1916, while leading a patrol probing the enemy's lines. His father, a barrister-at-law who lived at Lara House, Rathdrum, County Wicklow, had already received word of two other sons missing in action, one of whom subsequently proved to be dead: **Lieutenant Edward Spread Mulcahy-Morgan**, 3rd Royal Irish Rifles, was killed on October 27, 1914, and is commemorated on the Le Touret Memorial, Pas-de-Calais; his brother, Captain Thomas Westropp Mulcahy-Morgan had been living in Kenya before the war and served in the Royal Flying Corps. In a cruel twist of fate, his son, **John Anthony Mulcahy-Morgan**, a flight-lieutenant pilot in 213 Squadron, R.A.F. Volunteer Reserve, was killed in the last year of the Second World War and is buried in Belgrade War Cemetery, in former Yugoslavia. *(Pier and Face 15A and 15B)*

Lieutenant James Dermot Neill, of the 108th Machine Gun Corps, was one of the first to join the 13th Royal Irish Rifles. Educated at Royal Belfast Academical Institution, he later attended colleges in England, Switzerland and Germany. The 29-year-old, a director in his father's firm, had been an active member of the U.V.F., the Royal North of Ireland Yacht Club and Holywood Golf Club. His younger brother, **Robert Larmour Neill**, of the 5th Royal Irish Rifles attached to the 1st battalion, was killed in May, 1915, at Frommelles. His name is recorded on the Ploegsteert Memorial in Belgium. *(Pier and Face 5C and 12C)*

Second Lieutenant Donal Charles O'Connell was on attachment to the 8th Royal Inniskilling Fusiliers from the 4th Connaught Rangers when killed on September 9, 1916. The 21-year-old was the son of James John O'Connell, of Clonskea,

Private Thomas Joyce served in the 36th (Ulster) Division with the 9th Royal Irish Fusilliers and, like so many of his comrades, was killed on July 1, 1916 (Pier and Face 15A)

Courtesy of the Somme Heritage Centre

Lieutenant Finlay Kerr, 22, above, from Kingstown, County Dublin, served with the 2nd Royal Irish Regiment and was killed on July 5, 1916

Courtesy of the Somme Heritage Centre

Lieutenant James Dermot Neill, centre, of the 108th M.G.C., had been a director in his father's company

Courtesy of Lester Morrow

Rifleman John Orr, from Castlemount, Bangor, County Down, was with the 11th Rifles when killed on July 1, 1916 (Pier and Face 15A and 15B)

Courtesy of the North Down Heritage Centre

County Dublin, manager of the National Bank on College Green, Dublin. *(Pier and Face 15A)*

Captain Douglas Hill O'Flaherty, of the 15th Royal Irish Rifles, was 36 years old when killed on July 1, 1916. He had been a member of the Ulster Centre of the Motor Cycle Union and played cricket with the North of Ireland club. He left a widow, Beatrice, at Myrtlefield Park, Belfast. *(Pier and Face 15A and 15B)*

Lance Corporal William Robert Ogle, of the 6th Black Watch Territorials, had worked with the General Post Office in Bangor, County Down, where his father was an official. Following his death on July 30, 1916, his uncle, Cecil A. Ogle, a signaller who had previously worked as a draughtsman in the Harland and Wolff shipyards, wrote to the family to tell them of the tragedy. His letter was followed by one from Second Lieutenant A. D. Muir, who said: "His death was quite painless – a bullet wound and caused him no disfigurement." *(Pier and Face 10A)*

Second Lieutenant Patrick Gilbert Warwick O'Hara, 3rd East Surrey Regiment but on attachment to the 1st/4th Royal Berkshire Regiment, was the eldest son of Major Patrick H. A. O'Hara, formerly of the East Surrey Regiment, of Mornington, Crookedwood, County Westmeath. He was 19 years old when killed on August 14, 1916. *(Pier and Face 6B and 6C)*

Second Lieutenant Hugh Montgomery Archdale Olphert, 3rd Royal Munster Fusiliers attached to 7th Leinster Regiment, was killed on September 9, 1916. The 18-year-old was a son of Canon John Olphert, Urney Rectory, Sion Mills, County Tyrone, and grandson of the Very Rev. Thomas Olphert, former Dean of Londonderry. *(Pier and Face 16C)*

Second Lieutenant H. Corry Osborne, 12th West Yorkshire (Prince of Wales's Own) Regiment was killed on July 23, 1916. He was the eldest son of Joseph Osborne, Hopefield Terrace, Antrim Road, Belfast, and had attended the Royal Belfast Academical Institution. Before the war he had worked as a chartered accountant in his father's business, Osborne, Cook and Co., in the Scottish Provident Buildings. He had only been at the front two months. *(Pier and Face 2A, 2C and 2D)*

Sergeant Alfred Owens, 109th Machine Gun Corps, was killed in No-Man's-Land with Second Lieutenant Wedgwood (see Mill Road Cemetery, page 217) as they led their gun team across. The 24-year-old, from University Street, Belfast, was a member of the Ulster Cricket Club and Malone Rugby Club, where he played for the senior XV, and had worked for Workman and Clark shipbuilders in Belfast. *(Pier and Face 5C and 12C)*

Corporal William John Peake was awarded the Military Medal for his actions on June 26-27 when, commanding a blocking party of the 13th Royal Irish Rifles in a German trench, he had searched several dugouts and taken two prisoners, and then marshalled his men with coolness as they waited at the Sunken Road during an enemy retaliatory artillery barrage. The 24-year-old was killed days later on July 1, though initially he had been reported as missing in a telegram to his parents, John and Elizabeth, at Ballywalter Park, Ballywalter, County Down. *(Pier and Face 15A and 15B)*

Captain William Francis Henry Pelly, of the 9th Royal Inniskilling Fusiliers, was the son of the Rev. Charles Pelly, a former rector of Killybegs, County Donegal, and retired chaplain of Madras Ecclesiastical Establishment. He was 42 and related to Lieutenant-Colonel R. T. Pelly, commander of the 8th Royal Irish Rifles. *(Pier and Face 15A and 15B)*

Lieutenant John Pollock, of the 13th Royal Irish Rifles, was educated at Coleraine Academical Institution and Royal School, Armagh. He worked with his father in the firm of Lyle and Pollock, Dunbar Street, Belfast, and lived at The Priory, Marino, County Down. Regarded as one of the best golfers in the country, the 23-year-old had been a member of Holywood Golf Club and played for the North of Ireland Cricket Club. Lieutenant Pollock, who had formerly been in the U.V.F., was commissioned in October, 1914. *(Pier and Face 15A and 15B)*

Corporal Joseph Quinn, 8th Royal Inniskilling Fusiliers, had previously served during the Boer War in South Africa. From Washingford Road, Dungannon, County Tyrone, he had been awarded the Military Medal just three weeks before his death on September 6, 1916, for rescuing wounded comrades under heavy rifle and shell fire. *(Pier and Face 4D and 5B)*

Second Lieutenant William Turner Richardson, on attachment to the 103rd Machine Gun Corps, had formerly served with the 12th Royal Irish Rifles. He was reportedly shot through the head as he climbed out of the British trenches at the start of the assault. From Raheny, County Dublin, he had been a well-known sportsman before the war, playing golf, tennis and taking part in athletics events as a sprinter, as well as being a prominent member of the Old Wesley Football Club. He had worked for the Midland Great Western Railway. *(Pier and Face 15A and 15B)*

Captain John Ritty, 7th Royal Inniskilling Fusiliers, was the son of former **Royal Navy Lieutenant John Ritty** and wife Jenny, of Harbour View, Sligo. He had been awarded the Military Cross in June, 1916, for conspicuous gallantry, but was killed on September 9 that year. He was 22 years old. His family later moved to Lee-on-the-Solent, Hants., naming their new home "The Somme". *(Pier and Face 4D and 5B)*

Captain Maxwell Alexander Robertson, of the 10th Royal Inniskilling Fusiliers, was 42 years old and had been working as a barrister in London where he was also editor of a law journal. His mother was from Limavady. He was being helped back to his own lines by two junior officers after being wounded when a shell exploded above them, striking down all three. *(Pier and Face 4D and 5B)*

Private Herbert John Rogan, 6th Black Watch, was part of a Lewis gun section when killed on July 31, 1916. A son of former R.I.C. Sergeant John Rogan, who had been based in Monaghan, the 23-year-old lived at Victoria Terrace, off the Cregagh Road, Belfast. He had just completed his apprenticeship in the linen business with Bedford Street Weaving Company when the war started. *(Pier and Face 10A)*

Captain John Forrest Ruttledge, 2nd West Yorkshire Regiment (Prince of Wales's Own), was the eldest son of the Rev. L. W. Ruttledge, rector of Derryvullen, County Fermanagh, and Lifford, County Donegal. Born at Tamlaght in 1882, he had previously served in the old Donegal Artillery Miltia and the Royal Garrison Artillery. He had been ranching in Argentina when war broke out and returned home to serve. *(Pier and Face 2A, 2C and 2D)*

Second Lieutenant Hugh Alexander Small, from Keady, County Armagh, died on July 10, 1916, while serving with the 20th King's (Liverpool) Regiment. The 25-year-old had been awarded the Military Cross five weeks earlier following which he had been allowed home on leave. He was an only son. *(Pier and Face 1D, 8B and 8C)*

Captain William Alan Smiles was the fourth son of William Holmes Smiles, of Strandtown, Belfast. The 34-year-old solicitor was an active fundraiser for the Ulster Hospital for Children and Women in Templemore Avenue, Belfast. He received a commission in the 9th Royal Irish Rifles, was later transferred to the 17th battalion at Ballykinlar, County Down, and returned to the front in March, 1916, with the 2nd Rifles. *(Pier and Face 15A and 15B)*

Some of the Connaught Rangers dead remembered on the memorial walls

Lieutenant John Pollock, of the 13th Rifles, was considered one of the best golfers in Ireland

Courtesy of Lester Morrow

Captain William Haughton Smyth, 37, had been a director of the Banbridge, County Down, firm of William Smyth and Company, and a prominent member of the Unitarian Church before joining the 13th Royal Irish Rifles. *(Pier and Face 15A and 15B)*

Second Lieutenant Leonard William Hugh Stevenson, of the 9th Royal Inniskilling Fusiliers, was the youngest son of Isaac Stevenson, Hampstead Hall, Londonderry. He had been awarded the Military Cross shortly before his death on the opening day of the Somme battle. He died during the taking of the German second line. *(Pier and Face 4D and 5B)*

Lance Corporal William Stringer was just 18 and the eldest son of Thomas and Mary Stringer, of Milford, County Armagh. He had worked for McCrum's factory in his home village and had been a member of the local U.V.F. unit. He was serving in the machine-gun section of the 9th Royal Irish Fusiliers when killed. An officer, writing to the family, recorded: "There seems fairly conclusive evidence that Stringer behaved most magnificently. He got as far as the German wire and got his gun alone into action but the Boches apparently concentrated machine guns on him and he could hardly have survived many minutes. Considering the terrific fire of the Boche machine guns and artillery, which so few of our men survived, his performance was absolutely magnificent. He must have known it meant certain death and yet he evidently never hesitated a moment." *(Pier and Face 15A)*

Captain Lancelot Joseph Moore Studholme, of the 7th Leinster Regiment, was 31 when killed on September 9, 1916. From Ballyeighan, Birr, King's County, he was on his mother's side the grand nephew of Irish patriot Thomas Davis.

At the outbreak of war Captain Studholme, a justice of the peace and former High Sheriff of King's County, enlisted in the Leinster Regiment as a private until commissioned. He was reportedly killed attempting to rescue one of the workers from his estate who had joined up with him and was lying wounded in No-Man's-Land. *(Pier and Face 16C)*

Captain Charles Bernard Tate, 15th Royal Irish Rifles, was 27 when killed on July 1, 1916. His father John lived at Rantalard, Whitehouse, and was a well-known member of Belfast Rural District Council. Captain Tate, who had formerly worked for Richardson Sons and Owden Ltd., had been badly wounded in the shoulder at the third German line and had to be abandoned as his comrades were forced back. *(Pier and Face 15A and 15B)*

Corporal William Nathaniel Thom had been a national school teacher in Cookstown, County Tyrone, before taking up a management position in a factory. He was a son of Margaret Thom, of Donore Terrace, South Circular Road, Dublin, and aged 27 when killed while serving with the 9th Royal Inniskilling Fusiliers. *(Pier and Face 4D and 5B)*

Captain Alfred Maurice Thomson, of the Royal Army Medical Corps, was attached to the 7th Royal Sussex Regiment when killed on July 7, 1916. Although born in Brussels, Belgium, he was the only son of Alfred Thompson, of Marlborough Park, Belfast, and had been educated at the Royal Belfast Academical Institution and Queen's University. The 30-year-old had stopped to attend the wounds of the battalion adjutant, some 80 yards in front of his own lines, and then used a waterproof sheet to drag him back to within a few feet of the trenches only to be fatally wounded by shrapnel. *(Pier and Face 4C)*

Second Lieutenant Richard William Topp, of the 6th Royal Inniskilling Fusiliers but attached to the 11th, was last seen alive but wounded in a German trench on July 1, 1916. He was the eldest son of Richard and Emily Topp of Newry, County Down, though the 18-year-old lieutenant had been living in Omagh, County Tyrone, at the time he joined up. *(Pier and Face 4D and 5B)*

Private Frederick Charles Trench served in the 1st/14th London Regiment (London Scottish) under the name of Bloomfield. He was the younger son of the late Henry Bloomfield Trench, of Huntington, Portarlington, King's County. He had lived at Greystone Hall, Limavady, which had belonged to his wife's family, she being Catherine Lecky, the only child of Sir Thomas Lecky. Private Trench had saw active service in South Africa with the Royal Inniskilling Fusiliers and along with **Captain Claude Proctor** (killed the same day, July 1, 1916, and buried at the nearby Mill Road Cemetery), founded the U.V.F. in Limavady. He was reportedly killed close to the German barbed wire. *(Pier and Face 9C and 13C)*

Second Lieutenant Thomas White, 2nd Loyal North Lancashire Regiment, attached 8th battalion, was educated at the Royal Belfast Academical Institution and lived at Winston Gardens, Knock, before going to London to work. He died on July 8, 1916. *(Pier and Face 11A)*

Second Lieutenant James Alfred Williams, 3rd Royal Irish Rifles attached to the 7th battalion, was just 18 when he died and the youngest son of James Williams, Northland Road, Londonderry. Educated at Foyle College, he had been a medical student at Edinburgh University at the outbreak of war. Initially he enlisted with the Royal Scots and was in Dublin during the Easter Rising. Second Lieutenant Williams was one of four brothers serving, two also with the Rifles and one in the Royal Inniskilling Fusiliers. One of these, **Captain Charles Beasley Williams**, 20, was killed in August, 1915. He was serving with the 2nd Rifles and

An historical group, dressed as First World War soldiers, taking part in a July 1 ceremony at the Thiepval Memorial.

had been a divinity student at Trinity College, Dublin, before the war. His name appears on the Menin Gate in Ypres, Belgium. *(Pier and Face 15A and 15B)*

Rifleman David Williamson, 14th Royal Irish Rifles, was 26 when killed on July 1, 1916. Lieutenant S. H. Monard, writing to David's father at Market Street, Tandragee, County Armagh, said: "During the battle he never left my side, and he was with me in the fourth line of the German defences. We were the only two of the battalion to get to the fourth line. Here we met a party of six Germans, who pretended to surrender. One of them, however, had a bomb and was making to throw it at us when Davy shot him dead. The others commenced to run, but we shot them all except one and a bayonet thrust from Davy accounted for him. Our troops had all retired, so we made our way back to the third line, and joined our company again. We stayed in that line six hours under heavy shell fire, and Davy was cracking jokes with everybody and was very cool and happy. Towards dusk a strong counter-attack by the enemy made it necessary to fall back to a stronger position, and a rearguard of a few men kept up a heavy fire on the enemy to cover the retirement of our troops. Davy was one of this rearguard and, while exposing himself to get a better view of the enemy, a bullet went through his head, and he died instantaneously. You have every reason to be eternally proud of your son." *(Pier and Face 15A and 15B)*

Captain Samuel Willis was 43 years old and serving with the 14th Royal Irish Rifles. From Mountcharles, County Donegal, he had been on the teaching staff at Coleraine Academical Institution in 1914. His widow, Mary Christine Willis, later moved from the family home in Adelaide Avenue, Coleraine, to Lyncrest, on the Coleraine Road, Portrush. *(Pier and Face 15A and 15B)*

Captain Alexander Allen Wright, of the 1st/4th The King's Own (Royal Lancaster

Lieutenant Matthew Wright was killed on the eve of battle by a German shell in Thiepval Wood. His family later erected their own headstone – now in the Ulster Tower for safe keeping – at the site

Courtesy of Lester Morrow

Regiment) was killed on August 6, 1916. The former Collegians rugby player had been educated at the Ulster Provincial School in Lisburn, regularly attended St. Paul's Church on York Road, Belfast, and had worked in the Audit Office of Belfast's City Hall before the war. His father, Joseph S. Wright, also worked for Belfast Corporation in the Rates Department. *(Pier and Face 5D and 12B)*

Second Lieutenant Matthew J. Wright, of the 14th Royal Irish Rifles, was one of three sons of the Rev. Dr. William Wright, a Newtownards clergyman, to join the Colours. A former employee of James P. Corry Ltd., in Belfast, he had been injured in May, 1916, in an accident while acting as an instructor in a bomb throwing school. Sent home to recuperate, the 28-year-old refused an offer to extend his leave so he could return to "the boys". He was killed while still in Thiepval Wood and his family later erected a stone memorial in his memory near the spot where he fell. It can still be seen today in the Ulster Tower. *(Pier and Face 15A and 15B)*

The ornate gateway and impressive frontage of the Pozieres Memorial to the Missing stands on a busy road yet inside, enclosed by its panelled walls, it is tranquil. It commemorates close to 15,000 men who died in the latter part of the war, and particularly during the German offensives of March-April, 1918, and the subsequent Allied march to victory

POZIERES MEMORIAL

What matter though the wily Hun
With bomb, and gas and many a gun
In futile fury, lashes out,
Don't wonder what it's all about – "Stick it"

From "The B.E.F. Times"
(a successor to the Wipers Times)
on the eve of the German assault of March, 1918

The Pozieres Memorial to the Missing stands as a tribute to the 14,644 men of the Fifth Army who died during the German offensive of 1918 and later Allied counterattacks but who have no known graves. Much smaller than the memorial to the missing at Thiepval, it was designed by W. H. Cowlishaw to allow the visitor to view the panels more comfortably. It is situated four miles east of Albert, on the main road to Pozieres. Along its inner walls at the sides and back are the stone tablets bearing the names of the dead grouped by regiments. The walls enclose Pozieres British Cemetery, which holds more than 2,700 graves, the majority of which were added after the war. The village from which it takes its name was attacked on July 23, 1916, by the 1st Australian and 48th divisions and secured the following day. It was lost again in the German attacks of March, 1918, and was not to return to Allied hands until August 24.

Among those recorded as having served with the Royal Irish Rifles is Lieutenant Richard Brereton Marriott-Watson, of the 2nd battalion, who is best remembered for his poem Kismet. A holder of the Military Cross, he was leading a party of men round the enemy-held village of Cugny when challenged. Cyril Falls records: "Lieutenant R. B. Marriott-Watson, M.C., called out a reassuring answer in German, and quietly approached. There was a short and bloody scuffle in the darkness, and the Germans were bayoneted." The following morning, March 24, 1918, the lieutenant was killed as his company manoeuvred in a bid to prevent the Germans

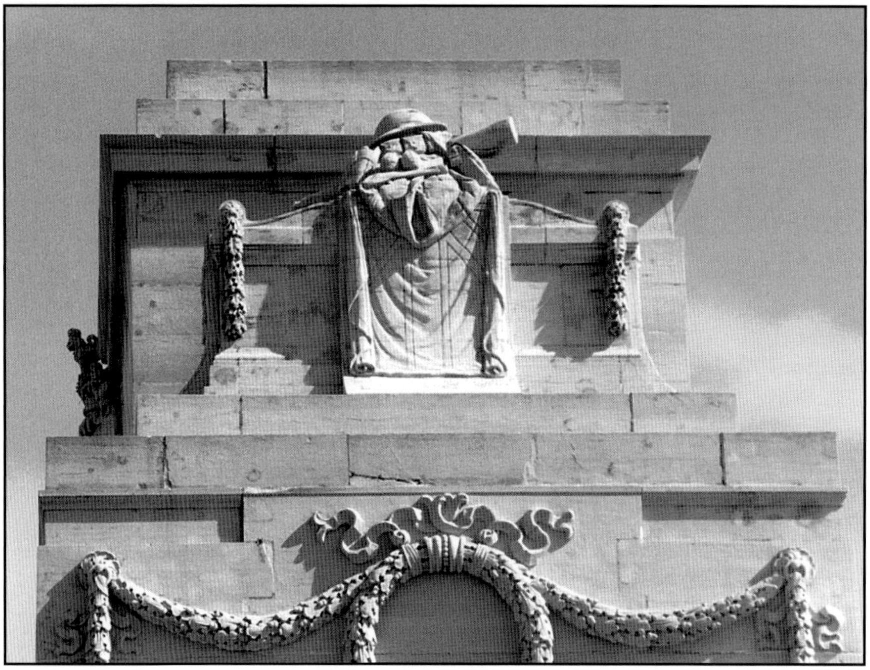

Some of the beautifully sculptured stone work on the Pozieres Memorial

pushing beyond Cugny. The name of the Rifles' Victoria Cross winner Second Lieutenant Edmund De Wind, of the 15th battalion, killed three days earlier on March 21, 1918, is similarly recorded on the memorial walls.
As with the Thiepval Memorial, the names listed below are but a small proportion of the thousands of lives whose loss is recorded at Pozieres. Details of Pozieres British Cemetery are included in the next section.

Captain Hugh Montgomery Baillie, 16th Royal Irish Rifles, was from Ellerslie, Ravenhill Road, Belfast. He was killed on March 21, 1918. He had joined up in 1914, leaving his job as an apprentice in the legal firm of Carson and McDowell, Royal Avenue, Belfast. His brother, Lieutenant R. Baillie, also of the Rifles, was wounded in 1916. *(Panel 74-76)*

Captain Arthur Cyril Bateman was from Kingstown, County Dublin. A member of the Royal Army Medical Corps, he was on attachment to the 7th Cameron Highlanders in March, 1918, and died as he retired in the face of the German onslaught on the 28th of that month. The 27-year-old, previously awarded a Military Cross for his courage, was initially reported missing. His colonel, writing to the family, reported: "Captain Bateman manfully stuck to his post until the Germans were within a few yards of him, when he started to retire along with his orderlies. Unfortunately he was hit, and fell into the hands of the enemy. I feel his loss very much. He was one of the best of fellows, and it will be difficult for any other M.O. to fill his place." *(Panel 95)*

Second Lieutenant Richard Gardiner Brewster was commissioned into the South Irish Horse. The cavalry officer later formed part of the 7th (S.I.H.) Royal Irish Regiment, created by the merging of two units. He was 25 when reported missing on March 21, 1918, and was later determined to have died on that date by the War Office though his body was never found. His family home had been at Audenville, on the Iona Road, Glasnevin, Dublin. (Panel 6)

Among the names inscribed on the memorial panels is that of Second Lieutenant Edmund de Wind, who won the Victoria Cross attempting to hold back the German assaults of March 21, 1918

Captain John Brown, 8th Royal Irish Rifles attached to the 1st battalion, was 23 years old when killed on March 21, 1918. The holder of a Military Cross and bar, he had proved himself a hero both at home and abroad. He won his medal for an action at the opening of the Battle of the Somme in July, 1916, during which he was wounded. While back in his native Belfast recuperating in September, 1916, he had shown his courage again when he saved someone from drowning, for which he was awarded the Royal Humane Society's Bronze Medal and certificate. He returned to the trenches, winning the bar to his M.C. in 1917. In civilian life he had worked for Messrs. Richardson, Sons and Owden Ltd. as a linen warehouseman. His father, Samuel S. Brown, was the Assistant Postmaster of Belfast and lived at Ailsa Terrace, Strandtown. *(Panel 74-76)*

Second Lieutenant Tomas Laurence Cahill enlisted in the Irish Guards in January 1915, serving with the 2nd battalion. He was wounded exactly a year later, in the opening month of 1916. Commissioned into the 8th Royal Dublin Fusiliers in 1917, by which time he was already the holder of a Military Medal, he was on attachment to the 1st battalion when killed on March 26, 1918. The family home was on Poplar Square, Naas, County Kildare. *(Panel 79 and 80)*

Captain John Leslie Chalmers was 27 when killed on March 27, 1918. His family had Scottish connections though he was living in Ceylon and working as a planter when the war started. He returned home to secure a commission. He was initially with the 10th (Irish) Division and took part in the landing at Suvla Bay and storming of Chocolate Hill, where he was wounded. On recovery he was posted to France and during the Somme offensives of 1916 he was again injured. The then Second Lieutenant Chalmers won the Military Cross for his actions at Cambrai in November, 1917. He was with the 1st Royal Irish Fusiliers, on attachment from the 5th battalion, when killed. *(Panel 76 and 77)*

Second Lieutenant Thomas Lipton Clements had worked in the Banbridge, County Down, branch of the Ulster Bank before the war. He was killed on March 23, 1918, while serving with the 9th Royal Inniskilling Fusiliers, on attachment from the 11th battalion. His father, David, was a Justice of the Peace and lived at Wesley Lodge, on the Dublin Road, Omagh, County Tyrone, while one brother was an officer in the United States army and two others were serving in the Royal Navy. *(Panel 38-40)*

Lieutenant Thomas Patrick Craig, 7th Royal Leinster Regiment, was killed on March 22, 1918. He was the only son of Samuel Craig, of Liscolman, Dervock, County Antrim, and a nephew of Judge J. Walker Craig, the Recorder of Belfast. The 27-year-old had passed through Dublin University O.T.C. *(Panel 78)*

Captain Thomas Horsfall Crofton, attached to the 6th Connaught Rangers from the 3rd battalion, was 28 when killed on March 21, 1918. He was the son of Sir Malby and Lady Crofton, of Longford House, Ballisodare, County Sligo. *(Panel 77)*

Lieutenant William Leonard Price Dobbin, 20, was the holder of the Military Cross. He had been born in Victoria, Australia, but had been living in Ireland where his father, Major William Dobbin, was governor of the borstal at Clonmel. Lieutenant Dobbin was serving with the Royal Irish Rifles when killed (along with **Lieutenant Gilbert Edwin Lynch**, on attachment to the Rifles from the Durham Light Infantry and also commemorated on the Pozieres Memorial) on the evening of March 21, 1918, leading D Company in an attack against vastly superior numbers in the village of Contescourt. His family later moved to Dunmurry, on the outskirts of Belfast. *(Panel 74-76)*

Lieutenant Gilbert Donnelly had been gazetted from Queen's University O.T.C. to the 1st Royal Munster Fusiliers. The 20-year-old's father, John, was superintendent of Postal telegraphs at the General Post Office in Belfast and lived at Glastonbury Avenue in the city. *(Panel 78-79)*

Second Lieutenant Robert Wallace Gilmour, of the 9th Royal Inniskilling Fusiliers, was killed in action on March 21, 1918. The former Ulster Bank employee, formerly employed at the Baggot Street branch in Dublin, was from the Diamond, Coleraine, County Londonderry. *(Panel 38-40)*

Second Lieutenant Percy Harold Green, 9th Royal Inniskilling Fusiliers, was the eldest son of Herbert Green, a Customs and Excise officer who lived with his wife Jessie at Limehurst, Holland Park, Knock, Belfast. The former Methodist College pupil had been working for Messrs. James Ireland and Co., woollen manufacturers based in May Street, Belfast, when the war started. He had initially joined the 20th (Public Schools Battalion) Royal Fusiliers in September, 1914, but had been wounded at Mametz Wood in July, 1916. After recovering he attended cadet school at Newmarket in England, being gazetted to the Inniskillings in August, 1917. (His posting coincided with the death of his brother, **Second Lieutenant Arthur Vivian Green**, a former Methodist College and Belfast Institutional College pupil, who was killed on August 17, 1917, while serving with the Royal Dublin Fusiliers. His body was never found and his name is recorded on the Tyne Cot Memorial in Belgium.) Second Lieutenant Green was killed in the fighting of March 26, 1918. *(Panel 38-40)*

Captain John Forsyth Harvey, of Inverary, Downshire Road, Cregagh, Belfast, was 24 when killed with the 9th Royal Inniskilling Fusiliers on March 23, 1918. Prior to the war he had worked for Messrs. Richardson, Sons and Owden Ltd. in the damask department of their Donegall Square North premises in Belfast city centre. He initially enlisted but was granted a commission in July, 1916, and had been commanding his own company since August, 1917. *(Panel 38-40)*

Second Lieutenant Arthur Oswald Houston was killed on March 26, 1918. The 26-year-old clerk with the Upperlands, County Londonderry, firm of Wm. Clark and Sons, had volunteered as a private with the Royal Inniskilling Fusiliers and was a corporal when commissioned into the 9th battalion of the regiment. He had lived at Summerhill, Maghera, County Londonderry. *(Panel 38-40)*

Lieutenant James Kerr, of the 1st Royal Irish Rifles, was killed on March 21, 1918 – a year and a day after the death of his brother, **Private Jack Kerr**, of the 21st battalion of the Australian Imperial Forces. Neither body was found, with James mentioned at Pozieres and John at Villers-Bretonneux Memorial, also on the Somme. Their father was Frank Kerr, of Altafort, Myrtlefield Park in Belfast, a well-known solicitor of his day with offices in both Belfast and Dublin. *(Panel 74-76)*

Lieutenant W. S. Kidd, of the 2nd Royal Munster Fusiliers, was initially posted as "wounded and missing" but had actually died on March 21, 1918, the first day of the German assault. He was the youngest of three officer brothers, with one, Major G. M. Kidd, M.C., serving in Palestine and the other, Captain J. A. C. Kidd in the Royal Army Medical Corps. Their father was the late Dr. F. W. Kidd, of Dublin. *(Panel 78-79)*

Sergeant Andrew Kinsella, wounded at the Battle of the Somme in 1916 and pictured with a friend while he was recuperating, was killed by a sniper near Epehy on March 29, 1918

Courtesy of the Royal Dublin Fusiliers Association

Sergeant Andrew Kinsella served with both the 8th and 1st battalions of the Royal Dublin Fusiliers. The former postman had lived with his wife, Mary, at Ivar Street, off Oxmantown Road, Dublin, before the war. He enlisted with the 8th Dubs in 1914, and arrived in France just before Christmas the following year. Sergeant Kinsella was wounded at Ginchy in September, 1916, and transferred to the 1st Royal Dublin Fusiliers on his recovery. The 36-year-old was killed by a German sniper near Epehy on Good Friday, March 29, 1918. In addition to a widow, he left six children without a father. *(Panel 79-80)*

Lieutenant Gilbert Edwin Lynch was originally with the 7th Durham Light Infantry before joining the Royal Irish Regiment, being a member of the 7th (South Irish Horse) battalion. The 27-year-old Englishman was killed leading a company of the 2nd battalion in an attack on the village of Contescourt on the evening of March 21, 1918, from which barely 40 men survived to withdraw. *(Panel 68-72)*

Second Lieutenant Dalton Prenter, left, spent 16 months in the ranks before being commissioned

Lieutenant Gilbert Donnelly, centre, joined the Munsters from Queen's University O.T.C.

Lieutenant Arthur Star, right, was a Trinity College graduate

Second Lieutenant Anderdon McFarran was attached to the 2nd Royal Irish Rifles from the 5th battalion when killed on March 21, 1918, at the age of 20. He was already the holder of the Military Cross and, as the battalion intelligence officer, had gone forward at 10am on the day of his death to reconnoitre the German advance. He was killed near Grugies, in the Forward Zone. His father was a major in the Royal Engineers. *(Panel 74-76)*

Captain Thomas Edward Morton had formerly served in the South Irish Horse before its merger into the 7th (S.I.H.) Royal Irish Regiment. The eldest son of Thomas Morton, of Drogheda, he had been living at Blackrock, County Dublin before the war. He died of wounds received on March 26, 1918. *(Panel 6)*

Lieutenant Paul O'Kane, of the 1st Royal Irish Rifles, was from Ballycastle, County Antrim, though had an address in Belfast. His father was a journalist living in the city. He was commissioned into the 4th Royal Irish Rifles in 1915 and was sent to the front the following year. At the time of his death the 23-year-old had been attached to the 107th Trench Mortar Battery. He died of wounds in a field ambulance on March 21, 1918. *(Panel 74 to 76)*

Lieutenant Samuel William Palmer had previously been serving with the 10th Royal Dublin Fusiliers but was technically on attachment to the 19th home-based battalion when killed on the Somme on March 27, 1918. The 21-year-old was the third son of David Palmer of Tandragee, County Armagh, and before the war had been working in the National Health Insurance Office. A brother, **Captain David Adam Palmer**, was killed just two days later (see Buried In A Distant Grave, pages 194-195) *(Panel 79 and 80)*

Second Lieutenant Dalton Prenter, 9th (North Irish Horse) Royal Irish Fusiliers, was killed in action on March 21, 1918. The 27-year-old Belfast man, whose family lived at Fitzroy Avenue in the city, had joined the 14th Royal Irish Rifles in September, 1914, and had completed 16 months in the ranks before being commissioned. He had worked for Messrs. Moore and Weinberg, Linenhall Street, Belfast, before the war. Second Lieutenant Prenter's brother Thomas served with the Canadian forces. *(Panel 76-77)*

Lieutenant Marcus Ralph Russell was an only son of William and Caroline Russell of Mount Temple, Moate, County Westmeath. He was 29 and serving with the 8th (King's Royal Irish) Hussars, to which he had been attached from the cavalry reserve, when killed on March 22, 1918. His widow, Margaret, lived at Newell, Sherborne, Dorset in England. *(Panel 6)*

Lieutenant Arthur James Starr was on attachment to the 9th Royal Inniskilling Fusiliers from the 11th battalion when killed on March 22, 1918. The 25-year-old was the youngest son of William and Jane Starr, Newtownhamilton, County Armagh. A past pupil of Drogheda Grammar School, he was an undergraduate of Trinity College and was commissioned in August, 1915, after attending Dublin University Officers' Training Corps. *(Panel 38-40)*

Second Lieutenant John Crawford Thompson, of the 5th Royal Irish Rifles but attached to the 1st battalion, was the only son of James Thompson, of Gayerville, Chlorine Gardens, Belfast. He was killed on March 21, 1918. His captain, writing to the family, said: "No more gallant or splendid boy has ever given his life for his country. Pluckiest of the plucky, although quiet and calm, he literally did not know what fear was." Born in the Shankill area, he had attended Wesley College, Dublin, and Methodist College, Belfast, playing rugby for the Medallion XV at the latter in 1912. He had been working as an agent for woollen manufacturers James Ireland & Co., May Street, Belfast. *(Panel 74-76)*

Corporal Bernard Ward, of the 2nd Royal Dublin Fusiliers, had been employed in the Accounts Department of the Guinness brewery in Dublin before the war. *(Panel 79-80)*

Lieutenant Fred William Wilson was 24 when killed on March 25, 1918, while serving with the 9th Royal Inniskilling Fusiliers. From Belmore Street, Enniskillen, County Fermanagh, he had worked in the manager's office of the Sligo, Leitrim and Northern Counties Railway. (Panel 38-40)

A cross of sacrifice stands in all Commonwealth War Graves Commission cemeteries on the Western Front

BURIED IN A DISTANT GRAVE

Though buried in a distant grave,
Amidst the shot and shell,
For Country's sake his life he gave,
He stood his trial well.

Who could have dealt that horrid blow,
On one we loved so well?
We never knew the pain he bore,
No mortal tongue can tell.

No matter how we think of him –
His name we oft recall –
There is nothing left to answer,
But the photo on the wall.

From a memorial card to Private Thomas Marcus,
Royal Inniskilling Fusiliers, killed July 1, 1916

It is a tradition in the British army to bury war dead as close as possible to where they fell, a policy which was reinforced during the First World War by the government's decision to forbid those who could afford it bringing the bodies of loved ones home. The static nature of the fighting meant, therefore, that countless cemeteries grew up within a few miles of the front line, while others were clustered around the field hospitals and medical centres which stretched as far back as the French coast. After the war most of the smaller plots were concentrated into larger sites in the immediate area, the land given over in perpetuity by the French. This process reduced to 410 the number of Commonwealth War Graves Commission cemeteries in the Somme department, of which close to 250 are sited on the 1916 battlefield. Some hold the remains of thousands of the fallen, and others barely a few dozen comrades. By comparison, the French, which held this sector up until the middle of 1915, have just 19 cemeteries on the Somme, all huge and often placed on main thoroughfares. Perhaps understandably, the French were disinclined to be generous in the allocation of plots to their enemy. Just 14 German cemeteries are in the region, with the shortage of space necessitating four or more bodies being buried per cross and most interred in mass graves. Today, the cemeteries are the most poignant, and visible, sign that remains of the tragedy played out during the Great War.

It was official policy to treat all the war dead equally, but the war wasn't equitable

The soldier sons of the Love family. Top: Walter, Samuel, Thomas, Joseph; bottom, Robert, David, George and John

Courtesy of the Down County Museum

in sharing out the suffering. While grateful families were relieved to get their sons and husbands back home, though often scarred physically and emotionally, at the end of the hostilities, others bore a heavier burden. It is not unusual to find sets of brothers and cousins among the casualties, some dying side-by-side such as the Hobbs boys (see Thiepval Memorial) and others spread across campaigns and even countries, like the loss endured by the Lynn family (see Auchonvillers Military Cemetery below). The Love family sent eight sons off to war. Three didn't return at all, of which two lie on the Somme, and a fourth came home so badly injured that he died six months after the Armistice: Sapper Samuel Love, 26th Field Company Royal Engineers was killed on April 8, 1916, at the age of 23 and is buried at St. Patrick's Cemetery, Loos; Sergeant John Love was 30 when killed on July 1, 1916, with the 13th Royal Irish Rifles. His body was never found and his name is recorded on the Thiepval Memorial (Pier and Face 15A and 15B); Sergeant George Love, who had been serving with the 2nd Royal Irish Rifles at the outbreak of war, died on September 30, 1916. The 34-year-old is buried at Puchevillers British Cemetery, some 13 miles north-east of Amiens on the Somme; Sergeant William Love, of 1st Royal Irish Rifles, was severely wounded at Neuve Chapelle early in the war. He was ultimately brought home to Scotch Street in Downpatrick, County Down, but died on May 10, 1919, and is buried in Down Cathedral New Cemetery.

Bangor man Alex Angus lost all three of his sons within weeks of each other in 1916, with none of their bodies recovered: his youngest boy, Blair, died on July 1 with the 13th Royal Irish Rifles, and is commemorated on the Thiepval Memorial along with his 23-year-old brother Robert, killed eight days later with the 2nd Royal Scots, while his remaining son, James, was killed in September with the 29th Canadian Infantry, with his name recorded on the Vimy Memorial; Frank Skelton, who had been a prominent U.V.F. member before the war, was sent home to Clones to die, having been severely wounded while serving with the 9th Royal Irish Fusiliers. He passed away on June 8, 1916, and is buried at St. Tighernach Church of Ireland in the border town. Three months later, his parents received word of the death of his brother, Private Gibson Fitzgerald Skelton of the 10th Canadian Infantry (Alberta Regiment), who was killed on September 12. He was laid to rest in Albert Communal Cemetery extension; John Orr, of Ballywhisken, Millisle, County Down, had five sons, a brother and three half-brothers in the services, of which three were killed: his son Andrew, serving with the Canadians, his brother Hugh, who was in the ranks of the Highland Light Infantry, and a half-brother Francis, with the Royal Irish Rifles; two of Belfast man Arthur Newell's three serving sons were already dead, one in July, 1915, and the second in March the following year, when he received word that his surviving boy had been wounded on the Somme on July 20, 1916. He recovered only to be killed in action in August, 1917; the widowed Mrs Hamill, of Finlay Street, Ligoniel, Belfast, lost two sons, one of whom, 21-year-old Rifleman Samuel George Hamill, of the 13th Royal Irish Rifles, lies in Doullens Communal Extension on the Somme. A third son was wounded; and brothers Joseph McCann, 19, of the 10th Royal Irish Rifles, and William, 5th Seaforth Highlanders, died a month apart on July 1 and August 2, 1916, respectively. Their parents lived at Ravenscroft Street in Belfast.

Behind each death lay a personal tragedy. Second Lieutenant Adam Clark Capper, attached to the 7th Royal Irish Rifles, was 23 when he was killed. A quirk of fate had saved him from the slaughter endured by the Ulster Division on July 1, 1916, but his own determination to see action sooner rather than later resulted in his death just over two months later. From the Malone Road in Belfast, he had attended the Royal Belfast Academical Institution and was working for his father's yarn business, based in the city's Brunswick Street, before the war. A member of the North of Ireland football club and Malone golf club, he was commissioned early into the 36th Division and worked in its recruiting office at the City Hall for three months. However, he caught measles just as the division was embarking for France and so was sent to the Army Service Corps School at Woolwich instead, later spending six months with the Transport Train of the South African Division at Borden. He applied and received a transfer to the 20th Royal Irish Rifles, being sent to the training camp in Newtownards in July, 1916, just days after the slaughter of his former colleagues on the Somme. He quickly secured his travel papers, allowing him to join the 7th Rifles of the 16th (Irish) Division in August and was killed on September 9, 1916. This young officer was buried nearby but his grave was lost in subsequent fighting and a special memorial at Delville Wood Cemetery marks his death; Captain P. A. C. Maginn, of the 18th London Regiment (London Irish Rifles) was killed on September 15, 1916. The 21-year-old had been wounded twice previously and was the holder of a Military Cross and bar, the latter for leading his platoon through a heavy barrage to relieve another battalion. He is buried at Flat Iron Copse Cemetery, Mametz.

The death of Second Lieutenant Richard Shaw Purdy turned his wife into a widow little more than a month after their wedding. The 25-year-old member of the 6th Royal Inniskilling Fusiliers was attached to the 8th battalion when killed on September 11, 1916. The only son of Belfast man Joseph Purdy, he had worked for Workman and Clark shipbuilders in the city before the war. On July 6, while home on leave, he married his sweetheart Annie Maud, from Bushmills, County Antrim, at St. Anne's Cathedral in Belfast and set up home on the Ormeau Road. He had been back at the front six weeks when killed in action. He is buried at Corbie Communal Cemetery Extension.

Many of those who joined up were driven by patriotic fervour, such as Gunner Harold Couser Simms, from Bridge Street in Banbridge, County Down. A civil engineer and architect by training, he was employed by the General Valuation Office in Belfast. In October, 1915, he was in the north of England working on the construction of a munitions factory when he took the decision to enlist in the 142nd Siege Battery of the Royal Garrison Artillery. He was killed on September 2, 1916, and is buried at Dive Copse British Cemetery, some 14 miles east of Amiens. Edward Percival Harpur returned with his family from Canada to join up. The son of a Methodist clergyman, the 25-year-old left his wife Eileen at Blackrock, County Dublin, before taking up a commission in the 7th Royal Irish Rifles. Lieutenant Harpur had already been wounded twice in the months leading up to his death and had only rejoined his battalion a week before being killed on September 11, 1916. He is buried at La Neuville British Cemetery, Corbie. Likewise, old soldier Captain Charles Stevenson Murray came home from South Africa, initially to enlist in the U.V.F. before returning to the Colours. The 44-year-old, who lies in Warloy-Baillon Cemetery, had formerly served in his father, Colonel Alexander Murray's Royal Irish Rifles battalion before settling in Matabeleland, where, as a member of the Matabele Mounted Police, he was awarded the Queen's and King's medals for service during the Boer War. His two brothers both served during the war, one in the 8th Rifles and the other with General Botha in German South West Africa. Major John Harold McErvel was another veteran. Educated at the Masonic Boys School, Dublin, and the Officer Training Corps, Queen's University, Belfast, he had served in the Royal Irish Fusiliers. He had returned to live at Eglantine Avenue, Belfast, after his initial service but was recalled to the Colours in 1914, initially with the 1st King's (Liverpool Regiment) then later attached to the Manchester Regiment. He had fought at Ypres, Neuve Chapelle, Richebourg, Loos and the Somme. The 32-year-old, who was engaged to be married, was killed on August 8, 1916, and is buried in Bernafay Wood British Cemetery, seven miles east of Albert. Another officer, Major Alfred Bellingham Cairnes, from Listoke, Drogheda, was an "old man" of 40 in 1916. The youngest son of Thomas Cairnes, from Stameen, County Louth, he was serving in the 7th Royal Irish Rifles having previously been a member of the defunct Louth Militia. He was killed on September 9, 1916, and is buried in the Guards Cemetery, Lesboeufs.

Major Cairnes' brother was the managing director of the Castlebellingham and Drogheda breweries and many of the officers killed were related to prominent figures in the business and political communities. Captain Oswald Brooke Webb, for example, was the son of Charles Webb, a justice of the peace and founder of the Old Bleach Linen Company at Randalstown, County Antrim, and a brother of W. H. Webb, a prominent member of the Ulster Unionist Council. The 37-year-old, who died on July 4, 1916, was serving with the 11th Royal Irish Rifles. He is buried at Warloy-Baillon Communal Cemetery Extension, about 14 miles north-east of Albert. His cousin, Captain Gilbert Watson Webb, a Campbell College old boy, had been wounded in May, 1915, while serving with the 2nd Rifles and had transferred to the Royal Flying Corps, returning to the front in May, 1916, only to be shot down on July 1; Second Lieutenant James Countney Laughlin, from University Street in Belfast, was killed on July 1, 1916, with the 20th King's (Liverpool Regiment). His father ran the firm of R. G. Laughlin and Sons in Skipper Street in the city, though he had been employed with another company in Anne Street. He passed through Queen's University Officer Training Corps and had been at the front three months. Another brother was serving with the 14th Royal Irish Rifles and a third with the 5th Lancashire Fusiliers; Second Lieutenant Robert Simmie Ross, King's Own Scottish Borderers, died on September 3, 1916. He had been educated at St Andrew's College, Dublin, and Campbell College, Belfast, after which he trained as a chartered accountant with the Belfast firm of Steward Blacker Quinn and Company. His father, George Ross, was manager of the Anglo-American Oil Company in the city. Second Lieutenant Ross, who had been a member of Knock Rugby Club and had played for the Ireland water polo team against Scotland, was in Calcutta, India, when the war started and returned home, living at North Road, Bloomfield, east Belfast, while waiting for his commission to come through. He had only been at the front 10 days when killed at the age of 25. He is buried at Delville Wood Cemetery.

War, of course, is no respecter of rank whether it is social, civil or military. Lieutenant Colonel Barry Lyons, of the 2nd Royal Munster Fusiliers, was mortally wounded as he inspected trenches recently won by the 16th Division on the Somme. Major A. W. Blockley reported of the Belfast man's death: "We had on the previous day taken over an advanced line of trenches in a recently won area, the sort of place where trenches as one usually finds them do not exist. Colonel Lyons, with his orderly, pushed forward into a small sap, and was looking over the parapet when he was shot through the head by a sniper who was concealed in a shell hole, the orderly says, not more than 15 yards in front." Colonel Lyons died on September 4, 1916, and is buried at Abbeville Communal Cemetery, close to where the River Somme enters the sea; Lieutenant-Colonel Alfred Durkan Murphy, of the 2nd Leinster Regiment, was killed on November 6, 1917. The 27-year-old, the son of Lieutenant-Colonel E. W. Murphy of Ballinamona, Cashel, County Tipperary, was the holder of a Distinguished Conduct Medal and Military Cross. He is buried in Roisel Communal Cemetery Extension on the Somme, some seven miles east of Peronne; Captain Mervyn Stronge Richardson, 1st Royal Welsh Fusiliers, was a member of an old Ulster family, being related through his mother to Colonel Sir James Stronge, of Tynan Abbey. Captain Richardson, who earlier had been mentioned in despatches, was killed on March 19, 1916,

Captain Oswald Brooke Webb, (grave pictured left) and Second Lieutenant James Countney Laughlin were both sons of prominent businessmen

Courtesy of the Somme Heritage Centre

Lieutenant-Colonel Alfred Durkan Murphy was commanding the 2nd Leinster Regiment when killed in November, 1917

while inspecting the barbed wire in front of his own lines at Fricourt. He is buried in Point 110 New Military Cemetery, Fricourt; Captain Michael Charles Lawrence, of the Coldstream Guards, was the son of General Sir Herbert Lawrence, London, and a grandson of Lord Lawrence, of Londonderry, who is credited with securing India for the Empire. He was killed, aged 21, on September 16, 1916, and is buried at Grove Town Cemetery, Meaulte, south of Albert; Second Lieutenant R. Nolan, attached to the 2nd Royal Irish Regiment, was one of three brothers serving from Cahir. He was 21 when killed on September 3, 1916, and is buried in Delville Wood Cemetery, Longeuval. Second Lieutenant Nolan's father, Walter, was the Clerk of the Crown and Peace for Tipperary.

The battles of 1918 condemned many more Irishmen to graves on the Somme, such as Private Reginald George Armstrong, a 20-year-old member of the North Irish Horse killed on March 26, 1918, reportedly while carrying out a reconnaissance mission to establish how close the Germans were to the retreating infantry. The eldest son of Charles Armstrong, of Beechfield House, Clontarf, Dublin, he was educated at St. Andrews College and had been a member of the 14th Boys' Brigade in the city. He had joined the N.I.H. on his 18th birthday in November, 1915, and shipped out to France in October, 1916. Private Armstrong is buried at Toutencourt Communal Cemetery, 12 miles south-east of Doullens; fellow cavalry man Lieutenant Richard Nigel Perceval-Maxwell, of the 16th (The Queen's) Lancers, was four years older at 24 when killed on March 30, 1918. He was the only son of Stephen and Mabel Perceval-Maxwell of Ballydugan House, Downpatrick, County Down, and Moore Hill, County Waterford. He lies in Moreuil Communal Cemetery Allied Extension, 12 miles south-east of Amiens.

Captain David Adam Palmer, formerly of the Royal Dublin Fusiliers, was serving with the recently formed 3rd Tank Corps when killed on March 25, 1918.

The holder of a Military Cross, won in 1916, he is buried at Dernancourt Communal Cemetery Extension, less than two miles south of Albert. He died two days after his brother, Lieutenant S. W. Palmer, whose name is recorded at Pozieres. The 25-year-old, from Tandragee, County Armagh, had been working in Dublin before the war. Fellow Dublin Fusilier Lieutenant Hebron Barrett, of the 10th battalion, was 25 when he died on March 27, 1918, the black-rimmed telegram arriving at the Dublin home of his parents, Robert and Jane Barrett, soon after. He is buried at Namps-au-Val British Cemetery, some 10 miles south-west of Amiens. Another lieutenant, P. L. Cahill, of the 4th Royal Munster Fusiliers, was a year younger at 24. Lieutenant Cahill had been in Canada when the war started and joined the cavalry there before being commissioned into the Munsters. Described by the Irish Times as a "man of fine physique" who excelled at sport, he was killed on March 21, 1918, and is buried at Epehy Wood Farm Cemetery, some 12 miles north-east of Peronne. His parents were Colonel John Nugent Cahill and Emily, of Ballyconra House, Ballyragget, County Kilkenny; Lieutenant Cecil John Kenny, 3rd Royal Irish Regiment, had been attached to the Machine Gun Corps after his recovery from a wound sustained in July, 1916. The 25-year-old son of Harry Brisco and Elizabeth, of Clyduffe House, Roscrea, County Tipperary, was killed on March 24, 1918, and buried at Ham British Cemetery, some 14 miles south-west of St. Quentin; Second Lieutenant William Andrew Wilkinson, of the Royal Inniskilling Fusiliers, died on the first day of the German offensive. The 30-year-old is buried at Templeux-le-Guerard British Cemetery, some 16 miles east of Peronne. He had been secretary of the Winnipeg Y.M.C.A. in Canada and worked with the organisation in Le Harve in France for a year before joining the ranks in 1916 while awaiting a commission. His parents lived at Creeslough, County Donegal.

Major John George Brew, of the 9th (North Irish Horse) Royal Irish Fusiliers suffered a lonely death. The 41-year-old was commanding his battalion on the retreat when he was taken prisoner along with a General Staff officer and his driver, both of whom were injured, and M. J. Furnell, who was in charge of the 1st battalion of the regiment, as they returned by car from seeing their brigadier. In a letter to Major Brew's widow, Annie, at her Portadown, County Armagh, home, in April, 1921, Furnell described what happened: "After being searched we were being marched back to the German headquarters by an escort, when some Germans who evidently mistook us for British troops opened fire on us; your husband was walking alongside me and was hit." After the confusion in the darkness subsided it was discovered that Major Brew had been shot through the lung but "it was impossible to move him without help from the Bosche which they refused to give and only beat us with the butts of their rifles when we asked them to move your husband. We moved him to the side of the road and made him as comfortable as possible, he couldn't speak much. The Bosche were trying to hurry us on all the time so didn't have much chance of doing anything and said goodbye to your husband and he was able to shake hands with me." Major Brew's body was later recovered and is buried at Roye New British Cemetery, some 28 miles south-east of Amiens.

Among the Irishmen killed serving with non-Irish regiments and units was Captain John Arnott, more commonly known as Punch, who was a member of the 15th (The King's) Hussars. The 32-year-old holder of the Military Cross was the son of Sir John Alexander Arnott of Merrion Square, Dublin, and had been educated at Eton and Cambridge University where he excelled as an athlete. At the outbreak of war he initially served on the General Staff but asked to be transferred to his old regiment, where he served as adjutant. He won his M.C. at the Second Battle of Ypres in May, 1915, and is buried at Fouilloy Communal Cemetery, 12 miles south of Albert; Captain Percival St. George Findlater, Army Service Corps, was reportedly killed by shell fire on March 28,

Major John George Brew suffered a lonely death. He is buried at Roye New British Cemetery

Courtesy of the Royal Irish Fusiliers Museum

1918. After attending St. Stephen's Green School and Harrow, he went on to graduate in engineering from Trinity College, Dublin. His father, Sir William Findlater, who predeceased him, had lived at Fitzwilliam Square, Dublin. Captain Findlater had spent much of the war on the French front, where he had earned mentions in despatches. He is buried at Mollines-au-Bois Communal Cemetery on the Somme; Second Lieutenant William James Knox Bell, of the 9th Siege Battery Royal Garrison Artillery, was 28 when killed on April 5, 1918. A holder of the Military Cross and an only son to parents James, an Inland Revenue Officer, and Fanny Jane who lived at Ashbrook, Coleraine, County Londonderry, he is buried at Bertrancourt Military Cemetery, just beyond the village of Mailly-Maillet. Major R. H. Clarke, in a letter to the family, said Second Lieutenant Bell had been killed early in the morning by a stray shell as he slept. "In him I had a really good and absolutely fearless officer and whom I have recommended for the work he did on March 21st." A former pupil of Coleraine Academical Institution, he had been working at the National Education Office in Dublin before the war. He enlisted initially as a motor cycle despatch rider and only sought a commission in 1916; Captain Ambrose Augustine Shearman, of the 2nd/7th London Regiment, was 26 when killed on April 20, 1918. The son of Johanna and Edward Shearman, of High Street, Kilkenny, he is buried at Picquigny British Cemetery, eight miles north-west of Amiens. Captain Shearman was educated at the Christian Brothers School, Kilkenny, and Rockwell College, before joining the National Bank where he worked at branches in Killarney and Baltinglass, County Wicklow.

Visitors to the Somme battlefields pass cemetery after cemetery, no matter which route they choose. Many of these will, undoubtedly, include Irish graves. What follows, therefore, is not an attempt to cover the entire range of cemeteries in the region. Instead, using the Ulster Tower as a central point (on the grounds that it is the most impressive and regularly visited of the Irish memorials on the Somme) I have described a selection of the cemeteries which, for the most part, lie within less than a 10 minute drive away. A few are further away and have been included for specific reasons – perhaps because they hold the body of the first soldier to die in a particular Irish unit, such as at Doullens, or better represent a significant phase in the fighting. I have included details on some of those who are buried at each of these locations but it is not, nor is it intended to be, exhaustive but rather is the starting point for a visit. A walk along the headstones, with the cemetery register in hand, will prove emotive and worthwhile. It is only by witnessing the rows upon rows of white headstones, by noting the ages of those who lie there, some of whom were little more than boys and others old enough to be grandfathers, and by reading the messages of love from those left behind, that the human cost can be appreciated in terms of individuals rather than military statistics.

(1) Serre Road Cemetery No.1

Started in the spring of 1917, the majority of the graves were added after the war. Of the 2,412 buried here, only three in every 10 can be identified by name. The cemetery is three miles north-east of the Ulster Tower and just outside the Somme department in Pas de Calais.

Only 10 of the dead from Irish regiments who lie in this cemetery are known by name, though more than three times that number could be identified as having served with Irish units. Undoubtedly there are many more within the ranks of the unknown.

As is often the case, the Royal Irish Rifles form the biggest group, with men from the 13th battalion killed on July 1, 1916, accounting for four of the regiment's five graves. The exception is Lance Corporal R. N. Leckey, who died on July 15, 1916, while technically still with the 5th Rifles, based at Palace Barracks, Holywood, County Down, at this time.

Private W. Ferguson, from Balleer, Tassagh, County Armagh, was just 17 when killed in action on July 1, 1916. He is one of three from the 9th Royal Irish Fusiliers buried here, his comrades being 21-year-old Private J. Lyness from Lurgan, County Armagh, and R. McCann, who likewise died on the opening day of the Battle of the Somme.

Michael O'Donovan, an 18-year-old Limerick private in the 7th Royal Inniskilling Fusiliers, part of the 16th (Irish) Division, was killed on September 6, 1916. He is the only member of his regiment known by name in this cemetery. Likewise, Private John Fagan, 29, from Knockdrin, Mullingar, County Westmeath, is the only representative of the Irish Guards. He died on September 16, 1916, while serving with the 2nd battalion.

Among those unknown by name are soldiers of the Royal Irish Regiment, Leinster Regiment and Royal Dublin Fusiliers.

(2) Serre Road Cemetery No.2

With an open frontage to the roadway, and climbing up a gradual incline, this cemetery is an impressive sight with its row upon row of headstones. It holds 7,139 graves, making it the largest cemetery on the Somme front. The vast majority of those buried here, 4,944, are unknown by name.

This cemetery was hugely expanded after the war, with some of the bodies brought long distances from where they had fallen. Almost 100 men serving with 10 different

LINES WRITTEN ON JAMES TATE,

WHO FELL IN HEROIC CHARGE OF THE ULSTER DIVISION, ON JULY THE FIRST, 1916.

When war's dread challenge first was heard
Throughout our Island home,
Our boys responded to the call,
And hastened o'er the foam :

To fight for King and Country,
A brave and noble band,
To crush out German cruelty
From out our peaceful land.

And one among those gallant lads—
Only a boy was he—
Left parents, all he held most dear,
To cross the bright blue sea.

Only a boy ; but O ! so brave,
His young heart knew no fear,
On that fatal July morning,
Though he knew that death was near.

He nobly did his duty,
'Mid the storm of shot and shell ;
In a hero's grave, "Somewhere in France,"
Sleeps him we loved so well.

He little thought when he left home
That he would ne'er return ;
But now he lies in that far-off land,
And we are left to mourn.

God knows best, and He alone
Can take away the pain
From the hearts he loved so dearly,
Though he'll ne'er see them again.

Some day we shall meet him,
In that happy home above,
When war's dread sound is heard no more,
Where all is peace and love.

LIZZIE SMYTH, Ballyminstra.

Writing to Mrs. Tate, under date 3rd October, 1916, the late Sergeant James Tate's platoon officer says :—

I have great pleasure in saying that your son was in my platoon for sixteen months. He was very much liked by his comrades. He was always anxious to do his duty, and was a most capable Sergeant. He was a first-class musketry instructor and a good shot. In the trenches he was exceptionally cool and seemed indifferent to danger. On the First of July he had his section over the parapet and was keen and eager in the attack. I was always glad to have him with me.

I can understand your feelings and sympathise with you, but pride in his sacrifice must be your consolation. With kindest regards.—Yours sincerely,

G. T. C. ARMSTRONG.

A printed memorial card for Sergeant James Tate, one of the 13th Royal Irish Rifles soldiers who lies in Serre Road Cemetery No.1

Courtesy of the Somme Heritage Centre

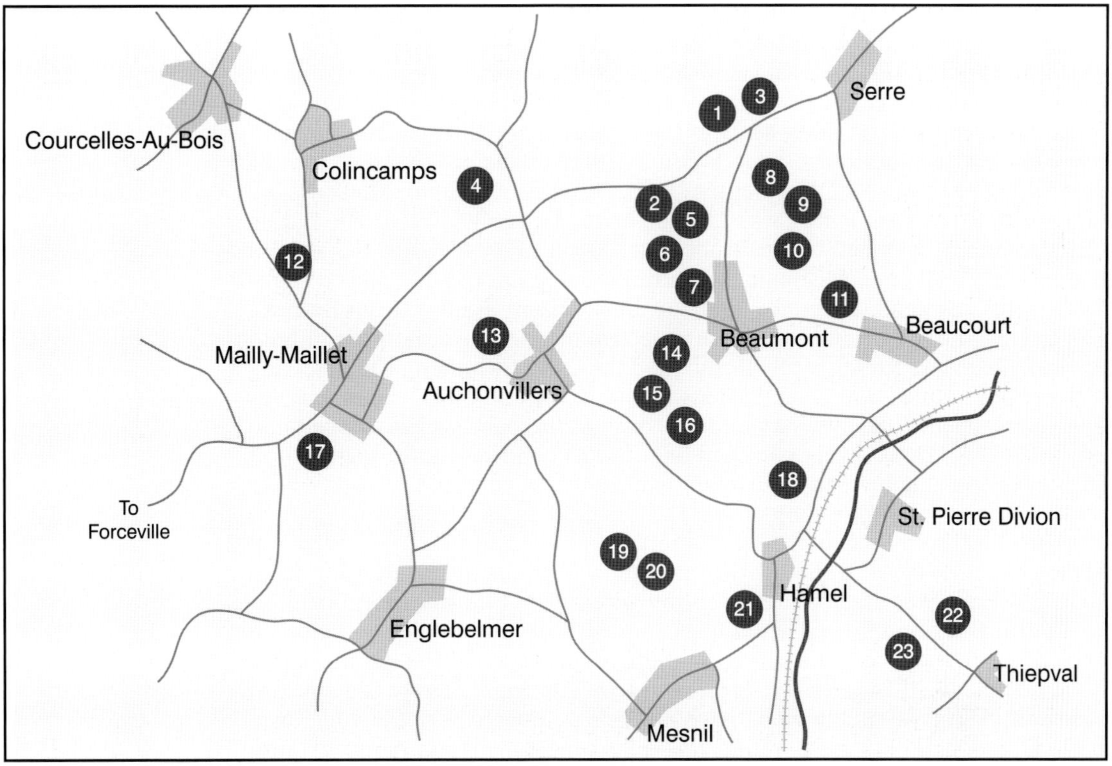

Irish regiments are known by name, with more than that number again having been identified as being in Irish units.

Captain James Samuel Davidson, of the 13th Royal Irish Rifles, was attached to 108th Machine Gun Corps when killed on July 1, 1916. The 39-year-old was the only surviving son of Samuel Clelland Davidson, of Seacourt, Bangor, founder and owner of the Sirocco engineering works in Belfast and an extremely wealthy man. Captain Davidson, a U.V.F. volunteer, had worked as general manager in his father's business before becoming a director. A keen yachtsman, tennis player and motorist, he was a member of the Ulster Club, Ulster Reform Club, Royal Ulster and Royal North of Ireland yacht clubs, and a governor of his old school, the Royal Belfast Academical Institution. He was injured in the enemy trenches and shot dead by a German sniper as he was helped back across No-Man's-Land. Captain Wilfred Spender, general staff officer with the Ulster Division, wrote to his father: "I am told that your son fell after gallantry which deserved the Victoria Cross, and was killed when his men had at last persuaded him to consent to letting them carry him back. Though badly wounded, he had insisted on 'carrying on'."

Another officer of note is Lieutenant Albert Edward Kinghan. The 24-year-old, who had earlier in the war been mentioned in despatches, was a son of the cloth, his father having been a minister in Dublin. He was serving with the 8th Royal Irish Fusiliers when fatally wounded in September, 1916. His mother had the following words added to his headstone:

True Love by Life,
True Love by death is Tried,
Live Thou for England,
He for England died.

Captain Thomas Gordon Fitzpatrick was in the same battalion and also had a clergyman father. From Kingstown, County Dublin, it is recorded that he was educated at "Corrig School, Kingstown, H.M.S. 'Conway,' Rock Ferry". Before the war he had worked for the London and North Western Railway Company, which handled the Irish mail, as a clerk at Dublin's North Wall. The 35-year-old, who had been in France since February, 1916, being promoted to captain in May that year, was killed on September 6. Lieutenant William McCluggage, of the 12th Royal Irish Rifles, was 23 when he died on July 1, 1916. The Larne, County Antrim, man had been a student at Queen's University in Belfast and had just taken an engineering degree before joining up. He had played rugby for both his town and university. Sergeant James Henry Rainey, from Belfast's Upper Newtownards Road, had been an active man, being a member of both the Sydenham and Knock football clubs and the Otter Swimming Club. Serving with the 15th Rifles, the 35-year-old was said to have bombed the enemy for four hours despite being twice wounded, once in the hand which stopped him using his rifle. "He was very cool and full of pluck, and was never the least bit frightened in doing his duty," his widow was told by a comrade.

In an army of young men, John Daly and Michael Drum stand out as 40-year-olds. From Leighlinbridge, County Carlow, Private Daly was killed on September 9, 1916, with the 8th Royal Dublin Fusiliers. Private Drum, from Newrath, Kells, was killed a month earlier with the 2nd Leinster Regiment.

Private Benjamin Powell, from Cork, had already seen action on Gallipoli and service in India before arriving on the Somme. The 31-year-old was killed on September 3, 1916, with the 2nd Royal Irish Regiment. There is no record of Private Alfred John Dilley's native home, but as a member of the 4th (Royal Irish) Dragoons, killed on March 25, 1918, his headstone is comparatively rare and stands among those of men from the Irish Guards, Royal Munster Fusiliers, Royal Inniskilling Fusiliers and Connaught Rangers.

Lieutenant James Greer McKay, of the Australian Machine Gun Corps, was born at Cookstown, County Tyrone. His father had moved to Leeds to continue his business, and it was from there that James had emigrated to Australia.

Captain James Samuel Davidson was killed by a sniper as he was helped back across No-Man's-Land after being wounded in the German lines

Courtesy of the North Down Heritage Centre

(3) Serre Road Cemetery No.3

Started in the spring of 1917, it holds 80 graves and commemorations, of which 35 are known by name.

There is, to the best of my knowledge, just one soldier with Irish connections in this cemetery. Private Mason Simonton, the son of William Simonton, Malone Park, Belfast, was 21 when killed on July 20, 1916, serving with the 20th Royal Fusiliers (Public Schools Battalion).

(4) Sucrerie Military Cemetery

A particularly beautiful cemetery, with well spaced graves, it is situated to the south-east of the village of Colincamps, and about three miles north-west of the Ulster Tower. Named after a sugar beet factory which used to be nearby, it contains 1,104 graves and was started by the French then used by the British from July, 1915, until December 1918.

Samuel Williamson was just 16 when killed on March 29, 1916, one of the youngest to die on the Somme front. The son of Samuel and Mary Williamson, of Dee Street, Belfast, he had served in the 9th Royal Irish Rifles. Another Belfast teenager, William Thomas McCombe, of the 10th battalion, was only a year older when killed three days before Christmas, 1915. Lance Corporal W. J. Cummins, of the same unit, was one of a number of men who died on Christmas Day, while 15th battalion riflemen John Freeman, 21, from Trafalgar Street in Belfast, and 19-year-old J. Baird, of Arlington Street in the city, were both killed on December 24, 1915.

A long line of nine Irish soldiers just inside the cemetery gate includes the grave of James Crozier, of the 9th Royal Irish Rifles, who was shot at dawn on February 27, 1916, for desertion. The 18-year-old from Battenberg Street, in the Shankill area of Belfast, was believed to be suffering from shell-shock when found out of his sector without his rifle or pack (see Leaving The Trenches, page 103).

All told, more than 100 Irishmen lie buried here, a third of them from the Royal Dublin Fusiliers, including Corporal W. Hefferman, of the 2nd battalion, who would have been one of the first British casualties buried here following his death on July 28, 1915. In addition, there are the dead of the Royal Irish Fusiliers, Royal Irish Regiment, Royal Inniskilling Fusiliers, and Royal Munster Fusiliers. Irishmen serving with non-Irish units include Corporal George Henry Waddell, 26, from Tullyrush, Seskanore, County Tyrone, who was with the 2nd Canterbury Regiment of the New Zealand Expeditionary Force when killed on August 23, 1918; Sapper Alexander McKee, of Richhill, County Armagh, was 20 when he died on November 21, 1915, with the 150th Company of the Royal Engineers; and James McGinn, 29, a driver with the Royal Field Artillery serving with the 7th Division's Armoured Column, was killed in March, 1917. He left a widow, Annie, at St. Patrick's Villas, Ringsend, Dublin.

Another Irish soldier not readily identifiable is Second Lieutenant David Buchanan, of the 2nd Seaforth Highlanders, the youngest son of William Buchanan, of Altanaros, Northland Road, Londonderry, and principal of the Derry firm of Buchanan Brothers. He joined the Colours at the outbreak of the war, going to France in May, 1915, with the Black Watch. After receiving his commission he was attached to the Seaforth Highlanders. He was killed in action on July 1, 1916.

Private George Jackson, 23, of the Royal Fusiliers, was killed on July 27, 1916, and lies here. His brother, Private Balfour Jackson, of the same regiment, was killed just four days later but his body was never found. He is commemorated on the Thiepval Memorial to the Missing (Pier and Face 8C, 9A and 16A). Both had been members of the Ulster Cricket Club with Balfour, 24, also playing rugby for Knock. Their father, William, of South Parade, Belfast, was a well-known figure in the linen trade.

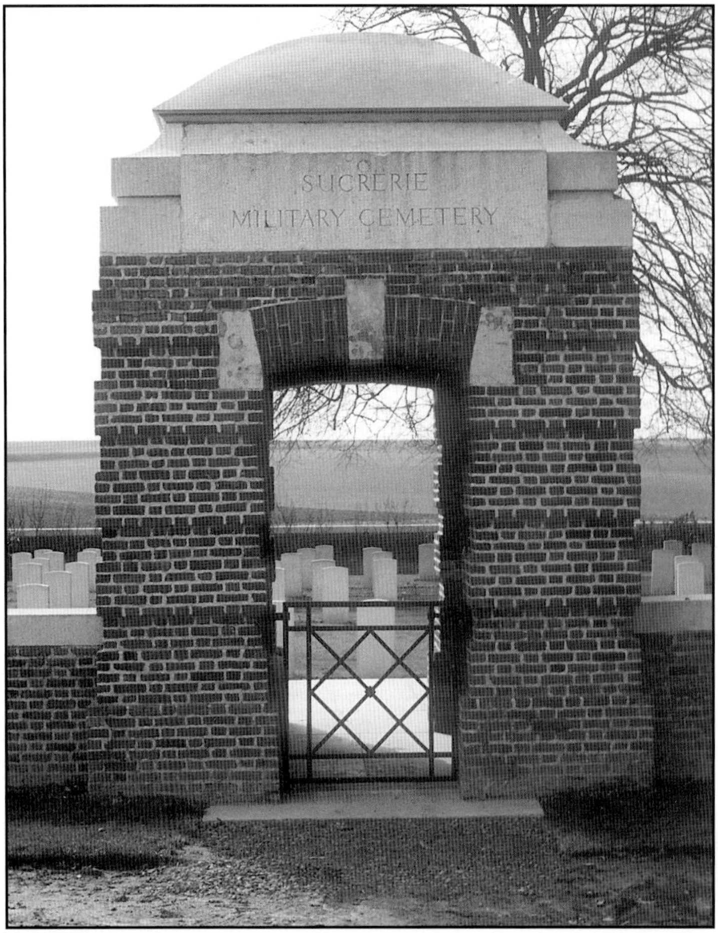

The entrance to Sucrerie Military Cemetery, named after a former sugar beet factory

(5) Redan Ridge Cemetery No.3

On the old German front line and next to the cemetery above, it holds just over 50 graves and commemorations, of which 33 are named. Special memorials record the names of 13 men.

There are no Irish regiments represented in this cemetery, though at least one Irishman is believed to rest here. Henry Charles Magrath, a sergeant with the 24th Royal Fusiliers, was killed in a final push of the Battle of the Somme on November 13, 1916. The 27-year-old was from Cork where his parents, William and Ann, lived in Washington Street. His name is one of those recorded on a special memorial after his grave was destroyed by shell fire latter in the war.

(6) Redan Ridge Cemetery No.2

One of three cemeteries on the Redan Ridge, some two miles north-east of the Ulster Tower, it sits less than 100 yards short of the old German front line. There are more than 250 graves and commemorations of soldiers killed between July-November, 1916, of which 155 are known by name.

Three soldiers of the 2nd Royal Dublin Fusiliers are the only representatives of the Irish regiments in this compact little cemetery. R. F. Hillhouse was just 17 and already a corporal. He, like his comrades, was killed on July 1, 1916, the first day of the Battle of the Somme. His parents lived at Ballincurra, Moyvore, Mullingar, County Westmeath; J. Flanagan, a 21-year-old private, was from Academy Street, Navan, County Meath; nothing but his name, rank and date of death are recorded for R. Wackrill.

There is at least one other Irishman within this cemetery. Private Bernard Patrick Morahan, 26, was serving with the 1st Hampshire Regiment when he was killed on July 1, 1916. He was from Carrick-on-Shannon, County Leitrim. Another man killed on the first day of battle with an admittedly tenuous Irish link was Captain Edward Granville Matthey, of the 1st Lancashire Fusiliers. Although he lived in Kensington, London, he was the son of a former officer in the Royal Inniskilling Fusiliers.

Nearby is Redan Ridge Cemetery No.1. Started in the spring of 1917, it holds 150 graves, of which 81 are known by name. There are no apparent Irish connections.

(7) Beaumont-Hamel British Cemetery

Small and narrow, Beaumont-Hamel British Cemetery lies off the road out of the village towards Mailly-Maillet, about two miles north-west of the Ulster Tower. There are 176 graves of which 82 are unknown by name. Park below the impressive 8th Argyll and Sutherland Highlanders Memorial and the cemetery lies a short distance away on your right.

There are only two Irish regiment graves in this cemetery: Private M. Harvey, of the 1st Royal Dublin Fusiliers, was killed on July 1, 1916; while Rifleman William Dunbar, a 19-year-old from Downpatrick Street in Belfast, who was serving with the 8th Royal Irish Rifles, died the following day.

Second Lieutenant S. MacDonnell Campbell, of the 13th Lanchashire Fusiliers, was the son of Robert Campbell of Dungiven, County Londonderry. The former bank clerk had been attached to the 86th Trench Mortar Battery and on July 1, 1916, was coordinating with a French mortar battery.

(8) Munich Trench British Cemetery

This cemetery was started in the spring of 1917 as part of the clearing of the battlefield following the German withdrawal. The nearby village of Beaumont-Hamel only fell in November, 1916, while the German trench, from which the cemetery derives its name, wasn't taken until two months after the end of the battle, in January, 1917. There are 128 graves, of which 28 are unknown by name.

Just one Irish soldier lies in this cemetery to the best of my knowledge. Private J. Sherriff, of the 2nd Manchester Regiment, was the son of Fred Sherriff, of Speowale House, Bailieborough, County Cavan. He died on November 18, 1916, days after a group of soldiers, principally of the 16th Highland Light Infantry, had become trapped in the nearby Frankfurt trench during a final tidying-up operation, holding out there for the best part of a week until forced to surrender after repeated raids to rescue them failed.

(9) Waggon Road Cemetery

A small cemetery of just 195 graves, most from November, 1916. It sits two miles north of the Ulster Tower amid a row of similarly sized cemeteries. Its name comes from the term used by the troops for a road which ran north of Serre.

Six soldiers of the 2nd Royal Inniskilling Fusiliers, and two others unknown by name, who were killed on November 23, 1916, lie here. They include both Belfast and Fermanagh men, such as Private Wilson Cairns, 25, from Beechnut Street in the city, and Corporal George Albert Latimer, who was a year younger and from Hollybrooke, Lisnaskea.

The body of Corporal George Albert Latimer lies in Waggon Road Cemetery while fellow Inniskilling Fusilier Robert Henry Hill is buried in nearby Frankfurt Trench British Cemetery

(10) Frankfurt Trench British Cemetery

A small cemetery of just over 150 graves (of which 127 are known by name), Frankfurt Trench consists largely of Scottish soldiers who died in the final weeks of the Battle of the Somme. Created in the spring of 1917 during the clearing of the battlefields following the German withdrawal to the Hindenburg Line, it is some three miles north-west of the Ulster Tower on land formerly occupied by the Germans.

Frankfurt Trench was the scene of what is generally viewed as the final act in the Battle of the Somme. A party of Highlanders, trapped in a stretch of the trench following the last official attack before the battle was deemed to be at an end, fought on against the odds until eventually overwhelmed. Attempts to rescue them had to be abandoned after costing some 300 casualties.

There are only five Irish graves in this cemetery, with one of those unknown by name. All are from November, 1916. The first of these to die was Second Lieutenant James John Wahab Griffin, who was serving with the 6th Bedfordshire Regiment. The only son of Robert and Alice Griffin, of St. Catherines Park, Rathfarnham, Dublin, the 22-year-old was killed on the 15th of the month. Two days later, Private John Magee, of the 1st/4th Seaforth Highlanders, died. He was 28 and from Antigua Street, Belfast. Both Robert Henry Hill, a 19-year-old from Matilda Street, Belfast, and C. McGrath were privates in the 2nd Royal Inniskilling Fusiliers when killed on the same day, November 23. The soldier unknown by name was also an Inniskilling Fusilier. The battalion had reached the nearby notorious Munich Trench during an advance five days earlier, with bitter hand-to-hand fighting ensuing.

(11) New Munich Trench Cemetery

Near Beaumont-Hamel, it holds 128 identified casualties, none of whom appear to have Irish connections.

(12) Mailly-Maillet Communal Cemetery Extension

A small cemetery of only 126 graves built on a slight rise next to the civilian graveyard, Mailly-Maillet Communal Cemetery Extension lies just a short distance outside the village it is named after. It was started by the French in June, 1915, and used by British field ambulances and fighting units from August that year.

This cemetery was used by the Royal Irish Rifles battalions of the 36th (Ulster) Division to bury their early dead, with 14 members of the regiment interred here. Several of them died in and around Christmas, 1915, such as Rifleman W. Beattie, of the 10th battalion, killed on Christmas Eve; and 18-year-old corporal Thomas Bradshaw, of the 15th battalion, killed on December 23. Pity his parents, Thomas and Sarah, of Upper Townsend Street, Belfast, whose thoughts as they celebrated that Christmas would undoubtedly have been with their son little realising he was already dead. Or Annie Laverty, of Blythe Street, Belfast, whose rifleman husband William, 43, of the 10th battalion, had been killed on December 16, 1915.

Among the final members of the regiment to be buried here are Riflemen James Templeton, from Enfield Street in Belfast, and J. F. McCracken, aged just 19, who were both with the 15th battalion. They were shot at dawn on Sunday, March 19, 1916, for desertion. They are thought to have been executed in a nearby quarry, now abandoned, which can be clearly seen from the cemetery wall, on the far side of the roadway towards which the graves face. (See Leaving The Trenches, page 106)

The first and second battalions of the Royal Dublin Fusiliers are both represented, Private C. Doyle, of the 2nd battalion, from Brownstown, Kilcullen, County Kildare, being the first to be buried following his death on December 19, 1915. Privates T. Irwin and M. Territt, the latter from Chapel Hill, Athy, County Kildare, were both in the 1st battalion and died in April and June 1916 respectively.

There are three members of the 1st Royal Munster Fusiliers, all privates and each killed in April, 1916. Dan McCarthy was 34 and from Cork; P. Kelly hailed from Limerick; and Richard Lewis Pickles was a 25-year-old from Burnley.

(13) Auchonvillers Military Cemetery

Auchonvillers Military Cemetery was started in 1915 by the French who then occupied this part of the line. Burials practically ceased in February, 1917, when the Germans retreated, with only 15 more added after the war. Of the 528 graves in this cemetery, more than 50 are Irish-linked

The village of Auchonvillers lies approximately two-and-a-half miles north-west of the Ulster Tower, with the cemetery on its western fringes and farm buildings running up its right-hand side and open land to the rear and left. Battle of the Somme graves account for the majority of the Irish dead, though this is a cemetery which clearly illustrates the constant drain of lives lost, day after day and year after year, to trench warfare.

Ten Royal Irish Rifles are buried here, a number of whom died in the nearby trenches between January-March, 1916, then later with the opening of the Battle of the Somme. The most significant grave is that of Second Lieutenant Robert Wilson MacDermott, the first officer of the 36th (Ulster) Division to be killed. Serving with the 8th Rifles, the 25-year-old died on January 8, 1916. He was a son of the cloth, his father being Dr. John MacDermott, of the Belmont Manse, Belfast, and, had he lived, would have seen a nephew become Northern Ireland's Lord Chief Justice. By chance, a reporter from the News Letter newspaper in Belfast was on a visit to the trenches at the time. He reported in the edition of January 19, 1916:

On our return to billet quarters I noticed the badge of the Royal Irish regiment on two squads of men standing in a farmyard entrance, and spoke to them. They were the ration party of a battalion of the Belfast Brigade of the Ulster Division; the battalion was in the trenches. I heard sad news from them.

On the previous morning a shell from the enemy had landed in one of the trenches, and it killed Second-Lieutenant MacDermott, son of the Rev. Dr. MacDermott, of Belmont, and a corporal and private who were standing close to him. "We buried them over there this morning," said the corporal of the party, pointing to an orchard surrounding farm buildings on the opposite side of the road. The orchard had been converted into a little cemetery. All round its margin were ranged lines of neatly-made, white painted wooden crosses, each bearing the name of the dead hero who slept his last sleep below.

I crossed the road, passed into the little 'God's Acre', and spent a minute's solemn communion with the dead at the foot of my young friend's grave, for I had known him in his revered father's congregation. He was as fine a young man as ever came out of Ulster. When he joined to do his bit for King and country with the rest of his battalion of the Ulster Volunteers, Lieutenant MacDermott had all the prospects of a fine future before him. That future is gone, but his end was glorious – killed at the post of duty in the very front of the firing line. Such is war.

The funeral took place in the early hours of this (Sunday) morning by candlelight in the village hard by, under fire from machine gun and artillery. So Second Lieutenant MacDermott had a soldier's burial in very truth.

It is likely the men buried either side of this unfortunate officer – 23-year-old Rifleman George Parkinson Connor, of Brookfield, Moira, and Corporal Henry Murphy – were those killed in the incident described. A "very handsome little gravestone cut out of a block of chalk", as described by the journalist, has long since gone, as have the wooden crosses, to be replaced by the standard Commonwealth War Graves Commission headstones. At the time of their deaths, the 8th and 15th battalions of the Rifles were attached to the 4th Division and took their turn in the front line astride the Mailly-Maillet/Serre Road, just north of Thiepval. Part of the line included the Redan, described by the Ulster Division historian Cyril Falls as "a most unpleasant corner". He adds:

It was the one point in our trenches which received fairly constant attention from German gunners, and the average weekly casualties in this tine lozenge were probably higher than on the whole of the rest of the 4th Division's front.

The biggest contingent of Irish graves belongs to the Royal Dublin Fusiliers, numbering 24 in total including several not known by name. Some of the 2nd battalion members died while serving in this sector in October, 1915, but most are from the 1st battalion, part of the 29th Division which, along with the Royal Inniskilling Fusiliers (nine of whom are buried here), fought on the Ulster Division's left that day. They faced the Germans at Beaumont Hamel and Serre, with Auchonvillers just inside the northern fringes of their sector. Lieutenant Alfred Middleton Blackwood Rose-Cleland was 21 when he was killed on July 1, 1916, with the 1st Dubliners. He was the only child of Henry S. Rose-Cleland, of Redford House, Moy, County Tyrone. Educated at Dungannon Royal School and St. Columba's College, Rathfarnham, County Dublin, he was working for the building firm of McLaughlin and Harvey on a contract in Essex, England, when the war started. Returning home to enlist, he was a lance corporal in the 9th Royal

Second Lieutenant Robert Wilson MacDermott was the first officer of the 36th (Ulster) Division to be killed in action. He lies in Auchonvillers Military Cemetery

Inniskilling Fusiliers when commissioned in February, 1915. In a newspaper biography, Lieutenant Rose-Cleland is described as "the lineal descendant of a Scottish noble family of great antiquity, one of his ancestors being a cousin of the famous Sir William Wallace, the hero of Scotland, while another fought at Flodden Field in defence of James IV of Scotland".

On July 1, the 2nd Dubs and the 1st Royal Irish Fusiliers – which are well represented in this cemetery – were part of the 4th Division, and next in line to the north. Sergeant William Lynn, of the 1st Royal Irish Fusiliers, was killed by an artillery explosion on August 16, 1916, as he tended to a wounded comrade. He was one of four brothers to die. Driver Robert Lynn, 87th Battery, Royal Field Artillery, was killed in August, 1915; Private John Lynn, 1st Royal Irish Fusiliers, died in a military hospital in Belgium in August, 1916, from the effects of gas poisoning; and Sergeant James Lynn, Royal Army Services Corps, was 37, when he died on August 7, 1920 (possibly due to the influenza epidemic which swept the world that year) and is buried in Haifa War Cemetery, Israel. The bodies of eight Royal Irish Regiment soldiers include a number who died mid-September in the battles further east.

Among the Irishmen serving with other regiments was Corporal George Michael Anderson, of the Royal Garrison Artillery, a 27-year-old who left a widow at Evergreen Cottage, Lismore, County Waterford; Second Lieutenant Michael Bernard O'Connor, of the New Zealand Canterbury Regiment, who was 23 and originally from County Kerry; Private Patrick O'Leary, of the 1st Lancashire Fusiliers, who was born in India, had lived in Wales with his wife, and whose parents were in Ireland; Private John Parkinson, a 21-year-old Dublin-born lance corporal in the 6th Black Watch who had been working for the Irish Land Commission before the war; and Richard Henry Williams, 33, of the New Zealand Rifle Brigade, who is recorded as having been a "native of County Kerry, Ireland".

(14) Hawthorn Ridge Cemetery No.1

This cemetery is another started in the spring of 1917 following the German withdrawal from the area. It holds 150 bodies, of which only 82 could be identified by name. Most who lie here died either on July 1, 1916, as the Battle of the Somme began, or November 13, 1916, as it was closing. The cemetery is approached via a 200-yard path and the Commonwealth War Graves Commission warns that access can be difficult in bad weather or in the ploughing season.

Just four Irishmen are known to lie within the cemetery walls of Hawthorn Ridge, two of whom were serving with non-Irish regiments. Private Daniel Murphy was just 18 and serving with the 16th Middlesex Regiment. The son of John and Catherine Murphy, of Kellystown, Adamstown, County Wexford, he was killed on July 1, 1916. Five-and-a-half months later came the death of Donald McNair, a private in the 1st/5th Seaforth Highlanders. The 24-year-old, who died on November 13, 1916, was from Ferguson Drive in the Strandtown area of east Belfast.

Second Lieutenant D. R. Warner must have been freshly arrived from Ireland when he was killed on July 1, 1916, for he is officially listed as still serving with the home-based 4th Royal Dublin Fusiliers. Private T. Devlin, of the 2nd Royal Irish Regiment, died on July 20, 1918, just as the war was turning in the Allies' favour.

(15) Hawthorn Ridge Cemetery No.2

Hawthorn Ridge Cemetery No.2, holding 214 bodies of which 149 are known by name, lies to the left of the Newfoundland Memorial Park, north-west of the Ulster Tower. The majority of the soldiers buried here died in the early phases of the Somme battle, their bodies being collected in the spring of 1917, with further burials following the Armistice

This is a small, open cemetery approached through the preserved trenches and trees of Newfoundland Park. There are just 14 Irish graves, members of the 1st Royal Dublin Fusiliers, who faced a hail of machinegun fire as they attacked near here on July 1, 1916. Some left widows, such as 38-year-old Private Daniel King, notice of his death arriving with Harriet at their South William Street home in Dublin, and Lance Corporal William Charles Rowswell, 29, who had lived with his wife in Notting Hill, London. Others were too young for marriage, like 19-year-old privates Patrick Dunleavey, of Church Hill, Sligo, who died on June 28, 1916, and Donald Patrick McLean, of Martin Street, South Circular Road, Dublin, killed three days later. Other telegrams had further to go: the mother of 22-year-od Private Thomas Quinn, another killed on June 28 in the run-up to the "Big Push", lived at Wanganui, New Zealand.

(16) Y Ravine Cemetery

Situated within Newfoundland Park, a mile-and-a-half north of the Ulster Tower, Y Revine Cemetery holds the bodies of 366 men, of which 275 are known by name, and special memorials commemorate another 53 thought to be buried here. It was started in 1917 following the German withdrawal.

This is a nice cemetery with a strong Irish interest which takes in both the start and end of the Battle of the Somme. The 1st Royal Inniskilling Fusiliers fought here on July 1, 1916, and 48 of their dead, three unknown by name, are buried in the cemetery. Many of their headstones carry personal messages from home, such as that of 27-year-old Lance Corporal W. McClelland, from Lisnamallad, Omagh, County Tyrone, which has the words: "In our hearts we mourn the loss of one we loved so well. Missed by all." The family of Sergeant M. Dunne, of Barrack Street, Mullingar, County Westmeath, recorded: "He is gone but not forgotten, never shall his memory fade. From his sorrowing wife and children."

Memorials of any kind apart from those approved by the Commonwealth War Graves Commission are not permitted in the cemeteries but a surprisingly high number have been added over the years and a blind eye turned. One such in this cemetery takes the form of a brass cross, apparently left by the great nieces of Private Peter Rafferty, a 22-year-old from Coalisland, County Tyrone. Corporal John Henry Chatton, 21, was living in Suffolk, England, with his parents before the war but was "born in Ireland" according to the register. Another English-based soldier of the 1st battalion was 28-year-old Private James Cotter, the holder of a Military Medal. Corporal Robert Watt, of the 1st Inniskillings, died on July 1, 1916. Six weeks later, on August 13, his 34-year-old brother David, recalled to the 2nd Argyll and Sutherland Highlanders from the reserve list, was killed in action. His name appears on the Thiepval Memorial to the Missing (Pier and Face 15A and 16C). The brothers' mother, Jane Watt, lived in Kitchener Street, Belfast.

The 10th Royal Dublin Fusiliers stormed Beaumont Hamel on November 13, 1916, securing the village four-and-a-half months after the Inniskillings had been beaten back by fire from the village. Eight Dubliners lie buried here, one unknown by name. Included among them is Private Robert Patrick Brown, 21, of Upper George Street, Wexford; M. F. Tierney, 22, of Railway Cottage, Belturbet, County Cavan; and Lance Corporal Gilbert Melville Lemon, a 20-year-old from Dublin.

Hawthorn Ridge Cemetery No.2, in Newfoundland Park, holds just 14 Irish graves

(17) Mailly Wood Cemetery

The cemetery is next to woods off the road between Mailly Maillet and Amiens. It can be difficult to reach during the winter as the path crosses rough grassland. Started in the summer of 1915, it holds 720 burials and commemorations, of which 642 are known by name.

Just one headstone here bears the Irish harp and it belongs to Private Nathan Barker, of the 2nd Royal Irish Regiment, who was killed on July 17, 1918, aged 33.

However, the cemetery register reveals a number of others who served with non-Irish units. They are split equally between Scottish and English regiments and indicate a north-south divide within Ireland.

Both William James Hall, a 20-year-old private from Avon Street, off Dee Street in east Belfast, but originally from Seagoe, Portadown, County Armagh, and J. J. Gorman, 32, from Emerson Row, Ligoniel, Belfast, joined the Seaforth Highlanders, serving in the 5th and 1/6th battalions respectively; 18-year-old William McCord, from Cullybackey, County Antrim, but whose father lived at Larne, was in the 1st/8th Argyle and Sutherland Highlanders; while Arnold Wilkinson Todd, 21, a private in the 6th Black Watch, was from Coleraine, County Londonderry. All four died during a three-day period beginning November 13, 1916.

John Howarth, 21, was a native of Cork but was living in Chorlton-on-Medlock, Manchester, with his mother when he enlisted in the 10th Lancashire Fusiliers. He was killed on August 25, 1918; in the 15th battalion of the same regiment was 26-year-old Lance Corporal Joseph Quigley, from Drogheda, County Louth, whose family had moved to Preston before the war. He died in November, 1916; it is less clear how Private J. Duff, 20, from Templeogue, County Dublin, ended up in the 9th Essex Regiment, as his parents are recorded as living at Lisle House, Crumlin, County Dublin. He was killed at the start of May, 1918.

There is strong Irish interest in Y Ravine Cemetery, just north of the River Ancre

The only officer among the Irishmen in this cemetery is Lieutenant the Honourable Frederic Sydney Trench, of the 1st King's Royal Rifle Corps, who was killed on November 16, 1916. He was the eldest son of Frederic Oliver Trench, third Baron Ashtown, of Woodlawn House, Woodlawn, County Galway. Educated at Eton and Magdalen College, Oxford, he had received his commission in November, 1914.

Another officer who just might have had Irish blood in his veins, judging by his father's name, was Second Lieutenant Dennis John Freeland Bradbury, of the King's Own (Royal Lancashire Regiment). The 19-year-old was born in Antigua, in the British West Indies, where his father, Patrick Joseph O'Leary Bradbury, was the Director of Education.

(18) Ancre British Cemetery

Ancre British Cemetery lies in the middle of the old No-Man's-Land, about three-quarters of a mile north-west of the Ulster Tower. Long and narrow, and shielded from the roadway by a high bank, it stretches up a narrow valley with agricultural land on three sides. Begun in 1917, it was later expanded to take the dead of seven battlefield cemeteries making approximately 2,500 graves in total of which 1,206 are known by name. Close to 200 of the latter are Irishmen.

On July 1, 1916, two battalions of the Ulster Division advanced north of the River Ancre into the deep ravine. The 9th Royal Irish Fusiliers enjoyed some initial success but at considerable cost. Some 40 named members of the battalion lie in this cemetery. They include Major Thomas Joyce Atkinson, who died that day at the head of B Company. The 38-year-old graduate of Trinity College, Dublin, had given up a civilian job as a solicitor to volunteer for the front. His headstone has the family inscription: "A Son of Ulster, Your Memory Hallowed In the Land You Loved." He shares a grave with Corporal Ernest Turkington, of the same battalion, who lived at Brownlow Terrace, Lurgan. The 22-year-old was seen lying wounded by his brother, Alfred, but he followed orders and didn't stop to help. He went out into No-Man's-Land on the two successive nights following to search for Ernest, but to no avail. He did, however, discover his own officer and retrieved documents from his body, being promoted, according to newspaper reports, to sergeant the following day. Lieutenant Richard Stapleton Barry Townsend died at the head of his detachment as the Battle of the Somme got under way. The son of a resident magistrate from Cathedral Close, Armagh, he was 32 when killed.

The second battalion, the 12th Royal Irish Rifles, was less fortunate than the Fusiliers, running into a salient on the brow of the small hill around which the barbed wire was virtually intact. Raked by machinegun fire, they were beaten back. Two further attempts to advance were similarly repulsed under the withering hail. By 8am, just 30 minutes after the beginning of the battle, the Germans were again in full control of the front line trenches. The bodies of more than 20 Rifles soldiers are buried at this spot, including 34-year-old Captain John Griffiths, an Englishman who had been a science teacher at Larne Grammar School, County Antrim, and Private Robert Hayes, from Portstewart, the second member of his family to die in the war. He had lost a brother, Thomas, of the 6th Royal Irish Fusiliers, at the Dardanelles in August, 1915. (Thomas is commemorated on the Helles Memorial.)

There is a large contingent of Royal Inniskilling Fusiliers (at least 47, including those known to belong to the regiment but whose identity could not be established). Among their number is Lieutenant Colonel Robert Campbell Pierce, of the 1st battalion, who was killed on July 1, 1916. Another is Second Lieutenant William Porter, of the 6th Inniskillings but attached to the 1st battalion. He had been living in Canada when the Home Rule crisis began and returned home (his parents

A sergeant of the 9th Royal Irish Fusiliers pays homage at the graveside of Lieutenant Townsend killed July 1, 1916. The photograph is believed to have been taken in November, 1921, when veterans travelled back to the battlefield for the opening of the Ulster Tower

Courtesy of the Royal Irish Fusiliers Museum

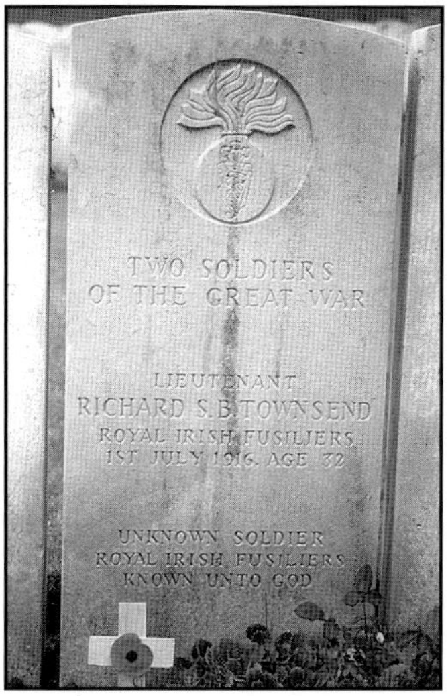

Lieutenant Townsend and, below, the stone headstone which replaced the original wooden cross in Ancre cemetery

Courtesy of the Royal Irish Fusiliers Museum

lived at Beechview, Balmoral Avenue, Belfast and an uncle, R. W. Bingham, was principal of the Royal School, Dungannon) specifically to join the Ulster Volunteer Force. He volunteered on the outbreak of war and was posted to the 10th (Irish) Division, being severely wounded in the chest during the landing at Suvla Bay in August, 1915. During his recovery he served in the west of Ireland as part of the coastal defence forces before returning to active service in France in time to take part in the opening day of the Battle of the Somme.

In excess of 40 Royal Dublin Fusiliers, of which 34 are named, lie here. They are, for the most part, members of the 10th battalion who died on November 13, 1916, during the Naval Division's successful advance that day. Among the dead is 21-year-old Patrick Joseph Mulheron, from Bennett Street in Londonderry, who was studying at Marlborough Training College in Dublin when the war broke out and presumably was swept into the ranks by the patriotic fervour. His headstone simply says: "Lord Have Mercy, Jesus Blest Grant My Darling Light and Rest." Another Ulster student of Marlborough College was Private Edward Reid Dallas. From Church Street in Coleraine, he enlisted with his lifelong friend Willie McGrath, from New Row in the County Derry town. The two were fatally wounded on the same day, November 13, 1916, with Eddie buried here and Willie surviving long enough to be taken to a field hospital at Etaples, on the coast, where he died the following day.

This cemetery is the final resting place for at least two Irish dead from the Allied push of 1918 – North Irish Horse privates Robert Ross, from the Springfield Road in Belfast, and W. McClelland, who died in August of that year.

The London Irish Rifles and King's (Liverpool) Regiment are both represented. Bertran St. George French, of the latter unit, has an address in

Canada and appears to have travelled back to enlist, having previously served with the Royal Inniskilling Fusiliers.

There are 45 bodies unknown by name but identified as belonging to Irish regiments. The majority of these are likely to have died on July 1-2, 1916, there bodies lying out in No-Man's-Land until the course of the war allowed their recovery.

(19) Mesnil Ridge Cemetery

Although difficult to reach, particularly during the winter months and spring ploughing season, this is a most pleasant cemetery to visit. The headstones are widely spaced and the isolation, with Knightsbridge Cemetery the only other man-made construction in sight, adds to the sense of tranquillity. There are nearly 100 burials, of which 94 are known by name.

Standing at the end of a deeply rutted dirt track in open countryside, some two miles west of the Ulster Tower, and almost a mile north of Mesnil-Martinsart, it is difficult to imagine that many, outside of those with family connections, bother to visit this lonely cemetery.

Almost a third of the bodies buried here are of Irish regiment soldiers, 29 in total and most members of the 36th (Ulster) Division. It served in this sector from shortly after its arrival in France through to the spring of 1916. The troops entered and left the line by a communication trench which emerged into the open between here and Knightbridge Cemetery. It is not hard to imagine them, tired, dirty and weary after sleepless nights in the trenches, surfacing to bury their comrades in rough and ready dawn ceremonies before marching back to billets and a straw bed. Although those buried here are not the earliest divisional casualties, they represent part of the blooding of the raw civilian volunteers as they came to terms with the tragedy in which they found themselves embroiled.

The biggest grouping is of Royal Irish Rifles, of which there are 14; nine are Royal Inniskilling Fusiliers; and three each from the Royal Irish Fusiliers and Royal Munster Fusiliers. Among the Ulster division casualties is Thomas Willoughby Stephens, a 25-year-old from Ardee, County Louth, but who travelled from Ballymoneean, Ashford, County Wicklow, to join the predominantly Protestant unit. He served in the 13th Rifles with County Down men such as Charles Newell, 19, from South Street, Newtownards, 21-year-old David McConnell, of Wallace Street in the same town, and Thomas Devlin, from Gilford, the latter three being killed in February, 1916. Stephens died a month later, on March 21, on the same day as Scotsman Donald McDonald, a lance corporal from Peterhead, Aberdeenshire, who had crossed the Irish Sea to enlist with the 13th Rifles. Omagh, County Tyrone, men Francis Hall, 29, a lance corporal from Gortmore Terrace, and Private James Ross Anderson, of Market Place, both died in May, 1916, one with the 1st Royal Inniskilling Fusiliers and the other the 9th battalion. Among the Munsters' dead is Private James Oliver Bridgewater, killed on April 18, 1916. The 30-year-old had served under the name Sutton, and left a widow, Francis Elizabeth, in Birmingham.

(20) Knightsbridge Cemetery

Along with the nearby Mesnil Ridge Cemetery, Knightbridge is one of the most difficult to reach, particularly in the winter months. The dirt track, off the main road at Mesnil-Martinsart, disappears eventually and the remaining journey has to be accomplished on foot. The cemetery, named after a communication trench which emerged into the open here, holds 548 graves. It lies a little less than two miles west of the Ulster Tower.

There are, by my reckoning, some 30 graves of soldiers serving in Irish regiments in this interesting but isolated cemetery. The Royal Dublin Fusiliers is the biggest grouping, making up more than two-thirds of the total. William Tallot, a 19-year-old private from Belmullet, County Mayo, died on July 1, 1916, fighting with the

1st battalion; Private James Fagan, 19, and from Walls Lane, Francis Street, Dublin, was listed as a member of the 5th battalion when he was killed on July 22, 1916; while most were serving with the 10th battalion in the bloody but successful attacks of November, 1916. These include a number of officers, all of whom died on November 13, including the distinctly un-Irish sounding Second Lieutenant St John Joseph Vincent Anthony Guisani, who was just 19, and had presumably been living with his doctor father Joseph on St Patrick's Hill, Cork; Second Lieutenant Henry Havelock Graham Cross, whose father was a clergyman in South Africa; and 22-year-old Lieutenant P. J. McCusker, of Dromore, County Tyrone, who had previously been living in Glasgow.

The remaining graves of Irish interest belong to soldiers of the Royal Inniskilling Fusiliers and Royal Irish Rifles, of which there are four each, and one man of the Leinster Regiment.

(21) Hamel Military Cemetery

A lovely little cemetery on the fringes of the village, Hamel Military Cemetery lies less than a mile due west of the Ulster Tower. It holds 487 graves and had already been open a year when the Battle of the Somme commenced. It was used both by fighting units who carried their fallen comrades out of the trenches and as a stop-off point for field ambulances.

Approximately one in six of the 411 known dead in this cemetery served in Irish regiments, mostly the Royal Irish Rifles and Royal Irish Fusiliers, accounting for more than 60 graves in total. Another 10 were members of the Royal Inniskilling Fusiliers.

Two men who were almost certainly related lie here: Private Alexander Hamilton and Corporal J. Hamilton joined the 9th Royal Irish Fusiliers together, their service numbers being 14287 and 14288 respectively, and both died on July 1, 1916. Alex was just 20 and the son of James and Maggie Hamilton, of 97 Avenue Road, Lurgan. He has no known grave but a special memorial indicates that he is believed to be buried somewhere in Hamel cemetery. Private James Alexander Hutchinson, of the same battalion, died near here on April 25, 1916. His parents, Maggie and John Hutchinson of Drummond, Richhill, County Armagh, received word in early July that a second son, Lance Corporal John Hutchinson, 21, had been killed on June 28, 1916. He is buried at Forceville Communial Cemetery Extension (see below). Private Harry Molloy was just 17 years old when killed on June 25, 1916. He lived at Drum, Clones, County Monaghan, but had been born at Newtownbutler, County Fermanagh.

Brothers Robert and William Ginn, both of the 1st Royal Inniskilling Fusiliers, were killed within days of one another in July, 1916. William, the younger of the two and the holder of a Distinguished Conduct Medal for his leadership in an earlier raiding party, lies in this cemetery, while Robert's name is recorded on the Thiepval Memorial to the Missing. In a letter to the men's father, Mr W. J. Ginn, of Derwent Street, Belfast, company commander Captain W. A. Morris, wrote: "As the only original officer of the Inniskillings I consider it my duty to tender to you my great sympathy in the all too sad loss of your two dead sons, who fell nobly in the face of the enemy. None braver. Your elder boy fell on the 1st inst to the great grief of his younger brother. He, poor lad, fell on the night of the 4th inst whilst out on patrol. Both their deaths were instantaneous and free from all pain. Your younger son was looked upon as one of our best and bravest sergeants, his Distinguished Conduct Medal being a true mark of appreciation of our officers who felt proud to bring the conduct to notice."

A name which catches the eye because of its historical significance is that of Randolph Churchill Bestall Campbell, a 21-year-old rifleman with the 14th (Y.C.V.) Royal Irish Rifles. It is perhaps fair to assume he was so titled as a tribute to the Conservative politician who, at the time of his namesake's birth, would have been fondly remembered among unionists for his anti-Home Rule stance and less charitably among his opponents for the coining of the phrase "playing the Orange card". Rifleman Campbell was killed on April 6, 1916. He had lived at Cyprus Park in Belfast, though was originally from Ballynahinch, County Down.

William Stephenson, also of the 14th Rifles, was buried here after being killed on April 6, 1916. His brother Andrew, attacking with the battalion on July 1, only narrowly avoided a similar fate. His letter to his father William at his Fitzwilliam Street home in Belfast, written from an English hospital, is understated but still gives a taste of the battle:

> *Our division went over the top at a part called Thiepval, about five miles north of Albert. We had no difficulty in taking the first three lines of German trenches. It was just like as if we had been out on an ordinary manoeuvre, except that they shelled us something awful, and the bullets were hissing all over the place. I had one or two very narrow escapes. While we were advancing I was carrying my rifle slung over my right shoulder, and a bullet hit the butt of it and shattered it to pieces. A bit of luck, wasn't it? Another time my shrapnel helmet saved me from what would have been a very nasty wound. But it only put a big bruise in it.*

Lieutenant Thomas Greenwood Haughton, of the 12th Rifles, was the youngest son of Thomas Wilfred Haughton, of Hillmount, Cullybackey, County Antrim, and had been managing director of the family's Frazer and Haughton firm prior to the outbreak of war. The 25-year-old had been a member of the Royal North of Ireland Yacht Club, the Ulster Gun Club and Cullybackey Golf Club. He was reportedly shot in the head and feet in front of the German wire and three officers who attempted to recover his body were all injured. For Private W. Brown, of the Ulster Division's pioneer battalion, the 16th Royal Irish Rifles, going to the aid of a comrade cost him his life. Hearing his cries, he climbed out over the parapet and carried the injured soldier back to the trench and was just climbing back in himself when shot dead by a German sniper. He was from Culnahey, New Ferry, Toomebridge.

Sapper John Malone, of the 121st Field Company of the Royal Engineers, was 22 when killed on May 23, 1916. His parents, William Henry and Margaret Malone, of Church Street, Downpatrick, County Down, were sent the wooden cross which originally marked his grave, later replaced by a headstone, by Church Army workers.

The wooden cross marking Sapper John Malone's grave was sent to his family in Downpatrick.

Courtesy of Eric Malone

(22) Mill Road Cemetery

Between the Ulster Tower and Thiepval village, and directly opposite Connaught Cemetery, Mill Road is approached on foot along a pathway from the road. It contains 1,304 graves, of which 815 are unknown by name.

There are approximately 100 known Irish graves in this cemetery, more than a fifth of the total, with many more presumed to be among the unidentified (of which fifteen were able to be confirmed as belonging to Irish regiments). Mill Road stands on the old German front attacked by the Ulster Division on July 1, 1916. Burials were started here in 1917, following the German

The Hewitt brothers: Holt, above, lies in Mill Road; William is commemorated on the nearby Thiepval Memorial; Ernest is remembered on the Le Touret Memorial

Courtesy of the North Down Heritage Centre

withdrawal, and continued after the war as the battlefields were cleared. A number of headstones have been laid flat as German tunnels underneath have made the ground liable to subsidence.

The Royal Inniskilling Fusiliers form the biggest group of graves, followed by the Royal Irish Rifles, with just two known members of the Royal Irish Fusiliers.

For many families July 1, 1916, proved a double or even a triple tragedy. Lieutenant Holt Montgomery Hewitt, of the 109th Machine Gun Corps, lies in Mill Road Cemetery. He was 29 and had worked before the war as a manager for a coal merchant, and played half-back for Bangor and later North of Ireland rugby clubs. A member of the 9th Royal Inniskillings, he had transferred to the Machine Gun Corps in January, 1916. His younger brother, Second Lieutenant William Arthur Hewitt, 23, of the 9th Royal Inniskilling Fusiliers, is commemorated on the nearby Thiepval Memorial. He had been assistant adjutant. On July 6, 1916, Colonel Ricardo wrote to the family: "Your little lad Willie led his platoon over our parapet, and the last I saw of him was his happy smile as I wished him luck. They got across to the German trenches, in front of which they came under an appalling machinegun fire. Your lad was hit, and Sergeant Lally, who is now in hospital wounded, was with him when he passed over." Parents, James – who was a well-known figure as manager of the Workshops for the Blind – and Jeannie Hewitt, of Altamont, Bangor, County Down, recorded him as "one of three brothers who fell" for a third son, Lieutenant Ernest Henry Hewitt, of 4th King's Own (Royal Lancaster) Regiment, had been killed over a year earlier, in June, 1915, and is commemorated on the Le Touret Memorial.

Philip E. Wedgwood, a second lieutenant with the 16th Royal Irish Rifles, the Ulster Division's pioneer battalion, is buried in this cemetery. His brother, 22-year-old Lieutenant Gilbert Colclough Wedgwood, of the 109th Machine Gun Corps, has his name engraved on a panel on the Thiepval Memorial. A chaplain, the Rev. Canon R. G. S. King, writing home, said Philip had been as "brave as a lion" during the assault. He added: "He was in the German trenches, and was taking prisoners in the dugouts. He and his party had bombs with them, and the Germans were at their mercy. He came to a dugout where there were some 20 Germans. He might have killed these but, instead, offered them their lives if they would come out and surrender. They did so, and all came out. He turned his back for a moment and one of them treacherously shot him dead." Gilbert

Wedgwood was a Methodist College old boy and had been working for the Ulster Bank before receiving his commission in October, 1914, later transferring to the Machine Gun Corps of his brigade. He was killed in No-Man's-Land during the initial stages of the attack. Their parents were the Rev. George Ryles Wedgwood, of University Road Methodist Church, Belfast, and a former Vice-President of the Methodist Conference, and Elizabeth Wedgwood, of Egerton, North Road, Belfast. A third son served in the Royal Navy.

It is likely that D. and M. Goodwin, both privates in the 9th Inniskillings, who died on July 1, 1916, were family. Their graves are just two rows apart in this cemetery; Likewise J. and R. White are probably related. Both were privates with the 11th Inniskillings and were killed on the same date. Of the latter it is recorded he was 42 and from Gortacorka, Drumkeerin, County Leitrim.

Another officer of note to lie buried here is Captain James Claude Beauchamp Proctor, of the 10th Inniskillings, killed like so many of his comrades on July 1, 1916. A graduate of Trinity College, Dublin, he had practiced law in his father's solicitors office in Limavady before joining the Bar as a member of the North West Circuit. He sat on the Ulster Unionist Council, was secretary to his local Unionist Club and had been second-in-command of the North Londonderry Ulster Volunteer Force. Two of his brothers served, one in East Africa and the other in the Australian forces in Egypt, while his younger sister was a military nurse.

Among the Royal Irish Rifles casualties was Lieutenant John Frederick Healy, a 19-year-old undergraduate of Trinity College, Dublin, who was attached to the 9th battalion. From Peafield, Blackrock, County Dublin, he is remembered on a special memorial as, though his grave has been lost, he is believed to have

Major Uprichard, chairman of his grandfather Forster Green's company before the war, was from Gilford, County Down

Courtesy of Lester Morrow

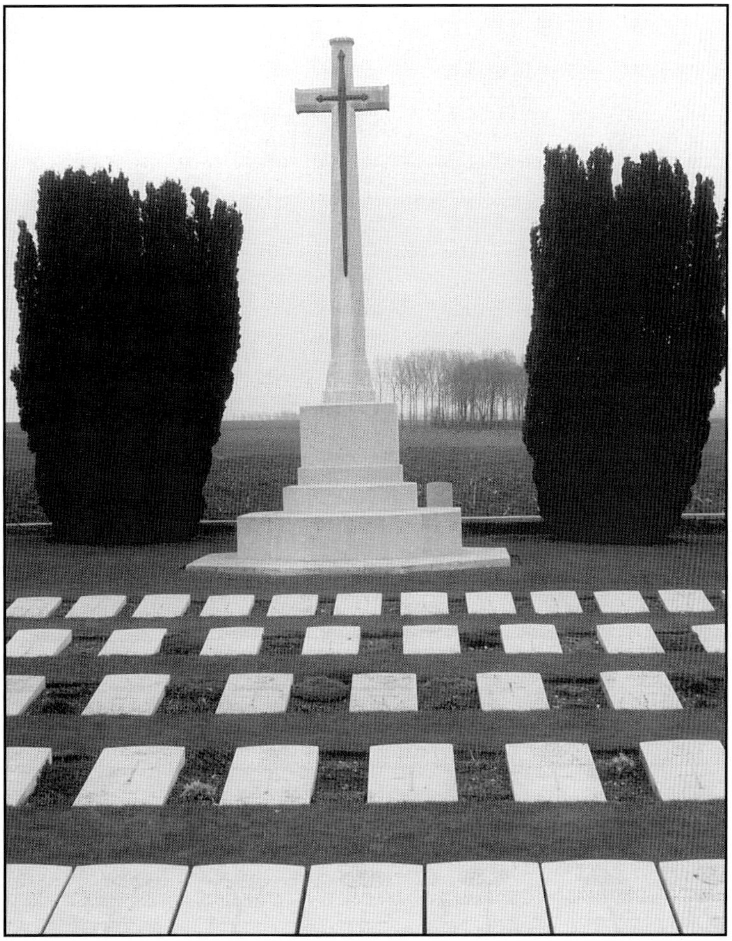

Many of the headstones in Mill Road Cemetery have had to be laid flat due to subsidence caused by German tunnelling

been buried here; Rifleman Samuel Glenn, 38, from Tullish, who left a widow, Sarah Anne, in Gilford, County Down; and T. Clarke, a 24-year-old private with the 9th battalion who had lived at Sefton Park, Liverpool. Lance Corporal David Foy, of the 14th Rifles, was among those killed on July 1, 1916, while his brother, Charles, was so seriously wounded that he had to be invalided out of the Army. A third brother, Second Lieutenant George Foy, also of the Rifles, was reported missing in March, 1918. Their father, also David, was the worshipful master of No.5 District (Sandy Row) Loyal Orange Lodge in Belfast.

Major Henry Albert Uprichard, of the 13th Rifles, was 36 when killed on July 1, 1916. He had lived at Bannvale House, Gilford, and was chairman of his grandfather Forster Green's company when he joined up. Company Sergeant-Major William Taylor stopped to help the major as he lay dying and was himself killed. A time-expired soldier who had been a leader and drill instructor to the South Down Regiment of the U.V.F., he left a widow and several children at James Street in Newry. The two men, despite the difference in ranks, had obviously been friends for in March, 1916, Major Uprichard had written to a friend: "Sgt-Major Taylor asked me to tell you that he is sending you some nose caps of shells that have been sent in or about our trenches. There is no one to touch Taylor; he is the cheeriest and best sergeant-major not only in the battalion but in the brigade." The sergeant-major is buried at Heath Cemetery, Harbonniers, between Amiens and St. Quentin.

Connaught Cemetery, built in front of the British trenches of July 1, 1916, from which the men of the 36th (Ulster) Division attacked

(23) Connaught Cemetery

Built on the roadway leading up to the Ulster Tower from thevillage of Thiepval, Connaught Cemetery sits in the No-Man's-Land over which the 36th Division advanced on July 1, 1916. There are 1,278 graves, many from the opening days of the battle, with almost half unknown by name.

This is a true frontline cemetery, the rows upon rows of headstones facing a now tranquil landscape which was once lined with German trenches and the infamous Schwaben Redoubt. There are many long, unbroken, sequences of Irish regimental badges on the headstones. Most are Royal Inniskilling Fusiliers, some 85 in total with many more among those who could only be identified by regiment. The Royal Irish Rifles have 39 of their dead recorded in the register, while among the headstones of those "known to God" is at least one Royal Munster Fusilier.

To the rear of the cemetery is Thiepval Wood, in which the Ulster Division sheltered as they waited on the order to attack. At zero hour, the Irish troops rushed the German trenches, taking the enemy's first and second lines with comparative ease. The German artillery and machineguns were more prepared for the second wave of attackers, mowing them down as they emerged from the cover of the trees. The official division history records:

And immediately the barrage left it, flanking machine-gun fire burst out from the dominating position of Thiepval cemetery. The 11th Inniskillings and 14th Rifles, as they emerged from the wood, were literally mown down, and No-Man's-Land became a ghastly spectacle of dead and wounded.

Buried here are close to 40 members of the 11th Royal Inniskillings and 13 officers and men of the 14th (Young Citizen Volunteers) Royal Irish Rifles mentioned above. They include my great uncle, John Reid Moore, who was attached to the 109th Light Trench Mortar Battery from the Rifles. Alongside him is the grave of 26-year-old Rifleman Samuel McIlroy, of the same battery, who was born in Belfast but had been living in Blackstock, South Carolina, America, prior to the war. It is possible, perhaps even likely, that these two young men, now bound together for eternity in death, fought and died alongside one another on July 1, 1916. Another member of the Y.C.V. battalion was Captain Charles Owen Slacke. The 44-year-old was a son of Sir Owen Randal Slacke and a grandson of the eminent architect Sir Charles Lanyon[1], who was responsible for so many of Belfast's finest buildings. Captain Slacke's wife Kate, who he married in 1902 and took home to Wheatfield in the city, was the daughter of the Right Honourable Sir Daniel Dixon, M.P., a former Lord Mayor of Belfast. The cemetery register records the captain as having "volunteered with the Ulster Division on the outbreak of war". He was reportedly killed at the German third line.

Among the Inniskillings is Company Sergeant Major J. Bennett, who had served with the 9th battalion. The Military Medal winner died on the first day of the Somme battle. More than 30 of his battalion comrades are buried here,

Captain Charles Owen Slacke, of the 14th Royal Irish Rifles, was a grandson of architect Sir Charles Lanyon

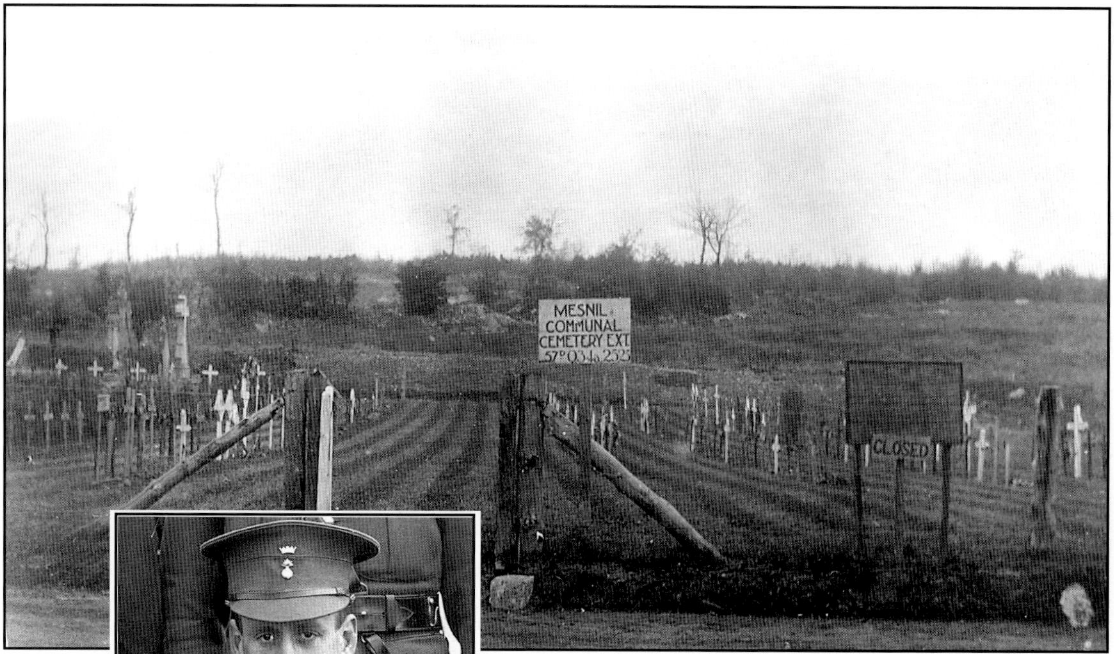

Mesnil Communal Cemetery Extension, photographed in 1921 under construction, holds the body of Captain Charles Moore Johnston, of the 9th Royal Irish Fusiliers, who is one of only four named Irish soldiers buried here

Courtesy of the Royal Irish Fusiliers Museum

men such as Private Richard Fowler, a 19-year-old from Lisnamallard, Omagh, County Tyrone, and Samuel Peter Hutchings, a 33-year-old private who had lived at Fitzgibbon Street, Dublin.

A number of volunteers for the Ulster Division, in some cases old soldiers eager to get back into the ranks, came from Liverpool and Scotland to enlist in Belfast. Private George Herbert Ledson, a 30-year-old with the 9th Royal Inniskilling Fusiliers and a native of Everton, Liverpool, and Private John Mackenzie, a 36-year-old from Glasgow serving with the 11th Royal Inniskilling Fusiliers, may have been two such men. A number of fellow countrymen who served with Irish regiments are at rest in this cemetery.

Just one solitary representative of the Royal Irish Fusiliers known by name could be found: Private Thomas Farr, a 29-year-old of the 9th battalion, was from Mall View, Armagh and, like so many in this cemetery, died on July 1, 1916.

[1]Another grandson, Captain William Mortimer Lanyon, from Lismara, Whiteabbey, County Antrim, was commissioned into the Royal Irish Rifles in 1899. A sniper shot him in the head, killing him instantly, at the beginning of his first full day in the trenches on April 5, 1915. He is buried at Rue-du-Bacquerot Graveyard, Laventie, Pas-de-Calais.

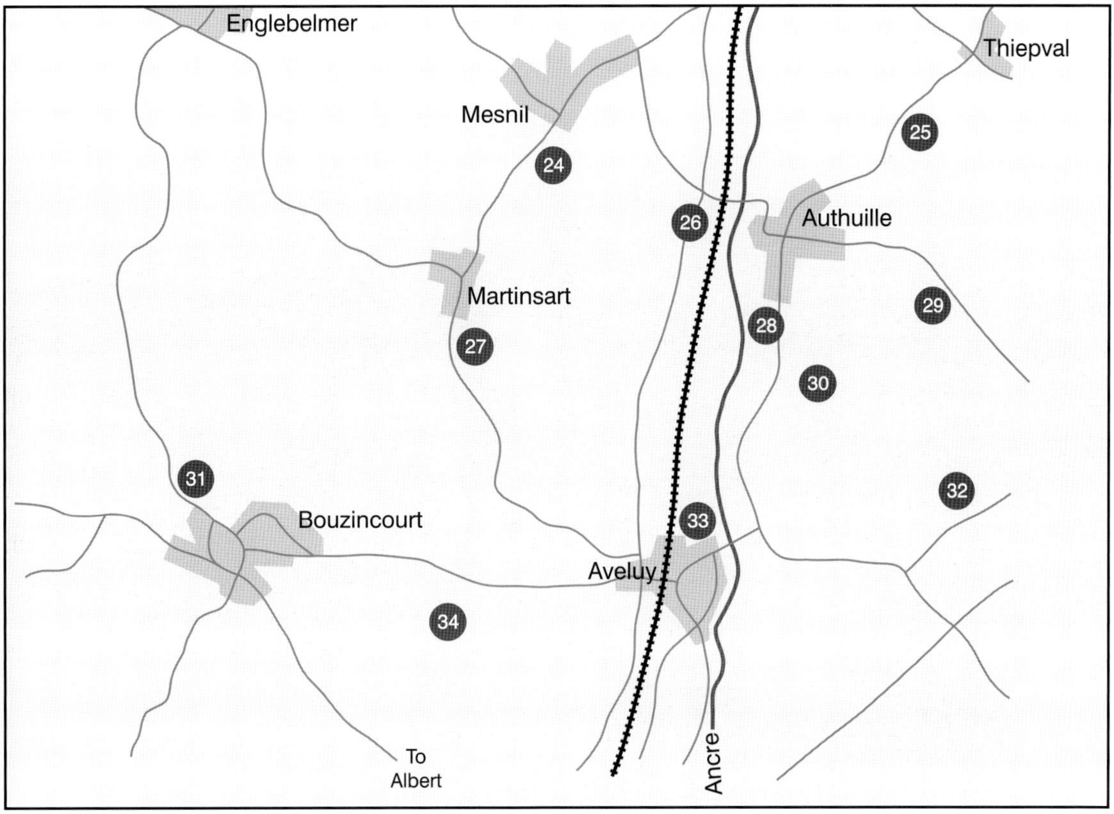

(24) Mesnil Communal Cemetery Extension

Mesnil Communal Cemetery Extension adjoins the French civilian graveyard and, as is always the case, looks much neater and more orderly by comparison. Just under two miles south-west of the Ulster Tower, it contains the graves of 333 men, 240 known by name, and was started in July, 1916, but extended after the war.

There are only four named Irish soldiers and one sailor in this cemetery that I could find. Captain Charles Moore Johnston, a 30-year-old from Carrickblacker Avenue, Portadown, where his widow Muriel received the black-rimmed telegraph, died on the opening day of the Battle of the Somme, July 1, 1916, as did Private F. Houston, a 26-year-old killed in action. Both served with the 9th Royal Irish Fusiliers, part of the 36th (Ulster) Division. Other members of this regiment are among those in the cemetery unknown by name. J. Dardis, who was 28 when killed on October 23, 1916, with the 10th Royal Dublin Fusiliers, was from Joanstown, Rathowen, County Westmeath. The fourth Irish soldier is Bombardier Robert Poag, a 26-year-old who was serving with the 67th Anti-Aircraft Battery of the Royal Garrison Artillery. He died on September 6, 1916. His death was the second heartbreak for his family on the Woodstock Road, Belfast, as another son, Lance Corporal James Stevinson Poag, 27, of the 2nd Royal Irish Rifles, had been killed in October, 1914. The former Belfast City Tramway employee left a widow, Mary, in William Street, Donaghadee, County Down. He is remembered on Le Touret Memorial, Pas-de-Calais. A third son, William, was wounded at Gallipoli while serving with the Royal Marines.

The Royal Navy man is Sub-Lieutenant Jack Caton, a member of the Royal Naval Volunteer Reserve before the war. He was serving in the Anson Battalion of the Royal Naval Division and was killed on March 27, 1918. He was the only

Thiepval Memorial Cemetery symbolises the Anglo-French tragedy played out at the Somme, with 300 soldiers from each nation lying either side of the Cross of Sacrifice

son of John and Eliza Caton, of Ross Villa, Muckamore, County Antrim, and had been employed at the York Street Flax Spinning Company in Belfast before the war.

(25) Thiepval Memorial Cemetery

Created in 1932-33 at the rear of the Thiepval Memorial to the Missing, the cemetery consists of 300 British and 300 French graves, symbolising the joint sacrifice during the Battle of the Somme. Barely a third on the British side are known by name.

There are nine Irish soldiers in this highly symbolic cemetery, built on what was the old German front line. Only two of these are known by name: Rifleman James Ritchie, of the 14th Royal Irish Rifles, who died on July 1, 1916, lies to the rear of the second block; the grave of Private Patrick Martin, 39, 1st Royal Irish Fusiliers, who was killed on October 12, 1916, and who came from Ballyjamesduff, County Cavan, is on the front row of the same block.

There are five unknown Royal Dublin Fusiliers, as well as unnamed members of the Royal Irish Rifles and Royal Irish Fusiliers.

The wording on the Sword of Sacrifice reads:

> *That the world may remember the common sacrifice of two and a half million dead here have been laid side-by-side soldiers of France and of the British Empire in eternal comradeship.*

(26) Aveluy Wood Cemetery

This cemetery, built in a clearing in Aveluy Wood, was initially named after a nearby supply dump. Used throughout 1916 and early 1917, burials halted with the German advance of March, 1918, but were started again later that year. There are 380 graves, including 26 Canadians. It lies some two miles north of Albert.

Despite there being so few Irish graves, the cemetery represents quite a spread of Battle of the Somme actions. There are six Royal Irish Rifles casualties, three of whom died in successive days: William John Keefe, of the 10th Battalion, a 34-year-old from Derwent Street in Belfast, killed on July 1; R. Atkinson, 25, from Woodcot Avenue in the city and posted to the 8th battalion, who died the following day; and Second Lieutenant D. Cole, of the 16th battalion, the divisional pioneers, who died from wounds on July 3.

One Royal Inniskilling Fusilier, Private J. Kerrigan, of B Company, 11th battalion, is known to lie here. The 39-year-old, from Mullanbouy, Castlefin, County Donegal, was killed in the July 1 fighting. Most of the Irish dead in this cemetery fell during the latter stages of the battle, including men of the 2nd Royal Irish Rifles killed on September 27, 1916, and six Royal Dublin Fusiliers, all but one of whom – 31-year-old Private P. Reynolds, who died on November 13, 1916 – are unknown by name.

(27) Martinsart British Cemetery

On the edge of the village, Martinsart British Cemetery is some two miles south-west of the Ulster Tower. It was started in 1916 by the Royal Irish Rifles and used again in 1918 and after the war as a concentration cemetery. There are 488 graves and commemorations, 333 known by name, marked by red Corsehill headstones instead of the usual white Portland.

In a continuous row along the back of Martinsart British Cemetery lie the bodies 14 Royal Irish Rifles soldiers who died instantly in the one incident just days before the start of the Battle of the Somme. On the evening of June 28, 1916, the 13th battalion was preparing to enter the line when a German shell fell in their midst, ultimately claiming the lives of 24 men. The official history records:

> *On the evening of the 28th, 'Y' day, the battalion was relieving the 11th Rifles in Thiepval Wood, and marching out of Martinsart by platoons at two hundred yards' interval. As number 11 Platoon and battalion headquarters were about to march out together a shell fell right in the midst of the party. Fourteen were killed on the spot, and ten more died later. Almost all the rest were wounded, including the second-in-command, Major R. P. Maxwell, and the adjutant, Captain Wright. The confusion in the pitch darkness, with scarce a man on his feet, was appalling. Fortunately a platoon of the 11th Rifles, just relieved from the trenches, appeared on the scene, and the street was speedily cleared.*

Among the dead were Company Sergeant Major Joseph McCoy, a 46-year-old originally from Monaghan but with an address in Blythe Street, Belfast, at the time of his death, and Regimental Sergeant Major J. Beatson. On the headstone of Rifleman J. Carson, 30, were added the words: "Ever Remembered by His

Martinsart British Cemetery, unusual because of its red Corsehill headstones, was started in June, 1916, after 14 members of the Royal Irish Rifles were killed nearby when a German shell landed in their midst. It also holds the remains of Colonel Bernard, below, who died leading his men across No-Man's-Land

Courtesy of the Somme Heritage Centre

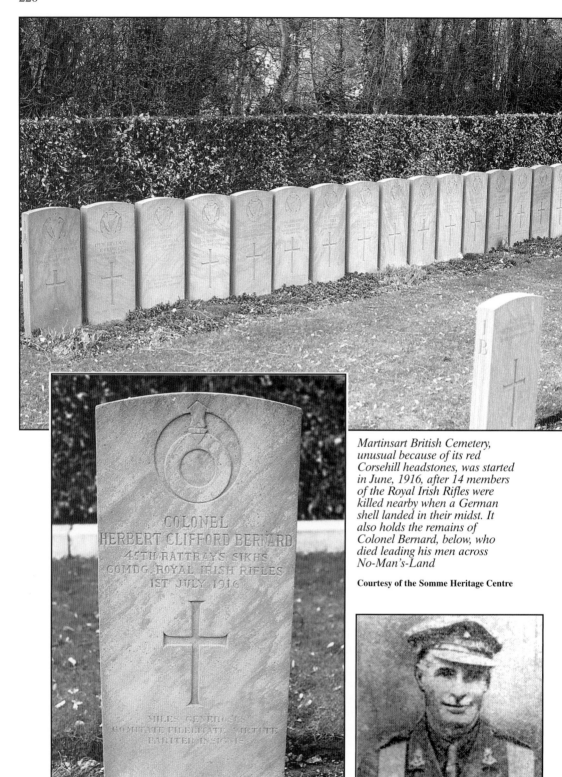

Loving Wife and Son, M. and J. Carson, Banbridge." As if to emphasis that message, two Poppy crosses had recently been planted by the grave at the time of my visit.

Alongside those who died in the blast are the graves of two second lieutenants. Charles Frederick Craig, 24, of the 10th battalion, had lived at Kildare Street, Newry, County Down. He was fatally wounded in a bombardment of the rear area and died a few days later. Second Lieutenant Craig had attended the Model and intermediate schools in Newry and had been working as a Bank of Ireland clerk for four years, serving in branches in Tipperary, Cavan and Waterford. He had only been at the front a month before his death. David Bertram Corbett was another recent arrival at the front for he was still formally recorded as being with the home-based 17th battalion. He lived at Ardsallagh, Derryvolgie, Belfast. Both died on July 3, 1916.

Further along that same back row is the grave of Colonel Herbert Clifford Bernard, commander of the 10th Royal Irish Rifles and one of the most colourful characters in the Ulster Division. Aged 50 at the time of his death, on July 1, 1916, he had disobeyed orders to lead his men into battle. Born in Cheltenham, he was a veteran of the Burmese War of 1885-91 and had only just retired from the Indian Army – where he had commanded the 45th Raltray's Sikhs from 1909 to 1914 – prior to the outbreak of the European war. He was a cousin of the Archbishop of Dublin and the last surviving son of Royal Navy doctor Robert Bernard, deputy inspector general of Hospitals and Fleets and honorary surgeon to the Queen. Colonel Bernard's nephew, Lieutenant Robert Bernard, of the Royal Dublin Fusiliers, son of the archbishop, was killed at Sedd-el-Bahr in 1915.

Crozier refers to Colonel Bernard on a number of occasions in his book A Brass Hat in No Man's Land, and obviously held him in the highest esteem. In one incident he recalled how the "old warrior", as he referred to him, lost his trousers:

> *One morning I go down to the right to meet Colonel Bernard at our junction, in order to decide a tactical consideration. We are to meet at 10am. I wait. The colonel is late, a most unusual thing for him. I stay on till 11am and am on the point of departure when I hear a sound. I look up. What do I see? It is Bernard all right, but he walks gingerly. What has he got on? Socks, shirt, tunic, cap, nothing else! He roars with laughter as he approaches. I regard him with amazement! 'You may well look' he says. 'I got bogged. Luckily they heard me. My trench boots were wedged, so they pulled me out of them. I had slacks on in order to free the circulation, so I undid the braces and thigh straps and got them to pull me out of the lot. Your HQ is nearer than mine, so I have told them to send me along a pair of breeks and some boots!' As it is very cold we move on to dry ground in a hollow and make for my dugout, my orderly carrying the colonel on his back, as his feet are cut.*

The pair spent part of the evening of June 30, 1916, in Thiepval Wood, eating sandwiches and discussing the coming battle and the situation in Ireland before grabbing a few hours' rest sitting against a tree trunk. Of his death, Crozier says:

> *The adjutant of the 10th tells me Colonel Bernard is no more. The colonel and half his men walked into the barrage of death during the advance. All died behind him as he resolutely faced the edge of the wood in an impossible effort to walk through a wall of raining iron and lead, which had lifted for us that brief five minutes.*

There are three Royal Irish Rifles graves in this cemetery unknown by name and including an officer, and one Royal Irish Fusilier, 20-year-old John Joseph Kells, of the 9th battalion, killed on July 1, 1916. He was from Lisboduff, Cootehill, County Cavan.

Major Robert Carson, of the Royal Garrison Artillery, was killed in August, 1916, as he tried to get his men under cover during an enemy bombardment

Courtesy of the North Down Heritage Centre

P. J. Kelly, a private in the Lancashire Fusiliers, killed on April 14, 1918, was an Irishman, as was Robert Carson, a major with the Royal Garrison Artillery who died on August 24, 1916. The latter was aged 37 and had been a member of the Ulster Yacht Club and Royal Belfast Golf Club, and played for the first XV of the North of Ireland Rugby Club. He joined the army in 1900, spending eight years in India. Major Carson was killed in an enemy bombardment as he checked his men were under cover. His father, a former clerk of the peace for Belfast, lived at Carnalea House, Carnalea, County Down, and he left a widow, Helen, in Broadwater, Kent.

(28) Authuille Military Cemetery

The approach to Authuille Military Cemetery, down a narrow track off a back street in the village, gives no indication of its picturesque setting on the river bank. From its entrance it slopes away, with views across the tree-lined water to the railway track beyond. Of the 472 graves here, well over a fifth belong to men from the 36th (Ulster) Division. The cemetery, which lies some two miles north of Albert, was used by field ambulances and includes burials from 1915-18.

On February 7, 1916, the 36th (Ulster) Division took over its first stretch of line between the Ancre and the Mailly-Maillet/Serre Road, with its headquarters at Acheux. Bar one heavy bombardment, which caused no casualties, it suffered more from the weather than the enemy.

After a short spell out of the line, the division was back at the front. May 7 marked its first raid on the enemy, with the 9th Royal Inniskilling Fusiliers inflicting heavy casualties on the Germans in their dugouts only to be pinned down on the sunken Thiepval-Hamel road for two hours by retaliatory artillery fire, during which a number were killed and injured. The following week, in the build-up to the "Big Push", there were more raids and counterattacks by the Germans.

On June 5, the 12th Rifles attacked a sap north of the Ancre, bombing dugouts and destroying two tunnels leading toward the British lines. Five nights later, the Germans retaliated on William Redan, a little salient jutting out into No-Man's-Land held by the 15th Rifles, during which bitter hand-to-hand fighting took place in the trenches.

The casualties from these spells in the line make up the majority of the Irish graves at Authuille, with May and June, 1916, figuring more prominently than the earlier months.

There are at least 66 Royal Inniskilling Fusiliers graves, of which all but five are named, and close to 50 Royal Irish Rifles soldiers known by name. One block is made up of a continuous line of Ulster graves, 23 in all, consisting of 14 Inniskilling Fusiliers and nine Rifles.

Among the Rifles dead is 18-year-old Charles Francis Hill, from Ravara, Ballygowan, County Down, who was serving with the 13th battalion; Corporal Victor Thomas Law, 19, from Anchor Lodge, Newcastle, County Down, killed on June 27, 1916, while raiding the German trenches; and Second Lieutenant Robert McCalmont Pettigrew, of the 8th battalion, from Eglantine Avenue in Belfast, who was 20. Many of the Inniskillings were Tyrone men, including privates George Neely of Summer Hill in Clogher and Thomas James Mossey, from Augher, both members of the 9th battalion. Not all the Inniskilling Fusiliers buried here were with the 36th Division. Thomas Woodburn was a soldier of 12 years' experience when he was killed in February, 1916. The Cookstown, County Tyrone man was 31 and had been serving with the pre-war regular 2nd battalion.

Authuille Military Cemetery sweeps around the hillside next to a tree-lined river

Courtesy of the Somme Heritage Centre

There is one member of the 6th Dragoons (Inniskillings), Albert Henry Nicholson, whose rank is given as Bandsman. The 23-year-old son of an army captain died in September, 1915.

(29) Lonsdale Cemetery

A particularly peaceful cemetery, Lonsdale lies just under a mile-and-a-half due south of the Ulster Tower on what was the British front line. Begun in 1917, and named in honour of the 11th (Lonsdale) battalion of the Border Regiment which stormed the Leipzig Salient from here, it was greatly expanded after the war. There are in excess of 1,500 graves of which more than half are unidentified by name.

This typical concentration cemetery includes the graves of a wide variety of units and time periods, though the vast majority of the casualties are from the Battle of the Somme in 1916. Just a handful of soldiers who served in Irish regiments lie here, with only the Royal Irish Rifles and Royal Inniskilling Fusiliers represented. Among the Rifles dead is Second Lieutenant John Francis Stein, 31, from Blackrock, County Dublin, who is recorded as being a member of the 3rd battalion on attachment to the 2nd battalion. Killed in September, 1916, he was his parents' only son.

Most of the Inniskilling dead are from the pre-war regulars of the 2nd battalion, and include lance corporals T. Neill, a 20-year-old from the Donegall Road in Belfast, and Maurice Lawson Banks, 22, from Small Heath, Birmingham, both killed on July 1, 1916.

Second Lieutenant James Ekin, killed on July 1, 1916, with the 8th York and Lancaster Regiment, was born in Sydney, Australia, though may have been of Irish descent. The 19-year-old's father was a bank official who had served with the Belfast Bank in Dungannon and Cookstown.

(30) Blighty Valley Cemetery

Lying little more than 1.5 miles south of the Ulster Tower, between Authuille and Aveluy, Blighty Valley Cemetery was called after the troops' name for the area. As a "blighty" was a wound which necessitated a return home for treatment, it is perhaps an indication of the ferocity of the war in the immediate area. The cemetery contains more than 1,000 graves, of which 491 are known by name. It was begun in July, 1916, and greatly extended after the war.

There are only four graves of Irish interest in this cemetery that I could find. Lieutenant Donard Irvine Smith, a 25-year-old of Annesley Mansions, Newcastle, County Down, was a member of the 5th battalion of the Royal Irish Rifles but on attachment to the 1st battalion. His father was J. Irvine Smith, a barrister-at-law of Ardkeen, Newcastle and Smithborough, County Monaghan, and his uncle was R. J. McMordie, M.P., a former Lord Mayor of Belfast. Lieutenant Smith had been working for the North Vancouver Engineers in Canada just prior to the outbreak of war. He died on July 1, 1916, at the head of D Company. Witnesses reported he was killed attacking the third German line, having earlier sustained a bayonet wound to the chest. Rifleman P. Collins, also of the 1st Rifles, was killed the same day.

Captain Bryan Dolphin Paull, although English by birth, had been attached to the 8th Royal Irish Rifles. The 19-year-old, who was killed on September 30, 1916, had originally been posted to the East Surrey Regiment. Second Lieutenant John Martindale Hall, of the 3rd Border Regiment attached 8th battalion, was killed on August 29, 1916. His father ran a musical instruments business in Royal Avenue and Wellington Place, Belfast, though the family, which later moved to Cumberland, may also have been English in origin.

(31) Bouzincourt Communal Cemetery and Extension

There are 33 soldiers' graves in the civilian cemetery with another 587 in the military extension to the rear. Bouzincourt lies to the south-west of the Ulster Tower, near Albert. Burials began here early in 1916. It was used by the field ambulances to leave off the bodies of soldiers who did not survive long enough to make it back to the main dressing stations. Further burials were added from 1919.

There are less than 30 Irish graves in Bouzincourt Communal Cemetery and Extension, only 20 of which can be identified by name.

The biggest representation is of Royal Inniskilling Fusiliers, their dates of death mostly being in June/July 1916. Among the dead of this regiment is another son of the manse, Second Lieutenant Claude Arthur Leonard Walker, whose father was the Rev. Robert Walker, of Shankill rectory in Belfast. The 21-year-old had joined the Public Schools Battalion at the outbreak of war in August, 1914, and had been selected to attend the Royal Military College at Sandhurst in December of that year. Commissioned in May, 1915, he was posted to the 2nd Royal Inniskillings Fusiliers and died of his injuries on July 10, 1916, reportedly having been hit in the head by a bullet. Second Lieutenant Arthur Henry Tottenham, who served in the same battalion, is buried nearby. A son of a former Royal Irish Constabulary district inspector who retired to Moy, County Tyrone, his grandfather had been the Venerable William Creek, Archdeacon of Kilmore and rector of Kildallon, County Cavan. The 20-year-old was killed on June 27, 1916 – in the same week that his family received confirmation that his older brother, Second Lieutenant Edward Tottenham, 21, had died during the fighting in Mesopotamia in April that year. His name is recorded on the Basra Memorial in Iraq. The two second lieutenants had been friends, and Walker had visited Tottenham's grave only days before he himself was laid to rest in the same cemetery.

In the days of Empire, people rallied to the Colours from around the globe. One such was Thomas William Hunte, a lance corporal with the 2nd Royal Irish Rifles, who was killed on October 19, 1916. The 25-year-old had been working as a Customs Officer in British Guiana when war broke out. His parents were recorded as living at the Ocean View Hotel, Hastings, Barbados, British West Indies.

Private James Agnew, of the 7th Royal Irish Fusiliers, didn't have quite as far to go to enlist. From Larne, County Antrim, the 30-year-old had been living in Glasgow before the war. Lance Corporal A. Vincent, who died on November 11, 1916, is the sole named member of the Royal Dublin Fusiliers in this cemetery. He served with the 9th battalion. There are two London Irish Rifles soldiers plus another, Rifleman P. E. John, from Northampton, who was attached to the 1/18 London Regiment from the Royal Irish Rifles.

Private Issac Freeman, 34, killed on the opening day of the Somme battle, was the first member of Belfast's Jewish community to die in the war. He had enlisted with the 17th Highland Light Infantry at the outset and had been in France since November, 1915. His parents lived at Avoca Street, Belfast.

Another grave of interest is that of Catholic priest the Rev. D. V. O'Sullivan, an army chaplain whose headstone backs onto the military extension from the adjoining civilian cemetery. The 26-year-old cleric, from Killarney, was killed on July 5, 1916. He was buried not with the men he served but with French soldiers whose bodies have since been removed. The grave, which has a standard Commonwealth War Graves Commission headstone, has its own surround which, while not unique, is fairly unusual. His brother, Mr J. J. O'Sullivan, worked at the Shankill Road Labour Exchange in Belfast. Whether the young priest was buried in the civilian cemetery to be with his co-religionists or, as is just as likely, to be as near as possible to the Cross of Sacrifice on the other side of the hedge has been lost in the mists of time.

Killarney priest the Rev D. V. O'Sullivan lies amongst the French civilians next to the soldiers' cemetery at Bouzincourt

(32) Ovillers Military Cemetery

This cemetery holds 3,436 bodies of which more than 70 per cent are unknown by name. In addition there are more than 100 French buried at Ovillers. It was started in the middle of 1916 and hugely expanded after the war.

This cemetery, some two-and-a-half miles south of the Ulster Tower, is the last resting place for the dead from a wide variety of Irish regiments which fought in the Somme area in both 1916 and 1918. Only 17 are known by name, with nearly as many again among the unknown having been identified as coming from Irish units.

The Royal Irish Rifles is the only regiment with a substantial number of casualties in this cemetery. A number of these are from the 2nd battalion's action near here in the middle of July 1916 and include Second Lieutenant T. E. Barton who, having missed the slaughter on July 1 with his own 14th Rifles, died while on attachment. Second battalion members J. Crawford and H. G. Dormer are remembered on special memorials, with their graves at Mash Valley Cemetery, one of those concentrated at Ovillers, unable to be found after the war, as is Rifleman Leo Vickers, of the 1st battalion. Thomas McEvoy, of the 1st Rifles, served under the name McDonald. He left a widow, Elizabeth, in Balkan Street, Belfast.

Of the remaining known dead, each is from a different regiment: Lance Corporal James Byrne, 29, was killed on October 23, 1916. From Sweetmount, Churchtown, Dundrum, County Dublin, he was serving with the 2nd Royal Dublin Fusiliers; Private Denis Halloran, killed on September 9, 1916, was with the 2nd Royal Munster Fusiliers; Frederick Christian Heneker is an interesting character. A lieutenant-colonel who had served with the Leinster Regiment, the 42-year-old was commanding the 21st Northumberland Fusiliers (Tyneside Scottish) when killed on July 1, 1916. His parents were living in Quebec, Canada, and his widow at Bickley, Kent; Adam Gordon Kelly, 28, was killed on August 26, 1918, while serving with the North Irish Horse. He was from Armaghbreague, Keady, County Armagh; Captain Cecil Cuthbert Thompson, 25, although technically attached to the home-based 4th Royal Inniskilling Fusiliers, was killed with the 2nd battalion on July 14, 1916. Among those unknown by name, but identified by regiment, are soldiers of the Irish Guards and Royal Irish Regiment.

An Irishman serving with a Welsh regiment is among the dead here. Second Lieutenant Charles Duncan McCammon, of the 9th Royal Welsh Fusiliers, was the youngest son of Andrew McCammon, of Drumgooland, Seaforde, County Down. The 24-year-old, killed on July 3, 1916, had already shown his courage by leading a patrol through barbed wire to bomb the enemy out of a row of trenches,

Riflemen Crawford, Dormer and Vickers were buried at Mash Valley Cemetery but their graves were later lost and they are now remembered with special memorials at Ovillers

for which he received a letter of congratulation from his commanding officer. Second Lieutenant W. C. Hickman, of the Royal Field Artillery, also lies in this cemetery. A nephew of Brigadier-General T. K. Hickman, who had commanded a brigade of the Ulster Division for a spell, he had returned home from Canada to join up. Second Lieutenant Andrew Hatch Jarman had been a manager at Workman, Clark shipyard in Belfast before the war and a member of Cliftonville cricket and hockey clubs. The 34-year-old, killed on July 1, 1916, was serving with the 20th Northumberland Fusiliers (Tyneside Scottish). The family home was at Ivydene, Antrim Road, Belfast.

Former Leinster Regiment officer Lieutenant Colonel Heneker was killed on July 1, 1916 when commanding the Tyneside Scottish

(33) Aveluy Communal Cemetery Extension

The village of Aveluy is south-west of the Ulster Tower, and almost three miles distant. The military cemetery is on a steep hillside overlooking the civilian graveyard below. The first burials were in August 1915 with 613 graves in total, though comparatively few are Irish.

Six Royal Irish Rifles, from both the 1st and 2nd battalions, lie in this cemetery, most having died in late June, 1916, in the final days of preparation for the Somme battle. Among their number is 28-year-old Lance Corporal E. Sutherland, originally from the Shankill Road in Belfast, who left a widow, Mary, at her Lisbon Street home in the east of the city. There are also three Royal Inniskilling Fusiliers, members of the 2nd battalion, killed between January and March 1916 when the regiment manned the lines east of here. Half-a-dozen men of the King's (Liverpool) Regiment, who died in two distinct periods, are buried in this cemetery, some from August and September 1915 and others from February-April 1917. It is likely, given its location, that many of those buried in this cemetery died from their wounds at a nearby Casualty Clearing Station.

An Irishman less easy to spot is Second Lieutenant Robert Clanrye McGaffin, of the 10th Siege Battery, Royal Garrison Artillery. He was the son of a Newry man who immigrated to Cape Town, South Africa, where he named his home "Donnybrook". Second Lieutenant McGaffin, 21, had been in France a month before his death on July 5, 1916.

(34) Bouzincourt Ridge Cemetery

This cemetery was started in September, 1918, after the British forces pushed the German army from the area. There are 709 burials and commemorations in total, of which 313 are unidentified and 396 can be named. It is reached via a 500 yard laneway situated a little more than a mile north-west of Albert, on the main road to Doullens.

Only four graves of soldiers who could be identified are men of Irish units. Three belonged to the London Irish Rifles, two of whom are stated to have been born in London. They are riflemen Arthur Edwin Northrop, 19, from Hampton Court, and W. C. Paisley, a 21-year-old from Bermondsey. Sergeant W. Oakley completes the trio, who all died on May 13, 1918.

The fourth soldier is Private G. Nelson, of the 9th Royal Irish Fusiliers, who was killed on the opening day of the Battle of the Somme on July 1, 1916. A walk along the rows of headstones indicates that there are at least another six burials of Irish regiment soldiers unknown by name. Four were Royal Irish Fusiliers with one each from the Royal Irish Rifles and Royal Inniskilling Fusiliers.

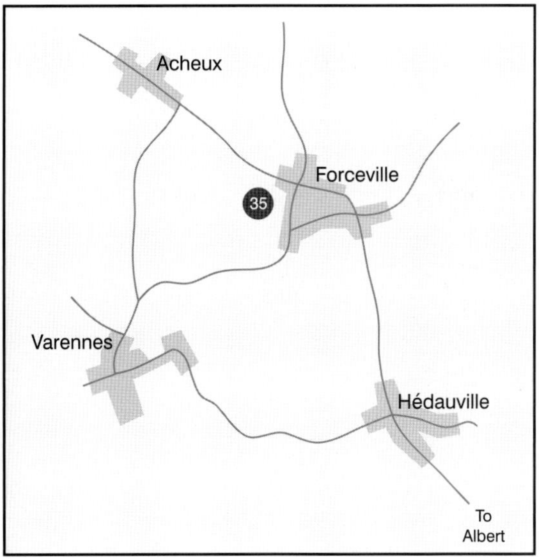

(35) Forceville Communal Cemetery Extension

On the road to Doullens, some seven miles north-west of Albert, Forceville Communal Cemetery Extension is another in which the majority of the Irish graves are pre-Battle of the Somme. It holds 304 bodies and was one of the first three cemeteries completed by the Imperial (now Commonwealth) War Graves Commission, with its design being effectively chosen as the template for the subsequent building programme. The cemetery was begun in September, 1915, and used by field ambulances to leave off the dead from February-July 1916.

The village of Forceville was a familiar sight to the soldiers of the 36th (Ulster) Division. A number of battalions had their headquarters here at various times in the months leading up to the Battle of the Somme and the 108th Field Ambulance's main dressing station was situated in the village throughout the early fighting.

Although it is just over five miles from the nearest part of the front line, it must have been an horrendous task to get the more seriously injured to the dressing station, part of the journey being made on roads that today are quiet and deserted but which, at the height of the battle, would have been packed with the walking wounded and those on stretchers.

The official history, in typically understated terms, says of the opening day of battle:

> *There was throughout no hitch in the medical arrangements, though at one period of the day the overcrowding of the Main Dressing Station at Forceville,*

Rifleman Tate was initially buried among the French civilians. Bangor man Samuel Moffett, right, of the 11th Royal Irish Rifles, was killed in March, 1916

Courtesy of North Down Heritage Centre

due to the strain upon the Motor Ambulance Convoy which evacuated the wounded to the Casualty Clearing Stations, gave rise to much anxiety.

Almost a quarter of the bodies buried at Forceville are Irish, with the majority of these members of the Ulster Division. More than 40 Royal Irish Rifles soldiers are interred here, the biggest single grouping, with burials having begun in November, 1915, and continued until early July, 1916. Private John Hamilton Cunningham had only joined the 11th Rifles in March, 1916, from the 18th battalion. Though originally from Carrickfergus, the 32-year-old had lived most of his life in Dromore, County Down. He died of wounds on June 26, 1916. Another member of the same battalion was 18-year-old Rifleman John Clay from Lambeg, Lisburn, County Antrim. He must have been popular with his comrades for after his death on March 28, 1916, they erected a wooden cross, now gone, which bore the words:

Soldier, rest, thy warfare o'er,
Sleep the sleep that knows no breaking;
Dream of fighting field no more,
Day of toil and night of waiting.

There are 18 members of the Royal Inniskilling Fusiliers buried in this quiet little cemetery, on the edge of the village. Private Jacob Laughlin, of the 9th battalion, who hailed from Ruskey, Dunamanagh, County Tyrone, is among them. His date of death is recorded as July 3, 1916, indicating he had been beyond help when he arrived at the Casualty Clearing Station yet had, perhaps, lingered for up to two days (the 9th Inniskillings having gone over the top on July 1) before succumbing to his wounds. There are five members of the Royal Irish Regiment, the earliest dating from the autumn of 1915. They include privates David Morrissey, a 35-year-old from Tipperary who died on September 5, 1915, while serving with the 2nd battalion, and Alderman Oliver Holden, just 22 and from Liverpool, who was killed the following month. There is one Royal Dublin Fusilier, 37-year-old Howth-born Private Peter Dowdall, of the 2nd battalion, who died on Boxing Day, 1915.

The cemetery, which adjoins the civilian graveyard, was completed by 1920. By "bending" its boundary hedge, it includes the grave of Rifleman J. P. K. Tate, of the Royal Irish Rifles, who following his death in February, 1916, was buried among the French civilians.

(36) Doullens Communal Cemetery Extension No.1

Doullens, once Marshal Foch's headquarters and the scene of an emergency Allied meeting in March, 1918, when the French commander was given overall command of all armies in the face of the German onslaught, is a large town much further west than most featured here. It was a major medical centre, with up to five Casualty Clearing Stations and a Canadian stationary hospital in the town. The cemetery, which can be seen in the mid-distance as you approach the town, is on the eastern fringes, a short distance off a major roadway which by-passes much of the commercial centre. It holds 1,729 graves, most of whom are identified by name.

Doullens is a particularly sad and, in appearance, unusual cemetery. After the British took over this sector of the front the town became a centre for medical units, and most of the burials were of men who arrived here beyond doctors' help. There are comparatively few Irish burials, little more than 30 in total and representing eight different regiments. It is, nonetheless, significant as it is the last resting place of the first Ulster Division soldier to be killed. Like other cemeteries which contain early burials, it somehow symbolises the loss of innocence the Irish soldiers experienced, cumulating in the 1916 slaughter on the Somme.

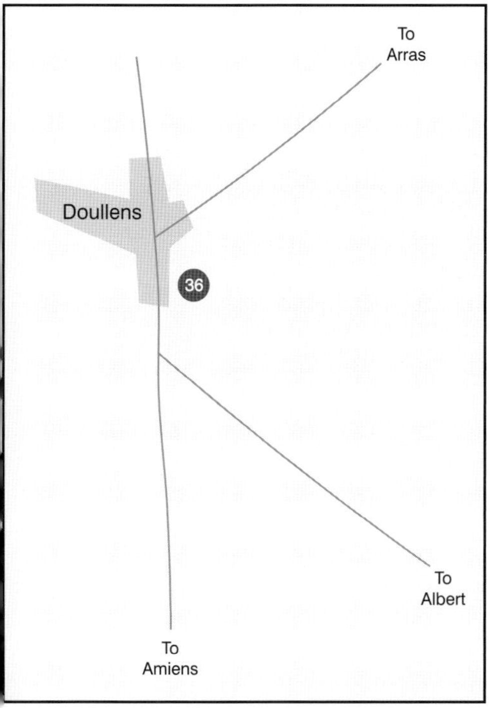

The Ulster Division's Staff officers had only landed in France at midnight on October 3, with the remainder of the division arriving during the 5th-9th of the month. The 107th Brigade was soon after attached to the 4th Division for five days' experience in trench warfare. It was followed by the 108th Brigade, which was split between the 4th and 48th divisions. On October 22, the Germans heavily shelled the frontline trenches, manned by the Warwickshire Fusiliers and their Ulster guests, though the expected trench raid by infantry failed to materialise. Two men were killed and more than a dozen injured. One of these was Rifleman Samuel Hill, of the 12th Royal Irish Rifles, who came from Rush Park, Whitehouse, Monkstown, on the outskirts of Belfast. He was taken back to a medical unit at Doullens but died from his wounds. His grave is to the right of the gateway, at the end of the second row from the back hedge.

Rifleman Hill is one of six Royal Irish Rifles buried at this cemetery. Another is Rifleman William Campbell, of Chief Street in Belfast. He was just 17, and serving with the 16th pioneer battalion, when he was fatally wounded, dying on July 16, 1916, a full two weeks after his division had been withdrawn from the fighting and sent further north. Rifleman Samuel George Hamill, from Ligoniel in Belfast, died of wounds on July 6, 1916.

The Irish Guards have the largest representation. Among their eight soldiers are privates Michael Lehane, 34, from Banteer, County Cork, and Joseph Kelly, who was 32 and from Moylough, Ballinasloe, County Galway. They were from the 1st and 2nd battalions respectively and died within a day of each other at the end of March, 1918.

The Royal Irish Fusiliers, Royal Dublin Fusiliers, and Royal Inniskilling Fusiliers each have six men buried within this cemetery. They include two medal holders, both serving with the Dubliners. Sergeant John McElhagga, who had served in the 1st battalion under the name McFarlane, held the Military Medal for bravery. From Azamar Street, on the Shankill Road in Belfast, he was 30 when he died on July 8, 1916. Corporal Walter Peter Curley, of the 2nd battalion, was the winner of a D.C.M. The 33-year-old, who passed away on July 6, 1916, was from Finstown, County Kildare, though may have been living with his wife in Plumstead, London, before the war.

There are two Irish cavalry men buried here. One is North Irish Horse soldier James McArow, who was killed on April 27, 1916. The 26-year-old trooper, from Mulrod, County Fermanagh, was a holder of the Medaille Militaire of France. The other is 6th Inniskilling Dragoon L. Jubb, killed on May 7, 1917.

London Irish Rifles soldier John Walter Gallacher, a 33-year-old rifleman from the south side of Glasgow who died in April, 1918, may be the sole representative of his battalion buried at Doullens.

Doullens Communal Cemetery Extension No.2

The second extension to the communal cemetery at Doullens is entered by a separate gateway to the left of the main graveyard. It holds 374 First World War graves. See above for further information.

Six Irish Guards lie in this part of the cemetery, which was built later in the war. The most interesting information available is for Second Lieutenant Harold Augustus Boyd Oliver, who died on May 26, 1918. The son of a London clergyman

Rifleman Samuel Hill was the 36th (Ulster) Division's first battlefield casualty. Injured by artillery fire on October 22, 1915, he was taken to a medical unit at Doullens but died of his injuries

and an actor by profession, he had joined up in November, 1914, and served in both France and Salonika with the 85th Field Ambulance. He was invalided home with malaria but remained determined to serve. He managed to secure a commission in the Irish Guards using the alias King and was on attachment to the 4th Guards Machine Gun Regiment when fatally wounded, aged 34. He is not the only one among this small group of guardsmen to show commitment. Private John O'Sullivan, a 23-year-old from Scarteen Street, Newmarket, County Cork, is recorded to have been "three times previously wounded" before finally being mortally injured in May, 1918. Thomas O'Brien, 25, from Athy, County Kildare, and another private with the 1st battalion, is simply stated to have been "a volunteer".

(37) Stump Road Cemetery

Lying to the east of the Ulster Tower, close to Grandcourt Road Cemetery, in what was once German-held territory. It holds the bodies of 263 soldiers, with most of the headstones bearing more than one name.

There is just one Irish soldier known to be buried in this cemetery: Rifleman J. Noble, of the 8th Royal Irish Rifles was, like his comrades in the nearby Grandcourt Road Cemetery, killed in action on July 2, 1916, after fighting his way deep into the German lines.

(38) Grandcourt Road Cemetery

Started in 1917, Grandcourt Road Cemetery is important in the story of the Ulster Division not so much for the number of Irish graves but for its location – close to a mile-and-a-half behind the German lines. It contains a total of 391 graves, with two or three bodies named per headstone, and more than a quarter unidentified.

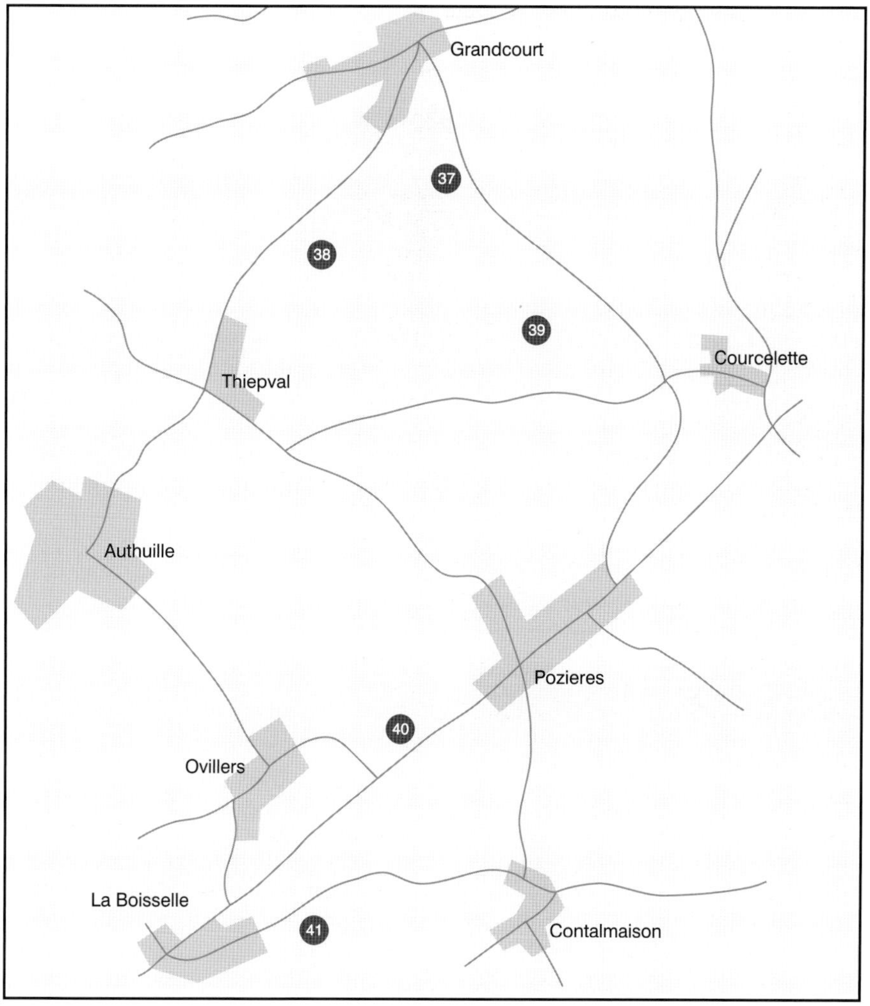

Grandcourt Road Cemetery is the story of what might have been. Lying beyond the German second line, with the formidable Stuff Redoubt out to the south, this area was temporarily taken by the Ulster Division on July 1. Some elements even reached the outskirts of the village of Grandcourt. Without reinforcements they were beaten back. Snuff Redoubt was not taken until early October, 1916, and the land in front of Grandcourt, so briefly held by the Ulstermen, was still being fought over as the Battle of the Somme came to an end in November.

It is an isolated spot, with a difficult approach along a narrow track which allows little room to turn a car, then a walk of several hundred yards across open farm land. The effort is worthwhile, however, as it provides great views across the battlefield and gives an indication of just how far those brave Ulster soldiers travelled that day under a barrage of artillery and machinegun fire. You can also appreciate the long haul back the survivors had to endure as they retired to the German front line, tired and weary, with the enemy closing in behind.

There are five Royal Irish Rifles soldiers known to be buried here, though almost certainly more are among the 108 unidentified. All are from the 8th battalion with their dates of death recorded as July 2, 1916. They are Rifleman H. H. Stewart, of Belvoir Street in Belfast; Rifleman M. Blyth, a 25-year-old who had been born at Selkirk, Scotland; Lance Corporal T. Sillars, the only N.C.O., who had lived at Ballyclare Street, Belfast; Rifleman T. Rippard of whom little is recorded in the cemetery book; and Rifleman A. Ranson, a 29-year-old from the Ravenhill Road in Belfast.

(39) Regina Trench Cemetery, Grandcourt

Named after a German trench system captured in November, 1916, the Regina Trench Cemetery holds 2,279 graves and commemorations, of which just under half, some 1,077, are unidentified by name.

Only four of those buried in this cemetery were serving with Irish regiments, with one of those on attachment to another unit. There are two Royal Inniskilling Fusiliers: Lance Corporal David Albert Porterfield was just 17 when killed on July 1, 1916. The son of John and Isabella Porterfield, of Lifford Common, County Donegal, he was a member of the 9th battalion. Fellow fusilier Private J. Chaters, of the 11th battalion, died the same day.

Captain John Ernest Motherwell was still officially a member of the 3rd Royal Irish Rifles, a reserve battalion back home in Ireland, when he was killed on the Somme on October 21, 1916. The 29-year-old from Somerset Terrace in Belfast was attached to the Loyal North Lancashire Regiment at the time. Rifleman Arthur Barker, 21, of the 2nd Royal Irish Rifles, was killed on the same date.

A cemetery of this size undoubtedly holds many more Irish burials, either among those unknown by name or serving in non-Irish regiments. A walk around the headstones with the cemetery register in hand is likely to prove a surprisingly profitable exercise for the visitor.

(40) Pozieres British Cemetery

An impressive structure some two-and-a-half miles south-east of the Ulster Tower, on the Albert-Pozieres road, this cemetery holds the graves of 2,733 soldiers, of which 1,381 are known by name. The vast majority of the bodies were added after the war. Around its walls are memorial tablets recording the names of 14,650 soldiers who died from March, 1918, but who have no known grave.

Despite the vast number of graves, there are comparatively few headstones displaying the cap badges of Irish regiments. Most of those that do show the harp and crown of the Royal Irish Rifles' 2nd and 13th battalions and are placed over men killed in the summer fighting of 1916. They include the likes of Thomas Howell, from Carrickmaclim, Carrickmacross, County Monaghan, who was already a sergeant at age 18 when killed on July 9, 1916, along with Rifleman Hugh Weir from Linwood Street in Belfast; Rifleman James McCagherty, 24, from Cochrane's Hill, Laurel Vale, Tandragee, County Armagh, who died the following month; and John Prentice, a 24-year-old rifleman from Ballynaris, Dromore, County Down, who was killed two days later on August 30, 1916, along with Rifleman Joseph Peters, 27, from Broughshane, County Antrim. All were members of the 2nd battalion.

Among the members of the 13th battalion, part of the 36th (Ulster) Division, buried here are riflemen Alexander Steele, 22, from Gilford, and J. Curran, 23, from Rathfriland Street, Banbridge, both County Down. They died on July 1, 1916, presumably several miles to the north-west at Thiepval, with their inclusion here indicating that their bodies were discovered later than most.

One grave of particular note is that of Lieutenant Harry Lister Villiers, of the 6th Dragoons (Inniskilling). The 19-year-old had managed to escape the mud of the trenches by getting himself attached to the Royal Flying Corps only to end up buried among so many of his earth-bound comrades following his death on February 4, 1917.

Private Richard Newell, of the 5th Battalion, Canadian Infantry (Saskatchewan

The Pozieres British Cemetery is one of the most impressive

Regiment), was reported to have been killed accidentally in an explosion on active service. He was the second son of S. C. Newell, a resident magistrate from Ballinasloe, County Galway, and Mrs Newell, Kingstown. Volunteering in 1915, Private Newell was sent to France in January the following year. His younger brother, Lieutenant Charles E. Newell, 8th Royal Inniskilling Fusiliers, aged just 19, was killed in May, 1915. He is buried in Bethune Town Cemetery, Pas-de-Calais.

(41) Gordon Dump Cemetery

This cemetery lies little more than a mile north-east of Albert, a short distance off the road to Bapaume. It was started in July, 1916, and greatly increased in size after the war. Only 623 of the 1,053 buried here are known by name

Only four Irish regiment soldiers are thought to lie in this cemetery, all members of the Royal Munster Fusiliers who died on July 15 or 16, 1916. Their names are recorded on special memorials by the Great Cross as, though they are "known or believed to be buried" in the cemetery, the exact location of their graves was lost because of subsequent fighting in the area. The soldiers involved are privates W. Gill, M. Guerin and J. Hannon, all members of the 2nd battalion, and Second Lieutenant Geoffrey J. Hewison, 21, who had only been at the front a few weeks when killed. His father, Edward Hewison, was one of the founders of the Leopardstown race meeting. Second Lieutenant Hewison, from Laurel Cottage, Killowen, near Rostrevor, County Down, was in training to be a dentist before the war.

Captain Claud Raymond Heygate was from a family with roots in Bellarens, County Londonderry. A member of the regular 2nd King's Own Yorkshire Light

The headstone and memorials to Royal Munster Fusilier soldiers Gill, Hannon and Hewison at Gordon Dump Cemetery

Infantry since 1906, but attached to the 10th battalion, the 29-year-old had fought at the battles of Marne, Aisne and First Ypres, where he was wounded. He had only returned to active service in June, 1916, and was killed days later on July 1.

(42) Carnoy Military Cemetery

The village of Carnoy is north of the Albert to Peronne road, just over six miles south-east of the Ulster Tower. Holding 837 graves, it was first used in August 1915, with field ambulance camps established nearby. The village was in German hands from March-August, 1918. A nearby German cemetery was removed in 1924.

This is a beautiful cemetery, on the fringes of the village from which it takes its name. It is also one of the most visited as it contains the body of Captain Wilfred Percy Neville, of the 1st East Yorkshire Regiment, who famously led the charge on July 1 by tossing four footballs into No-Man's-Land with the promise of a prize for the platoon which got it closest to the German trenches.

Although it has only little more that 20 Irish graves representing 10 regiments, the variety and ranks of those interred at Carnoy make it particularly interesting. Royal Irish Regiment soldier Private P. Pierce was killed in early September, 1916. Today the 20-year-old from Murrintown, Wexford, lies in exalted company, forming a trio of headstones with two lieutenant-colonels. Lieutenant Colonel John Staples Molesworth Lenox-Conyngham, one of four brothers serving, was the third son of Sir William Lenox-Conyngham, of Spring Hill, Moneymore, County Londonderry, the family home since the early 17th century. He had served with both the 1st and 2nd Connaught Rangers during a career spanning 30 years, from 1881-1911. He was recalled to service in October, 1914, to command the newly-formed 6th Connaught Rangers, and died on September 3, 1916, during the taking of Guillemont by elements of the 16th (Irish) Division. The 54-year-old was struck in the forehead by a bullet as he led his men, "whose ardour could not be restrained", out of the trenches. (A younger brother, Brevet Lieutenant-Colonel H. M. Lenox-Conyngham, of the Army Veterinary Corps, Fifth Army, died of wounds in March, 1918, and is buried at Kilgobbin Old Church Cemetery, County Dublin.) Next to him lies Lieutenant-Colonel Fitzroy Edmund Penn Curzon, formerly of the Royal Irish Rifles. He had retired from the army on half-pay in 1907 after having seen active service in the Sudan, Sierra Leone and South Africa. He had returned to the Colours to raise and train the 6th Royal Irish Regiment. He was still its commanding officer when he was killed six days after Lenox-Conyngham on September 9, 1916, as the Irish Division again covered itself in glory at the taking of Ginchy. The 57-year-old English-born son of a colonel was mentioned in despatches for the D.S.O. two months after his death.

Three Leinster Regiment officers, all of whom died in 1916, lie here: Captain Michael Cornelius Heenan had been on attachment to the 2nd Wiltshire Regiment when the 38-year-old was killed in January; Major John Carlon Markes, 36, from Glenlara, Tipperary, had formerly been a member of the Lancashire Fusiliers with which he had served in South Africa, earning a mention in despatches, before his death in the Leinsters' ranks in July; and Second Lieutenant H. T. B. Siddons, with an address in England, was with the 5th Leinsters when he died in August.

Soldiers from the Royal Dublin Fusiliers, Royal Irish Fusiliers, Irish Guards, Royal Munster Fusiliers and Royal Inniskilling Fusiliers, are buried in this plot, along with a lance corporal of the 6th Dragoons (Inniskilling), F. Bush, who had been on attachment to the Military Mounted Police when he was killed on July 13, 1916.

Lieutenant Colonel Lenox-Conyngham was killed at the head of the 6th Connaught Rangers at Guillemont. The wooden cross which originally marked his grave in Carnoy Military Cemetery is now in Armagh Church of Ireland Cathedral

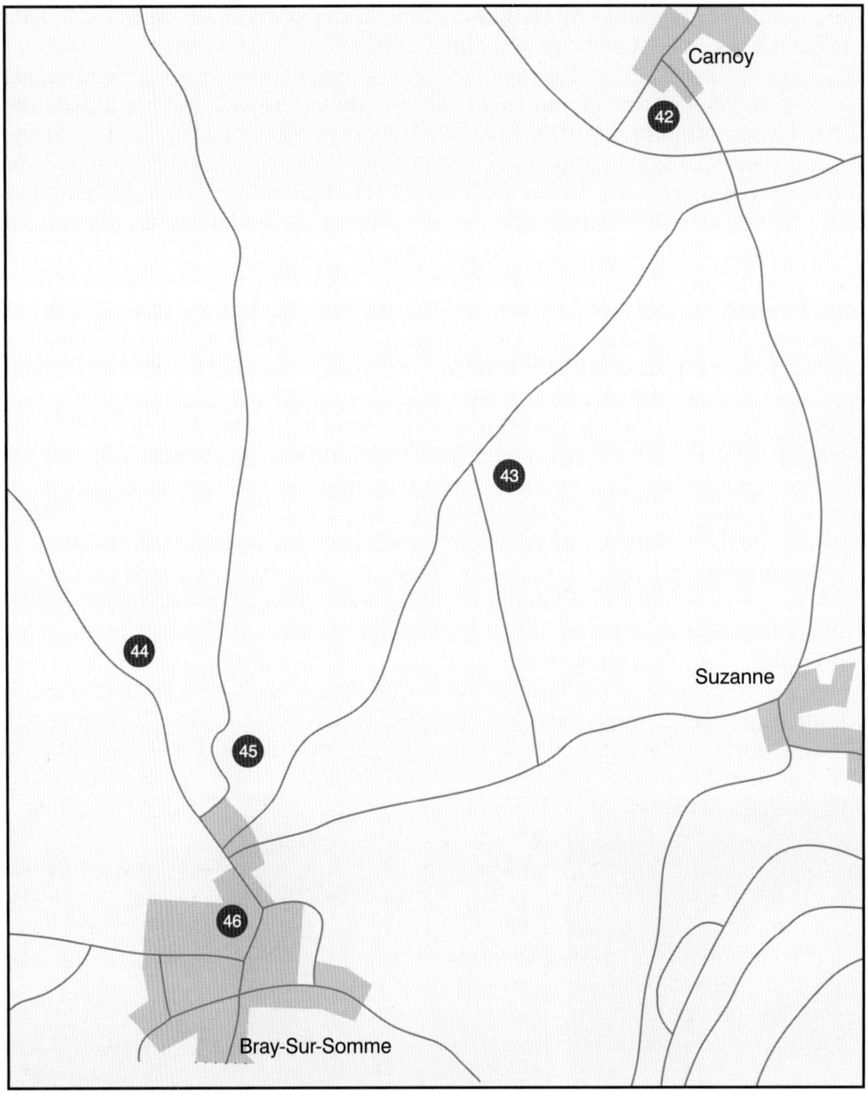

(43) Bronfay Farm Military Cemetery

There are 537 graves in Bronfay Farm Military Cemetery, on the fringes of Bray-sur-Somme next to the road to Maricourt. It was started in October, 1914, by the French and taken over by the British the following summer. The cemetery stands next to the farm buildings from which it gets its name and from where medical units operated from 1915. It holds 537 graves and commemorations, of which only 13 are unknown by name.

There are eight Irish regiment graves in Bronfay Farm Cemetery, representing six different units. The most senior in rank is Lieutenant-Colonel Hubert Pulteney Dalzell-Walton, of the 8th Royal Inniskilling Fusiliers, who was killed during the 16th (Irish) Division's successful attack on Ginchy on September 9, 1916. The 50-year-old warrior had served in the Bechuanaland expedition of 1884-85 and in Burma from 1886-1893, where he had been wounded twice, and in the South African War. His father was director general of telegraphs in Bombay and the Persian Gulf. A fellow regimental officer, Lieutenant G. Hawksley, of the 4th battalion but attached to the 7th/8th battalion, lies here. He died on March 22,

Lieutenant Colonel Dalzell-Walton, of the 8th Royal Inniskilling Fusilers, was killed at Ginchy in September, 1916

1918, on the second day of the German offensive which virtually destroyed his division.

Two Leinster Regiment officers are buried nearby. Captain Reginald Nicholas Barnewall was just 20 and attached to the 2nd battalion from the 5th battalion when he was killed on March 24, 1918. He was the son of the 18th Baron Trimlestown, of Willmount, Kells, County Meath. His fellow officer was Lieutenant A. M. Goudie, of the 2nd battalion but attached to the Machine Gun Corps, who had died during the second month of the Battle of the Somme, on August 18, 1916.

The other Irish soldiers who lie here are Private J. Conroy, of the 1st Irish Guards, who came from County Galway and was killed in September, 1916; Private J. Downey, of the 9th Royal Dublin Fusiliers died the same month; Private J. Fitzpatrick, 6th Royal Irish Regiment, was also a September, 1916, fatality; and Private Timothy Whelan, of the 1st Royal Munster Fusiliers, from Fairfield Street, Crumlin Road, Belfast, was killed on March 23, 1918.

(44) Bray Vale British Cemetery

Bray Vale cemetery, built on two levels, contains 279 bodies. Many of the earlier burials, on the top tier, are from 1918, while those nearest the road were added five years later when it was extended. More than 170 are unknown by name.

There are only a dozen men from Irish battalions known to be in this cemetery, which sits on the main road between Albert and Bray-sur-Somme, a short distance outside the latter. One of these is Major George Horner Gaffikin, a 30-year-old whose family lived at King's Castle, Ardglass, County Down. The 9th Royal Irish Rifles officer famously led his men into battle waving an Orange handkerchief, an act which took on a political symbolism in the telling though was based on military expediency – orange was the company colour.

Public school educated Gaffikin, a member of both the North of Ireland and Downpatrick cricket clubs, was a schoolteacher "of portly build" working in England when war broke out. He returned to Ireland to enlist but was lucky to escape serious trouble when caught drunk and incapable of commanding by Colonel, soon to be Brigadier-General, Frank Percy Crozier in a dugout at Hamel during one of the regiment's early stints in the front line just before Christmas, 1915. He had just lost two men in a German raid, which had apparently upset him greatly, and had ordered his men to prepare a retaliatory attack.

Crozier, in his book A Brass Hat in No-Man's-Land, records:

> *I enter the chalk cave which serves as a company headquarters. Gaffikin's old servant is there. He has done his best. I see no Gaffikin but I know where the bed is. A waterproof sheet now hides it. I lift it up. There is George, asleep. I poke him with my stick. He moves and grunts. I smell his breath. 'Drunk' I say, looking at an almost empty whisky bottle. I look at Gold. 'Don't let him leave here until I come back just before stand-to' I order. 'Take all the liquor away; also the ammunition.'*

Crozier returned later as promised. He writes:

> *I enter the dugout. George is sitting on his bed, his face covered by his hands, his elbows on his knees. As I approach, the old servant disappears. The officer commanding B Company stands up. 'Sit down,' I say and I do likewise, on an old backless kitchen chair, taken from some house. I look at the watch on my wrist – I wear it still – and stare George full in the face, for what seems like five minutes. His eyelids droop, his head bends down. At last I speak. 'Look at me,' I order, and he does so. 'Will you give me your word of honour*

not to touch liquor again so long as you are with the battalion? I don't care what you do when you're on leave,' I say slowly. 'I will, Sir,' comes the instant reply.

Gaffikin, then a captain and later promoted to major, went on to prove himself a capable officer, earning a mention in despatches from Sir Douglas Haig after holding the line in February, 1916, during a particularly vigorous assault by the enemy.

Of July 1, Crozier records a final meeting in No-Man's-Land:

George Gaffikin comes next waving an orange handkerchief. 'Good-bye, Sir, good luck,' he shouts to me, en passant, 'tell them I died a teetotaller, put it on the stone if you find me.' 'Good luck, George,' I say, 'don't talk rot, anyhow you played the game!' He died that day after behaving with magnificent courage and fortitude when stricken down.

There is, in fact, no mention of "teetotaller" on the headstone but, given Crozier's words, a perhaps more appropriate tribute has been added: "Write me as one that loves his fellow men." Gaffikin was fatally wounded in the German trenches on July 1 after organising a desperate bid to hold on to the Ulstermen's gains. He was 30 years old.

Another Royal Irish Rifles soldier in the cemetery is Cecil Marshall Elvy, though he didn't die in their ranks. The 19-year-old Londoner most likely joined the Ulster Division after the horrendous losses of the Battle of the Somme. He was later posted to the London Irish Rifles, where no doubt he felt more at home, only to be killed during the British advances of August, 1918. Another six of his London comrades are buried here, all having died that same month.

The Royal Inniskilling Fusiliers are the biggest Irish grouping, with 10 soldiers buried in this cemetery, though only four of these are named. They include two County Tyrone men, Corporal David Patterson Smyth from Newtownstewart and Sergeant Edward John Young, of Nurchasey, both members of the 9th battalion. The other two are Private Robert Cathcart, just 18, of the 11th battalion, who had lived at Black Lane, Ramelton, County Donegal, and 24-year-old Private W. Gray, 10th Inniskillings, who is recorded as having a sister living in Glasgow. Among the many unnamed in this cemetery is at least one grave known to belong to a soldier from an Irish regiment.

(45) Bray Military Cemetery

There are 875 graves in Bray Military Cemetery, which lies to the north of the village from which it takes its name. Many of those buried here died of their wounds at casualty clearing and dressing stations based in the Bray-sur-Somme area during the Battle of the Somme and beyond. The first burials were in April, 1916, with further graves added up until 1924. Some 127 are unidentified by name.

Sergeant M. Healy, of the 2nd Royal Munster Fusiliers, was a true hero and likely the most highly decorated soldier in this cemetery. The 25-year-old, from Ballinamuck, Dungarvan, County Waterford, was the holder of the Distinguished Conduct Medal, Military Medal and Bar, and Albert Medal, and died saving other members of his company. The regimental history records he won the D.C.M. after he was seen by his commanding officer displaying "reckless bravery" in both repelling the enemy's raids and carrying out his own on July 18, 1916, near Contalmaison, the battalion having taken over the line four days previously from the 1st Black Watch. The Official History of the Royal Munster Fusiliers records: "Rain fell again heavily during the night of the 17th; the trenches became waterlogged and many rifles unworkable. The enemy showed signs of having been reinforced, and about noon the following day heavy enemy bombing started, the object of the raiders being the left of the battalion, which rested near the junction of the old German first-line trench and a communication trench. No. 5130 Serjeant Healy came under the personal observation of the Commanding Officer, as did No. 7850 Private Hannon, for the reckless bravery they displayed both in repelling the enemy's raids and carrying out their own. They received the D.C.M. and M.M. respectively." Sadly, it was the careless toss of a grenade by a comrade which resulted in the sergeant's death less than nine months later. On March 1, 1917, he was in a trench when a grenade thrown by another soldier failed to clear the parapet and fell back, landing at the feet of an officer. A War Office letter records that "Sergeant Healy, fearing the party could not escape in time, made a most gallant attempt to seize and hurl the bomb from the trench. It exploded, however, and mortally wounded him. This was the last of Sergeant Healy's many acts of gallantry and devotion to duty. He was previously awarded the Distinguished Conduct Medal and the Military Medal and later a bar to his Military Medal." The date on the headstone indicates that he must have lingered for some hours as his death is given as March 2. After the war, his family had the words "Sacred Heart of Jesus, have mercy on his soul", added to the headstone. Four of his comrades are buried nearby.

The Royal Irish Rifles make up the biggest grouping of Irish regiment graves, with more than a dozen in total. Most died in 1917 and are from the 1st battalion, with a high proportion being English-born though not riflemen James Joseph Dempsey, 36, and J. Cleary, 24, who died in February and April, 1917, respectively. They came from opposite ends of Ireland: Cleary from Hydes Lane, Evergreen Road, Cork and Dempsey from English Street, Belfast. Edmund Westwood Flack, a 28-year-old lance corporal from the 22nd London Regiment who had been serving with the Royal Irish Rifles, is in good company as four members of the London Irish Rifles lie here.

(46) Bray-sur-Somme Communal Cemetery

The cemetery, at the heart of what was an important military town from 1915-18, used to hold 10 British graves. Seven of these were prisoners buried by the Germans during their occupation in 1918 and which were later removed to be interred elsewhere.

If you were to play with statistics, you could suggest that this cemetery is two-thirds Irish as two of the three soldiers' graves are linked to Ireland. One of these is Private G. Quinn, of the 2nd Leinster Regiment, who died on August 3, 1916, probably of wounds at one of the casualty clearing stations then based in the village. The other is John Percival Longfield, a captain in the 3rd Norfolk Regiment. The 29-year-old holder of an M.V.O. (Member of the Victoria Order for services to the Royal family) was killed on September 30, 1915. He was the son of Lieutenant-Colonel Augustus Henry Longfield and Florence Amy Longfield, of Waterloo, Mallow, County Cork.

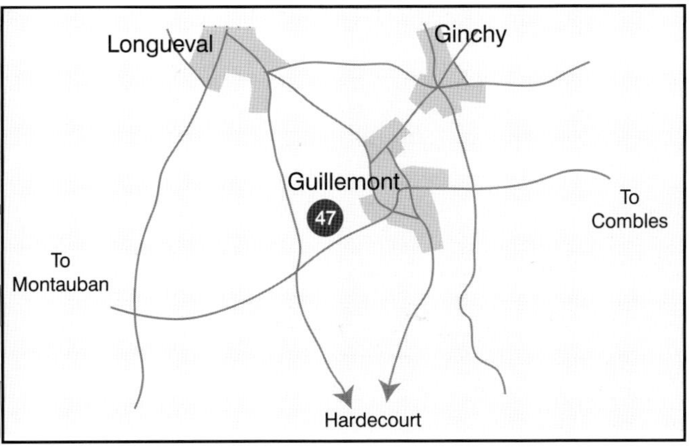

(47) Guillemont Road Cemetery

Considerably more than half the graves in this cemetery are unknown by name, some 1,523 unidentified out of a total of 2,263. Of the 741 named, surprisingly few are from Irish regiments. Guillemont Road Cemetery was started by the Guards Division in 1917 and greatly enlarged after the war.

There are only 37 soldiers from Irish regiments in this cemetery among those

Guillemont Road Cemetery, given its location, holds surprisingly few soldiers from Irish regiments. The 16th (Irish) Division suffered thousands of casualties in the taking of the village and nearby Ginchy.

known by name, though all the infantry regiments of the line are represented. The Royal Dublin Fusiliers and Royal Munster Fusiliers, with nine men each, are the largest groupings. Among the former are privates G. Graham, from Francis Street in Dublin where his foster mum Mary Timmins lived; and James Hunter, a 25-year-old from Celbridge, County Kildare, with a wife in Lucon, County Dublin; and 20-year-old Second Lieutenant Thomas Maxwell, whose doctor father lived in the capital. All were of the 8th battalion and died between the 6th and 9th of September, 1916. From the 9th battalion is Private T. Conlon, age 20, from Duleek, County Meath, who died on September 6, 1916; L. V. Keegan, also a private, was just a year older and died on the same day to the anguish of his parents at Charleville Mall, North Strand in Dublin; and Captain William Joseph Murphy, a 36-year-old whose family was from Tullow, County Carlow. He joined the Leinster Regiment's Cadet Corps in November 1914, being commissioned into the Dubliners in December that year. He is believed to be buried nearby but his body could not be found at the end of the war and so he is remembered on a special memorial. The Munsters include Private D. Moynihan, of Islandmore, Glenflesk, Killarney; 28-year-old Private D. McCarthy, from Ballincollig, Farran, County Cork; and 20-year-old Private T. Kelleher, who had lived with his mother Ellen on Foxes Street, Bandon, County Cork; and Lance Sergeant J. G. Atkins, 26, from Mohona, Dunmanway, County Cork; all members of the 1st battalion.

The three members of the Royal Irish Regiment who lie here are all privates from the 6th battalion: E. Coquelin was just 20 when killed on September 3, 1916. From Le Hurel Vale, Guernsey, he had presumably been one of the men of the Channel Islands who had been brought in to make up the numbers of the 16th (Irish) Division; J. O'Sullivan, a 31-year-old from Pembroke Passage West, County Cork; and Simon Cooney, from Lachanalooha, Mallow, County Cork, who was 45 when killed on September 9, 1916.

All the remaining regiments, the Royal Irish Rifles, the Leinster Regiment, the Royal Irish Fusiliers, Royal Inniskilling Fusiliers (of which Lance Corporal H. Millar, of the 1st battalion, stands out as he is the only one of the Irish soldiers buried here to have died in 1917), Connaught Rangers and Irish Guards all have less that five men buried among those known by name at Guillement, though one suspects there are many more among those unidentified. There is also a soldier of the London Irish Rifles.

Prime Minister Herbert Asquith was the man who introduced the Third Home Rule Bill which dominated and divided Ireland in the years leading up to the First World War. That, in turn, resulted in the formation of both the Ulster and Irish volunteer forces that ultimately formed the nuclei of the 36th and 16th divisions respectively. It is a sad irony, therefore, that Asquith's son Raymond should lie at Guillemont among men driven to take up arms by his father's political manoeuvrings. The 37-year-old was killed on September 15, 1916, while serving with the 3rd Grenadier Guards.

(48) Villiers-Faucon Communal Cemetery and Extension

The cemetery and extension hold a total of 680 British and 156 German graves, principally from 1917 and 1918, and special memorials to six men believed to be buried there.

This cemetery is comparatively rare in that it holds an Irish Victoria Cross winner. Second Lieutenant John Spencer Dunville, of the 1st Royal Dragoons, was the 21-year-old son of Whiskey baron John Dunville, who lived at Redburn, Holywood, County Down. He won his V.C. on July 26, 1917, being fatally wounded in the process. His headstone looks out over the French civilian cemetery, its dark irregular stonework in sharp contrast to the white uniformity of the British headstones, and backs onto a row of German dead. A second V.C. winner, Second Lieutenant H. F. Parsons, of the 14th Gloucesters, is buried nearby.

Two horsemen of the 8th (King's Royal Irish) Hussars, from opposite ends of the social spectrum, are buried here. Major the Hon. Robert Nathaniel Dudley Ryder was 34 when killed on November 30, 1917. He was the son of the fourth Earl of Harrow and lived in Cadogan Place, London; Private Jarlath Vincent Mooney, 23, lived in London, where he had worked as a clerk before the war. He was killed on March 27, 1917.

All told, more than 40 of the known dead here served in the 16th (Irish) Division, with most losing their lives in the final months of 1917 and early 1918, including at least two members of the Leinster Regiment. Lance Corporal C. H. S. Watson, of the 1st Royal Dublin Fusiliers, was one of many Englishmen serving with the division at the time, though it is likely he was a volunteer rather than a conscript as he had been an "Excise officer, stationed in Ireland" at the outbreak of war. Nineteen-year-old Private John O'Brien died on April 14, 1918, when this area had been under enemy control for almost a month. A member of the 2nd Royal Irish Regiment from Drawbridge Street, Cork, it is possible he was buried by the Germans after succumbing to wounds. William Frederick Colton, a 21-year-old private in the 7th (South Irish Horse) battalion of the same regiment was a late arrival in France, having volunteered in 1916. He was from Tullamore, King's County, and died on February 22, 1918.

Private P. Whitby, of the 6th Connaught Rangers, is one of those whose graves could not be found following later fighting in the area. His name is recorded on a special memorial in the cemetery. D. Allen, 20, a private in the 7th/8th Royal Inniskilling Fusiliers, was born in Glasgow but was likely of Irish extraction as his parents were recorded as living at Strand Terrace, Coleraine, County Londonderry. Private M. Keane, one of nine members of the Royal Munster Fusiliers buried in this cemetery, was with the 1st battalion but on attachment to the 47th Trench Mortar Battery when killed on February 19, 1918. He was from Mitchelstown, County Cork.

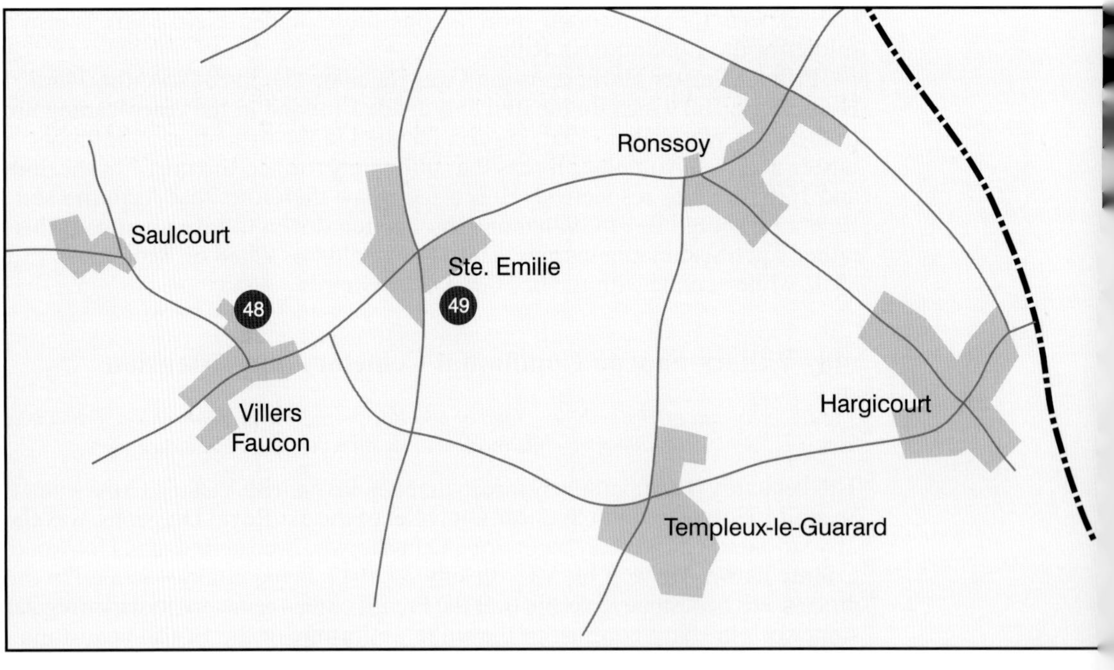

(49) Ste. Emilie Valley Cemetery

Further east than most other cemeteries featured, Ste. Emilie stands between Epehy and Roisel villages in an area reclaimed in March 1917 but lost again in the German advance of March, 1918. It holds 513 bodies, 222 of which have not been identified by name. There are special memorials to 21 soldiers believed to lie here.

Close to 60 of those known by name buried here served with the 16th (Irish) Division and were killed in the German advance of March, 1918. By this stage in the war recruitment in Ireland had slowed to such an extent that many of those serving in the division were English, Scottish and Welsh conscripts and this is reflected in the nationality of the fallen.

At least three of the Irish dead had been recognised for their bravery. Lieutenant Fenton King Cummins, 20, of the 6th Connaught Rangers, died on the opening day of the German offensive, March 21, 1918. The son of a doctor from Woodville, Glanmire, County Cork, he had been awarded the Military Cross. Two privates from the same battalion, Cork man P. Flynn and James Hughes, from Ballymena, County Antrim, held the 'other ranks' equivalent of the M.C., the Military Medal. Second Lieutenant Hugh Victor Moore had previously served with both the Connaught Rangers and Black Watch but was on attachment to the 48th Trench Mortar Battery when killed on March 21, 1918. The 31-year-old, with family at Auburn Terrace, Athlone, is remembered on a special memorial in the cemetery.

The Royal Munster Fusiliers dead form the largest group in the cemetery, amounting to 22 in total. They include Private Edward Birmingham, a 32-year-old from Evergreen Road in Cork and Michael Cooney, 22, of Cogan Place, Windmill Street, Limerick, both of the 1st battalion. There are half-a-dozen members of the Royal Dublin Fusiliers, most of them Englishmen. Private John Donnelly, 26, from Whitehead, County Antrim, and Lance Corporal Charles Dooley, 19, from Londonderry, both served in the merged 7th/8th Royal Irish Fusiliers. Private B. Devanny, 24, from Maiden Street, Newcastle West, County Limerick, was part of the 7th (South Irish Horse) Royal Irish Regiment when he was killed six days before the launch of the massive German assault.

The confusion which accompanied the fighting of March, 1918, is illustrated by the headstone of Private J. Gallagher. It is not known exactly when the 2nd Leinster Regiment soldier, from Glenview, Dundrum, Dublin, died, other than that it was some time between March 21-27. Private John Alexander Young, 22, from Balteagh, Limavady, was with the 8th Royal Inniskilling Fusiliers when killed on March 21, 1918. His grave, though subsequently lost, is believed to lie within Ste. Emilie Valley Cemetery and is recorded on a special memorial.

Appendix 1:

The 9th Royal Irish Fusiliers losses, July 1, 1916

July 14, 1916

Dear Fitzgerald,

Lieutenant Colonel Stewart Blacker

It is with a heavy heart I take up my pen to tell you the doings and losses of the Battalion on July 1.

After being five days in the trenches during the preliminary bombardment, we came out for two days' rest, then went on at midnight on June 30, and took up our positions ready for the assault which was for 7.30am, July 1.

The Battalion was on a four company front, each company being in a platoon front, thus being in four waves: two leading waves in frontline trench, 3rd wave in communication trenches, 4th wave in 2nd line trenches. Order of companies from right to left: A, B, C, D. These dispositions were completed by about 3am. We suffered 50 casualties while waiting. The opposing lines are about 400 yards apart, with a ravine some 70 yards wide with steep banks about 20 feet high, about halfway.

The order was for the leading wave to get within 150 yards from German line by 7.30am to be ready to assault the instant our barrage lifted at 7.30am. To do this the leading waves went over our parapet at 7.10am, 2nd waves at 7.15am, 3rd at 7.20am and the last waves at 7.30am.

Ensor, Atkinson, Johnston C, and Brew were in command respectively and 11 other platoon officers, that was all that were allowed in the actual assault: and about 600 men. Of these Johnston was killed, Atkinson, Townsend, Hollywood, Montgomery, Seggie, Stewart are missing, believed killed: and Brew, Gibson, Jackson, Shillington, Andrews, Smith, Barcroft, Capt Ensor are wounded and 516 other ranks are casualties.

57 killed
158 missing
303 wounded

Total 518

The 1st wave got away without suffering badly, the 2nd wave had many casualties and the 3rd and 4th waves were mown down by machinegun fire, frontal and enfilade, before they reached the ravine.

After the machinegun fire the Germans put a barrage between the ravine and our front line. A few of C and D companies got to the German front line, but a number of A and B companies got through the German line and reached their objective at Beaucourt Station, past the German 3rd line. Of these none have returned. Owing to the failures of Battalions on our left, they were cut off.

The gallant and splendid leading of the officers and steady advance of the men even after their officers were down, was magnificent, and makes me proud indeed to have been associated with such heroes.

For four nights after, parties went out and searched for the wounded and brought in several (Ensor and three others the 4th night), and then we moved back 12 miles and the Border regiment continued the search and rescued many of which we owe them deep gratitude. Cather was killed bringing in wounded in daylight, and Menaul slightly wounded. Alas, many of our best have gone and we only marched back 281 strong, including transport.

The Battalion in the hour of trial was splendid as I knew it would be, but I am heartbroken. The gallant friends and comrades we shall see no more. So few have come back unwounded it is hard to get any information as to individuals. Of the 48 Lewis gunners, only 7 are left.

In 'A' Company, Sgts Moore, Whitsitt, Hegan, Kirkwood, McCourt are wounded and Sgt Wilson is missing believed killed. In 'B' Company, Sgt Foster is killed and Sgts Caulfield, Keilty, Barr, Courtney, Johnston wounded. In 'C'Company, Sgts Hobbs and Bryans were killed and Sgts Brown, and or missing. In 'D' Company, Sgts Mullen, Gordon, Thornberry killed, Sgts Hare, Balmer, Sewell, Hughes wounded and Sgt Bunting missing.

McClurg, the Primate's chauffeur wounded. We want Lewis gunners badly, the Signallers escaped well, we still have over 30 available. Your draft of 53 came last night and I saw them today, very well turned out and a good lot.

What can you do further? I fear little – nearly all our bombing teams are gone. We are right back now, not more than 30 miles from Boulogne and we are hoping to get drafts and trying to refit and sort things out. Fortunately the four Company Sgt Majors and four Company Quarter Master Sgts were not allowed over the parapet so the Company Staff is intact.

Cather's loss is a severe one, he was quite wonderful as Adjutant, but his was a glorious death and his name had gone in for a posthumous Victoria Cross. He brought in one wounded man from about 150 yards from German wire in daylight! And was killed going out to a wounded man who feebly waved to him on his calling out to see if there were any more near.

There have been a lot of extravagant words written and published in the Press, which is a great pity. The Division behaved magnificently and the point does not want labouring. Please be careful that this epistle does not get into the Press.

I am still dazed at the blow and the prospect in front of us all, but we must not be downcast: and must remember the glorious example of the gallant band who so nobly upheld the honour of the Battalion, and who have died so gloriously, leaving their example to live after them, and to inspire those of us who are left.

Old Irwin wrote me wanting to hear details, perhaps you would send him on this when read to: East India Service Club, St James's Square, SW.

Yours ever, Stewart W Blacker

PS: Please let General "Hacket Pain" have this account to read.

(Letter courtesy of the Royal Irish Fusiliers Museum)

Appendix 2:

The King's farewell to disbanded Irish regiments

COLOURS HANDED OVER AT WINDSOR

The King received at Windsor Castle yesterday detachments from the Royal Irish Regiment, the Connaught Rangers, the South Irish Horse, the Prince of Wales's Leinster Regiment (Royal Canadians), the Royal Munster Fusiliers, and the Royal Dublin Fusiliers – the six South of Ireland regiments which are being disbanded – to receive from them their Colours, which are to be hung permanently on the grand staircase near to the famous and historic St. George's Hall. The detachments went by train to Windsor, and were welcomed at the station by a number of distinguished officers and officials, including Sir Douglas Dawson (State Chamberlain to his Majesty), Colonel the Hon. George Crichton (Controller in the Lord Chamberlain's Department), Major-General G. D. Jeffreys (commanding the London district), Lord Henry Seymour (commanding the 3rd Grenadiers), and a party of the King's gentlemen Ushers. In the Royal waiting room the Colours were unfurled, and having been saluted by an escort of Grenadiers, were carried at the head of the detachments through the crowded streets of Windsor and up Castle Hill to the Castle. The accompanying band meanwhile played the marches of the various regiments, leading off with "Come back to Erin," while, as the Colours were taken into St George's Hall, the band of the Grenadiers stationed in the Quadrangle immediately beneath the windows of the Hall, rendered "Auld Lang Syne."

The detachments were drawn up in line, and when presently the King arrived, the Colours were dipped in salutation for the last time, a Royal salute was given, and the band outside played the National Anthem. The King, who wore a Field Marshal's service uniform, was accompanied by the Queen, beautifully gowned in zephyr-like white material; the Duke of Connaught, in a Field-Marshal's service dress; Princess Mary and Viscount Lascelles, the Marquis and Marchioness of Cambridge and Lady Mary Cambridge, the Earl and Countess of Athlone, and the ladies and gentlemen-in-waiting. His Majesty proceeded to inspect the line, and then the Colour-bearers of each detachment in turn advanced to a position in front of their Majesties, knelt down, and surrendered the Colours. Immediately before they did so the King delivered the following speech with marked emphasis, and manifesting deep feeling:-

"We are here today in circumstances which cannot fail to strike a note of sadness in our hearts. No regiment parts with its Colours without feelings of sorrow. A knight in days gone by bore on his shield his coat-of-arms and tokens of valour and worth. Only to death did he surrender them.

"Your Colours are the record of valorous deeds in war, and of the glorious traditions thereby created. You are called upon to part with them today for reasons beyond your control and resistance. By you and your predecessors these Colours have been reverenced and guarded as a sacred trust, which trust you now confide to me.

"As your King, I am proud to accept this trust; but I fully realise with what grief you relinquish these dearly-prized emblems, and pledge my word that within these ancient and historic walls your Colours will be treasured, honoured, and protected as hallowed memorials of the glorious deeds of brave and loyal regiments."

When accepting the Colours, the King handed to the commanding officer of each battalion a message of farewell, a copy of which will ultimately be given to every officer and man of each regiment. Little more now remained to complete the ceremony. Then men grounded arms, the officers "returned" their swords, and the whole parade passed the saluting base in single file. The King and Queen stood side by side, and made a point of cordially shaking hands with every officer and man present. At intervals during the farewell ceremony the band on the Quadrangle had played plaintive airs, and at the conclusion they finished with the National Anthem.

By command of the King, the visitors were shown over the Castle, and were entertained to luncheon on the completion of their pathetic errand to Windsor.

(From the News Letter, Tuesday, June 13, 1922)

The arrival of the Irish regiments at Windsor Castle (from the News Letter report of June, 1922)

Appendix 3:

Opening of the Ulster Tower

A GREAT SACRIFICE COMMEMORATED

Under ideal conditions so far as the weather was concerned, the beautiful tower which the people of Ulster have erected at Thiepval, as memorial to the men from the province who made the supreme sacrifice in the war, was formally opened and dedicated on Saturday. It was a matter of regret to everybody interested in the movement that Lord Carson of Duncairn and Sir James Craig, Prime Minister of Northern Ireland, were prevented by indisposition, from taking the promised part that had been allotted them in a ceremony which was of historic importance, because it was largely through their enterprise, eloquence, and patriotic ardour that the Ulster Division, which won inperishable renown at Thiepval on 1st July, 1916, was brought into existence. Both gentlemen had fully made up their minds to be present, and it was only at the last moment, and in obedience to the imperative orders of their medical advisers that they reluctantly abandoned their intention of going to Thiepval and paying their tribute in person to the gallant dead on a spot that will be sacred for all time to the people of Ulster.

In a very small area of territory, hundreds of Ulstermen gave up their lives on that July morning as a token and a pledge of their love for their native country and the mighty empire with which it is allied. They will not be forgotten – no, not the humblest of them, for they died in a good cause; and we know that they gave up their lives like brave chivalrous men in order that we might live. The Thiepval Tower, built of white stone and standing on a eminence in the centre of a pastoral district which the merciless guns of the Germans, scattering death and destruction on all sides, have reduced to a baron wilderness – black, desolate, and chaotic – will stand as a permanent memorial not only to the sacrifices of the dead, but to the courage, endurance, and devotion of those who came through the awful ordeal with their lives spared to them. The men who lie buried in foreign soil at Thiepval did not give their lives in vain. They fought for noble ideals and the attainment of those ideals must inevitably be brought nearer by their heroic examples.

When Lord Carson ascertained definitely that it was impossible for him to visit Thiepval he wrote the following on Saturday:-

Please express my deep sorrow and disappointment at being compelled by peremptory orders from my doctor to abandon my visit to Thiepval. On 1st July, 1916, Ulstermen at Thiepval won undying fame for themselves, the Empire, and

Crowds gathered amid the devastation of the Somme for a religious ceremony marking the opening of the memorial

Courtesy of the Royal Irish Fusiliers Museum

their province. To quote from Col Buchan's history of the war "It was the anniversary of the Battle of the Boyne and the charge when the men shouted 'Remember the Boyne' will be forever a glorious page in the annals of Ireland. Nothing finer was done in the war. The splendid troops drawn from these Volunteers, who had banded themselves together for another cause, now shed their blood like water for the liberty of the world."

Ulster mourned, and continues to mourn, the loss of thousands of her best sons, but will appreciate with pride the monument which is dedicated today to their memory and which will forever record in the annals of the world's history the contribution that Ulster made to the civilisation of the world.

Every inch of ground on the battlefield of Thiepval is, and ever will be, sacred and revered by all those who feel grateful and thankful for the prowess of Ulster's sons, and this territory will be a link which binds us to the French nation in her maintenance of freedom and liberty. Their souls are in the care of All Mighty God and their bodies we leave as a sacred charge to the great French Republic. Let us reverently today – almost in their presence and amidst the fields and surroundings in which they shed their blood – resolve in our hearts that those who came after them at all costs follow their example, and maintain the freedom from the aggressor whether at home or abroad which they won at such heavy cost and thus prove themselves worthy citizens of the Empire to which they were so proud to belong.

Of my own personal feelings, I dare not attempt to write for every man who fell was a friend and a comrade and no lapse of time can ever obliterate from my memory the confidence and affection which long existed between us.

In the absence of Lord Carson and Sir James Craig it was necessary to revise the programme and as a result of the changes that were made, a signal compliment was paid to Ulster by one of the most distinguished soldiers of the present generation – General Weygand, Marshall Foch's Chief of Staff – and one of the organisers of the victory in the war, who consented to unveil the tablet that has been placed in the memorial chamber. This duty was to have been performed by Lord Carson, and it was fitting that as his deputy on this impressive and auspicious occasion his place should be taken by such a military genius. In physique, General Weygand does not quite realise one's expectations. He is short in stature, but he is very alert, and it is interesting and instructive to see the animation which lightens up his face when he is engaged in conversation. His bright eyes and his pleasant smile are indicative of his genial disposition but along with his geniality one can also detect both in his bearing and his facial expression wonderful force of character, and when one watches him closely one gets an idea of his great intellectual power and his capacity for acting quickly and decisively in an emergency. Sir Henry Wilson, who was no mean judge in these matters, declares that Weygand is incomparable in the role of chief of staff, and Marshall Foch apparently shares that view for the general was his right-hand man throughout the war and nothing was done by the Commander-in-Chief of the Allied armies without his opinion being asked.

Field-Marshall Sir Henry Wilson, who has never made any secret of his admiration for the Ulster people with their sterling loyalty and their enterprise and industry, had been invited to unlock the door of the tower, and he left London on Friday morning by the same train as conveyed the visitors of Ulster to their destination. From Dover to Calais the party had a very smooth crossing and on arriving at Amiens railway station they witnessed a spectacle which would have thrilled any Ulsterman with pride. On the platform there were waiting to receive Sir Henry Wilson as the Military Chief of the British Army the Mayor of the town, and a number of French Army officers of high rank. The members of the Ulster Patriotic Fund who were present were introduced to the Mayor and representatives of the French Army, and the whole of the party, numbering about 100, and including two men from each battalion of the Ulster Division, and several soldiers' widows, filed into the street, where they saw French troops lined up as a guard of honour for the British Field-Marshall. The street at this point was crowded with spectators, the residents having seemingly hurried out en masse, and Sir Henry Wilson was received with every mark of respect. A regimental band played the British and French national anthems, and the Chief of the Imperial General Staff then inspected the troops, whom he complimented on their smart appearance.

Pilgrims and veterans make their way along trenches at Thiepval following the opening of the Ulster Tower in 1921

Courtesy of the Somme Heritage Centre

Between nine and ten o'clock on Saturday morning the party left for Thiepval in charabancs and motor cars. There had been a keen frost overnight, and the roofs were still covered with rime, but the atmosphere was bright and clear with hardly a speck of cloud to mar the tender blue of the sky, and the 30 miles run to Thiepval was very exhilarating. There was plenty of food for sad and solemn meditation in the scenes which were witnessed. For some miles no trace of the havoc wrought by the war was discernible, and in the fields the ploughmen were going about their work as though France had not suffered any such catastrophic change as was produced by the horrors which extended over a period of four years. But on approaching Albert, which is only about four miles from Thiepval, the picture underwent a sharp and depressing change. Before the war Albert was a peaceful and prosperous little town, boosting of the possession of a stately cathedral and more than one solid and ornate public building. At the present time the town is in ruins. It is literally true to say that not one house, shop, church, or other building which existed in 1914 remains today. The destruction is inconceivable and indescribable. Where everyone looks there are heaps of ruins. There is not a stone-built house or shop in the place. The people were driven out of their homes by the fierce and prolonged artillery fire to which the town was exposed and many of them were unable to find shelter when they left with the small quantities of baggage which they were able to carry. They are now gradually returning, for attachment to their birthplace is a remarkable trait in the French character and accommodation is being made for them in huts or cabins. There may be districts which sustained greater financial loss in the war than Albert through destruction of property, but none can have suffered more complete desolation. Albert offers a striking object lesson in the tragedy and the barbarity of modern warfare, and no-one can gaze upon its ruins and think of the agony of its people without realising the blessing of peace, and praying that they may be vouchsafed to us and our descendants.

The road from Albert to Thiepval is badly cut up, but in the course of time it will doubtless by much improved.

The Ulster War Memorial Tower is now Thiepval's principal landmark. Like Helen's Tower it is "dominant over sea and land", and in the glittering sunshine which flooded the landscape on Saturday, relieving it of much of the drabness which the ravishes of the war have imposed on it, the building looked exceedingly beautiful. It has been erected on the site of the Schwaben Redoubt, a strongly fortified post, which the Ulster Division eventually captured from the enemy. The approach is by means of a narrow road, which is at present very badly cut up. In the view from the front, Albert seems quite close at hand, whilst immediately to the right there are the German trenches in very much the same condition now as they were when the Ulster Division made their attack in 1916. The Prefect of the Somme has generously undertaken to preserve the trenches in order that they may be visible to future generations of people who visit the historic spot where the men of Ulster proved "how nobly they fight and die".

Most of the visitors walked along the first trench, and those who were on the lookout for souvenirs had no difficulty in satisfying their wants for the ground was littered with the weapons and implements of warfare. Scores of rifles rendered useless by exposure to the weather are still lying about and there are pieces of shell, spades, picks, steel helmets, bayonets, and even articles of clothing. The barbed wire, by which the trenches were protected, has fallen and it is a danger to people who wander over the ground as some of the visitors on Saturday realised to their cost as a result of their garments being torn by sharp projections.

(From the News Letter, Monday, November 21, 1921)

Appendix 4:

Unveiling of 16th (Irish) Division Cross

MARSHAL JOFFRE PRAISES IRISH WAR HEROES

It was a tired party that arrived here last evening, after a long and fatiguing journey by road from Wytschaete. The route lay right down the old line through Armentietes and La Bassie, by Loos and Aeux les Mines to Arras, and thence through Bapaume and Albert to Amiens.

This morning we set out for Guillemont at about half past nine, after having spent the night in Amiens, and arrived in the little Picardy village shortly before half past eleven, the hour at which the unveiling ceremony was scheduled to begin.

Every old soldier knows the road from Amiens to the Somme – that long avenue of poplars and birch trees that runs as far as Albert through well-tilled fields of corn and pasture, and then leads on to the front – to Montauban, to Mametz, to Guillemont and Ginchy on the one side, and to Peronne, Beaumont, Hamel, and Thiepval on the other.

Albert is almost as wonderful as Ypres. I was there five years ago, when hardly one stone of the town stood on another. The people were living in dugouts and roughly improvised shelters of various kinds. There was an old army hut which served as a *mairie*, and the whole place was a horror of desolation.

Now all that has changed. Albert is back to normal again. It has five shops, broad, well laid-out streets, and the only outward and visible sign of the war that it bears today is the wrecked cathedral, which is much as it was during the war, save for the fact that it no longer has the leaning statue of the Virgin, which became a legend in those days.

Even Montanbai is a civilised little spot again. Houses have been re-built everywhere, the old trenches and shell-holes have been filled in, corn grows abundantly over the fields that saw so much battle, and everywhere there are poppies, thousands and thousands of them – they call them coquelicots in Picardy – throughout the fields and on the roadsides.

You can drive right up to Guillemont, and if you did not pass a few British cemeteries, you would not see a trace of the war. At Guillemont, however, right at the head of the village, on the top of that nasty little hill which gave so much trouble to the troops, stands the memorial cross which was unveiled this morning.

It is an exact replica of that at Wytschaete, and both are fashioned on the model of the original Ginchy Cross, which was made by Irish pioneers out of some old beams from a French farmhouse. The cross at Guillemont bears the following inscription:-

"1914-1918.

"Do Cum Gloire De Agus Onora Na Il-Eireann

"In commemoration of the Victories of Guillement and Ginchy, September 3 and 9th, 1916.

"In Memory of those who Fell Therein, and of all Irishmen who gave their Lives in the Great War."

When I arrived slightly in advance of the main party I found a band of men and women working feverishly at the memorial.

Profuse decorations had been put up by the local inhabitants, and the whole village was en fete in honour of its Irish visitors. At every one of the three entries to the "square" a banner was stretched across the road with the words "Vive l'Irlande" in large lettering, while all round the site of the cross itself paper shamrocks and green bunting were intermingled with Union Jacks and brand new French tricolours, whose brilliant crimson ends might have been dipped in the heart's blood of France.

A French officer was supervising the arrangements, and all was agog in anticipation of this great event in the history of the village. The local fire brigade, resplendent in shining helmets and blue uniforms, was in full force, and the little bandmaster fussed around in fine style, ensuring that everything was in order.

General Hickie was among the first of the Irish pilgrims to arrive, and, with the very capable assistance of Mr. M. J. Nolan – who, by the way, has borne the brunt and burden of the day since the pilgrimage began – lost no time in setting matters to rights.

One by one motor cars and coaches unloaded their batches of visitors, and at 11.30 there were several hundreds of pilgrims at the cross, which was covered with a single Union Jack.

General Hickie allotted positions to all the chief members of the party, and, having given us a short sketch of the fighting that resulted in the capture of Guillemont and Guinchy by the 16th (Irish) Division after several other Divisions had tried in vain to capture them, he proceeded to drill us in the general salute so that we should make no mistake on the arrival of Marshal Joffre, who had been appointed by the French Ministry of War to unveil the memorial.

Even the womenkind were requested by the General to stand to the salute in honour of the venerable old soldier, whose name, as was said afterwards by the bishop of Amiens, has become "Toute une Epopee", an epic in itself.

Twice he made us stand uncovered while the buglers of the Irish Guards startled the grazing sheep with their pealing calls, and, as we were beginning to become proficient, a motor horn at the foot of the hill sent a rustle through the crowd. But it was a false alarm, which was not without its humorous aspect.

Instead of the Marshal's limousine what was it but a lorry load of fine fat pigs on the way to the fair at Amiens?

"Local colour," whispered an eminent Irish officer somewhat irreverently; "they know where we come from." But the incident relieved the solemnity of the proceedings, and a good laugh did nobody any harm.

The inscription on the Guillemont Cross

In a few moments, however,

Marshal Joffre poses for photographs after the unveiling with, to his left, Irish generals Sir Bryan Mahon and Sir William Hickie

the General Salute was sounded, this time for the Bishop of Amiens, a typical French ecclesiastic, tall of stature and of dignified mien. He was received by General Hickie, and went with the Rev. Fathers O'Connell and Stafford to the local Presbytery, where he robed for the ceremony. Time began to hang heavy on our hands; for the Marshal was slightly late, but shortly before mid-day his car arrived at the bottom of the village.

A procession was formed at the mairie with Generals Hickie, Mahon and Beauchamp Doran, Sir Edward Bellingham, and two other Irish officers, headed by mounted gendarmes, in the van.

Immediately behind them came the Bishop of Amiens, with his crozier and mitre, accompanied by two French priests and the two Irish padres. They were followed by the local band, composed of war veterans, some of whom were limping from the effects of old war wounds.

Then came the frail form of the grand old Marshal of France – Joffre, hero of the Marne and architect of that marvellous retreat from Mons in which the chief executive part was played by Sir John French, Ireland's most distinguished soldier.

Joffre has grown old since the war. He is a bit bent now, but the old white moustache bristles bravely as of yore, and the keen grey eyes flash beneath snowy brows.

At Wytschaete yesterday General Borremans, of the Belgian Army, was laden with jewels and Orders, but Joffre's uniform was as simple as it was in those days when the safety of civilisation depended on his word. A wonderful veteran of the world war; Joffre – Grandpere de la Victoire.

The mounted gendarmes took up their positions with drawn sabres on the roadside, facing the cross. The Marshal was given a chair just in front of the little metal gate, and then Sir Bryan Mahon, stepping forward at the salute, asked him to unveil the memorial.

The old man straightened himself up, throwing off his shoulders the weight of heavy years, and assisted by General Hickie, pulled down the flag that covered the cross.

Yesterday's ceremonial was repeated in every detail, but this time the monument was blessed by the Bishop of Amiens, whose elaborate intonation was in marked contrast to the simple office of the Irish priests.

The wreaths were far more numerous than at Wytschaete. Captain Tuite, of the Connaught Rangers, a wounded survivor of the terrible times, laid a crown of laurels and poppies at the foot of the cross on behalf of his Regimental Association, and there was a touching scene when about a score of children, some of them tiny little tots, hardly able to walk, gave their childish tributes of wild flowers – culled from that unofficial cemetery which is the rich soil of Picardy – in memory of the men who freed their poor little village from the invader's grasp.

These were the children of Guillemont, sons and daughters as the Bishop said, of France's soldiers, and, as they were led round the Cross by Father Stafford, and a burly fireman, one saw the pity of it all – the ghastly horror of that awful sacrifice.

Most of those children were not born when the village of Guillemont was captured by the Irish troops, but throughout their lives the Celtic cross which stands there now will be a constant reminder of their debt to Ireland, and they will be required by their sorrowing mothers to tend to that memorial with pious care.

The principal event of the ceremony was the speech which was delivered by the Bishop of Amiens. Trained in the school of the great French prelates of the eighteenth century, his lordship made an eloquent oration that lasted half-an-hour. He spoke with all the fire and passion of the Gallic race, and, in the course of his remarks, spoke in the most eulogistic terms of the Irish people and their friendship with France.

He reminded us that Marshal MacMahon's stock came from Limerick, that for a hundred years an Irish Brigade had fought in the service of his country, and that in the Great War Irish soldiers had shed their blood on every battlefield from Belgium to the Swiss frontier.

Le belle Irlande and La douce France, the Isle of Saints and La France Catholique, they had been sisters in sorrow, and today both rejoiced in a freedom that had been won at bitter cost.

The Bishop's speech was greeted by loud applause. He had spoken with such fervour that he was quite exhausted when he sat down, and General Hickie shook him warmly by the hand in token of his appreciation of his magnificent eloquence.

Marshal Joffre also spoke in simple, touching words, innocent of rhetorical effort, but clear and vigorous as ever. He spoke highly of the military achievements of General Hickie, and having asked us to regard his presence as a tribute from France, retired to his chair.

Another speech from a French Senator and some further remarks by General Hickie concluded the proceedings, and after the Marseillaise and the National Anthem had been played, the party set out on the homeward journey, halting at Thiepval, where a wreath was laid on the splendid memorial tower to the 36th Ulster Division.

This act of homage from one gallant band of Irish soldiers to another – from the Roman Catholic South to the Protestant North – marked the end of the official programme of the tour.

(From the Irish Times, August 24, 1926)

Appendix 5:

Young Citizen Volunteers revisit Mesnil

Mesnil, a village in the Somme, near the town of Albert, defended with wonderful gallantry by the 14th Battalion Royal Irish Rifles (the Y.C.V.s of the Ulster Division) was the scene of a happy little ceremony yesterday.

Sixty ex-members of the battalion, mostly from Belfast, who are at present doing a tour of the battlefields, visited the village this forenoon and were received by the Mayor (Monsieur A. Maguier). Major J. A. Mulholland, M.C., presented his old comrades-in-arms, and the company repaired to the spot where the old church stood, where the ceremony took place.

During the defence of the village these hands of the church clock in some mysterious way moved at very irregular intervals, usually after or previous to the relief of troops. Whether it was the action of a spy or the occasional vibration from the explosion of shells it was never ascertained, but to prevent any mistake about the matter the hands were removed. A short time after the church was demolished by German artillery fire.

The hands have since been in the possession of the officer who gave instructions for their removal, and to-day they were presented to the Mayor in a unique and appropriate form.

The hands are set at Armistice hour – 11am – and on the right are the crossed flags of England and France, having in the centre the Croix-de-Guerre, the Croix-de-Guerre having been presented to the Commune by the French Government. On the left is the badge of the Royal Irish Rifles and the regimental motto underneath.

A short history of the clock hands in French and English is printed in ivory on each side of the shield.

These hands were presented to the Mayor by Major Mulholland on behalf of the 14th Battalion Royal Irish Rifles.

The Mayor was also presented with a gold-mounted regimental stick by the men of the party.

In making the presentation, Major Mulholland said:- It was with feelings of both pleasure and sadness that they as ex-members of the 14th Battalion Royal Irish Rifles visit the village that day, because although they had some happy days in that neighbourhood they had also very sad memories of their sojourn in that area. The majority of us, he continued, lived and fought around here for many months, and whilst we can recall hours of fun and laughter when resting in the surrounding villages, there is ever present with us the memory of many of our comrades who lie buried in the military cemeteries close to Mesnil.

We have returned to-day to do honour to their memory, to walk over the ground which they so nobly defended, to think more deeply of their gallantry and self-sacrifice, and we trust that visits such as this will help, if indeed help is needed, to maintain the friendship which exists between our two countries.

We are taking the opportunity when here to give back to you the hands of your old church clock, which was destroyed by German artillery when we occupied the village, and we feel that they will be received by you in the spirit in which we restore them. It would be our earnest hope and belief that they will be treasured not alone by the old residents, but by their children, and that they will be a reminder of the part played in the Great War by their village.

Need I explain the import of the words "C'est fini?" Whilst they, together with the setting of the hands at eleven o'clock indicate the cessation of hostilities, are they not the last words of Him who made the great sacrifice and set the example to all mankind, that it is greater to lay down one's life for one's friend than to gain the whole world?

There is also a Croix-de-Guerre affixed to the shield, and I would here congratulate your commune on that honour which has been conferred upon you by the French Government.

I should refer to the motto of our regiment which you see on the shield. "Quis Separabit," or "Who shall separate us." Is it not appropriate and applicable to our two nations, who fought side by side in the greatest of wars?

I have now very great pleasure, Mr Mayor, in handing over to you this shield on behalf of our old battalion.

The Mayor acknowledged the gifts in a brief speech.

HOW VERDUN WAS SAVED

A further report of the visit of ex-members of the 14th Royal Irish Rifles (Y.V.C.s) to the Flanders battlefields shows that this itinerary was an extensive one. It was the first organised tour of the battlefields by members of this unit of the 36th (Ulster) Division.

The party included five of the battalion's officers – Major J. A. Mulholland, M.C.; Major H. Clokey, M.C.; Major J. W. Harper; Lieut. W. J. Allen; Lieut. E. Morrow and about 60 ex-N.C.O.s and men.

The tour commenced in Belgium, the jumping-off point being Ostend, from whence the party proceeded to Ypres, where a day was spent in visiting the various sectors in which the battalion had fought.

Leaving Ypres the party proceeded on a two-day motor tour. Among the places visited were Wytschaete, Dranoutre, Bailleul, Bethune, Vimy Ridge, Arras, Bapaume, the Australian Memorial in Delville Wood, Contalmaison and Albert.

The culminating point of the trip was the visit on Wednesday to Mesnil, a small village in the Somme Department, close to Thiepval, which was held by the 36th Division prior to the attack of 1st July, 1916.

While the 14th Royal Irish Rifles held the village the clock on the church was destroyed by German artillery fire, and the hands have since that time been in the possession of Major J. A. Mulholland, M.C., who was second in command of the battalion. Major Mulholland, with the intention of returning the clock hands to the town, had them mounted on a shield, together with a battalion badge and a Croix de Guerre – which honour was conferred upon the town by the French President. Also on the shield is an inscription in English and French and the words "c'est fini" (it is finished).

On arriving in Mesnil the party formed up in front of the *Mairie* (a wooden hut) and Major Mulholland handed over the shields to the Mayor (M. Maovier) in a telling speech published in earlier reports of the ceremony.

The Mayor in his reply thanked Major Mulholland, the officers and men for their gift, which would be much appreciated by the present and future generations. He understood the purpose of their tour and sympathised with them in their great losses and the trials they had passed through.

Referring to the attack of the 1st July, he said that when the French Army was being hard pressed at Verdun and there was great danger of a breakthrough, the Somme Battle was launched. The enemy rushed his reserves to that front and Verdun was saved. They all knew and appreciated the great and glorious part played by the 36th (Ulster) Division of the British Army in the first days of the attack when they lost so heavily.

He wished on behalf of the town and himself to pay tribute to the gallantry of the 14th Battalion of the Royal Irish Rifles and in particular to Major Mulholland.

Major Mulholland was then presented with a bouquet by a schoolboy, and a gold-mounted "swagger" cane was given to the Mayor by ex-Sergeant James Diamond, the presentation being made by Major Harper.

Subsequently the school children of the village placed flowers on the Cross of Sacrifice in the British War Cemetery.

In the afternoon the party visited the 36th Division Memorial Tower at Thiepval and a wreath was laid in the memorial chamber of the tower by ex-Sergeant R. Stewart.

After these ceremonies the tour of the battlefields was continued. The last two days, Thursday and Friday, are being spent in Paris.

(From the Belfast Telegraph of July 14 and 15, 1927)

The old clock hands, still on the plaque presented by the men of the 14th (Y.C.V.) Royal Irish Rifles, still takes pride of place at Mesnil Mairie

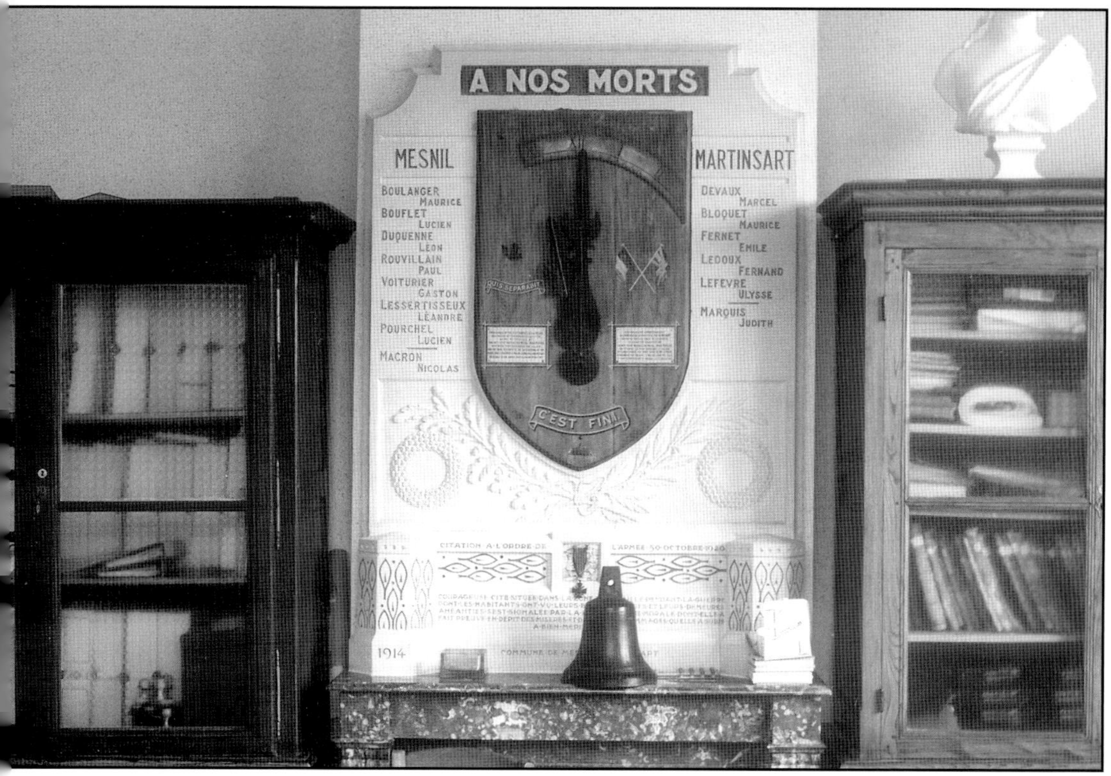

ACKNOWLEDGEMENTS

Writing a book is considered a lonely occupation, yet throughout this work I have happily walked in the company of eminent historians, First World War enthusiasts and, most rewarding of all, retraced the footsteps of hundreds of soldiers through their memoirs, letters or obituaries. To all these men and women I owe a huge debt of gratitude.

A number of individuals and organisations have been of particular assistance: the staff at the Somme Heritage Centre and Somme Association, Newtownards, especially Billy, Carol, Craig and Noel, who gave freely of their expertise, resources – the majority of the photographs in this publication were supplied by them – and patience; Amanda Moreno, curator of the Royal Irish Fusiliers Museum in Armagh was generous with her time and knowledge and contributed many superb illustrations, including the front cover photograph; Lester Morrow invited me to his home to view his impressive collection and granted permission to use a number of his photographs; Ian Wilson and his staff at North Down Heritage Centre were most helpful in allowing me to view, copy and reproduce photographs from the Bangor War Memorial Book, a terrific resource which has yet to be fully appreciated; the staff at Bangor Library, Belfast Central Library and the adjoining Newspaper Library, where I have blissfully spent countless days looking through old books and papers; Mike King at the County Down Museum for his help and especially for providing the photographs of the tragic Love brothers; and Tom Burke of the Royal Dublin Fusiliers Association for permission to use a number of photographs from their website.

So many friends and colleagues at the News Letter, particularly in the production, marketing and editorial departments, have played a vital part in this project. To each and everyone goes genuine thanks for a job well done.

And finally my wife Heather and sons Nicholas, Andrew and Christopher, who have been supportive as always, and my father John Moore, who did the initial proof reading.

BIBLIOGRAPHY

Arthur, Max, (in association with the Imperial War Museum), *Forgotten Voices of the Great War* (Elbury Press, London, 2002)

Barnett, Correlli, *The Great War* (Park Lane Press, London, 1979)

Bredin, Brigadier A. E. C., *A History of the Irish Soldier* (Century Books, Belfast, 1987)

Brown, Malcolm, *The Imperial War Museum Book of the First World War* (Sidgwick and Jackson, London, 1993)

———, *The Imperial War Museum Book of the Somme* (Sidgwick and Jackson, London, 1996)

———, *The Imperial War Museum Book of 1918: Year of Victory*, (Pan Books, London, 1999)

Coombs, Rose E. B, *Before Endeavours Fade: A Guide to the Battlefields of the First World War* (After the Battle Publication, London, 1983)

Corbally, Lt-Col M. J. P. M., *The Royal Ulster Rifles, 1793-1960* (Paramount Press, Glasgow, 1960)

Corns, Cathryn, and John Hughes-Wilson, *Blindfold And Alone: British Military Executions in the Great War* (Cassell, London, 2001)

Crozier, Brigadier-General F. P., *A Brass Hat in No Man's Land* (Jonathan Cape, London, 1930)

Denman, Terence, *A Lonely Grave: The Life and Death of William Redmond* (Irish Academic Press, Blackrock, Co. Dublin, 1995)

Doherty, Richard, *The North Irish Horse: A Hundred Years of Service* (Spellmount, Staplehurst, Kent, 2002)

———, Richard and David Truesdale, *Irish Winners of the Victoria Cross* (Four Courts Press, Dublin, 2000)

Falls, Cyril, *The History of the 36th (Ulster) Division* (McCaw, Stevenson and Orr, Belfast, 1922)

———, *The History of the First Seven Battalions: The Royal Irish Rifles in the Great War, Volume 2* (Regimental Committee, Aldershot, 1925)

Gilbert, Adrian, Terraine, John, Consultant Editor, *World War 1 in Photographs*, (Orbis Book Publishing Corporation, London, 1986)

Haines, Keith, *North Down Memories* (Blackstaff Press, Belfast, 2000)

Harris, H. E. D., *The Irish Regiments in the First World War* (Mercier Press, Cork, 1968)

Harris, Henry, *The Royal Irish Fusiliers* (Leo Cooper Ltd, London, 1972)

Harris, R. G., (revised by H. R. G. Wilson), *The Irish Regiments 1683-1999* (Spellmount, Steplehurst, Kent, 1999)

Hart, Liddell, *History of the First World War* (Papermac, Macmillan, London, 1997. First published 1930)

Holmes, Richard, *The Western Front* (BBC Worldwide Ltd, London, 1999)

Holts, Major and Mrs, *Battlefield Guide to the Somme* (Leo Cooper, London, 2000)

James, Robert Rhodes, *Gallipoli* (Pimlico, London, 1999)

Jeffery, Keith, *Ireland and the Great War* (Cambridge University Press, 2000)

Johnstone, Tom, *Orange, Green & Khaki: The Story of the Irish Regiments in the Great War*, 1914-18 (Gill and Macmillan Ltd., Dublin, 1992)

Keegan, John, *The First World War* (Pimlico, London, 1999)

Livesey, Anthony, *Great Battles of World War I* (Angus Books, London, 2003)

Macdonald, Lyn, *Somme* (Papermac, Macmillan, London, 1984)

———, *1914*, (Penguin Books, London, 1989)

———, *The Roses of No Man's Land* (Papermac, Macmillan, London, 1984)

Mackey, Brian, *Lisburn: The Town and its People* (Blackstaff Press, Belfast, 2000)

McCarthy, Chris, *The Somme: The Day-by-Day Account* (Brockhampton Press, London, 1998)

Middlebrook, Martin, *The First Day on the Somme, Allen Lane* (Penguin Books, London, 1971)

———, Martin and Mary, *The Somme Battlefields: A Comprehensive Guide from Crecy to the Two World Wars* (Penguin Books, London, 1994)

Moreno, Amanda, and David Truesdale, *Angels and Heroes: The story of a Machine Gunner with the Royal Irish Fusiliers, August 1914 to April 1915* (The Royal Irish Fusiliers Museum, Armagh, 2004)

Neillands, Robin, *The Great War Generals on the Western Front 1914-18* (Robinson Publishing Ltd., London, 1999)

Orr, Philip, *The Road to the Somme: Men of the Ulster Division Tell Their Story* (Blackstaff Press, Belfast, 1987)

Pollock, John, *Kitchener* (Robinson, London, 2002)

Sheen, John, *Tyneside Irish: 24th, 25th, 26th & 27th (Service) Battalions of the Northumberland Fusiliers* (Pen and Sword Books Limited, Barnsley, South Yorkshire, 1998)

Shermer, David, *World War 1* (Octopus Books, London, 1973)

Taylor, James W., *The 1st Royal Irish Rifles in the Great War* (Four Courts Press, Dublin, 2002)

Thompson, Robert, *Bushmills Heroes 1914-1918* (published by author, 1995)

The Great War: A Tribute to Ulster's Heroes 1914-1918, (Pretani Press, 1991. First published by Citizens Committee, City Hall, Belfast, 1919)

INDEX

A reference in a footnote is indicated by *n* after the page number and in a photograph caption by the use of *italics*